Customizing the Microsoft® .NET Framework Common Language Runtime

Steven Pratschner

PUBLISHED BY
Microsoft Press
A Division of Microsoft Corporation
One Microsoft Way
Redmond, Washington 98052-6399

Library of Congress Control Number: Pending

Printed and bound in the United States of America.

2 3 4 5 6 7 8 9   QWE   9 8 7 6 5

Distributed in Canada by H.B. Fenn and Company Ltd.

A CIP catalogue record for this book is available from the British Library.

Microsoft Press books are available through booksellers and distributors worldwide. For further information about international editions, contact your local Microsoft Corporation office or contact Microsoft Press International directly at fax (425) 936-7329. Visit our Web site at www.microsoft.com/learning/. Send comments to mspinput@microsoft.com.

Acquisitions Editors: Robin Van Steenburgh and Ben Ryan
Project Editor: Kathleen Atkins
Copy Editor: Christina Palaia
Indexer: William S. Meyers

Body Part No. X11-04145

To Erin, Katherine, and Maraye

*Maraye, Your love makes me look forward
to spending the rest of my days with you.
I love being your husband.*

*Kate and Erin, You make me so
very proud to be your father.
I'll always be here for you.*

Contents at a Glance

Table of Contents

What do you think of this book?
We want to hear from you!

Microsoft is interested in hearing your feedback about this publication so we can continually improve our books and learning resources for you. To participate in a brief online survey, please visit: *www.microsoft.com/learning/booksurvey/*

Foreword

In October 1999, someone I knew at Microsoft asked me if I would do some consulting work on the Microsoft .NET Framework team. At that time, I knew very little about the .NET Framework, but what I did know impressed me quite a bit, and I immediately joined the team.

At that time, the .NET Framework was internally called COM+ 2.0. But Microsoft knew that this new way of programming deserved a better name than that. Before its first release, the .NET Framework had many other names. One code name was "Lightning." This name was chosen because earlier versions of Microsoft Visual Basic had the code name "Thunder," and "Thunder & Lightning" sounded cool. (By the way, Microsoft's reference implementation of the Shared Source CLI [*http://MSDN.Microsoft.com/net/sscli*] is code-named "Rotor" because it is another meteorological term.) The .NET Framework was also called "NGWS" at one time, which stands for Next Generation Windows Services or Next Generation Web Services, depending on whom you ask.

Another code name for the .NET Framework was "URT," which stands for Universal Runtime. In my mind, this code name was particularly telling and indicated that Microsoft's goal was to make the CLR universally available. In other words, for Microsoft, the CLR would be *the* programming model for all its applications and servers. Any application that offered any kind of programmability would offer that programmability through the CLR. The full fruition of this vision is many years away, but today managed code can be written to extend the capabilities of Microsoft SQL Server, Microsoft Excel, Word, and Outlook.

However, the CLR wouldn't truly be universal unless other companies could also incorporate it into their products, enabling end users to extend these applications using managed code as well. Today, many companies do incorporate the CLR into their applications. Like SQL Server, IBM's DB2 database incorporates the CLR, enabling developers to write stored procedures in managed code. Also, AutoDesk allows users to extend its AutoCAD products by using managed code.

By incorporating the CLR into your own applications and servers, you will gain many benefits. Here's a list of just a few:

- Users can extend your application using any .NET programming language.
- Microsoft (and other companies) provides editors, wizards, debuggers, profilers, and other tools to aid your users.
- The managed objects are garbage collected so that there are no memory leaks or corruption.
- The code is verified to ensure that only safe operations are performed.
- Code can run in a secure AppDomain so that the hosting application can limit what the user's code can do.

- XCopy deployment means that it is easy to deploy, back up, restore, move, and uninstall managed assemblies.

- Users have access to all the types in the Microsoft .NET Framework Class Library as well as types created by other companies to help them in building their code.

As I said, these are just some of the benefits of incorporating the CLR into your applications and servers. The perfect resource to learn about more of these features and, more important, how to incorporate them and use them effectively is the very book you are holding in your hand!

I met Steve Pratschner in 1999 when I started consulting on the COM+ 2.0/Lightning/NGWS/ URT/.NET Framework team. At the time, Steve was a program manager responsible for the CLR's loader and assembly versioning stuff. He was quite helpful to me when I was working on my book *Applied Microsoft .NET Framework Programming* (Microsoft Press, 2002), and we immediately became friends. Later, Steve became the program manager responsible for the CLR's hosting capabilities that were added to version 2.0 of the .NET Framework. This, of course, makes Steve uniquely suited to write a book like this. He has the deep knowledge of how the system works and also has the experience of talking to customers to understand their needs and can therefore explain why the CLR team was motivated to add the features they did.

When Steve told me that he wanted to write this book, I immediately asked him if I could review it as he wrote it because I wanted to learn about all this stuff myself. I am very impressed at how good a job Steve has done. Even if you aren't interested in incorporating the CLR into your own applications and servers, this book will offer you insight into how the CLR works that no other book comes close to supplying. If you are familiar with *Applied Microsoft .NET Framework Programming*, you will find this book to be a great complement to it.

As you read this book, you will gain a different perspective on the CLR that will no doubt give you a new appreciation for it. This book can open your mind to new possibilities of how to use the CLR, and I'm sure that you will get as much out of it as I have.

Jeffrey Richter (*http://wintellect.com*)

Acknowledgments

Writing this book has been a daunting task at times. I've relied on several people throughout this project for everything from technical assistance to help with the logistics of writing a book to encouragement and support. In particular, I thank Jeff Richter for his help throughout the project. Not only did Jeff help me get started, but his technical expertise and writing experience have been absolutely invaluable.

In addition, the following individuals helped make sure this book is technically accurate and easily readable: Dennis Angeline, Mason Bendixen, Chris Brown, Christopher Brumme, Alessandro Catorcini, Suzanne Cook, Mike Downen, Patrick Dussud, Greg Fee, Brian Grunkemeyer, Jonathan Hawkins, Jim Hogg, Jonathan Keljo, Sonja Keserovic, Jim Kieley, Raja Krishnaswamy, Tim Kurtzman, Bryan Lamos, Sebastian Lange, WeiWen Liu, Rudi Martin, Frank Peschel-Gallee, Sonia Pignorel, Mahesh Prakriya, Michael Rayhelson, Beysim Sezgin, Alan Shi, Craig Sinclair, Tarik Soulami, Jan Stranik, Sean Trowbridge, Dino Viehland, Kimberly Wolk, and Junfeng Zhang.

The people at Microsoft Press put in untold numbers of hours making sure everything fits together just so. They do an incredible job. As a first-time author, I certainly needed extra help at times. Thanks so much to Kathleen Atkins, Ben Ryan, Christina Palaia, Sally Stickney, and Robin Van Steenburgh for guiding me through this project and producing my book.

Finally, I'm eternally grateful for the people in my personal life who continue to give me so much love and support. In addition to my daughters Erin and Katherine and my wife Maraye, I'd also like to thank Zo Van Eaton and my parents Joe and Audrey Pratschner. I wouldn't have been able to reach this goal without all of you there to help me.

Introduction

The introduction of Microsoft .NET Framework 2.0 marks the third major release of the core component in the Microsoft .NET platform strategy. With each subsequent release of the .NET Framework, the reach of the .NET platform is extended as the managed code programming model is made available in more application models. For example, .NET Framework 2.0 is the first version of the .NET Framework that will be integrated with the Microsoft SQL Server database system. In addition, many key architectural changes have been made in .NET Framework 2.0 in preparation for its deeper integration with future versions of the Windows operating system.

The presence of the .NET programming model in so many different application environments is possible only because the .NET Framework's core execution engine, the Common Language Runtime (CLR), is flexible enough to support application environments with a wide range of requirements. In .NET Framework 2.0, several new extensibility points have been added that make the CLR much more customizable than in previous releases. Fortunately, the same techniques that Microsoft uses to integrate the CLR into products such as Internet Explorer, SQL Server, and Internet Information Server are available for you to achieve the same level of integration between the CLR and your own product.

What Makes This .NET Framework Book Unique?

Numerous books have been written about the .NET Framework and the CLR since their introduction in early 2002. This book is different in that it is targeted at those developers who want to dig deeper into the subject of .NET Framework programming and expand their overall knowledge of how the CLR works. Most of the topics I cover in this book aren't found in introductory books about the .NET Framework. Instead, I cover those advanced and unfamiliar topics that will help you (once you are familiar with them) write more flexible, reliable, and secure applications.

A few years ago, I worked on a CLR subteam responsible for integrating the CLR into products like SQL Server and Windows. During that time, I realized that many of the features the CLR team was building to support these application models make the CLR much more flexible and customizable in a way that enables developers outside of Microsoft to integrate the CLR into their own applications as well. To that end, many of the topics I cover in this book are of direct use to those developers hoping to integrate the CLR into their existing products, to write applications that are extensible, or to customize the way the CLR works by default. The following list gives you a flavor of the topics I cover, many of which are new to .NET Framework 2.0:

- Using the CLR hosting APIs to customize the CLR from unmanaged code
- Configuring the CLR startup parameters, including version and build type

- Using application domains to isolate effectively groups of assemblies running in a process

- Configuring application domains to best meet your specific requirements

- Managing multiple application domains easily by writing an application domain manager

- Understanding strategies for dynamically loading assemblies into your application domains

- Diagnosing assembly loading failures

- Loading assemblies from custom file formats and locations

- Specifying your own assembly version policy

- Using domain-neutral assemblies to reduce the amount of memory consumed by applications that use several application domains

- Customizing the Code Access Security (CAS) system to restrict the permissions granted to the code running in your process

- Using a new feature named *host protection* to enforce programming model constraints that are specific to your application

- Controlling the way the CLR behaves in the face of exceptional conditions, such as out of memory errors and stack overflows, to protect the integrity of your process

- Configuring the CLR's garbage collector

- Replacing the primitives the CLR uses to allocate memory to track memory usage or restrict the amount of memory the CLR can use

- Integrating the CLR into an environment that relies on Win32 fibers or any other mechanism that requires cooperative task scheduling

Even if CLR integration or extensibility isn't your current goal, a deeper understanding of .NET Framework programming will help make the applications you're writing today better. For example, learning about the subtleties that can occur when multiple versions of the .NET Framework are installed on the same machine can help you design your application so that it is not affected when a new version of the .NET Framework gets deployed; knowing how application domains are used for isolation can help you build applications that are more reliable and secure. Also, if you happen to be a developer who writes components for use within other applications, this book can help you understand how the applications that use your components are likely to be designed. This knowledge can help you write add-ins that more seamlessly integrate with the applications that host them.

The .NET Framework 2.0 Prereleases

This book is based on prerelease versions of .NET Framework 2.0. At the time of this writing, the latest publicly available prerelease is the October Community Technology Preview. I expect there will be a few more Community Technology Previews and at least one more beta before the final version of .NET Framework 2.0 is released. The October Community Technology Preview can be downloaded from *http://lab.msdn.microsoft.com/vs2005/downloads/default.aspx* .

Because I've written this book based on prereleased software, you might find some differences between what I've written here and the final version of the product. I don't expect significant design changes to occur between now and the final release, but some small differences might appear as the new .NET Framework 2.0 APIs are finalized because the team has responded to customer feedback.

Sample Code and System Requirements

I demonstrate most of the topics I cover using sample code. Throughout the book, you'll find a mix of small examples and complete sample programs. All of the sample programs are provided in the form of Microsoft Visual Studio projects built with the October Technology Preview of Visual Studio 2005.

The samples that accompany this book can be downloaded from the Microsoft Press site at

http://www.microsoft.com/learning/books/products/6895/

The samples will be updated as needed. To build and run the samples, you'll need a machine running a version of Windows that's supported by Visual Studio 2005, such as Windows 2000, Windows Server 2003, or Windows XP.

This book assumes that you have a working knowledge of Microsoft .NET Framework programming and a familiarity with the C# programming language. In addition, many of the samples are written in a combination of managed and unmanaged code. As a result, a background in native C++ programming will enable you to get the most from the samples.

Comments, Corrections, and Support

Every effort has been made to ensure the correctness of the text and the sample code in this book. However, especially because this book is based on prerelease software, you might find some errors. If you have comments, would like to suggest ways to make this book better, or would like to report any errors, please send them to Microsoft Press at the following address:

mspinput@microsoft.com

Microsoft Press also provides corrections and additional content for its books through the World Wide Web at

http://www.microsoft.com/learning/support/

Chapter 1
CLR Hosts and Other Extensible Applications

The Common Language Runtime (CLR) lies at the heart of the Microsoft .NET initiative. It is the CLR that provides the runtime services required to execute the code you write to expose as Web services, Microsoft ASP.NET applications, rich client applications, database stored procedures, and so on. If you've worked much with the .NET Framework, you're probably familiar with many of the high-level benefits of the CLR, such as automatic memory management (garbage collection), the common type system, and Code Access Security (CAS). However, the CLR possesses another key characteristic that you might not have spent as much time working with directly: its tremendous flexibility.

The extensibility points offered by the CLR enable it to be customized to run in a variety of application environments that have a wide range of requirements. For example, these extensibility points have enabled the CLR to be integrated into Microsoft SQL Server 2005, Internet Information Services (in the form of ASP.NET), and the Internet Explorer Web browser, among others. The ability of a core runtime system to be customized so extensively is crucial for a platform to achieve broad adoption. Imagine how differently the .NET Framework would be perceived if it were only a platform that supported rich client applications or Web applications, but not both, or if it supported the application models developed by Microsoft, but didn't allow third parties to develop their own. The absence of extensibility severely limits the reach of a platform. The CLR's flexibility has been a key factor in the overall success of the .NET Framework to date.

This book describes how to use the various extensibility points provided by the CLR to customize it to work well in your particular application. Almost every major subsystem of the CLR is customizable. For example, the CLR has a well-defined set of default rules it uses to locate assemblies that are referenced within an application. However, although these default rules can work great in many scenarios, it's clear that one model cannot satisfy the requirements of every application. In light of that problem, the CLR allows the rules for loading assemblies to be customized completely.

In a similar way, the .NET Framework ships with a default policy that governs the security permissions granted to applications running on a particular machine. Again, if this default policy doesn't meet your needs, you're free to define programmatically your own policy that can directly affect the permissions granted to the code running in your process. The release of the CLR included in Microsoft .NET Framework 2.0 dramatically increases the amount of customization possible. Many of the new ways you can customize the CLR result from the work done to integrate the CLR into SQL Server 2005 and into future versions of the Microsoft Windows operating system. The customization available in .NET Framework 2.0 is so extensive that you can even replace the basic primitives the CLR uses to allocate memory, create threads, and so on. In essence, the .NET Framework 2.0 CLR enables you to substitute your own mechanism for providing basic services for which the CLR typically relies on the operating system. In this way, you can achieve a high degree of integration between your application and the CLR.

This book covers a variety of topics, ranging from how to make the most effective use of application domains to how to replace the basic primitives used for memory allocation. Many of the customizations covered can be accomplished directly from within your managed application. However, some CLR customization scenarios require the use of unmanaged code. In most cases, unmanaged code is required for two main types of customizations: those that must take place before the CLR begins executing managed code, such as the selection of which version of the CLR to use; and those that require a deep integration with the CLR engine, such as the ability to customize the format in which assemblies are stored.

The CLR provides an unmanaged collection of functions and interfaces called the *CLR hosting APIs* for those times when you must customize the CLR from unmanaged code. Generally speaking, applications that are written to take advantage of the CLR hosting APIs can customize the CLR to a much greater extent than those applications written completely in managed code. The applications that take advantage of the CLR hosting APIs are called *CLR hosts*. CLR hosts are a specific example of an *extensible application*. In the context of this book, an extensible application is any application that defines an extensibility model that allows *add-ins* to be loaded dynamically into its process. Following are a few concrete examples of extensible applications:

- **Database servers** Today's database servers provide extensibility models that enable developers to add custom code to the database in a variety of ways. Stored procedures, user-defined types, and custom aggregate functions are all ways to extend the built-in functionality of the database. The database server is the extensible application, and the stored procedures, types, and so on defined by the third-party developer are the add-ins.

- **Web browsers** Historically, Web browsers have included an extensibility model that allows custom code to run when a Web page is accessed. For example, many Web browsers include a Java Virtual Machine that allows Java applets to be loaded and run dynamically. Also, Microsoft Internet Explorer supports add-ins in the form of controls written with the .NET Framework.

- **Web servers** ASP.NET is a great example of an application environment that provides an extensibility model for Web servers. ASP.NET enables developers to write custom application code that is hosted on the Web server. In this example, the code that is written as part of the Web application serves as the add-in.

- **Productivity applications** Many productivity applications offer extensibility models. For example, most e-mail programs now allow custom code to be executed when various events, such as the sending and receiving of e-mail, occur. Similarly, many word processors, spreadsheet programs, and other client-side applications allow users to write add-ins to add dynamic behavior to documents. In some cases, the extensibility model provided by these applications is so extensive that the program almost becomes a programming environment in itself.

A key property of extensible applications is that they are dynamic. In particular, the set of add-ins that will be loaded into the extensible application is determined dynamically instead of when the application is built, which means, in part, that the number of add-ins that will be loaded and where they will come from is unknown. These characteristics result in some unique requirements in many areas, including security, assembly loading, and reliability. For example, the fact that add-ins can come from unknown sources generally requires the authors of extensible applications to take a conservative approach to security. Also, the individual add-ins in an extensible application often are isolated to ensure that unrelated add-ins cannot interfere with each other. Many of the topics I discuss in this book are aimed at solving the problems encountered in extensible applications. As you'll see, the CLR allows itself to be customized in a variety of ways that help it adapt to the unique requirements of extensible applications, including CLR hosts.

Most extensible applications have several common architectural components as shown in Figure 1-1.

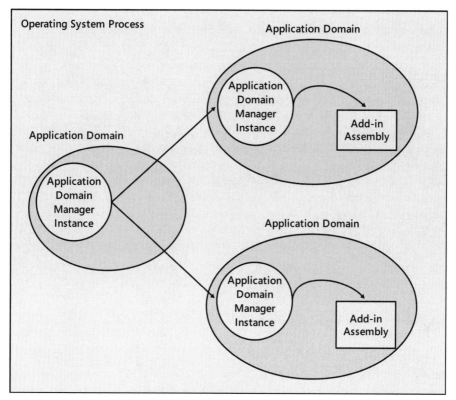

Figure 1-1   Common elements of an extensible application

I use the basic architectural framework in Figure 1-1 throughout the book as I describe the various CLR customizations from within the context of extensible applications. The key architectural elements of an extensible application include the following:

- **Add-ins**   Add-ins are the extensions that are dynamically added to your application. Because add-ins often come from unknown origins and the set of add-ins you'll load is determined dynamically, applications that provide an extensibility model have unique requirements as described earlier. Examples of add-ins include stored procedures in SQL Server 2005, Web pages containing code in ASP.NET, and controls loaded in a Web browser.

- **Application domains**   An application domain is a construct used to isolate groups of assemblies running within an operating system process. Extensible applications typically use application domains to make sure that unrelated add-ins can't interfere with each other. Several application domains can exist in a given process simultaneously. As you'll see, application domains provide many benefits of process-based isolation at a much lower cost.

- **Application domain manager**   The .NET Framework 2.0 release of the CLR includes a new concept called an application domain manager that makes it much easier to write applications that use multiple application domains. As the author of an extensible application, you provide a class that derives from an application domain manager base class, and the CLR takes care of automatically creating an instance of your domain manager in each new application domain created. This infrastructure enables you to load assemblies into application domains much more efficiently and to configure the various settings that control how application domains behave within your process.

In many ways, writing a CLR host (or any extensible application) defines a new application model in which managed code can be run. For example, without the SQL Server 2005 host, stored procedures could not be written in managed code. Similarly, without the integration of the CLR with Internet Explorer using the CLR hosting API, browser controls written with .NET Framework could not be used in Web pages. Both of these application models are examples that leverage the techniques described in this book to enable managed code to be used in many more scenarios. Each new effectively written CLR host extends the reach of the .NET platform.

Summary

This book describes the many ways the CLR can be customized to satisfy the unique requirements of your application. Throughout this book, these customizations are described within the context of CLR hosts and other extensible applications. A CLR host is an application that uses the CLR hosting APIs to customize the CLR. Examples of CLR hosts include SQL Server 2005, Internet Explorer, and ASP.NET.

Now that I've defined some basic terms and discussed the typical architecture of an extensible application, let's get started with a broad overview of what you can achieve by customizing the CLR using the hosting APIs.

Chapter 2

A Tour of the CLR Hosting API

The common language runtime (CLR) hosting API is a set of unmanaged functions and interfaces that a host uses to customize the CLR for its particular application model. Because the CLR has been designed to adapt to a variety of application scenarios, the amount of customization available through the hosting APIs is quite extensive. In most cases, you'll find that your scenario requires only a subset of the total functionality provided by the API. The overview of the hosting API provided in this chapter is intended to give you an idea of the possible customization options so that you can decide which ones apply most to your application's requirements.

Most of the individual features introduced here have entire chapters dedicated to them later in the book. This chapter merely provides the big picture. In addition to explaining the features, I'll describe the design pattern used in the interfaces and provide enough background and samples to get you started using them.

The hosting API is defined in the file mscoree.idl, which can be found in the Include directory in the Microsoft .NET Framework software development kit (SDK). These programming interfaces consist of both unmanaged functions and a set of COM interfaces. The unmanaged functions are public exports from mscoree.dll. Most of these functions are used primarily for CLR initialization, but some are used to discover basic information about the CLR after it is running, such as which version was loaded and where the CLR installation resides on disk.

CorBindToRuntimeEx and *ICLRRuntimeHost*

The primary unmanaged function you'll use is *CorBindToRuntimeEx*. This function is used to initialize the CLR into a process and is therefore the first of the hosting APIs you're likely to call. One of the return parameters from *CorBindToRuntimeEx* is a pointer to an interface named *ICLRRuntimeHost*–the *initial* COM interface in the hosting API. I say "*initial*" because *ICLRRuntimeHost* is the first interface you'll use when hosting the CLR. Given an interface pointer of type *ICLRRuntimeHost,* you gain access to all the other hosting functionality provided by the API. Figure 2-1 provides a sampling of the breadth of functionality a CLR host can access given a pointer to the *ICLRRuntimeHost* interface.

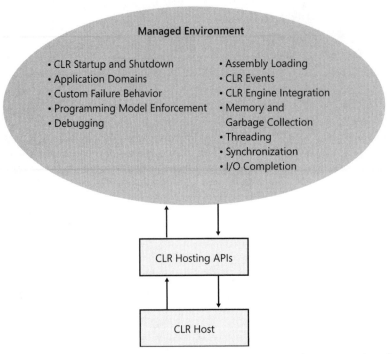

Figure 2-1   The CLR hosting interfaces as the gateway to the managed environment

Because of its role as the initial interface that hosts use to customize the CLR, *ICLRRuntime-Host* plays a part in every CLR host you'll write. As such, this interface will show up in one way or another in almost every chapter in this book. Table 2-1 provides an overview of the capabilities of *ICLRRuntimeHost* by briefly describing each method. The table also describes where in the book to look for more detail about each method.

Table 2-1   The Methods on *ICLRRuntimeHost*

Method	Description
Start	Starts the CLR running in a process. Details provided in Chapter 3.
Stop	Stops the CLR once it has been loaded into a process. Details provided in Chapter 3.
GetHostControl	Used by the CLR to discover which other interfaces the host implements. This method is described in more detail later in this chapter. See the "Hosting Manager Discovery" section.
GetCLRControl	Used by a CLR host to obtain a pointer to one of the hosting interfaces implemented by the CLR. This method is described in more detail later in this chapter. See the "Hosting Manager Discovery" section.
UnloadAppDomain	Unloads an application domain from the process. Details provided in Chapter 5.

Table 2-1   The Methods on *ICLRRuntimeHost*

Method	Description
GetCurrentAppDomainId	Returns the unique numerical identifier for the application domain in which the calling thread is currently running. I discuss this method and the overall role of application domain identifiers in Chapter 5.
ExecuteInDomain	Executes a callback function in a particular application domain. See Chapter 7 for details.
ExecuteApplication	Executes an application defined by a formal application manifest. Application manifests are a new concept in Microsoft .NET Framework 2.0. I don't cover application manifests or the *ExecuteApplication* method at all in this book. See the Microsoft .NET Framework SDK for details.
ExecuteInDefaultAppDomain	Executes a given method in the default application domain. This method is handy for CLR hosts that use only one application domain. This method is discussed more in Chapter 7.

CLR Hosting Managers

The COM interfaces in the hosting API that the host and the CLR use to communicate with each other are grouped into what are called *hosting managers*. A hosting manager is nothing more than a convenient way to categorize a set of interfaces that work together to provide a logical grouping of functionality.

For example, a host can use the hosting interfaces to provide a set of allocation primitives through which the CLR will direct requests to allocate memory. This manager is referred to as the *memory manager* and consists of the interfaces *IHostMemoryManager* and *IHostMalloc*. As another example, consider the manager that lets a host control various aspects of how assemblies are loaded in a process. Four interfaces are involved in providing this customization: *IHostAssemblyManager*, *IHostAssemblyStore*, *ICLRAssemblyIdentityManager*, and *ICLRAssemblyReferenceList*. These interfaces are grouped into what is called the *assembly loading manager*.

Both of the managers in the preceding examples consist of multiple interfaces, as many managers are. In these cases, one of the interfaces is designated the *primary interface*. The main role of the primary interface (apart from implementing some of the functionality of the manager) is to participate in the discovery process, or the steps that are taken to identify which managers the host and the CLR implement. (More on this in the section entitled "Hosting Manager Discovery" later in this chapter.)

A few important points about the hosting managers are worth highlighting. First, some managers are implemented by the CLR, some are implemented by the host, and some are split, in that both the host and the CLR implement portions of the manager that complement each other. The hosting interfaces follow a naming convention that makes it easy to tell whether a particular interface is implemented by the CLR or by the host. All interfaces that are implemented by the

CLR start with *ICLR*, whereas those implemented by the host start with *IHost*. Second, the factoring of the API into a set of managers gives the host the flexibility to customize some, but not all, aspects of the CLR. Every manager is optional; that is, the host implements only those managers that support the customizations they require. However, if you decide to implement a particular manager, you must implement all of it. You cannot implement just those methods you choose and delegate the rest to the CLR defaults, for example. The fact that hosts get to pick only those customizations that are specific to their needs is what makes the CLR so adaptable to a variety of scenarios.

Table 2-2 briefly describes all the managers in the CLR hosting API. (The primary interface for each manager is shown in boldface.)

Table 2-2   The CLR Hosting API Managers

Manager	Purpose	Interfaces in the Manager
assembly loading	Used by hosts to customize various aspects of the assembly loading process.	**IHostAssemblyManager** IHostAssemblyStore ICLRAssemblyReferenceList ICLRAssemblyIdentityManager
host protection	Enables enforcement of a host-specific programming model.	**ICLRHostProtectionManager**
failure policy	Enables the host to customize the way failure conditions are handled by the CLR.	**ICLRPolicyManager** IHostPolicyManager
memory	Enables the host to provide a set of allocation primitives through which the host will allocate memory. The CLR uses these primitives instead of their Microsoft Win32 equivalents.	**IHostMemoryManager** IHostMalloc ICLRMemoryNotificationCallback
threading	Enables the host to provide primitives to create and manipulate tasks (an abstract notion of a "unit of execution"). The CLR uses these primitives instead of their Win32 equivalents. The threading manager also enables a host to trap all calls into and out of the CLR.	**IHostTaskManager** ICLRTaskManager IHostTask ICLRTask
thread pool manager	Enables the host to provide a custom implementation of the thread pool used by the CLR.	**IHostThreadPoolManager**
synchronization	Enables the host to provide a set of synchronization primitives such as events and semaphores. The CLR will use these primitives instead of their Win32 equivalents.	**IHostSyncManager** ICLRSyncManager IHostCriticalSection IHostManualEvent IHostAutoEvent IHostSemaphore

Table 2-2 The CLR Hosting API Managers

Manager	Purpose	Interfaces in the Manager
I/O completion	Enables the host to plug in a custom implementation to handle overlapped input/output (I/O).	**IHostIoCompletionManager** *ICLRIoCompletionManager*
garbage collection	Enables a host to force a collection, obtain statistics about recent collections, and receive notifications when collections begin and end. Unlike the other managers, the interfaces in the Garbage Collection Manager are discovered independently; hence, there is no primary interface.	**IHostGCManager**[1] *ICLRGCManager*
debugging	Enables a host to customize how debugging works in its particular scenario.	**ICLRDebugManager**
CLR events	Enables a host to receive information about various events happening in the CLR, such as the unloading of an application domain.	**ICLROnEventManager** *IActionOnCLREvent*[2]

1 Neither of the interfaces in the garbage collection manager can be considered a primary interface. These two interfaces are independent and don't need to be used together, so one isn't obtained from the other.

2 *IActionOnCLREvent* is implemented by the host. As such, it should probably have been named IHostActionOn-CLREvent to follow the naming convention that indicates whether the implementation for a given interface is provided by the CLR or by the host.

Given this background, let's begin our tour of the hosting API by looking at how to initialize and load the CLR in a process.

CLR Initialization and Startup

As described, *CorBindToRuntimeEx* is the API you'll call to initialize the CLR. I briefly describe the API in this section, and then we'll dig into the details in Chapter 3.

There are four configuration settings you can specify when calling *CorBindToRuntimeEx*:

- **Version** You either can specify an exact version of the CLR to load, or you can default to the latest version installed on the machine.

- **Build type** The CLR comes in two flavors—a workstation build and a server build. As their names suggest, the workstation build is tuned for workstations, whereas the server build is tuned for the high-throughput scenarios associated with multiprocessor server machines.

- **Garbage collection**   The CLR garbage collector can run in either concurrent mode or nonconcurrent mode. The garbage collection mode is very closely tied to the type of build you select. Concurrent mode is used exclusively with the workstation build of the CLR because it's tuned to work best with applications that have a high degree of user interactivity. Typically, nonconcurrent garbage collection is used with the server build of the CLR to support the high-throughput requirements of applications such as Web servers or database servers.

- **Domain-neutral code**   The term *domain neutral* refers to the capability of sharing the jit-compiled code for an assembly across all application domains in a process. Much more is explained about domain-neutral code in Chapter 9.

Here's a sample call to *CorBindToRuntimeEx* that demonstrates how you'd specify these configuration settings. In this call, I've specified that I want to run with only version 2.0.40103 of the CLR. In addition, I'd like to always run the workstation build with the garbage collector in the concurrent mode.

```
ICLRRuntimeHost *pCLRHost = NULL;
HRESULT hr = CorBindToRuntimeEx(
      L"v2.0.40103",
      L"wks",
      STARTUP_CONCURRENT_GC,
      CLSID_CLRRuntimeHost,
      IID_ICLRRuntimeHost,
      (PVOID*) &pCLRHost);
```

CorBindToRuntimeEx is implemented in mscoree.dll. mscoree.dll does not contain the implementation of the CLR engine, but rather is a shim whose primary job is to find and load the requested version of the CLR engine. As such, you'll often hear mscoree.dll referred to as the *CLR startup shim*. The startup shim is required to support the side-by-side architecture of the CLR and the .NET Framework. Side-by-side refers to the ability to have multiple versions of the core CLR and the .NET Framework assemblies installed on a machine at the same time. As we see in Chapter 3, this architecture helps solve the "DLL hell" problems associated with platforms such as Win32 and COM. To keep multiple installations separate, each version of the CLR is installed into its own subdirectory under %windir%\microsoft.net\framework. (Some files are also stored in the global assembly cache.) The startup shim ties the multiple versions of the CLR together. Specifically, the shim tracks which versions are installed and is capable of finding the location on disk of a specific version of the CLR. Because of its role as arbitrator, the shim is not installed side by side. Each machine has only one copy of mscoree.dll installed in %windir%\system32. All requests to load the CLR come through the startup shim, which then directs each request to the requested version of the CLR. Figure 2-2 shows the side-by-side architecture of the CLR and the .NET Framework. We cover this topic in much greater detail in Chapter 3.

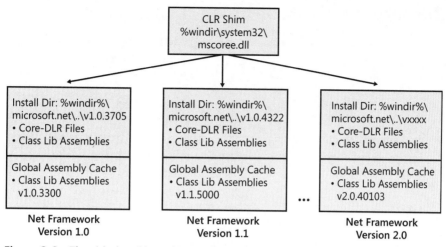

Figure 2-2   The side-by-side architecture of the CLR and the .NET Framework

A call to *CorBindToRuntimeEx* sets the version, garbage collection, build type, and domain-neutral parameters, but it does not actually start the CLR running in a process. My definition of *start* is that the version-specific CLR DLLs are loaded into the process and managed code is then ready to run. Starting the CLR occurs when the host calls the *Start* method on the *ICLRRuntimeHost* interface. You'll notice in the preceding code that *CorBindToRuntimeEx* returns an interface pointer of type *ICLRRuntimeHost* as its last parameter as I discussed earlier. In this way, *CorBindToRuntimeEx* serves two roles as far as a host is concerned: it initializes the CLR and returns an interface pointer from which all interaction between the host and the CLR begins.

The combination of *CorBindToRuntimeEx* and *ICLRRuntimeHost::Start* gives you explicit control over several aspects of the CLR including some basic settings and the exact time at which the CLR is loaded. However, calling these functions isn't strictly required to load the CLR into a process. If explicit calls to *CorBindToRuntimeEx* and *Start* are not made, the CLR will be loaded implicitly in certain scenarios. Although this can be convenient in some cases, implicit loading of the CLR removes your ability to configure it in the way I've been describing. One scenario in which the CLR is often started implicitly is when a managed type is created in a process through COM interoperability. If the CLR has not been initialized and started explicitly, the COM interoperability layer starts the runtime automatically to load and run the type. There might also be cases when you don't want to load the CLR when the process starts, but you still want to configure some of the startup options. For example, you might want to lazily load the CLR to avoid having to pay the cost of starting the CLR when your process starts. You can use the hosting API *LockClrVersion* to register a callback that the CLR will call at the times when it would have loaded itself implicitly. This callback gives you the chance to call *CorBindToRuntimeEx* to initialize the CLR as you see fit. See Chapter 3 for a sample that uses *LockClrVersion*.

As we've seen, gaining control over CLR startup is easy—it takes just a few lines of code. Controlling startup in this way is just one small but useful example of the type of control you obtain through the hosting API with relatively little investment. Chapter 3 covers the use of *CorBindToRuntimeEx* and *LockClrVersion* in much more detail.

Other Unmanaged Functions on mscoree.dll

Although *CorBindToRuntimeEx* is the most commonly used export from mscoree.dll, it is probably not the only one you'll ever use. Table 2-3 briefly describes some of the other commonly used exports that are of interest to hosts.

Table 2-3   Other Commonly Used Exports from mscoree.dll

API Name	Description
GetCORVersion	Returns the version of the CLR that is loaded in the process. *GetCORVersion* returns null if called before the CLR is started.
GetCORSystemDirectory	Returns the directory on disk in which the loaded CLR is installed (see Figure 2-2). This function is useful for locating compilers and others tools that are located in the CLR installation directory.
LockClrVersion	Enables you to register a callback so you can lazily control CLR initialization.
GetRequestedRuntimeInfo	Enables you to determine whether a given version of the CLR is present on the machine.

Hosting Manager Discovery

The COM interfaces in the hosting API are factored into a set of pluggable managers, as described earlier. This factoring allows a host to implement only the managers of interest in a particular scenario. The fact that a host can optionally provide a particular manager means the hosting interfaces must include a protocol by which the CLR can determine which, if any, managers a host chooses to implement. Remember, too, that some managers are implemented completely on the CLR side, such as the host protection manager used to enforce host-specific programming model considerations. These managers are always provided by the CLR if a host asks for them. As such, there must also be a mechanism for a host to ask for a particular CLR-implemented manager.

The discovery of the managers supported by a host and the managers supplied by the CLR are arbitrated through two interfaces named *IHostControl* and *ICLRControl*. As their names suggest, *IHostControl* is implemented by the host and *ICLRControl* is implemented by the CLR.

IHostControl contains a method called *GetHostManager* that the CLR uses to determine which managers a host supports, whereas *ICLRControl* contains a method called *GetCLRManager* that the host calls to obtain an interface pointer to one of the CLR managers.

Figure 2-3 shows the relationship between the host, the CLR, the control interfaces, and the hosting managers. For those managers in which the implementation is split between the CLR and the host, the primary manager interface is always provided by the host.

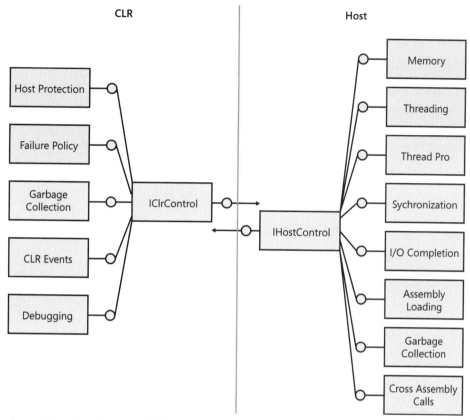

Figure 2-3 IHostControl, ICLRControl, and the hosting managers

Discovering Host-Implemented Managers

Now that we've looked at all the pieces, let's take a look at how the CLR determines which managers a host implements.

Step 1: The Host Supplies a Host Control Class

After the host's call to *CorBindToRuntimeEx* returns, the host initializes an instance of its host control class (that is, a class derived from *IHostControl*) and informs the CLR of its existence by calling *ICLRRuntimeHost::SetHostControl*. It's important to note that the host *must* do this before *ICLRRuntimeHost::Start* is called—calls to *SetHostControl* that occur after *Start* have no effect.

Given a host-implemented control class such as the following:

```
class CHostControl : public IHostControl
{
public:
    // Methods from IHostControl
    HRESULT __stdcall GetHostManager(REFIID riid,
                          void **ppObject);

    // Additional methods, including those from IUnknown, omitted for clarity
};
```

the code in the host to set the host control object looks like this:

```
ICLRRuntimeHost *pCLR = NULL;
// Initialize the clr
HRESULT hr = CorBindToRuntimeEx(L"v2.0.40103",
                    L"wks",
                    STARTUP_CONCURRENT_GC,
                    CLSID_CLRRuntimeHost,
                    IID_ICLRRuntimeHost,
                    (PVOID*) &pCLR);

// Initialize a new instance of our host control object
CHostControl *pHostControl = new CHostControl();

// Tell the CLR about it...
pCLR->SetHostControl((IHostControl *)pHostControl);
```

Step 2: The CLR Queries the Host Control Class

After *CorBindToRuntimeEx* returns, the CLR begins the process of setting itself up to run managed code. As part of this initialization, the CLR checks to see whether a host control has been registered (that is, the host called *ICLRRuntimeHost::SetHostControl*). If not, the host does not implement any managers as far as the CLR is concerned, and initialization proceeds. If a host control class has been registered, the CLR will call *IHostControl::GetHostManager* once for every manager for which the primary interface is implemented by the host. Specifically, *GetHostManager* will be called once for the following IIDs:

- *IID_IHostMemoryManager*
- *IID_IHostTaskManager*
- *IID_IHostThreadPoolManager*
- *IIE_IHostIoCompletionManager*
- *IID_IHostSyncManager*
- *IID_IHostAssemblyManager*
- *IID_IHostGCManager*
- *IID_IHostPolicyManager*

If a valid interface pointer is returned for a given IID, the host is said to implement that manager. If *E_NOINTERFACE* is returned, the host does not implement that manager.

Here's a sample host's implementation of *IHostControl::GetHostManager* that supports just the memory manager and the assembly loading manager:

```
HRESULT __stdcall CHostControl::GetHostManager(REFIID riid, void **ppObject)
{
    if (riid == IID_IHostMemoryManager)
    {
        // The CLR is asking for a memory manager.  Create an instance of the
        // host's memory manager and return it. Note: This snippet assumes
        // the host's implementation of the memory manager is in
        // a class named CHostMemoryManager
        CHostMemoryManager *pMemManager = new CHostMemoryManager();
            *ppObject = (IHostMemoryManager *)pMemManager;
             return S_OK;
    }
    else if (riid == IID_IHostAssemblyManager)
    {
        // The CLR is asking for an assembly loading manager.  Create an
        // instance of the host's manager and return it.  Note: This
        // snippet assumes the host's implementation of the Assembly Loading
        // Manager is in a class named CHostAssemblyManager
        CHostAssemblyManager *pAsmManager = new CHostAssemblyManager();
        *ppObject = (IHostAssemblyManager *)pAssemblyManager;
        return S_OK;
    }
    // This host doesn't support any other managers - so just return
    // E_NOINTERFACE
    *ppObject = NULL;
    return E_NOINTERFACE;
}
```

After the series of calls to *GetHostManager*, the CLR has a complete picture of which managers the host supports. From this point on, the CLR's interaction with the managers goes directly through each manager's primary interface. The host control object's only job is to return managers to the CLR. After that, it's out of the picture.

Obtaining CLR-Implemented Managers

As described earlier, the CLR provides a set of managers that hosts can use to customize various aspects of a running CLR. These managers are implemented completely on the CLR side. A host's interaction with these managers is very simple because the communication is all one way—from the host to the CLR.

The process a host uses to obtain interface pointers to the CLR-implemented managers is relatively straightforward. First, the host obtains an interface pointer to an *ICLRControl* by calling *ICLRRuntimeHost::GetCLRControl*. Next, the host calls *ICLRControl::GetCLRManager*, passing in the IID of the interface corresponding to the manager of interest. For example, the following code obtains a pointer to the failure policy manager, which is used to customize the way the CLR behaves in the face of resource failures:

```
// Get a pointer to an ICLRControl (pCLR is of type ICLRRuntimeHost *)
ICLRControl *pCLRControl = NULL;
pCLR->GetCLRControl(&pCLRControl);

// Ask for the Failure Policy Manager
ICLRPolicyManager *pPolicy = NULL;
pCLRControl->GetCLRManager(IID_ICLRPolicyManager, (void **)&pPolicy);
```

Once the desired interface pointer is returned, the host saves it and calls the methods relevant to the customization it desires. The semantics of when each of the managers can be called and which settings can be configured varies by manager. The rest of this chapter provides an overview of each of the major hosting managers. Details about how to use these managers are provided in subsequent chapters in this book.

Overview of the Hosting Managers

Earlier in the chapter, I described the manager architecture, listed each manager and its interfaces, and talked about how the CLR and the host go about obtaining manager implementations. In this section, I take a brief look at each manager to understand how it can be used by an application to customize a running CLR.

Assembly Loading

The CLR has a default, well-defined set of steps it follows to resolve a reference to an assembly. These steps include applying various levels of version policy, searching the global assembly cache (GAC), and looking for the assemblies in subdirectories under the application's root directory. These defaults include the assumption that the desired assembly is stored in a binary file in the file system.

These resolution steps work well for many application scenarios, but there are situations in which a different approach is required. Remember that CLR hosts essentially define a new application model. As such, it's highly likely that different application models will have different requirements for versioning, assembly storage, and assembly retrieval. To that end, the assembly loading manager enables a host to customize completely the assembly loading process. The level of customization that's possible is so extensive that a host can implement its own custom assembly loading mechanism and bypass the CLR defaults altogether if desired.

Specifically, a host can customize the following:

- The location from which an assembly is loaded

- How (or if) version policy is applied

- The format from which an assembly is loaded (assemblies need not be stored in stand-alone disk files anymore)

Let's take a look at how Microsoft SQL Server 2005 uses the assembly loading manager to get an idea of how these capabilities can be used.

As background, SQL Server 2005 allows user-defined types, procedures, functions, triggers, and so on to be written in managed languages. A few characteristics of the SQL Server 2005 environment point to the need for customized assembly binding:

- **Assemblies are stored in the database, not in the file system.**   Managed code that implements user-defined types, procedures, and the like is compiled into assemblies just as you'd expect, but the assembly must be registered in SQL before it can be used. This registration process physically copies the contents of the assembly into the database. This self-contained nature of database applications makes them easy to replicate from server to server.

- **The assemblies installed in SQL are the exact ones that must be run.**   SQL Server 2005 applications typically have very strict versioning requirements because of the heavy reliance on persisted data. For example, the return value from a managed user-defined function might be used to build an index used to optimize performance. It is imperative that only the exact assembly that was used to build the index is used when the application is run. If a reference to that assembly were somehow redirected through version policy, the index that was previously stored could become invalid.

To support these requirements, SQL Server 2005 makes extensive use of the assembly loading manager to load assemblies out of the database instead of from the file system and to bypass many of the versioning rules that the CLR follows by default.

It's important to notice, however, that not all assemblies are stored and loaded out of the database by SQL. The assemblies used in a SQL Server 2005 application fall into one of two categories: the assemblies written by customers that define the actual behavior of the application (the add-ins), and the assemblies written by Microsoft that ship as part of the Microsoft .NET Framework. In the SQL case, only the add-ins are stored in the database—the Microsoft .NET Framework assemblies are installed and loaded out of the global assembly cache.

In fact, it is often the case that a host will want to load only the add-ins in a custom fashion and let the default CLR behavior govern how the Microsoft .NET Framework assemblies are loaded. To support this idea, the assembly loading manager enables the host to pass in a list of assemblies that should be loaded in the normal, default CLR fashion. All other assembly references are directed to the host for resolution.

Those assemblies that the host resolves can be loaded from any location in any format. These assemblies are returned from the host to the CLR in the form of a pointer to an *IStream* interface. For hosts that implement the assembly loading manager (that is, provide an implementation of *IHostAssemblyManager* when queried for it through *IHostControl::GetHostManager*), the process of binding generally works like this:

1. As the CLR is running code, it often finds references to other assemblies that must be resolved for the program to run properly. These references can be either static in the calling assembly's metadata or dynamic in the form of a call to *Assembly.Load* or one of the other class library methods used to load assemblies.

2. The CLR looks to see if the reference is to an assembly that the host has told the CLR to bind to itself (a Microsoft .NET Framework assembly in our SQL example). If so, binding proceeds as normal: version policy is applied, the global assembly cache is searched, and so on.

3. If the reference is not in the list of CLR-bound assemblies, the CLR calls through the interfaces in the Assembly Manager (*IHostAssemblyStore*, specifically) to resolve the assembly.

4. At this point, the host is free to load the assembly in any way and returns an *IStream ** representing the assembly to the CLR. In the SQL scenario, the assembly is loaded directly from the database.

Figure 2-4 shows the distinction between how add-ins and the Microsoft .NET Framework assemblies are loaded in SQL Server 2005.

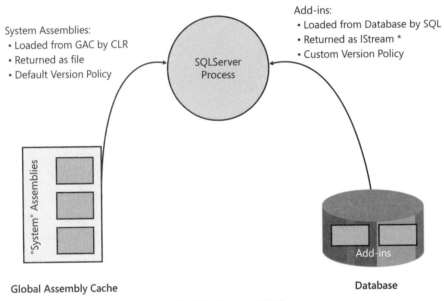

Figure 2-4   Assembly loading in the SQL Server 2005 host

Details of how to implement an assembly loading manager to achieve the customizations described here is provided in Chapter 8.

Customizing Failure Behavior

The CLR hosting APIs are built to accommodate a variety of hosts, many of which will have different tolerances for handling failures that occur while running managed code in the process. For example, hosts with largely stateless programming models, such as ASP.NET, can use a process recycling model to reclaim processes deemed unstable. In contrast, hosts such as SQL Server 2005 and the Microsoft Windows shell rely on the process being stable for a logically infinite amount of time.

The CLR supports these different reliability needs through an infrastructure that can keep a single application domain or an entire process consistent in the face of various situations that would typically compromise stability. Examples of these situations include a thread that fails to abort properly (because of a finalizer that loops infinitely, for example) and the inability to allocate a resource such as memory.

In general, the CLR's philosophy is to throw exceptions on resource failures and thread aborts. However, there are cases in which a host might want to override these defaults. For example, consider the case in which a failure to allocate memory occurs in a region of code that might be sharing state across threads. Because such a failure can leave the domain in an inconsistent state, the host might choose to unload the entire domain instead of aborting just the thread from which the failed allocation occurred. Although this action clearly affects all code running in the domain, it guarantees that the rest of the domains remain consistent and the process remains stable. In contrast, a different host might be willing to allow the questionable domain to keep running and instead will stop sending new requests into it and will unload the domain later.

Hosts use the failure policy manager to specify which actions to take in these situations. The failure policy manager enables the host to set timeout values for actions such as aborting a thread or unloading an application domain and to provide policy statements that govern the behavior when a request for a resource cannot be granted or when a given timeout expires. For example, a host can provide policy that causes the CLR to unload an application domain in the face of certain failures to guarantee the continued stability of the process as described in the previous example.

The CLR's infrastructure for supporting scenarios requiring high availability requires that managed code library authors follow a set of programming guidelines aimed at proper resource management. These guidelines, combined with the infrastructure that supports them, are both needed for the CLR to guarantee the stability of a process. Chapter 11 discusses how hosts can customize CLR behavior in the face of failures and also describes the coding guidelines that library authors must follow to enable the CLR's reliability guarantees.

Programming Model Enforcement

The .NET Framework class libraries provide an extensive set of built-in functionality that hosted add-ins can take advantage of. In addition, numerous third-party class libraries exist that provide everything from statistical and math libraries to libraries of new user interface (UI) controls.

However, the full extent of functionality provided by the set of available class libraries might not be appropriate in particular hosting scenarios. For example, displaying user interface in server programs or services is not useful, or allowing add-ins to exit the process cannot be allowed in hosts that require long process lifetimes.

The host protection manager provides the host with a means to block classes, methods, properties, and fields offering a particular category of functionality from being loaded, and therefore used, in the process. A host can choose to prevent the loading of a class or the calling of a method for a number of reasons including reliability and scalability concerns or because the functionality doesn't make sense in that host's environment, as in the examples described earlier.

You might be thinking that host protection sounds a lot like a security feature, and in fact we typically think of disallowing functionality to prevent security exploits. However, host protection is not about security. Instead, it's about blocking functionality that doesn't make sense in a given host's programming model. For example, you might choose to use host protection to prevent add-ins from obtaining synchronization primitives used to coordinate access to a resource from multiple threads because taking such a lock can limit scalability in a server application. The ability to request access to a synchronization primitive is a programming model concern, not a security issue.

When using the host protection manager to disallow certain functionality, hosts indicate which general categories of functionality they're blocking rather than individual classes or members. The classes and members contained in the .NET Framework class libraries are grouped into categories based on the functionality they provide. These categories include the following:

- **Shared state**   Library code that exposes a means for add-ins to share state across threads or application domains. The methods in the *System.Threading* namespace that allow you to manipulate the data slots on a thread, such as *Thread.AllocateDataSlot*, are examples of methods that can be used to share state across threads.

- **Synchronization**   Classes or members that expose a way for add-in to hold locks. The *Monitor* class in the *System.Threading* namespace is a good example of a class you can use to hold a lock.

- **Threading**   Any functionality that affects the lifetime of a thread in the process. Because it causes a new thread to start running, *System.Threading.Thread.Start* is an example of a method that affects thread lifetime within a process.

- **Process management**   Any code that provides the capability to manipulate a process, whether it be the host's process or any other process on the machine. *System.Diagnostics.Process.Start* is clearly a method in this category.

Classes and members in the .NET Framework that have functionality belonging to one or more of these categories are marked with a custom attribute called the *HostProtectionAttribute* that indicates the functionality that is exposed. The host protection manager comes into play by providing an interface (*ICLRHostProtectionManager*) that hosts use to indicate which categories of functionality they'd like to prevent from being used in the process. The attribute settings in the code and the host protection settings passed in through the host are examined at runtime to determine whether a particular member is allowed to run. If a particular member is marked as being part of the threading category, for example, and the host has indicated that all threading functionality should be blocked, an exception will be thrown instead of the member being called.

Annotating code with the category custom attributes and using the host protection manager to block categories of functionality is described in detail in Chapter 12.

Memory and Garbage Collection

The managers we've looked at so far have allowed the host to customize different aspects of the CLR. Another set of managers has a slightly different flavor—these managers enable a host to integrate its runtime environment deeply with the CLR's execution engine. In a sense, these managers can be considered abstractions over the set of primitives or resources that the CLR typically gets from the operating system (OS) on which it is running. More generally, the COM interfaces that are part of the hosting API can be viewed as an abstraction layer that sits between the CLR and the operating system, as shown in Figure 2-5. Hosts use these interfaces to provide the CLR with primitives to allocate and manage memory, create and manipulate threads, perform synchronization, and so on. When one of these managers is provided by a host, the CLR will use the manager instead of the underlying operating system API to get the resource. By providing implementations that abstract the corresponding operating system concepts, a host can have an extremely detailed level of control over how the CLR behaves in a process. A host can decide when to fail a memory allocation requested by the CLR, it can dictate how managed code gets scheduled within the process, and so on.

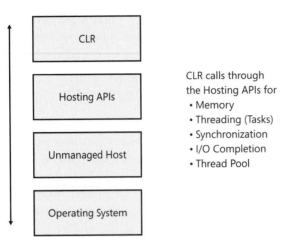

Figure 2-5 The hosting APIs as an abstraction over the operating system

The first manager of this sort that we examine is the memory manager. The memory manager consists of three interfaces: *IHostMemoryManager*, *IHostMalloc*, and *ICLRMemoryNotification-Callback*. The methods of these interfaces enable the host to provide abstractions for the following:

■ **Win32 and the standard C runtime memory allocation primitives** Providing abstractions over APIs such as *VirtualAlloc*, *VirtualFree*, *VirtualQuery*, *malloc*, and *free* allow a host to track and control the memory used by the CLR. A typical use of the memory manager is to restrict the amount of memory the CLR can use within a process and to fail allocations when it makes sense in a host-specific scenario. For example, SQL Server 2005 operates within a configurable amount of memory. Oftentimes, SQL is configured to use all of the physical memory on the machine. To maximize performance, SQL tracks all memory allocations and ensures that paging never occurs. SQL would rather fail a memory allocation than page to disk. To track all allocations made within the process accurately, the SQL host must be able to record all allocations made by the CLR. When the amount of memory used is reaching the preconfigured limit, SQL must start failing memory allocation requests, including those that come from the CLR. The consequence of failing a particular CLR request varies with the point in time in which that request is made. In the least destructive case, the CLR might need to abort the thread on which an allocation is made if it cannot be satisfied. In more severe cases, the current application domain or even the entire process must be unloaded. Each request for additional memory made by the CLR includes an indication of what the consequences of failing that allocation are. This gives the host some room to decide which allocations it can tolerate failing and which it would rather satisfy at the expense of some other alternative for pruning memory.

■ **The low-memory notification available on Microsoft Windows XP and later versions**   Windows XP provides memory notification events so applications can adjust the amount of memory they use based on the amount of available memory as reported by the operating system. (See the *CreateMemoryResourceNotification* API in the Platform SDK for background.) The memory management interfaces provided by the CLR hosting API enable a host to provide a similar mechanism that allows a host to notify the CLR of low- (or high-) memory conditions based on a host-specific notion, rather than the default operating system notion. Although the mechanism provided by the operating system is available only on Windows XP and later versions, the notification provided in the hosting API works on all platforms on which the CLR is supported. The CLR takes this notification as a heuristic that garbage collection is necessary. In this way, hosts can use this notification to encourage the CLR to do a collection to free memory so more memory is made available from which to satisfy additional allocation requests.

In addition to the memory manager, the CLR hosting API also provides a garbage collection manager that allows you to monitor and influence how the garbage collector uses memory in the process. Specifically, the garbage collection manager includes interfaces that enable you to determine when collections begin and end and to initiate collections yourself.

We discuss the details of implementing both the memory and garbage collection managers in Chapter 13.

Threading and Synchronization

The most intricate of the managers provided in the hosting APIs are the threading manager and the synchronization manager. Although the managers are defined separately in the API, it's hard to imagine a scenario in which a host would provide an implementation of the threading manager without implementing the synchronization manager as well. These managers work together to enable the host to customize the way managed code gets scheduled to run within a process.

The purpose of these two managers is to enable the host to abstract the notion of a *unit of execution*. The first two versions of the CLR assumed a world based on physical threads that were preemptively scheduled by the operating system. In .NET Framework 2.0, the threading manager and synchronization manager allow the CLR to run in environments that use cooperatively scheduled fibers instead. The threading manager introduces the term *task* as this abstract notion of a unit of execution. The host then maps the notion of a task to either a physical operating system thread or a host-scheduled fiber.

The scenarios in which these managers are used extensively are likely to be few, so I don't spend too much time discussing them in this book. However, the subject is interesting if for no other reason than the insight it provides into the inner workings of the CLR.

The set of capabilities provided by the threading manager is quite extensive—enough to model a major portion of an operating system thread API such as Win32, with additional features specifically required by the CLR. These additional features include a means for the CLR to notify the host of times in which thread affinity is required and callbacks into the CLR so it can know when a managed task gets scheduled (or unscheduled), among others.

The general capabilities of the threading manager are as follows:

- **Task management**   Starting and stopping tasks as well as standard operations such as join, sleep, alert, and priority adjustment.

- **Scheduling**   Notifications to the CLR that a managed task has been moved to or from a runnable state. When a task is scheduled, the CLR is told which physical operating system thread the task is put on.

- **Thread affinity**   A means for the CLR to tell the host of specific window during which thread affinity must be maintained. That is, a time during which a task must remain running and must stay on the current thread.

- **Delayed abort**   There are windows of time in which the CLR is not in a position to abort a task. The CLR calls the host just before and just after one of these windows.

- **Locale management**   Some hosts provide native APIs for users to change or retrieve the current thread locale setting. The managed libraries also provide such APIs (see *System.Globalization.CurrentCulture* and *CurrentUICulture* in the Microsoft .NET Framework SDK). In these scenarios, the host and the CLR must inform each other of locale changes so that both sides stay synchronized.

- **Task pooling**   Hosts can reuse or pool the CLR-implemented portion of a task to optimize performance.

- **Enter and leave notifications**   Hosts are notified each time execution leaves the CLR and each time it returns. These hooks are called whenever managed code issues a PInvoke or Com Interoperability call or when unmanaged code calls into managed code.

One feature that perhaps needs more explanation is the ability to hook calls between managed and unmanaged code. On the surface it might not be obvious how this is related to threading, but it ends up that hosts that implement cooperatively scheduled environments often must change how the thread that is involved in the transition can be scheduled.

Consider the scenario in which an add-in uses PInvoke to call an unmanaged DLL that the host knows nothing about. Because of the information received by implementing the threading and synchronization abstractions, the host can cooperatively schedule tasks running managed code just fine. However, when control leaves that managed code and enters the unmanaged DLL, the host no longer can know what that code is going to do. The unmanaged DLL could include code that takes a lock on a thread and holds it for long periods of time, for example. In this case, managed code should not be cooperatively scheduled on that thread because the host cannot control when it will next get a chance to run. This is where the hooks come in. When a host receives the notification that control is leaving the CLR, it can switch the scheduling mode of that thread from the host-control cooperative scheduling mode to the preemptive scheduling mode provided by the operating system. Said another way, the host gives responsibility for scheduling code on that thread back to the operating system. At some later point in time, the PInvoke call in our sample completes and returns to managed code. At this point, the hook is called again and the host can switch the scheduling mode back to its own cooperatively scheduled state.

I mentioned earlier that the threading manager and synchronization manager are closely related. The preceding example provides some hints as to why. The interfaces in the threading manager provide the means for the host to control many aspects of how managed tasks are run. However, the interfaces in the synchronization manager provide the host with information about how the tasks are actually behaving. Specifically, the synchronization manager provides a number of interfaces the CLR will use to create synchronization primitives (locks) when requested (or needed for internal reasons) during the execution of managed code. Knowing when locks are taken is useful information to have during scheduling. For example, when code blocks on a lock, it's likely a good time to pull that fiber off a thread and schedule another one that's ready to run. Knowing about locks helps a host tune its scheduler for maximum throughput.

There's another scenario in which it's useful for a host to be aware of the locks held by managed tasks: deadlock detection. It's quite possible that a host can be running managed tasks and tasks written in native code simultaneously. In this case, the CLR doesn't have enough information to resolve all deadlocks even if it tried to implement such a feature. Instead, the burden of detecting and resolving deadlocks must be on the host. Making the host aware of managed locks is essential for a complete deadlock detection mechanism.

Primarily for these reasons, the synchronization manager contains interfaces that provide the CLR with implementations of the following:

- Critical sections
- Events (both manual and auto-reset)
- Semaphores
- Reader/writer locks
- Monitors

We dig into more details of these two managers in Chapter 14.

Other Hosting API Features

We've now covered most of the significant functionality the CLR makes available to hosts through the hosting API. However, a few more features are worth a brief look. These features are discussed in the following sections.

Loading Code Domain Neutral

When assemblies are loaded domain neutral, their jit-compiled code and some internal CLR data structures are shared among all the application domains in the process. The goal of this feature is to reduce the working set. Hosts use the hosting interfaces (specifically, *IHostControl*) to provide a specific list of assemblies they'd like to have loaded in this fashion. Although domain-neutral loading requires less memory, it does place some additional restrictions on the assembly. Specifically, the code that is generated is slightly slower in some scenarios, and a domain-neutral assembly cannot be unloaded until the process exits. As such, hosts typically do not load all assemblies domain neutral. In practice, the set of assemblies loaded in this way often are the system assemblies—add-ins are almost never loaded domain neutral so they can be dynamically unloaded while the process is running. This is the exact model that hosts such as SQL Server 2005 follow. Domain-neutral code is covered in detail in Chapter 9.

Thread Pool Management

Hosts can provide the CLR with a thread pool by implementing the thread pool manager. The thread pool manager has one interface (*IHostThreadPoolManager*) and provides all the functionality you'd expect including the capability to queue work items to the thread pool and set the number of threads in the pool. The thread pool manager is described in detail in Chapter 14.

I/O Completion Management

Overlapped I/O can also be abstracted by the host using the I/O completion manager. This manager enables the CLR to initiate asynchronous I/O through the host and receive notifications when it is complete. For more information on the I/O completion manager, see the documentation for the *IHostIoCompletionPort* and *ICLRIoCompletionPort* interfaces in the .NET Framework SDK.

Debugging Services Management

The debugging manager provides some basic capabilities that enable a host to customize the way debuggers work when attached to the host's process. For example, hosts can use this manager to cause the debugger to group related debugging tasks together and to load files containing extra debugging information. For more information on the debugging manager, see the *ICLRDebugManager* documentation in the .NET Framework SDK.

Application Domain Management

Application domains serve two primary purposes as far as a host is concerned. First, hosts use application domains to isolate groups of assemblies within a process. In many cases, application domains provide the same level of isolation for managed code as operating system processes do for unmanaged code. The second common use of application domains is to unload code from a process dynamically. Once an assembly has been loaded into a process, it cannot be unloaded individually. The only way to remove it from memory is to unload the application domain the assembly was in. Application domains are always created in managed code using the *System.AppDomain* class. However, the hosting interface *ICLRRuntimeHost* enables you to register an application domain manager[1] that gets called by the CLR each time an application domain is created. You can use your application domain manager to configure the domains that are created in the process. In addition, *ICLRRuntimeHost* also includes a method that enables you to cause an application domain to be unloaded from your unmanaged hosting code.

Application domains are such a central concept to hosts and other extensible applications that I dedicate two chapters to them. The first chapter (Chapter 5) provides an overview of application domains and provides guidelines to help you use them most effectively. The second chapter (Chapter 6) describes the various ways you can customize application domains to fit your application's requirements most closely.

CLR Event Handling

Hosts can register a callback with the CLR that gets called when various events happen when running managed code. Through this callback, hosts can receive notification when the CLR has been disabled in the process (that is, it can no longer run managed code) or when application domains are unloaded. More details on the CLR event manager are provided in Chapter 5.

Summary

The set of APIs described in this chapter allow the CLR to be customized to work in a variety of application environments. The extent of the customization allowed ranges from configuring basic startup parameters to controlling critical runtime notions such as how code is loaded into the process, how memory is managed, and when code is scheduled to run. The hosting API is factored into a set of managers that group logically related interfaces together. As the author of a CLR host, you get to choose which of these managers you'd like to implement so you can customize only those aspects of the CLR that are most important to your scenario.

This chapter provides an overview of the hosting API to give you an idea of the various ways the CLR can be customized. Throughout the rest of this book, we dig into different parts of the API in greater detail.

---

1. The term "manager" as used here can be a bit confusing given the context in which we've used it in the rest of the chapter. An application domain manager isn't a "manager" as specifically defined by the CLR hosting interfaces. Instead, it is a managed class that you implement to customize how application domains are used within a process.

Chapter 3

Controlling CLR Startup and Shutdown

A number of configurable settings determine the basic characteristics of the CLR that gets loaded into the process. For example, various settings enable you to select the version of the CLR to load, configure the basic operations of the garbage collector, and so on. All these settings must be specified before the CLR is loaded.

If you're writing a CLR host, you can have full control over all the settings that control CLR startup. It's worth noting that you might not have to write the host yourself to configure the startup options that your scenario requires. Most hosts provide some mechanism to enable application developers or administrators to customize at least some of the CLR startup options. For example, the default CLR host offers a high degree of customization through application configuration files. The options available when using the default host are described in Chapter 4.

In this chapter, I concentrate on what you do to customize CLR startup when writing your own host. Writing your own host enables you to set all of the startup options and offers you flexibility to control when the CLR is actually loaded into the process.

I start by describing the details of the CLR startup settings, and then I describe how to use the unmanaged function *CorBindToRuntimeEx* to set them explicitly. When you're talking about controlling CLR startup, it's natural to also talk about controlling CLR shutdown. Although you can't completely unload the CLR from a process and reload it later, the CLR hosting API essentially enables you to disable the CLR. I end the chapter with a discussion of exactly what it means to disable the CLR and how to do it.

The CLR Startup Configuration Settings

Four primary settings can be configured as part of CLR startup. Once set, these options affect all code running in the process and cannot be changed (although the domain-neutral settings can be further refined). These options are as follows:

1. The version of the CLR to load into the process

2. Whether you'd like the server or workstation build

3. Garbage collection options

4. Settings to control domain-neutral loading of code

The following sections describe these settings in detail.

Version

Setting the CLR version arguably requires the most thought because several criteria go into making the right choice.

Multiple versions of the CLR can be installed on a given machine at one time. Establishing how your host behaves when multiple versions of the CLR are present is one of the most critical up-front decisions you have to make. This decision is especially important because only one version of the CLR can be loaded into a process, and once that version has been loaded, it cannot be unloaded and replaced with another version. In general, you have two choices when choosing a version. First, you can specify that you always want to run using a specific version. Or you can choose always to run with the latest version of the CLR installed on the machine.

You'll see throughout this section that the trade-off is between isolating your host from version changes made to the CLR over time (to the extent possible) and always being upgraded to the CLR containing the newest functionality, the most bug fixes, and the latest performance enhancements.

In practice, most hosts choose to select a specific version and stay with it. Sticking with a single version gives the host the most control over its own environment because it minimizes the amount of changes made to the CLR the host runs with (however, you'll see in a bit that you can't completely isolate yourself from change because of service releases made to the CLR). When you specify a particular CLR version to use, if a new version of the CLR is released that you wish to support, you must update your code to specify the version number of the new CLR and then test your code against that release before shipping the new host to your customers. On the other hand, clearly, scenarios exist in which it is preferable for an application always to run with the latest CLR version. I explore both options throughout this section.

Side by Side: A Technique to Avoid DLL Hell

When multiple versions of a piece of software are installed on one computer and can be run at the same time, they are referred to as existing *side by side*. From the very beginning, the concept of side by side has been a specific design goal and has been built directly into the CLR.

To avoid confusion, I want to clarify that the concept of side by side can be viewed from a few different perspectives. The first perspective is the notion of side-by-side applications and assemblies. As part of the core versioning story in the CLR, multiple versions of a specific application or assembly can be installed and run simultaneously. This is in direct contrast to the Win32 and COM models in which the last version of an application or component to be installed is the one that everyone uses. This *use latest* approach led directly to the phenomenon referred to as "DLL Hell"—the all-too-common scenario we've all experienced when the installation of one application breaks some existing application on the machine.

A major portion of the Microsoft .NET Framework approach to solving this problem is to leverage side by side as a default rather than use latest. In the side-by-side model, the installation of a new version doesn't overwrite existing versions and both versions can be run at the same time. This form of isolation through side by side is key to solving DLL Hell.

However, you can't completely isolate applications from changes unless the platform on which the application is running installs and runs side by side as well. This is the other perspective of side by side: the fact that the entire .NET Framework (including the CLR) installs side by side and that hosts or individual applications get to pick which version they'd like to run. As you can see, side by side of the platform is a direct follow-on to side by side at the application level. The two concepts are closely related and tend to bleed together rather easily when you're discussing either one specifically.

At the time of this writing, three side-by-side versions of the .NET Framework (which includes the CLR) have been shipped: Microsoft .NET Framework 1.0, .NET Framework 1.1, and .NET Framework version 2.0. Any, or all, of these can be present on a machine to which your application is deployed. The primary focus of this section is to help you determine the best course of action for selecting which version your application should run with when more than one version is installed.

The criteria that typically go into selecting a CLR version include the following:

- The version your application was built and tested against
- Any functionality available in a certain release on which either your application or extensions to your application depend
- The Microsoft strategy for issuing service releases to the .NET Framework
- The compatibility of the .NET Framework between releases

You can start to imagine the complexities you might run into when considering multiple versions of a platform coexisting—especially if you've written a host with one version of the CLR and are asked to run a component from one of your customers written with another version!

Choosing a versioning strategy starts by considering how multiple versions of the CLR coexist on the same machine and how a particular version gets selected and loaded.

The Side-by-Side Architecture of the .NET Framework

At a high level, the .NET Framework consists of two big pieces: the CLR and the .NET Framework class libraries. Drawing a distinction between the core CLR files and the .NET Framework class libraries is useful when talking about how a side-by-side version of the .NET Framework is installed and loaded. One reason the distinction is useful is because the version numbers for the core CLR files appear differently than the version numbers for the class libraries when you view them using Windows Explorer, which can be confusing. Throughout this section, I point out where the versions appear differently and why.

For purposes of this discussion, I define the CLR as the set of unmanaged files that make up the CLR execution engine plus the managed assembly that contains the base class library. The core engine files include such items as the engine (mscorwks.dll), the jit compiler (mscorjit.dll), the base portion of the security system (mscorsec.dll), and so on. The file for the assembly containing the base class library is mscorlib.dll. The .NET Framework class libraries include all the managed assemblies that contain the classes that make up the API to the .NET platform, including system.dll, system.xml.dll, system.windows.forms.dll, and many others.

Four interesting things happen (at least from the perspective of side by side) when a version of the .NET Framework is installed:

1. Registry entries that indicate a new version of the .NET Framework has been installed are made.

2. The CLR files and a copy of the .NET Framework class libraries are installed into a sub-directory of your Windows directory.

3. The .NET Framework class libraries are installed in the global assembly cache (GAC).

4. The CLR startup shim is installed in the Windows system directory if the version of the CLR you are installing is newer than any other version that already exists on the machine. The shim is the centerpiece of the side-by-side architecture as I explain in a minute.

.NET Framework Registry Keys   The registry key under which all .NET Framework–related keys are written is as follows:

HKEY_LOCAL_MACHINE\SOFTWARE\Microsoft\.NETFramework

Information about the versions of the .NET Framework installed on the machine is kept under the *Policy* subkey. Each time a new version of the .NET Framework is installed, a new subkey is written under the *Policy* key. Figure 3-1 shows the state of the registry after both .NET Framework 1.0 and .NET Framework 1.1 have been installed.

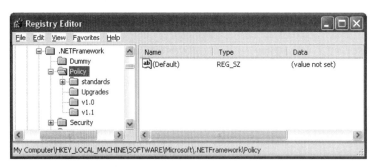

Figure 3-1   Registry entries when multiple versions of the CLR are installed

The version numbers written into the registry are those of the core CLR files. The CLR contained in .NET Framework 1.0 has a major and minor version number of 1.0 as indicated by the v1.0 subkey, whereas the CLR in .NET Framework 1.1 has a major and minor version of 1.1 (the v1.1 subkey). Furthermore, each version of the CLR also has a build number that you should consider when determining which version to load. The build number is stored as a value under the key that describes the major and minor numbers. For example, the build number for .NET Framework 1.0 CLR is 3705, as shown in Figure 3-2.

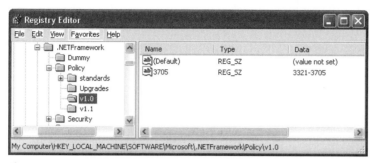

Figure 3-2 Registry entries showing the version number for the CLR contained in .NET Framework 1.0

As you can see, the registry is the central point for determining which versions of the .NET Framework are installed on your machine. You can get this list easily using the standard Win32 registry functions.

The Versioned Installation Directory   The core CLR files and the class libraries are written to a subdirectory of your Windows directory under Microsoft.NET\Framework. Figure 3-3 shows the state of this directory after both .NET Framework 1.0 and .NET Framework 1.1 have been installed.

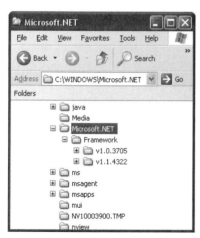

Figure 3-3 Contents of %windir%\Microsoft.NET with multiple versions of the .NET Framework installed

Notice that the subdirectories are named by CLR version and that those versions match the names of the keys and values in the registry. The fact that the names in the registry match the names in the file system is not a coincidence. The CLR startup shim uses this mapping to determine the presence of a given CLR version and to apply any upgrades in the appropriate scenarios (more on this later).

The Global Assembly Cache   The .NET Framework setup program installs each of the class library assemblies into the GAC. The GAC maintains the side-by-side storage of assemblies automatically, so the setup program just calls the GAC install APIs and lets the GAC sort out the storage needs. As expected, installing two versions of the .NET Framework results in two copies of each class library assembly in the GAC, as shown in Figure 3-4.

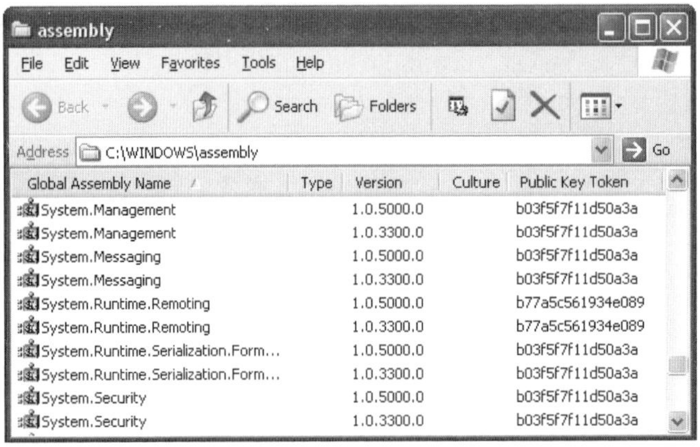

Figure 3-4   Contents of the GAC with multiple versions of the .NET Framework installed

You'll notice that the version numbers displayed for the class library assemblies are different than the version numbers displayed for the core CLR files shown earlier. Assemblies have two different version numbers (there's actually more than two, but let's ignore the rest!). Because managed code is stored in standard executable files, each assembly has a Win32 version number just as executable files containing unmanaged code do. In addition, managed code files have an assembly version number that the CLR uses when resolving references to assemblies. When you navigate to the GAC with Windows Explorer, view the GAC with the .NET Framework Administration tool, or look inside an assembly with the Microsoft IL Disassembler SDK tool (ildasm.exe) you see the assembly version number—not the Win32 version number. If you were to use Windows Explorer to look at the properties of a managed assembly, you'd see the Win32 version there as well. This version number would be the same as the version number used to name the installation directory or to identify that version of the .NET Framework in the registry.

Table 3-1 shows the mapping between Win32 version numbers and assembly version numbers for each release of the .NET Framework.

Table 3-1 **Win32 and Assembly Version Numbers for the .NET Framework**

	Win32 Version Number	Assembly Version Number
Microsoft .NET Framework 1.0	1.0.3705	1.0.3300
Microsoft .NET Framework 1.1	1.1.4322	1.0.5000
Microsoft .NET Framework version 2.0	2.0.41013	2.0.3600

Why Are Two Copies of the Class Library Assemblies Installed?

It might seem odd that two copies of the class library assemblies are installed during setup: one copy is installed in the version subdirectory (%windir%\Microsoft\.NET-Framework\v*XXXX*), while another copy is installed in the GAC. The reason this is done is to support both compile-time and run-time scenarios with the same install. None of the compilers that target the CLR (at least that I'm aware of) has the ability to compile against a reference to an assembly in the GAC. That is, you cannot supply an assembly name as input to the compiler and have it automatically found in the GAC. Instead, you must supply the path to the file containing the manifest. The copies of the assemblies in the version directory are there so you can reference them on the command line for your compiler. By the way, if you use a development tool such as Microsoft Visual Studio 2005, this is all hidden from you because Visual Studio takes care of passing the filenames of the assemblies you reference to the compiler for you.

The CLR Startup Shim

Every aspect of these two installations I've discussed so far aims to keep the two versions of the .NET Framework completely separate: registry entries are stored under version-specific keys, files are installed in subdirectories based on version, and the GAC separates the storage of multiple versions of the same assembly. At this point, nothing in the architecture ties these multiple versions together. Specifically, some software component must be aware of which versions exist and have the ability to map a request to load a certain version or a request to run a certain application into a specific version of the CLR. This is the job of the CLR startup shim. The shim code is contained in the file mscoree.dll, which is installed in the Windows system directory. The shim is *not* installed side by side. That is, installing a new version of the .NET Framework overwrites the version of mscoree.dll that was there previously. The shim is not installed side by side out of necessity because of the reasons just stated—it is the component that acts as a broker between the host application and a specific version of the CLR. In fact, the only way to load a version of the CLR is to go through the shim. Because the shim is not installed side by side, its requirements for backward compatibility are extremely high. Complete side by side is not possible on all operating systems that the .NET Framework supports, so in essence Microsoft has dramatically reduced the surface area for backward-compatibility problems down to one small DLL. Every effort is made to keep the functionality in this DLL as simple and straightforward as possible. The relationship between the shim and multiple versions of the .NET Framework is shown in Figure 3-5.

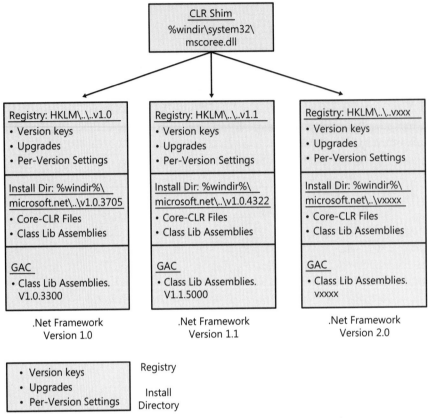

Figure 3-5   The shim and multiple versions of the .NET Framework

Two primary pieces of functionality in the shim relate to side by side. The first is the *CorBind-ToRuntimeEx* API that was introduced in Chapter 2. *CorBindToRuntimeEx* takes a version number (among other things) and loads that version of the CLR into the process. The other important piece of functionality in the shim is the default CLR host. The default CLR host is used in various scenarios, the most common of which is when executables are launched from the command line. The default CLR host is also invoked if a request comes in to instantiate a managed class through the COM Interoperability layer. Chapter 4 describes the inner workings of the default CLR host, including how you can configure the CLR startup options using application configuration files.

Given the earlier installation discussion, it's relatively easy to see how the shim maps a version number to the actual implementation of that version using registry keys and directory names. The one piece of information missing is the root directory under which all versions of the CLR are installed. This information is captured in the *InstallRoot* registry under

HKEY_LOCAL_MACHINE\SOFTWARE\Microsoft\.NETFramework as shown in Figure 3-6. The setup program always sets this to %windir%\Microsoft.NET\Framework\ and currently doesn't offer an option to change it.

Figure 3-6   The InstallRoot registry value

The shim's ultimate goal is to construct a path to the requested version of the core CLR engine DLL, mscorwks.dll. The formula it uses is straightforward:

Path to CLR engine DLL = Contents of the InstallRoot registry value (i.e., "C:\Windows\ Microsoft\.NETFramework\") + Name of the Major.Minor key (i.e., "v1.1") + Value of the Build number key (i.e., "4322") + Filename of core engine DLL ("mscorwks.dll")

So, given a version number of "v1.1.4322," the shim will load C:\Windows\Microsoft\.NET-Framework\v1.1.4322\mscorwks.dll.

It might seem unnecessary to use the version information in the registry. After all, the combination of the *InstallRoot* value plus the requested version leads right to the appropriate directory. The registry lookup is done for few reasons. The first is as an extra sanity check that the installation of the CLR is coherent. The more important reason, though, is for scenarios involving the default CLR host in which a request for a particular CLR version is upgraded to another version. In these situations, the information in the registry is required. If you're writing your own host (i.e., calling *CorBindToRuntimeEx* yourself), these automatic upgrades don't apply.

Once the core CLR DLL (mscorwks.dll) is loaded, the other unmanaged supporting DLLs such as the JIT compiler and class loader are loaded from the same directory. In addition, the version of mscorlib.dll that matches the given CLR is loaded. mscorlib.dll is an interesting case because even though it is a managed assembly (it contains base classes such as *String*, *Object*, and *Exception*), a given version of mscorlib.dll is directly tied to the same version of mscorwks.dll and cannot be loaded independently. The two are tied closely together because they share data structures that must be in sync. Once you've picked a version of the CLR to load in the process, you have no say over which version of mscorlib.dll gets loaded.

Other than mscorlib.dll, the class library assemblies aren't tied to a particular version of mscorwks.dll, but nevertheless selecting a version of the core CLR files also influences the versions of the class libraries used. As discussed earlier, the .NET Framework consists of two major pieces: the core CLR and the class libraries. A version of the core CLR and the corresponding version of the class libraries are built and tested to work together. Using this matched set together results in the most consistent, predictable experience.

Once a CLR is loaded in the process, all requests to load one of the class library assemblies results in the loading of that version of the assembly that matches the CLR in the process. This is true even if the application running in the process references a different version. For example, say a developer has built an add-in that references the version of *System.Windows.Forms* that shipped with .NET Framework 1.0 (that is, version 1.0.3300). Now, say that control is hosted in a process that has loaded .NET Framework 1.1 Even though the control was compiled with a reference to version 1.0.3300, the version of *System.Windows.Forms* that is used at run time will be the version that shipped with .NET Framework 1.1 (that is, version 1.0.5000).

At first glance, this design can seem overly restrictive, especially in scenarios like the one I've been discussing in which a host can load add-ins written with various versions of the .NET Framework. This is one point where the different perspectives on side by side described earlier begin to blur. It is also a point at which the discussion about the compatibility between multiple versions of the .NET Framework comes into play. Earlier I said that the ability to run multiple versions of a given assembly simultaneously within a process was a key to solving DLL Hell because it loosened the backward-compatibility requirements for a given assembly. But on the other hand, I just discussed a design that doesn't use that side-by-side capability when it comes to the .NET Framework assemblies themselves. If a single version of a given assembly is always going to be loaded, its requirements for backward compatibility are very high.

Thankfully, the situation isn't as inconsistent as it seems because the behavior I've just described is only the default. You can use application configuration files to indicate that you'd like a version of a given class library assembly loaded different than the one that matches the CLR in the process. These overrides can be specified for each application domain in the process. I examine the details of how to do this in Chapter 7. Furthermore, it's likely that a future version of the CLR might have a more flexible solution to the compatibility concerns brought on by forcing only a particular set of assemblies to be loaded into a process.

The CLR and the Class Library Assemblies Are Not Automatically Matched When You Use .NET Framework 1.0

The behavior I just described, whereby picking a version of the CLR automatically redirects all assembly references to the matching set of class library assemblies, is implemented only in .NET Framework 1.1 and .NET Framework version 2.0. As a result, if the CLR that shipped with .NET Framework 1.0 is running in your process, you won't see this behavior. Instead, the versions of the class libraries that the CLR attempts to load are the ones referenced by the assembly that is running. This can be an issue if you are running an application that contains assemblies built with different versions of the .NET Framework.

Let's take a look at a specific example to see how this can affect you. Say you have a host that loads two add-ins: Addin2002.dll and Addin2003.dll. As its name suggests, Addin2002.dll was built with .NET Framework 1.0 and therefore has references to the versions of the class libraries that shipped with that version. Similarly, Addin2003.dll was built with .NET Framework 1.1 and contains references to the 1.1 libraries. If .NET Framework 1.1 is installed and your host runs with that version, all of the references to the 1.0 class libraries contained in Addin2002.dll would be automatically upgraded to the 1.1 versions. As a result, that assembly would run just fine (ignoring potential compatibility issues). Clearly, because Addin2003.dll was built with 1.1, that would run too, so the whole scenario works fine. In contrast, if you are running the CLR from .NET Framework 1.0 in your process, the references to the 1.1 class libraries contained in Addin2003.dll would *not* be "downgraded" and therefore won't be found at run time. This is because the CLR that shipped in .NET Framework 1.0 does not automatically redirect references to a matching set of class libraries as described earlier. Fortunately, there is a way out of this. You can use an application configuration file to specify additional version statements to get this scenario to work. I describe the details of how to do that in Chapter 7.

.NET Framework Updates

One of the basic decisions a host has to make as part of its overall versioning strategy is what its tolerance is for handling updates to the CLR it has chosen to run with. The decision whether to load a specific CLR version always or to take the latest is a direct consequence of the degree to which the host would like to be insulated from potential compatibility issues caused by updates made to the CLR it uses.

A simple example helps illustrate the basic point. Consider a scenario in which two hosts, HostFix.exe and HostFloat.exe, exist on a machine that has .NET Framework 1.1 installed. HostFix.exe specifies that .NET Framework 1.1 should always be used, whereas HostFloat.exe indicates it would like to run with the latest version on the machine. At some later point in time, .NET Framework 2.0 is installed. The next time HostFix.exe starts, it uses .NET Framework 1.1 just as it always has. In contrast, HostFloat.exe now begins to use .NET Framework 2.0. In this scenario, the installation of .NET Framework 2.0 directly affects HostFloat.exe, but HostFix.exe remains unaffected. By choosing to specify an exact version, HostFix.exe has insulated itself from this particular update to the CLR.

It's important to notice, however, that although specifying an exact version means you won't be affected by major product releases like in the scenario just described, you still *will* be affected by bug fix updates made to the version of the CLR you have specified.

To understand the degree to which you are exposed to these kinds of updates, you must be aware of the following types of .NET Framework releases and how they are applied:

■ **Single bug fix releases** These releases consist of a fix for a single bug and are usually made available in response to a request from a specific customer or because a general issue related to security was found. You might have heard these releases referred to as hot fixes or something similar. These fixes usually affect only one file and are typically made available through Microsoft Windows Update or a similar mechanism aimed at wide distribution. When deployed, the affected file overwrites the existing file on disk. The host can't explicitly control whether to accept this fix—once the administrator installs the fix, the host begins to use it.

- **Service packs** Service packs are collections of bug fixes. From a host's point of view, a service pack behaves just as a single bug fix release does in that the affected files are overwritten, thus automatically affecting the host.

- **Feature releases** These releases contain new feature work and are installed side by side. The releases used as examples throughout this chapter (.NET Framework 1.0 and .NET Framework 1.1) are examples of feature releases. Because feature releases are installed side by side, the host has the flexibility to decide whether to pick up the new release automatically.

Choosing Your Strategy: Fix or Float

I've discussed how multiple versions of the .NET Framework are installed, how the shim loads a particular version, the implications that has on the class libraries loaded, and what the basics of the CLR upgrade story are. Given all that, how do you pick whether to always load a specific CLR version (and if so, which one) or to always take the latest?

In practice, the majority of hosts choose always to load a specific version of the CLR (and therefore the class library assemblies). Clearly, the primary advantage in this approach is control: you as a host can control your runtime environment to the greatest extent possible. We've all experienced incompatibilities from time to time when forced to upgrade to a new version of a platform without explicit consent. Also, bug fix updates still can affect you, but the .NET Framework team has built in the concept of side by side specifically to enable hosts and other applications to remain isolated. That said, the version with which you choose to run should be straightforward: always run with the version you have built and tested against. If you're unsure whether that version exists on all machines you must run on, you can always play it safe and redistribute the version of the .NET Framework you require along with your application. A primary benefit of side by side is that even when you redistribute a version of the .NET Framework along with your application, other applications on the machine do not start using it by default. So you can be assured that installing your application won't affect other applications.

The Server and Workstation Builds

The second startup setting is the choice between build types. The CLR comes in two flavors—a workstation build and a server build. As the names suggest, the workstation build is tuned for workstations, whereas the server build is tuned for the high-throughput scenarios associated with multiprocessor server machines.

The difference between the two builds is in the way the garbage collector works. The server build creates garbage collection heaps based on the number of processors and can therefore take advantage of the fact that multiple processors exist to make collections parallel. The server build of the CLR is so optimized for multiprocessor machines that the startup shim doesn't even allow it to be run on machines with just one processor! If you specify the server build on a uniprocessor machine, the workstation build is always loaded instead.

The default build type is always workstation. That is, if you don't specify a preference, the workstation build is always used. You might assume that the default build on multiprocessor machines is the server build, but it isn't. The default is always workstation regardless of the number of processors on the machine. Therefore, if you have a server-based application, you'll always want to request the server build specifically so you're sure you'll get it on multiprocessor machines.

Concurrent Garbage Collection

If you are using the workstation build of the CLR, you can specify another startup setting to configure the garbage collector. The CLR garbage collector can run in either concurrent mode or nonconcurrent mode. If you are running on a computer with more than one processor, concurrent mode causes garbage collections to happen on a background thread at the same time that user code is running on foreground threads. If your computer has only one processor, garbage collections happen on the same threads that are running user code. Concurrent collections are appropriate for applications that have a high degree of user interactivity. The goal of the concurrent collection mode is to keep the application as responsive as possible. In contrast, the nonconcurrent garbage collector does the collections on the same threads on which the user code is running. It might seem counterintuitive at first, but nonconcurrent collections result in much higher throughput overall. The primary reason for the increased throughput is because collections are done on the same thread, so there is no need to synchronize the threads doing the collections with the threads running user code.

Remember, too, that the concurrent garbage collection mode is available only when running the workstation build. If you select the server build, you'll always run with nonconcurrent collections. If you specify the server build and concurrent collections, the concurrent collection setting will be ignored—you'll always get nonconcurrent collections.

The following points summarize how the concurrent garbage collection settings relate to the two CLR builds.

- **Server build**   When using the server build, you'll always get nonconcurrent collections as noted earlier. This combination is used when server-style applications that require high throughput are run on multiprocessor machines (recall, the server build doesn't run on uniprocessor machines). Microsoft SQL Server and Microsoft ASP.NET are examples of hosts that use this combination.

- **Workstation build—UI-intensive applications**   If your application requires a high degree of user interactivity, likely you'll be best off using the workstation build and concurrent collections. Applications based on Microsoft Windows Forms or a similar class library are examples of the type of application benefiting from this scenario.

■ **Workstation build—batch (non-UI) applications**   If you're running the workstation build, but your application does not display UI (or at least not much), whether to enable concurrent collections isn't as clear. The best thing to do is to run your app in both modes and measure the performance. Several people have found that their batch-*style* apps perform better using nonconcurrent collections when the workstation build is used.

A more in-depth discussion of concurrent and nonconcurrent garbage collection is beyond the scope of this book. Jeffery Richter's book *Applied Microsoft .NET Framework Programming* from Microsoft Press dedicates an entire chapter to garbage collection and is widely considered the most in-depth, accurate, and well-explained description of the CLR garbage collector.

Domain-Neutral Code

Domain neutral refers to the ability to share the jit-compiled code for an assembly across all application domains in a process, thus reducing the amount of memory used. Unlike the rest of the settings discussed throughout this chapter, you don't have to specify your domain-neutral settings at startup time. These settings can be specified in a few different ways, most of which can be done later. In addition to the startup settings, you can configure domain-neutral behavior through custom attributes, using application domain configuration settings or by implementing the *IHostControl* interface introduced in Chapter 2. A full description of domain-neutral code and the various ways it can be configured is given in Chapter 9. Here, I just discuss the options available for configuring domain-neutral code at startup.

At startup time, you can choose from three options to configure how the CLR loads domain-neutral code:

■ No assemblies are loaded domain neutral (except mscorlib, which is always loaded domain neutral)

■ All assemblies are loaded domain neutral

■ Only assemblies with strong names are loaded domain neutral

In practice, it turns out that having just these three general options doesn't work very well in most hosting scenarios. Almost all CLR hosts contain some managed code in addition to the unmanaged code that is used to initialize and start the CLR. Ideally, the managed portion of the host would be loaded domain neutral because it is guaranteed to be used in all application domains. As a result, hosts written before the .NET Framework version 2.0 release typically choose to give the managed portion of their host a strong name and load all strong-named assemblies domain neutral. However, choosing this setting means that all add-ins that happen to be strong named are loaded domain neutral as well. The primary disadvantage of this, because assemblies loaded domain neutral cannot be unloaded, is that some add-ins exist in the process until it is shut down, thus using memory that ideally could be reclaimed for better purposes. To support this scenario, the *IHostControl* interface includes a method that enables a host to supply the specific assemblies that should be loaded domain neutral. In this way, a host can elect to load only its own implementation domain neutral, not any add-ins.

I expect the scenarios in which hosts must use the preceding three options to decrease as a result of the more flexible support provided by *IHostControl*.

Setting the Startup Options Using *CorBindToRuntimeEx*

Once you understand the CLR startup options, setting them using *CorBindToRuntimeEx* is easy. The version and build type options map directly to parameters to the API, and the concurrent garbage collection and the domain-neutral options are specified as flags.

Here's the definition of *CorBindToRuntimeEx* from mscoree.h:

```
STDAPI CorBindToRuntimeEx(LPCWSTR pwszVersion,
                          LPCWSTR pwszBuildFlavor,
                          DWORD startupFlags,
                          REFCLSID rclsid,
                          REFIID riid,
                          LPVOID FAR *ppv);
```

Table 3-2 describes the parameters to *CorBindToRuntimeEx* and how they are used to set the CLR startup options.

Table 3-2 *CorBindToRuntimeEx* **Parameters to Configure CLR Startup**

CLR Startup Setting	Parameter	Legal Values	Default
Version	*pwszVersion*	A string describing the version of the CLR to load or specifying NULL.	NULL
		The string must be in the following form:	
		v.*major.minor.build*	
		For example, to load the CLR that comes with .NET Framework 1.0, you'd pass	
		v1.0.3705.	
		Passing NULL loads the latest version of the CLR installed on the machine.	
Build	*pwszBuildFlavor*	A string describing whether to load the server or workstation build. The following are valid values: svr and wks.	wks
		Remember, too, that svr value is ignored on uniprocessor machines. The workstation build is always loaded in such cases.	
Concurrent garbage collection	*startupFlags*	Concurrent garbage collection is turned on by passing *STARTUP_CONCURRENT_GC* to *startupFlags*. This flag, along with the flags for the domain-neutral options, is specified by the *STARTUP_FLAGS* enumeration in mscoree.h.	Enabled

Table 3-2 *CorBindToRuntimeEx* Parameters to Configure CLR Startup

CLR Startup Setting	Parameter	Legal Values	Default
Domain-neutral code	*startupFlags*	The following are valid values from *STARTUP_FLAGS*: *STARTUP_LOADER_OPTIMIZATION_SINGLE_DOMAIN.* No assemblies are loaded domain neutral. *STARTUP_LOADER_OPTIMIZATION_MULTI_DOMAIN.* All assemblies are loaded domain neutral. *STARTUP_LOADER_OPTIMIZATION_MULTI_DOMAIN_HOST.* Strong-named assemblies are loaded domain neutral.	No assemblies loaded domain neutral (except mscorlib)

You'll notice that *CorBindToRuntimeEx* has three parameters in addition to the ones described in Table 3-2: *rclsid*, *riid*, and *ppv*. These parameters are used to get an interface pointer of type *ICLRRuntimeHost* through which to access all the functionality in the COM interfaces that are part of the CLR hosting APIs. The capabilities available through *ICLRRuntimeHost* are described in Chapter 2. Table 3-3 describes the parameters used to get a pointer to *ICLRRuntimeHost*.

Table 3-3 *CorBindToRuntimeEx* Parameters to Return *ICLRRuntimeHost*

Parameter	Description
rclsid	[in][1] The CLSID of the object containing the *ICLRRuntimeHost* interface. Always pass *CLSID_ClrRuntimeHost*.[2]
riid	[in] The IID of *ICLRRuntimeHost*. Always pass *IID_ICLRRuntimeHost*.
ppv	[out] The address of the returned *ICLRRuntimeHost* pointer.

1 [in] means that the parameter is passed in to the function. [out] means the parameter is returned from the function.

2 The need to pass the CLSID and the IID for the runtime host interface might seem unnecessary. The reason these parameters exist is so the API can return interfaces of different types in a future release.

Starting the CLR

Calling *CorBindToRuntimeEx* sets the CLR startup options and loads the core runtime engine DLL (mscorwks.dll) into the process. However, the runtime must still be "started" before any managed code can be run. Once initialized, starting the CLR is easy. Just call the *Start* method on the *ICLRRuntimeHost* pointer you got back from calling *CorBindToRuntimeEx* as shown in the following example.

```
// Set the CLR startup options
    HRESULT hr = CorBindToRuntimeEx(
        L"v2.0.41013",
        L"svr",
        NULL,
```

```
        CLSID_CLRRuntimeHost,
        IID_ICLRRuntimeHost,
        (PVOID*) &pCLR);

    // Use ICLRRuntimeHost to start the CLR
    hr = pCLR->Start();
    assert(SUCCEEDED(hr));
```

Handling Failures from *CorBindToRuntimeEx*

Recall that only one copy of the CLR can be loaded in a process at a time. So calling *CorBind-ToRuntimeEx* multiple times has no effect. If you do so, *S_FALSE* is returned on all but the first call. Successful calls to the API return *S_OK*, as you'd expect.

If you pass in a version that is not present on the machine, *CLR_E_SHIM_RUNTIMELOAD* (defined in CorError.h in the .NET Framework software development kit) is returned. In addition, the dialog box shown in Figure 3-7 is displayed instructing the user to install the desired version of the CLR.

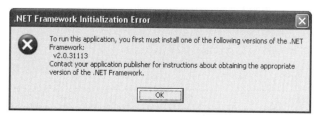

Figure 3-7   Incorrect version dialog box

Clearly, scenarios exist, especially in server applications, in which a host would not want to display UI when the requested version of the CLR is not present. You can prevent this dialog box from appearing by calling the *SetErrorMode* Win32 API before calling *CorBindToRun-timeEx*. *SetErrorMode* takes a single parameter that controls whether dialog boxes are displayed for certain types of errors. Be sure to pass *SEM_FAILCRITICALERRORS*:

```
SetErrorMode(SEM_FAILCRITICALERRORS);
```

Deferring CLR Initialization and Startup

In some scenarios a host might elect to delay the initialization and loading of the CLR until it is actually needed rather than doing it upfront. Loading the CLR lazily can reduce both your startup time and startup working set. However, waiting until later to call *CorBindToRuntimeEx* opens a window in which a copy of the CLR might get loaded into the process without your knowledge and therefore without an opportunity for you to set the startup options you want.

The classic case in which this can occur is with COM interoperability. If your host doesn't initialize the CLR at startup and some unmanaged code in your process loads a managed type through COM, the activation of that type brings the CLR into the process. Because the host is out of the loop at this point, the default settings chosen by the default CLR host are used (refer to Chapter 4 to see how the default CLR host chooses these settings). This can result in loading a CLR that does not match what the host would have chosen. For example, a different version of the CLR might be loaded or the wrong build type might be chosen.

Fortunately, hosts can use a function on the shim called *LockClrVersion* to close this window. When you call *LockClrVersion*, you're essentially stating that you are the only one allowed to initialize the CLR in this process. When the shim receives the first request to run managed code, it will call a function that you provide to enable you to initialize the CLR the way you see fit. In the preceding scenario, the host's function would have been called when the managed type was accessed through the COM interoperability layer, thereby giving the host a chance to initialize and load the CLR.

Here's the definition of *LockClrVersion* as found in mscoree.h:

```
typedef HRESULT (__stdcall *FLockClrVersionCallback) ();
STDAPI LockClrVersion(FLockClrVersionCallback hostCallback,
              FLockClrVersionCallback *pBeginHostSetup,
              FLockClrVersionCallback *pEndHostSetup);
```

The parameters to *LockClrVersion* are summarized in Table 3-4.

Table 3-4   Parameters to *LockClrVersion*

Parameter	Description
hostCallback	[in] A pointer to a host-supplied function the shim will call when the CLR needs to be initialized
pBeginHostSetup	[out] A pointer to a CLR-supplied function that the host must call just before it begins to initialize the CLR
pEndHostSetup	[out] A pointer to a CLR-supplied function that the host must call after it has initialized the CLR

At first glance, *pBeginHostSetup* and *pEndHostSetup* might seem unnecessary. After all, the shim can tell when the CLR has been initialized after the call to *hostCallBack* returns. The reason these additional parameters are needed is to notify the shim about which thread the initialization is happening on. The shim needs this information mostly for internal implementation reasons relating to the fact that only one thread in the process is allowed to initialize the CLR. The shim also uses the information to block other threads that might enter the process and wish to run managed code from proceeding until the initialization is done.

Listing 3-1 from the sample DeferredStartup.exe shows how to use *LockClrVersion* to delay the loading of the CLR. In this example, I force the CLR into the process by activating a managed type through the COM Interoperability layer as in the scenario described earlier. When the managed type is activated, the host-supplied function is called to initialize the CLR.

Listing 3-1   Using *LockClrVersion* to Load the CLR

```
#include "stdafx.h"
#include <mscoree.h>

// Declare globals to hold function pointers to call to notify the shim when the
// initialization of the CLR is beginning and ending.
FLockClrVersionCallback g_beginInit;
FLockClrVersionCallback g_endInit;

// This function is registered as the host callback provided to the CLR by LockClrVersion.
//
 The shim will call this function the first time it receives a request to run managed code.
STDAPI InitializeCLR()
{
    // Notify the CLR that initialization is beginning
    g_beginInit();

    // Initialize the CLR.
    ICLRRuntimeHost *pCLR = NULL;
     HRESULT hr = CorBindToRuntimeEx(
        L"v2.0.41013",
        NULL,
        NULL,
        CLSID_CLRRuntimeHost,
        IID_ICLRRuntimeHost,
        (PVOID*) &pCLR);

    assert(SUCCEEDED(hr));

    // Start the CLR.
    pCLR->Start(NULL, NULL);

    // Notify the CLR that initialization has completed.
    g_endInit();

    return S_OK;
}

int main(int argc, char* argv[])
{
    HRESULT hr = S_OK;

    // Call LockClrVersion so the InitializeCLR always get called to set up the runtime.
    LockClrVersion(InitializeCLR, &g_beginInit, &g_endInit);

    // Initialize COM and create an instance of a managed type through COM Interop.  This
    // will require the CLR to be loaded—InitializeCLR will be called.
    CoInitialize(NULL);

    CLSID clsid;
    hr = CLSIDFromProgID(L"System.Collections.SortedList", &clsid);
    assert(SUCCEEDED(hr));

    IUnknown *pUnk = NULL;
    hr = CoCreateInstance(clsid, NULL, CLSCTX_INPROC_SERVER, IID_IUnknown, (LPVOID *) &pUnk);
```

```
    assert(SUCCEEDED(hr));

    pUnk->Release();

    CoUninitialize();

    return 0;
}
```

LockClrVersion can be used for another, less obvious purpose—to prevent the CLR from ever being loaded in a process. The scenarios in which you'd want to do this are clearly limited, but if you had a requirement to prevent managed code from running in your process completely, *LockClrVersion* is the way to do it. As you've seen, *LockClrVersion* takes a callback function that gets invoked when the CLR needs to be initialized. If you return a failure *HRESULT* from this callback, the CLR would not be loaded. In this way, you can prevent the CLR from ever entering your process.

> **Note**   There's another technique you can use to accomplish a subset of what *LockClrVersion* provides. Recall that *CorBindToRuntimeEx* has a *startupFlags* parameter. One of the flags you can pass is called *STARTUP_LOADER_SETPREFERENCE*. When you pass this flag to *CorBindToRuntimeEx*, the startup shim does not initialize the CLR, but rather just remembers the version number you've passed through the *pwszVersion* parameter. Later, when the CLR needs to be initialized—either implicitly (as happens when a managed type is created from COM) or explicitly by another call to *CorBindToRuntimeEx* that does not set *STARTUP_LOADER_SETPREFERENCE*—the shim loads the version of the CLR that it remembered earlier. In this way, you can use *CorBindToRuntimeEx* to indicate which version of the CLR to load in a delayed fashion.
>
> Using *STARTUP_LOADER_SETPREFERENCE* with *CorBindToRuntimeEx* is more limited than *LockClrVersion* in three key ways:
>
> - **You can specify only a version number**   *STARTUP_LOADER_SETPREFERENCE* remembers only the version number you passed to *CorBindToRuntimeEx*. It does not remember your preference for build type, your garbage collection settings, or your domain-neutral code settings. When the CLR is started later, defaults are used for these other settings.
>
> - **You cannot provide a callback to do extra processing**   As you've seen, *LockClrVersion* takes a callback that is invoked when the CLR needs to be initialized. In addition to calling *CorBindToRuntimeEx*, hosts often use this callback to create their host control object and report it to the CLR so the appropriate hosting managers are set up properly. If you don't use *LockClrVersion*, there's no way to accomplish this, or other related startup tasks, in a delayed fashion.
>
> - **You cannot prevent the CLR from entering the process**   You can use *LockClrVersion* to prevent the CLR from ever entering a process by returning a failure *HRESULT* from your callback. You can't do this using *STARTUP_LOADER_SETPREFERENCE* and *CorBindToRuntimeEx*.
>
> Even with these limitations, passing *STARTUP_LOADER_SETPREFERENCE* to *CorBindToRuntimeEx* can still be useful. If all you need to do is ensure a specific version of the CLR is loaded in a lazy fashion, you can do this with much less code than it takes to use *LockClrVersion* properly.

The CLR and Process Lifetime

Once loaded into a process, the CLR can never be completely removed. That is, there is no way to guarantee that all files and data structures associated with the CLR are cleaned up and all the memory they required is returned. You can, however, disable the CLR. Specifically, when you disable the CLR, it no longer is able to run managed code in the process. The process itself is not damaged in the sense that unmanaged code continues to run just fine, but further attempts to run managed code are not honored.

You disable the CLR by using the *Stop* method on *ICLRRuntimeHost*. Calls to *Stop* must be paired with calls to *ICLRRuntimeHost::Start*, which is discussed earlier in the chapter. That is, you must call *Stop* once for each call you made to *Start* for the CLR to be disabled. It's also important to note that once the CLR has been disabled using *Stop*, it can never be restarted in the same process again.

Summary

The *CorBindToRuntimeEx* API gives you explicit control over when the CLR is loaded and enables you to configure the basic settings that determine how the CLR behaves in your process. By using *CorBindToRuntimeEx* you can specify which version of the CLR gets loaded, whether the CLR is optimized for a server application or a workstation application, and how code is shared across the application domains in the process. Of these settings, determining the most appropriate version to load is the most complex because you must understand the implications of having more than one version of the .NET Framework installed on a single machine. In addition to understanding the basic side-by-side architecture of the CLR, you also must be aware of more subtle issues such as the impact of CLR servicing releases on the version you choose. Although the CLR has rich support to customize startup, the support to control CLR shutdown is less sophisticated. There is no way to remove the CLR from a process completely after it has been loaded, but you can disable it. Disabling the CLR prevents you from running managed code in the future and removes some of the CLR files and data structures from the process, but the shutdown isn't completely clean. In addition, even if you disable the CLR in this fashion, you cannot restart it again. You must start an entire new process to reinitialize the CLR.

Chapter 4

Using the Default CLR Host

The CLR ships with a default host that you can use to run managed code in any process without having to write your own CLR host. That is, you don't have to include code in your application to call *CorBindToRuntimeEx*, interact with the CLR through the *ICLRRuntimeHost* interface, and so on. The goal of this chapter is to provide enough details about the default CLR host to help you determine whether it meets the requirements of your scenario. If the capabilities provided by the default host meet your needs and if you don't require the additional functionality provided by the CLR hosting APIs, using the default host can save you time and effort.

The default host is invoked in one of two ways. First, the default host is used to run managed executables launched from the command line or from the shell. The second use of the default host is to run managed types that have been introduced to a process through the CLR's COM interoperability layer. This second method of invoking the default host can fit with a wide range of scenarios. Any application that exposes an extensibility model based on COM (or creates COM components as part of the application itself) can use the default host to extend the application with the capabilities of managed code.

Using the default host doesn't provide all of the flexibility you get by writing a host yourself, but you can configure many of the CLR startup options through application configuration files (see Chapter 3 for details on what the CLR startup options are). Understanding how the default host gets activated, what its default values are for the CLR startup options, and the degree to which these defaults can be customized helps you determine whether using the default host is appropriate in your application.

Invoking the Default Host: Running Managed Executables

The default host for running managed executables is implemented in the function *_CorExeMain* in the CLR startup shim (mscoree.dll). Control is passed to *_CorExeMain* differently depending on the operating system on which you're running. On computers running Microsoft Windows XP and later, the operating system loader has explicit knowledge of managed code executables and calls *_CorExeMain* directly when a managed executable is launched.

For earlier versions of the Windows operating system, the process for getting to *_CorExeMain* isn't as direct. When a compiler emits a managed executable, it sets the main routine (in the Portable Executable [PE] header) to a small stub that calls *_CorExeMain* instead of the executable's "real" entry point. Launching the executable thereby passes control to the CLR startup shim, where the process of running the program begins.

How Does Windows XP Determine Whether a File Contains Managed Code?

Managed executable files are stored in the standard PE format. An additional directory entry has been added to the standard file header that identifies whether the file contains managed code. You can see this directory entry by looking for the COM Descriptor Directory in the output from running *dumpbin /headers* on a file.

If a nonzero address is specified for the COM Descriptor Directory, the file contains managed code as shown in the following output from *dumpbin*:

```
OPTIONAL HEADER VALUES
             10B magic # (PE32)
            6.00 linker version
            1000 size of code
            2000 size of initialized data
               0 size of uninitialized data
            265E entry point (0040265E)
            2000 base of code
            4000 base of data
          400000 image base (00400000 to 00407FFF)
            2000 section alignment
            1000 file alignment
            4.00 operating system version
            0.00 image version
            4.00 subsystem version
               0 Win32 version
            8000 size of image
            1000 size of headers
           13331 checksum
               3 subsystem (Windows CUI)
             400 DLL characteristics
                   No safe exception handler
          100000 size of stack reserve
            1000 size of stack commit
          100000 size of heap reserve
            1000 size of heap commit
               0 loader flags
              10 number of directories
               0 [        0] RVA [size] of Export Directory
            2604 [       57] RVA [size] of Import Directory
            4000 [      860] RVA [size] of Resource Directory
               0 [        0] RVA [size] of Exception Directory
               0 [        0] RVA [size] of Certificates Directory
            6000 [        C] RVA [size] of Base Relocation Directory
            20A0 [       1C] RVA [size] of Debug Directory
               0 [        0] RVA [size] of Architecture Directory
```

```
    0 [        0] RVA [size] of Global Pointer Directory
    0 [        0] RVA [size] of Thread Storage Directory
    0 [        0] RVA [size] of Load Configuration Directory
    0 [        0] RVA [size] of Bound Import Directory
 2000 [        8] RVA [size] of Import Address Table Directory
    0 [        0] RVA [size] of Delay Import Directory
 2008 [       48] RVA [size] of COM Descriptor Directory¹
    0 [        0] RVA [size] of Reserved Directory
```

Invoking the Default Host: Activating Managed Types Through COM Interop

The Microsoft .NET Framework software development kit (SDK) includes a tool (regasm.exe) you can use to make managed types available through COM. In this way, a managed type can be brought into a process using any of the existing COM APIs. regasm.exe works by creating the registry entries necessary to make the type visible to COM. The default host for managed types activated in this way is also implemented in the CLR startup shim (mscoree.dll). In this scenario, the default host is activated because regasm.exe sets the CLR startup shim as the *InProcServer32* key under the COM registry entries for all managed types. Figure 4-1 shows the registry entries that regasm.exe would make to allow the managed type *System.Collections.SortedList* to be activated through COM.

Figure 4-1   Registry entries that expose a managed type to COM

When an instance of *System.Collections.SortedList* is created through COM, the shim loads the CLR in the process and returns a class factory through which COM can create the type. The CLR determines which type it needs to create by looking back in the registry for the globally unique identifier (GUID)/ProgID requested by COM. Notice in Figure 4-1 that regasm.exe adds some custom registry values under the *InProcServer32* key for a managed type. These values include the name of the type to create and the assembly in which the type is implemented.

---

1. A nonzero value identifies a managed code file.

Defaults for the CLR Startup Options

Once control reaches the shim through either of the activation paths described previously, the default host determines which values to use for the four CLR startup options (version, build type, garbage collection mode, and the domain-neutral settings). Determining the build type, the garbage collection mode, and the domain-neutral settings is easy: the default values are hard-coded into the host. The default values for these settings are as follows:

- **Build type** The workstation build is always loaded, regardless of the number of processors on the machine.

- **Garbage collection mode** The garbage collection mode is always set to concurrent.

- **Domain-neutral code** No assemblies (except mscorlib) are loaded domain neutral by default.

Selecting a CLR Version

The process for selecting the version of the CLR to load into the process is more involved and is different depending on whether the default host is activated to run a managed executable or to load a managed type through COM. The version to load is not hard-coded into the host as the other settings are, but rather varies based on which version of the CLR was used to build the assembly about to be run and which versions of the CLR are present on the machine.

Running Managed Executables

Embedded in every assembly is the version of the CLR used when the assembly was built. For example, if you build an assembly with the .NET Framework SDK 1.1 (included in Microsoft Visual Studio .NET 2003), your assembly will contain the version number 1.1.4322—the version of the CLR included in .NET Framework 1.1. Keep in mind that the version number I am discussing here is not related to the version you give to the assembly. The recording of the CLR version in your assembly happens completely under the covers when your assembly is compiled.

The samples for this book include a utility called clrversion.exe that can be used to display the version of the CLR used to build a particular assembly. Just invoke clrversion.exe from the command line with the name of the file containing the assembly you're interested in to display the version of the CLR used to build that assembly. Here's sample output from running clrversion.exe on a file called simpleexe.exe.

```
C:\>clrversion SimpleExe.exe
SimpleExe.exe was built with v1.1.4322 of the CLR
```

The tool clrversion.exe is useful for helping you determine why the shim is choosing a particular version of the CLR when many are installed on the machine.

When running a managed code executable, the default host begins by looking in the assembly to determine which version of the CLR was used to build the file. It then looks in the registry to determine whether that version of the CLR is installed on the machine. It also determines whether any upgrades to that version should be applied (more on this later in the chapter). If the version of the CLR used to build the executable is installed, the startup shim loads that version of the CLR to run the program. For more details on what these registry keys look like and how the shim maps a version number to a given CLR, see Chapter 3.

Upgrades   If the version of the CLR used to build the executable is not installed on the machine, the shim might choose to run the program with a later version of the CLR. It's important to remember that an upgrade is not applied in all circumstances. The shim chooses to run an application with a later version of the CLR only if the following two conditions are true:

- The version of the CLR used to build the application has not been installed.

- The application does not have a configuration file that explicitly states a preference for a specific CLR version(s).

If these two conditions are met, the shim looks to see whether a newer version of the CLR is present on the machine that is compatible with the version used to build the application. Information about whether a given CLR release is intended to be compatible with other releases is stored in the registry under the Upgrades key:

HKEY_LOCAL_MACHINE\SOFTWARE\Microsoft\.NETFramework\Policy\Upgrades

For example, the Upgrades registry key shown in Figure 4-2 indicates that version 1.1.4322 of the CLR is compatible with version 1.0.3705. Because 1.1.4322 is intended to be compatible with 1.0.3705, the shim will use version 1.1.4322 of the CLR to run an application built with 1.0.3705 (but remember, this happens only if 1.0.3705 isn't present on the machine and the application doesn't have a configuration file that states a version preference).

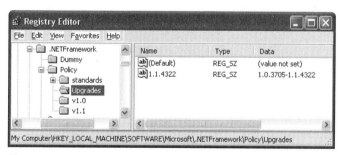

Figure 4-2   The Upgrades registry key

Let's look at a few examples to see how the shim behaves when the conditions for an upgrade are met. Say you have a program myapp.exe that was built with CLR version 1.0.3705. Regardless of whether a newer, compatible version of the CLR is present, myapp.exe will always be run with 1.0.3705 if that version is installed on the machine. Figure 4-3 shows the application running with the version it was built with, even though a newer, compatible version is present.

MyApp.exe

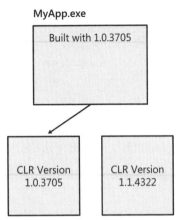

Figure 4-3   Applications run with the CLR version they are built with by default.

However, if CLR version 1.0.3705 is not installed, but version 1.1.4322 is, the application is run with 1.1.4322 because the Upgrades key identifies it as a suitable upgrade. This scenario is shown in Figure 4-4.

MyApp.exe

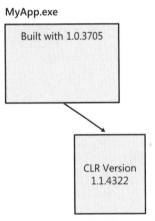

Figure 4-4   Applications can be run with a newer, compatible version of the CLR.

Remember that this behavior occurs only when the default host has not been customized using a configuration file. I explore the details of how to specify a CLR version using an application configuration file later in the chapter.

Activating Managed Types Through COM Interop

The shim's algorithm for picking a version in the COM interoperability scenario is much more straightforward—the latest version installed on the machine is always used. This "use latest" behavior might sound like taking the easy way out, but in fact the alternatives are no more desirable. In the interoperability scenario discussed previously, the executable that started the process clearly contains no information about CLR versions because it is not a managed code file. So no information is available when the process starts to hint at which version to use.

The managed assemblies that get loaded through COM interoperability do contain the version of the CLR they were built with just like managed executables do. It's tempting to think that the version of the CLR to load can be determined by looking at the assembly the shim has been asked to load through COM. This approach might work fine if the application were to load only one assembly, but it can fall apart if multiple assemblies are to be loaded. In this case, each assembly might have been built with a different version of the CLR. Therefore, the first one to be loaded determines the version of the CLR that would run all assemblies in the process (recall that only one version of the CLR can exist in a process). In many scenarios, the order in which multiple assemblies are loaded is not guaranteed. So basing the versioning decision on the first loaded assembly introduces unpredictability when multiple assemblies are involved.

For example, consider an application that supports an add-in model based on COM. The add-ins for this application can be written in managed code as long as the appropriate COM interfaces are provided to hook into the application. If the user selects which add-ins to load based on choices in a menu, the order in which the add-ins are selected determines which version of the CLR is used, which in turn influences how the application behaves.

Scenarios like these are the primary reason the shim always selects the latest CLR in situations in which managed code is first brought into the process through COM. Although choosing the latest version relies on a high degree of compatibility between releases of the CLR, it at least keeps the behavior of this type of application consistent.

This behavior of using the latest CLR will likely remain true as long as Microsoft continues to release versions of the CLR that are backward compatible (at least by design). If Microsoft decides to ship a version of the CLR that is intentionally not backward compatible, the logic for determining which CLR to load in these types of interoperability scenarios will likely have to change.

Customizing the Default Host Using Configuration Files

The default behavior described previously can be customized for the version, build type, and garbage collection settings using application configuration files. The only setting you cannot change using a configuration file is the specification for which assemblies should be loaded domain neutral. The domain-neutral settings can be set only by using the CLR hosting interfaces or through a custom attribute, as discussed in Chapter 9.

Application configuration files are Extensible Markup Language (XML) files that are associated with an application by naming convention and directory. When using the default host, configuration files must be placed in the same directory as the application and are named by simply appending *.config* to the name of the executable file for the application. For example, the configuration file for myapp.exe must be called myapp.exe.config.

Configuration files can be used to customize the settings for both the managed executable scenario and the COM interoperability scenario described earlier. It might seem odd that a configuration file can be used to customize the CLR in the COM interoperability scenario. After all, the configuration file has settings that are relevant only to managed programs, yet the main executable for the application in this scenario is unmanaged. This works because the shim looks for the configuration file based on the name of the executable that started the process (as obtained by calling the Microsoft Win32 API *GetModuleFileName*). The fact that the primary executable does not consist of managed code is irrelevant.

There are two ways to edit configuration files: by hand or with the .NET Framework configuration tool. For purposes of this discussion, the configuration tool is somewhat limited in that it doesn't enable you to set the CLR version that should be used to run the application. For this reason, and for a better understanding of what's going on under the covers, I stick to showing the XML itself. However, I point out the scenarios in which the tool can be used instead.

In the following sections, I describe how to use configuration files to customize the garbage collection, build type, and version settings.

Concurrent Garbage Collection

Recall that the default setting for concurrent garbage collection is on. That is, collections will happen on background threads while the application is running if the application is running on a multiprocessor machine. As described, the default for concurrent garbage collection and that of the build type (workstation) work nicely together. It is possible, however, to disable concurrent garbage collection through the configuration file.

The value for concurrent garbage collection is set using the *<gcConcurrent>* element in the configuration file. This element must always be nested inside the *<runtime>* element. (See the .NET Framework SDK documentation for a description of the complete configuration file schema.) The element *<gcConcurrent>* has a single attribute called *enabled* whose value is either the string "*true*" (the default) or "*false*". The following configuration file shows how to disable concurrent garbage collection for a given application:

```
<configuration>
  <runtime>
    <gcConcurrent enabled="false" />
  </runtime>
</configuration
```

Concurrent garbage collection is one of the settings that can be changed using the .NET Framework configuration tool as well. You can find a shortcut to the tool in Control Panel under Administrative Tools. I don't go into detail on using the tool here, but if you've never used the tool, an overview can be found in the SDK guide.

The options for concurrent garbage collection are shown in the Properties dialog box for an application, as shown in Figure 4-5.

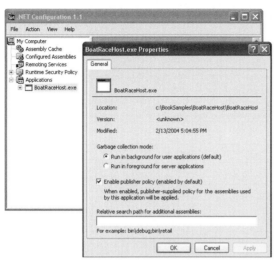

Figure 4-5   Setting concurrent garbage collection using the .NET Framework configuration tool

The Properties dialog box presents the options as a set of radio buttons under Garbage Collection Mode. The wording of the options conveys whether collections are done in the background or not. The option Run In Background For User Applications corresponds to the default of enabled, whereas the Run In Foreground For Server Applications option corresponds to not enabled.

Be careful not to confuse the term *server applications* in this dialog box with the server build of the CLR. By choosing this option, you are configuring the workstation build to run without concurrent garbage collection—you are not directing the shim to load the server build. You can specify that the server build should be used either by calling *CorBindToRuntimeEx* as described in Chapter 3 or by using a configuration file as described in the next section.

Build Type

You can change the default build type of workstation to server using the *gcServer* element in an application configuration file. The *gcServer* element has an attribute called *enabled* that you set to true if you'd like to run the server build. Keep in mind that the server build is loaded only on multiprocessor machines, however. Even if you set *gcServer* to true on a single-processor machine, the workstation build will be loaded. The following configuration file uses the *gcServer* element to specify that the server build of the CLR should be used:

```
<configuration>
  <runtime>
    <gcServer enabled="true" />
  </runtime>
</configuration>
```

Unlike the settings for concurrent garbage collection, there is no support in the .NET configuration tool for setting the build type—you must edit the XML directly.

As I explained in Chapter 3, you can also specify a build type using the *pwszBuildFlavor* parameter to *CorBindToRuntimeEx*. If you specify a build type using both *CorBindToRuntimeEx* and the *gcServer* element in the application's configuration file, the setting passed to *CorBindToRuntimeEx* takes precedence.

Changing the Build Type on Older Versions of the CLR

The ability to specify a build type using an application configuration file is new in .NET Framework 2.0. If you want to load the server build for executables running with either .NET Framework 1.0 or .NET Framework 1.1, you must write a small CLR host that uses *CorBindToRuntimeEx* to specify the build type. Fortunately, it's very easy to write an application launcher that calls *CorBindToRuntimeEx* to set the server build and then runs the original application.

The following sample does just that. svrhost.exe is a CLR host that can be used to run managed executables from the command line using the server build of the CLR. svrhost.exe takes the managed executable to run as a command-line parameter. In addition to the executable, you can also pass any command-line arguments for the managed executable to svrhost.exe as well. For example, say you have an application called paystub.exe that you normally invoke as follows:

```
C:\> paystub stevenpr  013103
```

To run paystub.exe with the server build of the CLR, you'd invoke it using svrhost.exe as follows:

```
C:\> svrHost paystub stevenpr  013103
```

The code for svrhost.exe is very straightforward, as shown in Listing 4-1. svrhost.exe uses *CorBindToRuntimeEx* to load the server build of the CLR. After the CLR has started, svrhost.exe gathers the name of the program to execute along with any arguments from the command line. It then uses the *ExecuteAssembly* method on the *System.AppDomain* class to run the specified program in the default application domain. Notice that svrhost.exe uses an interface called *ICorRuntimeHost* instead of the *ICLRRuntimeHost* interface I introduced in Chapter 2. *ICorRuntimeHost* is the primary hosting interface in .NET Framework 1.0 and .NET Framework 1.1. In .NET Framework 2.0, that interface is replaced with *ICLRRuntimeHost*. Because you want svrhost.exe to run on these older versions of the CLR, the sample sticks with *ICorRuntimeHost*.

Listing 4-1 svrhost.cpp

```
#include "stdafx.h"

// needed for CorBindToRuntimeEx
#include <mscoree.h>
```

```cpp
// include the typelib for mscorlib for access to the default AppDomain through COM Interop
#import <mscorlib.tlb> raw_interfaces_only high_property_prefixes("_get","_put","_putref")

using namespace mscorlib;

int _tmain(int argc, _TCHAR* argv[])
{
    if (argc < 2)
    {
        printf("Usage: SvrHost <Managed Exe> [Arguments for Managed Exe]\n");
        return 0;
    }

    ICorRuntimeHost *pCLR = NULL;

    // Initialize the CLR.  Specify the server build.  Note that I'm
    // loading the CLR from .NET Framework 1.1.
    HRESULT hr = CorBindToRuntimeEx(
        L"v1.1.4322",
        L"svr",
        NULL,
        CLSID_CorRuntimeHost,
        IID_ICorRuntimeHost,
        (PVOID*) &pCLR);

    assert(SUCCEEDED(hr));

    // Start the CLR
    pCLR->Start();

    // Get a pointer to the default AppDomain
    _AppDomain *pDefaultDomain = NULL;
    IUnknown   *pAppDomainPunk = NULL;

    hr = pCLR->GetDefaultDomain(&pAppDomainPunk);
    assert(pAppDomainPunk);

    hr = pAppDomainPunk->QueryInterface(__uuidof(_AppDomain),
                                        (PVOID*)&pDefaultDomain);
    assert(pDefaultDomain);

    // get the name of the exe to run
    long retCode = 0;
    BSTR asmName = SysAllocString(argv[1]);

    // Collect the command-line arguments to the managed exe.  These must be
    // packaged as a SAFEARRAY to pass to ExecuteAssembly.
    SAFEARRAY *psa = NULL;
    SAFEARRAYBOUND rgsabound[1];

    rgsabound[0].lLbound = 0;
    rgsabound[0].cElements = (argc - 2);
    psa = SafeArrayCreate(VT_BSTR, 1, rgsabound);
    assert(psa);
```

```
    for (int i = 2; i < argc; i++)
    {
        long idx[1];
        idx[0] = i-2;
        SafeArrayPutElement(psa, idx, SysAllocString(argv[i]));
    }

    // Run the managed exe in the default AppDomain
    hr = pDefaultDomain->ExecuteAssembly_3(asmName, NULL, psa, &retCode);
    assert(SUCCEEDED(hr));

    // clean up
    SafeArrayDestroy(psa);
    SysFreeString(asmName);
    pAppDomainPunk->Release();
    pDefaultDomain->Release();

    _tprintf(L"\nReturn Code: %d\n", retCode);
    return retCode; }
```

Version

Microsoft's goal is to keep each release of the CLR as backward compatible as possible with all previous releases. (I say *as possible* because we all know that complete compatibility can never be guaranteed.) This is the approach taken for years by other Microsoft products, including the Windows operating system, Microsoft Office, and Microsoft SQL Server. Because of the focus on backward compatibility, it is quite likely that an application built with one version of the CLR will run just fine on a later version of the CLR.

The default behavior of the shim is to run an application with the version of the CLR used to build it (minus the upgrades scenarios I discussed). However, it might be the case that you as an application author want to be able to take advantage of a new CLR when it is released without having to rebuild and re-release your application. Each new version of the CLR will undoubtedly contain numerous bug fixes and performance enhancements, and because backward compatibility is likely, you can choose to have the shim run your application with a new version when it becomes available.

The *<supportedRuntime>* Element

The default host enables you to state your desire to run with different versions of the CLR using the *<supportedRuntime>* element in your application configuration file. The *<supportedRuntime>* element has a single attribute called *version* that indicates the version of the CLR you support. By including a *<supportedRuntime>* element for a given version, you are telling the shim that you are willing to have your application run with that version of the CLR.

You might also specify more than one *<supportedRuntime>* element. This enables your application to run on any machine that has at least one of your supported versions. If, through testing, you determine that several different versions of the CLR are acceptable, supplying the full list can dramatically broaden the number of machines your application can run on without you having to worry about redistributing a given version of the .NET Framework.

Clearly, the safest way to determine which CLR versions your application can run on is through testing. As discussed earlier, backward compatibility cannot be universally guaranteed and can really be defined only within the context of a given application. Be aware of the potential for compatibility issues when specifying a <supportedRuntime> element for a version of the CLR you haven't tested with.

If you've specified multiple <supportedRuntime> elements, the order in which the elements appear in the configuration file is the order in which the shim will try to load those versions of the CLR. If none of the versions you specify can be found, the shim will display an error and your application won't run.

All <supportedRuntime> elements must be nested inside the <startup> tag of the runtime section of your configuration file. The value of the *version* attribute is a string in the following format:

"v + <major number> + <minor number> + <build number>"

For example, setting version to "v1.1.4322" indicates that your application can be run with the version of the CLR that shipped with .NET Framework 1.1. Recall from the previous discussion in Chapter 3 of how the shim locates a CLR that this string maps to the name of the subdirectory (under the main CLR installation root directory) in which the desired version of the CLR is installed.

Here's an example configuration file that causes the shim to attempt to run the application with the last two publicly released versions of the CLR. Note that the versions are specified from newest to oldest. In this way, the version with the latest bug fixes and performance enhancements is tried first.

```
<configuration>
  <startup>
    <supportedRuntime version="v2.0.41013" />
    <supportedRuntime version="v1.1.4322" />
  </startup>
</configuration
```

By design, the <supportedRuntime> element enables you to run your application with a version of the CLR that is different from the one used to develop the application. So it's important to use this element with caution. The whole premise behind the side-by-side architecture of the .NET Framework is to provide a platform where applications can remain isolated from changes made to the system without their knowledge. The <supportedRuntime> element is a handy tool to use when you have completed testing and are ready to make an explicit decision to allow your application to be upgraded. However, if you allow your application to be upgraded without explicit testing, you're opening yourself and your customers to potential unwanted compatibility problems.

The *<requiredRuntime>* Element and .NET Framework 1.0

The preceding section describes how the *<supportedRuntime>* element can make it easier to deploy your application when you're not sure which version of the CLR is installed on a given target machine. This statement is true with one exception: you cannot use the *<supportedRuntime>* element on a machine that has *only* the version of the CLR that shipped with .NET Framework 1.0. That original version of the CLR does not include support for this element. Instead, the design at the time used a different element that is now deprecated called *<requiredRuntime>*. This element is similar in spirit to *<supportedRuntime>* in that it is used to indicate which version of the CLR an application should run with. However, because *<requiredRuntime>* has been retired in favor of *<supportedRuntime>*, it really has use only when you have an application you've built with .NET Framework 1.1, but you want to make sure it runs on machines with only .NET Framework 1.0 installed. (Of course, this scenario also requires that you haven't used any features available only in the new releases, but I'm ignoring that fact for now.)

To support this scenario, you need a configuration file that contains a *<requiredRuntime>* element for the original version of the CLR and a *<supportedRuntime>* element for .NET Framework 1.1. Here's an example:

```
<configuration>
  <startup>
    <supportedRuntime version="v1.1.4322" />
    <requiredRuntime  version="v1.0.3705" />
  </startup>
</configuration>
```

This configuration file enables an application built with either .NET Framework 1.0 or .NET Framework 1.1 regardless of which version is installed on the machine.

> **Note** Applications built with .NET Framework 2.0 cannot be run on older versions of the CLR. The .NET Framework 2.0 release contains a few new features, such as support for generics, that required the format of the CLR metadata to change. Older versions of the CLR won't be able to read this new metadata and therefore can't run applications built with the .NET Framework 2.0.

As described earlier, the order of these elements in the configuration file determines their priority. Hence, if both versions 1.1.4322 and 1.0.3705 are installed, 1.1.4322 will be used. If neither of those versions is installed, the shim will run the application with v1.0.3705 (that is, .NET Framework 1.0) if it is present.

Unfortunately, your configuration file needs more work if you want to run an application built with .NET Framework 1.1 on .NET Framework 1.0. (Keep in mind, too, that these scenarios are restricted to the cases in which you're sure you don't rely on any features that aren't available in .NET Framework 1.0–and that you've tested your application on that version.) Recall that in Chapter 3 I said that when you pick a version of the CLR to run your application, you also get the matching set of class library assemblies by default. Recall also that this behavior occurs only when either .NET Framework 1.1 or .NET Framework 2.0 is installed on the machine.

If only .NET Framework 1.0 is available, you must include additional statements in the configuration file to redirect all assembly references back down to the versions that shipped with .NET Framework 1.0. You do this using the *<bindingRedirect>* tag in your application configuration file. You must include one *<bindingRedirect>* tag for each assembly that ships in the .NET Framework redistributable (unless you're sure there are assemblies you don't use). I know this sounds cumbersome, but fortunately, the same configuration file works for all applications, so once you get it right, you're set.

Here's the configuration file used earlier with *<bindingRedirect>* entries for the .NET Framework assemblies. (I haven't included them all for the sake of brevity but the entire configuration file is available from the Microsoft Press download site for this book. See the Introduction of this book for the URL.)

```
<configuration>
    <startup>
        <supportedRuntime version="v1.1.4322" />
        <requiredRuntime  version="v1.0.3705" />
    </startup>

    <runtime>
        <assemblyBinding xmlns="urn:schemas-microsoft-com:asm.v1">
            <dependentAssembly>
                <assemblyIdentity name="System.Security"
                    publicKeyToken="b03f5f7f11d50a3a" culture=""/>
                <bindingRedirect oldVersion="0.0.0.0-65535.65535.65535.65535"
                    newVersion="1.0.3300.0"/>
            </dependentAssembly>
            <dependentAssembly>
                <assemblyIdentity name="System.Runtime.Remoting"
                    publicKeyToken="b77a5c561934e089" culture=""/>
                <bindingRedirect oldVersion="0.0.0.0-65535.65535.65535.65535"
                    newVersion="1.0.3300.0"/>
            </dependentAssembly>
            <--! Lots of others need to be included here…..
        </assemblyBinding>
    </runtime>
</configuration>
```

If you've been following along closely and are familiar with how *<bindingRedirect>* statements work, you're probably thinking that the configuration file I've just shown works great if my application runs with .NET Framework 1.0, but what if my application runs with .NET Framework 1.1 or 2.0? Won't all my assembly references get redirected down to the versions of the class library assemblies that shipped with .NET Framework 1.0? Well, the answer is yes—the configuration file as I've defined it doesn't work with all versions of the .NET Framework. What I'd really like is for the *<bindingRedirect>* statements to apply as specified if my application runs with .NET Framework 1.0 but to be ignored if my application runs with a later version (because later versions will ensure that my references to system assemblies automatically get redirected to the version that matches the CLR I've chosen).

To accommodate this scenario, you must add the *appliesTo* attribute to the *<assemblyBinding>* element (under which all of your *<bindingRedirect>* statements lie) in your application configuration file. The value of the *appliesTo* attribute is the version of the CLR to which the statements in the *<assemblyBinding>* section of the configuration file apply. In other words, the *<bindingRedirect>* statements take effect only if the version of the CLR identified by the *appliesTo* attribute is loaded. In this case, I clearly want the *<bindingRedirect>* statements to apply only if version 1.0.3705 (also known as .NET Framework 1.0) is loaded. As a result, the final configuration file looks like this:

```
<configuration>
   <startup>
      <supportedRuntime version="v2.0.1111" />
      <supportedRuntime version="v1.1.4322" />
      <requiredRuntime  version="v1.0.3705" />
   </startup>
   <runtime>
      <assemblyBinding xmlns="urn:schemas-microsoft-com:asm.v1"
            appliesTo="v1.0.3705">
         <dependentAssembly>
           <assemblyIdentity name="System.Security"
              publicKeyToken="b03f5f7f11d50a3a" culture=""/>
           <bindingRedirect oldVersion="0.0.0.0-65535.65535.65535.65535"
                            newVersion="1.0.3300.0"/>
         </dependentAssembly>
         <dependentAssembly>
           <assemblyIdentity name="System.Runtime.Remoting"
                   publicKeyToken="b77a5c561934e089" culture=""/>
           <bindingRedirect oldVersion="0.0.0.0-65535.65535.65535.65535"
                            newVersion="1.0.3300.0"/>
         </dependentAssembly>
         <--! Lots of others need to be included here...
      </assemblyBinding>
   </runtime>
</configuration>
```

Summary

The CLR includes a default host that enables you to use application configuration files to specify which version and build type of the CLR to use and in which garbage collection mode to run. If you don't need to customize the settings for domain-neutral code and if you don't require any other features of the CLR hosting API, using the default host can save you time.

The configuration file used to customize the default CLR host enables you to list more than one version of the CLR with which to run the application. If multiple versions are listed, the order of the versions in the list determines their priority. However, it's always safest to list only the version of the CLR your application was built with because that's the version that offers the most predictable behavior at run time. If you choose to list additional versions, make sure you've completed sufficient testing to ensure that the other versions are backward compatible from the perspective of your application.

Finally, if you've determined that your application can run on a machine that has only .NET Framework 1.0 installed on it, you must include extra statements in your configuration file to upgrade these references manually because the CLR that shipped with .NET Framework 1.0 does not automatically upgrade all references to the .NET Framework assemblies to match the CLR.

Chapter 5
Using Application Domains Effectively

If you're writing an extensible application or have reason to unload code without shutting down an entire process, you'll likely want to take advantage of application domains. Application domains enable you to isolate groups of assemblies from others running in the same process. Oftentimes, the isolation provided by application domains is used to run multiple applications in the same Win32 process as is done by CLR hosts such as Microsoft ASP.NET and Microsoft SQL Server. However, application domains are useful in a variety of other scenarios as well. For example, some applications use application domains to isolate individual controls running in the same process, whereas others use domains simply to support their requirements for dynamically unloading code.

This book includes two chapters on application domains. This first chapter introduces the concept of an application domain and gives general architectural guidelines to help you make the most effective use of domains within your application. Topics covered in this chapter include the role of application domains, a discussion of their internal structure, guidelines to follow when partitioning a process into multiple application domains, the relationship between domains and threads, and the use of application domains to unload code from a running process. In Chapter 6, I describe the various ways you can customize application domains to fit your particular scenario.

The Role of Application Domains

To meet the reliability and security required by modern computing environments, operating systems and other software platforms must provide a means to isolate unrelated applications from one another at run time. This isolation is necessary to ensure that code running in one application cannot adversely affect another, thereby exploiting a security vulnerability or causing that application to crash.

The Microsoft Windows operating system uses processes to enforce this isolation. If you've used Microsoft Internet Information Services (IIS) and ASP in the past, you probably recall two configurations you could select that controlled where your application code ran relative to the code for IIS itself. In one configuration you chose to run your application in the same process as IIS. Your other option was to run your application in a different process than IIS. The tradeoff between these two options was one of reliability versus performance. Running in-process with IIS meant no process boundaries were crossed between your application and IIS. However, if some application running in the IIS process had a bug that caused it to access an invalid memory location, not only would that application crash, but the entire IIS process would go down, bringing your application with it. Choosing to run your application in a different process isolates you from this unpredictability, but that isolation comes at a performance cost. In this configuration all calls between your application and IIS must cross a process boundary, which introduces a performance penalty. This tradeoff between reliability and performance doesn't scale in many situations, including the Web server scenario just described.

One of the reasons process boundaries prove expensive as a way to enforce isolation is related to the way memory accesses are validated. Memory access in the Windows operating system is process-relative. That is, the same value for a memory address maps to two different locations in two different processes—each location is scoped to the process in which it is used. This isolation is essential in preventing one process from accessing another's memory. This isolation is enforced in hardware. Memory addresses in the Windows operating system are not references into the processor's physical memory. Instead, every address is virtual, giving the application a flat, contiguous view of memory. So each time memory is accessed by the application, its address must be translated by the processor from a virtual address to a physical address. This translation involves the use of a CPU register and several lookup tables examined by the processor. This CPU register holds a value that points to a list of physical pages available to the process. Each time a process switch occurs in the Windows operating system, the value of this register must be adjusted. In addition, the processor must take a virtual address and break it down into pieces that identify the page and the offset within the page of the physical memory being accessed. These checks must be done at the hardware level to ensure that all memory accesses are to valid memory addresses within the process. The reason that memory access must be validated on the fly in this fashion is because the Windows operating system cannot determine ahead of time which memory in the process the application will access.

Another factor in the cost of using processes as an isolation boundary is the expense of switching the context associated with execution from one thread to another. All threads in the Windows operating system are process-relative—they can run only in the process in which they are created. When processes are used to isolate IIS from your application, the transfer of control between the two processes involves a thread context switch. This thread switch, along with the cost of translating memory address and some overhead associated with communication between processes, accounts for most of the expense associated with using processes to achieve application isolation.

Type Safety and Verification

In contrast, the CLR can statically determine how a given process will access memory before it is actually run. This is possible primarily because the Microsoft Intermediate Language (MSIL) is at a higher level and much more descriptive than native processor instructions such as x86 or Intel Architecture 64 (IA-64). The CLR relies on this more descriptive instruction set to tell whether a given assembly is type safe, that is, whether all accesses to memory made from within the assembly go through public entry points to valid objects. In this way, the CLR can ensure that a given assembly cannot access invalid regions of memory within the process. That is, they cannot produce an access violation that can bring down the entire process. The practice of determining program correctness is referred to as verification.

Given code that is verified to be type safe, the CLR can provide the isolation typically associated with a process without having to rely on the process boundary. This is where application domains enter the picture. They are the CLR's construct for enforcing isolation at a cost lower than that of a process boundary, which means you can run multiple managed applications in the same operating system process and still get the level of isolation that previously was possible only by using a process boundary. In this way, application domains are the reason that applications such as ASP.NET scale much better than their unmanaged predecessors. Because of the isolation they provide within a single process, application domains are often described as subprocesses. Figure 5-1 shows a single Windows process running three separate, unrelated applications. Each application runs in its own application domain.

Windows Process

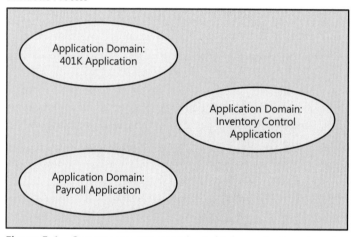

Figure 5-1   One process can contain multiple application domains.

Not all managed assemblies are verifiably type safe, however. If an assembly cannot be verified to be type safe, you cannot rely on application domains for isolation. Such code can make an invalid memory access just as unmanaged code can, causing the entire process to come down. Whether code is verifiable depends in part on the programming language used to write the assembly. The MSIL instruction set is built to support a wide variety of languages, including those that include support for direct pointer manipulation. As a result, your ability to generate verifiable code depends on whether the language you are using exposes some of the unsafe aspects of MSIL. For example, all code generated by the Microsoft Visual Basic.NET compiler is type safe. Visual Basic.NET exposes no language features that let you write unverifiable code. In contrast, C++ is typically not verifiable because C++ code often makes extensive use of pointers. C# is somewhere in the middle. By default, C# produces verifiable code. However, you can use pointers in C# by using the *unsafe* language keyword.

To leverage the full benefits of application domain isolation, you must ensure that only code that can be verified to be type safe is allowed to run in your process. You do this using the CLR's Code Access Security (CAS) system. I've talked about verifiability mostly from the perspective of reliability, but the ability to verify that code won't make random memory accesses is critical for security reasons as well. Verification can be relied on to make sure that code won't overrun buffers or access data it shouldn't, for example. In fact, CAS depends completely on verifiability—without type-safe code, CAS can offer you little protection. A complete description of CAS is beyond the scope of this book, but for now suffice it to say that the system works by granting a set of permissions to code based on some characteristic of that code that is meaningful to administrators or to the host application. Examples of permissions include the ability to write to the file system or the registry and the ability to read and write data from the network. Because the notion of verifiability is so central to security, one of the permissions defined by the Microsoft .NET Framework is the *SkipVerification*[1] permission—or the ability to run code that can't be verified. As a host, you can control which permissions are granted to code running in the application domains you create. Ensuring that nonverifiable code can never run in your process is simply a matter of customizing the CAS system to never grant *SkipVerification* permission. The details of how to accomplish this are explored in detail in Chapter 10.

Application Isolation

In the preceding section, I talked about isolation primarily from the perspective of preventing unwanted memory access. The isolation provided by application domains has many more dimensions, however. Application domains provide isolation for most everything you rely on process isolation to do, including the following:

- Type visibility
- Configuration data
- Security settings
- Access to static data and members

Type Visibility

Application domains form a boundary around the types that can be called from code running in that domain. Assemblies are always loaded into a process within the context of a domain. If the same assembly is loaded by code in two domains, the assembly is loaded twice.[2] Assemblies loaded into the same domain can freely use each other's public types and methods. How-

---

1. Technically, *SkipVerification* isn't permission itself in the true sense. It's a state of another permission called *SecurityPermission*. See the Microsoft .NET Framework SDK for details.

2. This is true in general; however, an optimization known as domain-neutral loading changes this loading behavior. Domain-neutral loading does not change any semantic behavior with respect to isolation though. I talk about domain-neutral code much more in Chapter 9.

ever, a type in one application domain can't automatically see and use public types in other application domains. Communicating across domains in this way requires a formal mechanism for discovering types and calling them. In the CLR, this formal mechanism is provided by the remoting infrastructure. Just as a process or a machine forms a boundary across which calls must be removed, so does an application domain. In this way, the remote domain must explicitly expose a type so it can be accessed from another domain, thereby enforcing that cross-domain calls come through known entry points.

Configuration Data

Each application domain has a configuration file that can be used to customize everything from the local search path for assemblies to versioning and remoting information. In addition, code running within the application domain can store its own settings in the configuration file. Examples of these settings include connection strings to a database or a most recently used files list.

Security Settings

Applications domains can be used to further scope the CAS permissions granted to code running within the domain. This further scoping must be set up explicitly by the extensible application—it is not enabled by default. Permission grants can be customized by the extensible application in two ways. The first is to define custom CAS policy for the domain. This policy maps a notion of code identity (called evidence) to a set of permissions that the code is granted. Examples of evidence include the location from which the code was loaded, its strong-name signature, an Authenticode signature, or any custom evidence provided by the host. Real-world examples of how application domain policy is used include SQL Server 2005 and ASP.NET. In SQL Server 2005, domain policy is used to restrict the permissions that code loaded out of the database is granted. ASP.NET uses domain policy to implement the Minimum, Low, Medium, High, Full permission scheme.

The second way to configure security for an application domain is to set security evidence on the domain itself. This evidence is evaluated by policy just as the evidence from an assembly is. The union of these two evaluations forms the final set of permissions that are granted to the assembly. If the grants from the domain are less than the grants from the assembly, the domain essentially wins. For example, the Microsoft Internet Explorer host uses this feature to make sure that no code running in the domain is granted more permissions than the Web site would get. This is implemented by setting domain-level evidence to the URL of the Web site from which the code was loaded.

The CAS system is so extensible that an entire chapter is dedicated to it later in the book. In Chapter 10, I describe how to implement both application domain CAS policy and domain-level security evidence.

Access to Static Data and Members

I've discussed how application domains are used to restrict access to types and their members. However, static data and members don't require instantiation of a type, but still must be isolated per domain to prevent either accidental or malicious leaking of data across domain boundaries. This behavior usually falls out naturally because assemblies are not shared across domains by default. However, when code is loaded domain neutral, the jit-compiled code is shared among all domains in the process to minimize the working set. In this case, the CLR provides this isolation by maintaining a separate copy of each static data member or method for each application domain into which the assembly is loaded.

Runtime Concepts Not Isolated by Application Domains

Not all resources that are isolated to a process in Win32 are isolated to an application domain in the CLR. In some cases, isolating these resources to an application domain isn't necessary because of type safety or other checks implemented by the runtime. In other cases, resources aren't isolated to an application domain because they are built on the underlying Win32 primitives, which, of course, have no notion of application domains.

Examples of resources not isolated to an application domain include the garbage collection heap, managed threads, and the managed thread pool. In the case of the garbage collection heap, the notion of type safety can be relied upon so that different heaps need not be maintained for each application domain. In the case of threads and the thread pool, the CLR has knowledge of which application domain a thread is currently running in and takes great care to ensure that no data or behavior is inadvertently leaked when a thread crosses into another domain. I talk more about this later in the "Application Domains and Threads" section.

The .NET Framework libraries provide a number of classes that enable add-ins to create and use synchronization primitives such as events and mutexes. These primitives are examples of managed concepts that are built directly on the unmanaged equivalents. Because the unmanaged notion of an event or mutex clearly has no knowledge of application domains, the managed equivalents are technically not constrained by the application domain boundary. However, application domain isolation of the managed synchronization primitives can be achieved in practice by controlling access to the name you give the object when it is created. For example, if you create an unnamed managed synchronization object, there would be no way that object could be manipulated directly from another domain unless you explicitly pass the underlying operating system handle to the other domain. Perhaps a "truer" notion of application domain–scoped synchronization primitives might show up in the future if the underlying Windows operating system were to add the notion of an application domain to its current process structure.

The other important aspect of process management that hasn't yet been scoped to the application domain level is debugging. In Win32 when a thread hits a breakpoint in one process, all threads in that process are suspended, but the threads in other processes continue to run.

Application domains don't mirror this same behavior yet, unfortunately. When you set a breakpoint in managed code, all threads in that process stop (regardless of which application domain they are running in at the time) instead of just the one you're debugging. Clearly, this behavior isn't ideal and is a significant restriction in many scenarios. There's no underlying technical reason why this can't be implemented given the current architecture. It just hasn't been done because of time constraints and priorities. It's likely this debugging behavior will be fixed in upcoming releases of the CLR.

Application Domain Structure

Internally, application domains are implemented as a set of data structures and runtime behavior maintained by the CLR. The application domain data structures contain many of the constructs you'd expect after reading the previous section, including a list of assemblies, security policy information, and so on. The elements of the application domain data structure, the fact that memory isolation can be guaranteed through type safety, and the additional checks performed by the CLR for threading-related activities are what enables an application domain to isolate multiple applications in a single process.

A graphical view of a CLR process and the corresponding application domain data structures are shown in Figure 5-2.

Windows Process

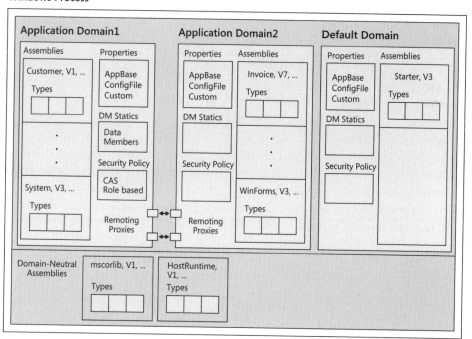

Figure 5-2   The internal structure of a CLR process with multiple application domains

As shown in the figure, each application domain holds several elements related to isolation. These include the following:

- A list of assemblies loaded in the application domain
- Security policy
- Application domain properties
- Copies of static data members
- Proxies for remote calls

These elements of the application domain data structures are described in the following sections.

Assembly List

Every assembly is loaded within the context of an application domain. The CLR maintains a list of the loaded assemblies per domain. This list is used for many purposes, one of which is to enforce the visibility rules for types within an application domain. The assembly list contains both assemblies that are written as part of the application and those that are shipped by Microsoft as part of the .NET Framework platform.

Security Policy

As described, security policy can be customized per domain. This policy includes both CAS policy and policy for role-based authorization checks.

Application Domain Properties

Each application domain has a list of properties associated with it. These properties fall into two general categories: those properties that are natively understood by the CLR and those properties that are provided by the extensible application for its own use. The properties known to the CLR include the base directory in which to search for assemblies and the file containing the configuration data for the domain. Application domains can be customized in numerous ways by setting these properties. The subject of application domain customization is covered in Chapter 6. In addition to the properties known to the CLR, the application domain includes a general-purpose property bag for use by applications. The property bag is a simple name-object pair and can be used to store anything you need for quick access from any assembly within the domain.

Statics for Domain-Neutral Assemblies

When an assembly is loaded domain neutral, it logically is loaded into every application domain. I say *logically* because the assembly is physically loaded only once, yet the CLR maintains enough internal data to make it appear to each domain that it contains the assembly. For example, in Figure 5-2, both *mscorlib* and the assembly called *HostRuntime* are available to all three domains in the process. So, Application Domain1 really contains the *Customer*, *System*, *mscorlib*, and *HostRuntime* assemblies.

A critical part of the data that is maintained in each domain for a domain-neutral assembly is a copy of each static data member or field defined in the assembly. As described earlier, this must be done to prevent static data from accidentally leaking between domains. When code in a particular domain accesses a static data member contained in a domain-neutral assembly, the CLR determines in which application domain the referencing code is running and maps that access to the appropriate copy of the static.

Proxies for Remote Calls

All communication between application domains must go through well-known channels. In the CLR these channels are remoting proxies. The CLR maintains a proxy for every object that the application hands out of the domain. Calls coming into the domain are fed through proxies as well. These proxies are an essential part of the domain boundary, both to regulate access and to make sure that application domains are unloaded cleanly. After a domain is unloaded, the proxy maintained by the CLR has enough information to know that the object is it referring to has disappeared. As a result, an exception is thrown back to the caller.

The Default Application Domain

I've said that every assembly must be loaded into an application domain. However, it's likely that you've created at least one managed application in which you didn't think about application domains at all. In fact, the vast majority of programs are written this way. To handle this most common scenario, the CLR creates a default application domain every time a process is started. Unless you take specific steps to load an assembly into an application domain you've created yourself, all assemblies end up in the default domain. For example, when you run a managed executable from the command line, the assembly containing the entry point is loaded by the CLR into the default domain. Furthermore, all assemblies statically referenced by that executable are loaded into the default domain as well. The default domain is also used in COM interop scenarios. By default, all managed assemblies that are loaded into a process through COM are loaded into the default domain as well.

The default application domain is very handy in a wide variety of scenarios. However, you should be aware of a key limitation if you are writing an extensible application: the default domain cannot be unloaded from the process before the process is shut down. This can be a hindrance if your architecture requires you to unload application domains during the process lifetime. For this reason, most extensible applications don't use the default domain to run add-ins. If they did, there'd be no way to ever unload it.

> **Note**   In .NET Framework version 1.0 and .NET Framework version 1.1, the default domain has a second limitation as well: many of the configuration options that can be set on application domains you create yourself couldn't be set on the default domain. Because the default domain couldn't be customized in any way, it wasn't of much use for many extensible applications. Fortunately, the ability to customize the default domain has been added in .NET Framework version 2.0, as discussed later in this chapter.

The AppDomainViewer Tool

It's relatively easy to build a tool to help visualize the relationship among processes, application domains, and assemblies on a running system. The AppDomainViewer tool (appdomainviewer.exe) included with this book shows this relationship in a graphical tree structure. AppDomainViewer is an executable that, when started, enumerates all the processes on the system that are currently running managed code. For each process, AppDomainViewer first enumerates the application domains within the process and then enumerates the assemblies loaded into each application domain.

Figure 5-3 shows the AppDomainViewer running on a machine that runs Microsoft Visual Studio 2005 and a number of purely managed executables.

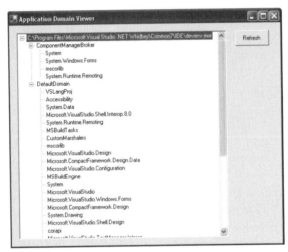

Figure 5-3   The AppDomainViewer tool

If you expand the tree view, the first level contains the application domains in the process. Notice that every process has at least one application domain. This is the default domain. When an application domain is created, it is assigned a friendly textual name. This is the name displayed in the user interface of AppDomainViewer. In most cases, the name of the default domain is simply Default Domain; however, applications can change this. I discuss how this is done in Chapter 6.

Expanding an application domain in the tree view shows the set of all assemblies loaded into that domain. Looking at the assemblies under each application domain gives me a good chance to expand on the concept of domain-neutral code touched on briefly earlier. Recall that domain-neutral assemblies are loaded once in the process and their code is shared across all application domains to reduce the overall working set of the process. However, from the programmer's point of view, these assemblies appear in every application domain (recall this is part of application domain isolation). In Figure 5-3, the assemblies *mscorlib*, *System*, and so on are loaded domain neutral. Even though these assemblies are loaded only once, they show up under every application domain in the tree view. I cover domain-neutral code in more detail in Chapter 9.

The AppDomainViewer uses the CLR debugging interfaces to get application domain and assembly information out of running processes. It might not occur to you to use the debugging interfaces for this purpose, but it's the only technique the CLR provides for inspecting processes other than the one in which you are running. Most of the functionality provided by the debugging interfaces is aimed at debugging, of course, but a set of interfaces referred to as the publishing interfaces can be used to look inside other processes.

The interfaces (*ICorPublish*, *ICorPublishProcess*, *ICorPublishAppDomain*, and a few others) are all unmanaged COM interfaces. However, the .NET Framework 2.0 software development kit (SDK) includes a set of managed wrappers around these interfaces. The AppDomainViewer is written in managed code and accesses the CLR debugging system through these managed wrappers as shown in Figure 5-4.

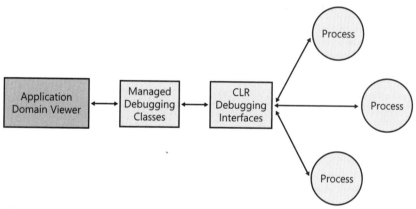

Figure 5-4   AppDomainViewer architecture

Listing 5-1 shows the source for the AppDomainViewer. I've omitted some of the boilerplate Microsoft Windows Forms code for clarity. The sample is generally straightforward, but there is one twist worth discussing. As described, the CLR debugging interfaces are COM interfaces. The underlying objects that implement these interfaces must run in a multithreaded apartment (MTA). However, the Windows Forms code used to display the user interface must run in a single-threaded apartment. To get around these conflicting requirements, I start an MTA thread whenever I need to call the debugging interfaces, then use the Windows Forms control method *Begin.Invoke* to marshal the data back to the user interface thread. You can examine this in the code for the *RefreshTreeView* method and look to see where it's called.

Listing 5-1 AppDomainViewer.cs

```csharp
using System;
using System.IO;
using System.Drawing;
using System.Collections;
using System.ComponentModel;
using System.Windows.Forms;
using System.Data;
using System.Threading;

// Include the namespaces for the managed wrappers around
// the CLR debugging interfaces.
using Microsoft.Debugging.MdbgEngine;
using Microsoft.Debugging.CorPublish;
using Microsoft.Debugging.CorDebug;

namespace AppDomainViewer
{

    public class ADView : System.Windows.Forms.Form
    {
        // Windows Forms control definitions omitted…

        // The background thread used to call the debugging interfaces
        private Thread m_corPubThread;

        // The list of tree nodes to display in the UI. This list gets populated
        // in RefreshTreeView.
        private ArrayList m_rootNodes = new ArrayList();


        // More Windows Forms setup code omitted…
        [STAThread]
        static void Main()
        {
            Application.Run(new ADView());
        }

        private void ADView_Load(object sender, System.EventArgs e)
        {
            // Populate the tree view when the application starts.
            RefreshTreeView();
        }

        private void btnRefresh_Click(object sender, System.EventArgs e)
        {
            // Populate the tree view whenever the Refresh Button is clicked.
            RefreshTreeView();
        }

        private void RefreshTreeView()
        {
            // The CLR debugging interfaces must be called from an MTA thread, but
            // we're currently in an STA. Start a new MTA thread from which to call
            // the debugging interfaces.
```

```
    m_corPubThread = new Thread(new ThreadStart(ThreadProc));
    m_corPubThread.IsBackground = true;
    m_corPubThread.ApartmentState = ApartmentState.MTA;
    m_corPubThread.Start();
}

public void ThreadProc()
{
    try
    {
        MethodInvoker mi = new MethodInvoker(this.UpdateProgress);

        // Create new instances of the managed debugging objects.
        CorPublish cp = new CorPublish();
        MDbgEngine dbg = new MDbgEngine();

        m_rootNodes.Clear();

        // Enumerate the processes on the machine that are running
        // managed code.
        foreach(CorPublishProcess cpp in cp.EnumProcesses())
        {
            // Skip this process-don't display information about the
            // AppDomainViewer itself.
            if(System.Diagnostics.Process.GetCurrentProcess().Id!=
                                               cpp.ProcessId)
            {
                // Create a node in the tree for the process.
                TreeNode procNode = new TreeNode(cpp.DisplayName);

                // Enumerate the domains within the process.
                foreach(CorPublishAppDomain cpad in cpp.EnumAppDomains())
                {

                    // Create a node for the domain.
                    TreeNode domainNode = new TreeNode(cpad.Name);

                    // We must actually attach to the process
                    // to see information about the assemblies.
                    dbg.Attach(cpp.ProcessId);
                    try
                    {
                        // The debugging interfaces (at least for this task) are
                        // centered on modules rather than assemblies.
                        // So we enumerate the modules and find out which
                        // assemblies they belong to. In the general case,
                        // assemblies can contain multiple modules.
                        // This code is simpler, however. It assumes one
                        // module per assembly, which might yield incorrect
                        // results in some cases.
                        foreach(MDbgModule m in dbg.Processes.Active.Modules)
                        {
                            CorAssembly ca = m.CorModule.Assembly;
                            // Make sure we include only assemblies in this
                            // domain.
```

```
                        if (ca.AppDomain.Id == cpad.ID)
                        {
                            // Add a node for the assembly under the
                            // domain node.
                            domainNode.Nodes.Add(new TreeNode(
                              Path.GetFileNameWithoutExtension(ca.Name)));
                        }
                    }
                }
                finally
                {
                    // Detach from the process and move on to the next one.
                    dbg.Processes.Active.Detach().WaitOne();
                }

                // Add the domain node under the process node.
                procNode.Nodes.Add(domainNode);
            }

            m_rootNodes.Add(procNode);
        }
    }

    // "Notify" the tree view control back on the UI thread that new
    // data is available.
    this.BeginInvoke(mi);

}
//Thrown when the thread is interrupted by the main thread-
// exiting the loop
catch (ThreadInterruptedException)
{
    //Simply exit....
}
catch (Exception)
{
}
}

// This method is called from the MTA thread when new data is
// available.
private void UpdateProgress()
{
    // Clear the tree, enumerate through the nodes of the array,
    // and add them to the tree. Each of the top-level nodes represents
    // a process, with nested nodes for domains and assemblies.
    // m_rootNodes is constructed in RefreshTreeView.
    treeView.Nodes.Clear();
    foreach(TreeNode node in m_rootNodes)
    {
        treeView.Nodes.Add(node);
    }
}

}
}
```

Guidelines for Partitioning a Process into Multiple Application Domains

If you're building an application that relies on application domains for isolation, especially one in which you'll be running code that comes from other vendors, determining how to partition your process into multiple domains is one of the most critical architectural decisions you'll make. Choosing your domain boundaries incorrectly can lead to poor performance or overly complex implementations at best, and security vulnerabilities or incorrect results at worst.

Oftentimes, determining your domain boundaries involves mapping what you know about application domain isolation into some existing concept in your application model. For example, if you have an existing application that currently relies on a process boundary for isolation, you might consider replacing that boundary with an application domain boundary for managed code. Earlier in the chapter, I described how the presence of the CLR enabled the ASP team to move from a process boundary in their first few versions to an application domain model in ASP.NET. However, replacing a process boundary with a domain boundary clearly isn't the only scenario in which application domains apply.

Application domains often fit well into applications that have an existing extensibility model, but haven't used process isolation in the past because of the cost or other practical reasons. A typical example is an application that supports an add-in model. Consider a desktop application that enables users to write add-ins that extend the functionality of the application. In the unmanaged world, these extensions are commonly written as COM DLLs that are loaded in-process with the main application. If the user loads multiple add-ins, you'll end up with several of these DLLs running in the same address space. In many unmanaged applications, often it isn't practical for the application author to isolate these DLLs in separate processes. Performance is always a concern, but it also might be the case that process isolation just doesn't fit with the application model. For example, the add-ins might need to manipulate an object model published by the application. Application domains work very well in scenarios such as these because they are lightweight enough to be used for isolation where a process boundary is too costly.

Earlier in the chapter, I talked about the various aspects of domain isolation, including access to types, scoping of configuration data, and security policy. Whether you're incorporating managed code into an existing extensible application or writing a new application from scratch, these criteria are a primary factor in determining where your domain boundaries lay. However, you must keep in mind other considerations as well. Performance, reliability, and the ability to unload code from a running process are all directly related to application domains and must be carefully considered. In particular, your design should be geared toward reducing the number of calls made between domains and should consider your requirements for unloading code from a running process.

Code Unloading

You might need to unload code from a running process in various scenarios, such as when you want to reduce the working set or phase out the use of an older version of an assembly when a new version is available.

To remove managed code from a process, you must unload the entire domain containing the code you want to remove. Individual assemblies or types cannot be unloaded. No underlying technical constraint forces this particular design, and in fact, the ability to unload an individual assembly is one of the most highly requested CLR features. It's quite possible that some day the CLR will support unloading at a finer granularity, but for now, the application domain remains the unit at which code can be removed from a process.

The nature of an application domain as the unit for unloading almost always plays a very significant role in how you decide to partition your process into multiple application domains. In fact, I've seen several cases in which a process is partitioned into multiple application domains for this reason alone. If you have a specific need to unload individual pieces of code, you must load that code into a separate application domain so it can be removed without affecting the rest of the process.

For more details on unloading, including how to unload application domains programmatically, see the section "Unloading Application Domains" later in this chapter.

Cross-Domain Communication

Calls between objects in different application domains go through the remoting infrastructure just as calls between processes or machines do. As a result, a performance cost is associated with making a call from an object in one application domain to an object in another domain. The cost of the call isn't nearly as expensive as a cross-process call, but nevertheless, the cost can be significant depending on the number of calls you make and the amount of data you pass on each call. This cost must be carefully considered when designing your application domain model.

Performance isn't the only reason for minimizing the amount of cross-domain calls, however. As described, the CLR maintains proxies that arbitrate calls between objects in different application domains. One of these proxies exists in the application domain of the code making the call (the caller), and one exists in the domain that contains the code being called (the callee). To provide type safety and to support rich calling semantics, the proxies on either side of the call must have the type definition for the object being called. So, the assembly containing the object you are calling must be loaded into both application domains.

Making an assembly visible to multiple application domains complicates your approach to deployment. Every domain has a property that describes the root directory under which it will search for private assemblies (i.e., assemblies visible only to that domain). In many cases, placing assemblies in this directory or one of its subdirectories is all you need. You've probably used this technique either with executables launched from the command line or ASP.NET applications. Deploying assemblies in this way is convenient and extremely easy. Unfortunately, the story isn't quite as straightforward for assemblies that must be visible to multiple domains. These assemblies are referred to as *shared assemblies*. Shared assemblies have different naming and deployment requirements than private assemblies do. First, shared assemblies must have a strong name. A strong name is a cryptographically strong, unique name that the CLR uses to uniquely identify the code and to make security checks. Second, unless you customize how assemblies are loaded (see Chapter 8), assemblies with strong names must be placed in either the global assembly cache (GAC) or in a common location identified through a configuration file. When placed in one of these locations, the ability to delete or replicate your application just by moving one directory tree is lost. Furthermore, shared assemblies deployed in this manner are visible to every application on the machine. In general, this might be OK, but it does open the possibility that your assembly could be used for purposes other than you originally intended, which should make you uneasy regarding security attacks. In short, making an assembly visible to more than one application domain requires some extra steps and is harder to manage.

A process is partitioned into application domains most efficiently when the amount of cross-domain communication is limited, for the reasons I've just described: the performance is better and the deployment story is more straightforward. However, communication between application domains cannot be completely eliminated. If it were, there would be no way to load and run a type in a domain other than the one in which you were running! Typical extensible applications, whether written entirely in managed code or written using the CLR hosting interfaces, contain at least one assembly that is loaded into every domain in the process. This assembly is part of the implementation of the extensible application and provides basic functionality, including creating and configuring new application domains and running the application's extensions in those domains. Throughout the remainder of this chapter, I refer to these assemblies as *HostRuntime assemblies*. In the most efficient designs almost all communication between application domains goes through these HostRuntime assemblies. The key is to partition your process in such a way that the add-ins you load into individual application domains have little or no need to communicate with each other—the less cross-domain communication you have, the better your performance will be. Figure 5-5 shows a scenario in which the communication between domains is limited to the HostRuntime assemblies.

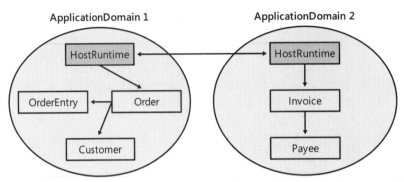

Figure 5-5   Communication between domains through HostRuntime assemblies

Sample Application Domain Boundaries

Often, the best way to understand how to partition your process into multiple application domains is to look at some examples of how other products have done it. In this section, I discuss the designs adopted by existing CLR hosts, including ASP.NET, SQL Server, and Internet Explorer.

ASP.NET

The Microsoft IIS Web server enables multiple Web sites to be hosted on the same physical machine through *virtual roots*. Each virtual root appears as its own site when accessing the Web server. Each virtual root has a base directory under which all content and code for that Web application are stored. In ASP.NET each virtual root is mapped to an application domain. That is, all code running in a particular application domain either originates in the virtual root's base directory (or a subdirectory thereof) or is referenced from a page or code contained in that directory. By aligning virtual roots and application domains, ASP.NET uses domains to make sure that multiple Web applications running in the same process are isolated from each other. Note, too, that all instances of particular Web applications are not necessarily run in the same application domain. That is, ASP.NET load balances instances of the application across multiple domains in multiple processes. So, although it's always true that a particular domain contains code from only one application, it is not necessarily true that all instances of the application run in the same domain.

ASP.NET's implementation of application domains is a perfect example of mapping a domain model to an existing construct that defines an application model (i.e., a virtual directory).

SQL Server

SQL Server 2005 maps the database concept of a schema to an application domain. A schema is a collection of database objects that are owned by a single user and form a namespace. These database objects include types, stored procedures, and functions that are written with managed code. A given application domain contains objects that are all from the same schema. In SQL Server it is possible for an object in one schema to reference an object in another schema. Because objects from different schemas are loaded in separate application domains, a remote call is required for calls between schemas. The less a given application calls objects in different schemas, the better its performance generally is.

Internet Explorer

Internet Explorer is the only CLR host I'm aware of that lets the developer programmatically control where the application domain boundaries lie. By default, an application domain is created per site (as in the ASP.NET model). In the vast majority of cases, this default works well in that it gathers all controls from a particular Web site into a single domain. This means that controls that run in the same Internet Explorer process, but that originate from different sites, cannot discover and access each other.

However, there are hosting scenarios in which it makes sense to define an application to be at smaller granularity than the entire site. Examples of this scenario include sites that allocate particular subdirectories of pages for individual users or corporations. In these scenarios, code running in a particular subsite must be isolated from code running in the rest of the site. To enable these scenarios, the Internet Explorer host lets the developer specify a directory to serve as the application's root. This directory must be a subdirectory of the site's directory and is specified by using a *<link rel=...>* tag to identify a configuration file for the Web application. You'll see in Chapter 6 how the creator of an application domain can set a property defining the base directory corresponding to that domain. When processing pages from the site, the Internet Explorer host loads all controls from pages that point to the same configuration file in the same application domain. In this way, the Internet Explorer host enables a developer to specify an isolation boundary at a level of granularity finer than a site. A full description of how to use the *<link rel= ...>* tag can be found in the .NET Framework SDK.

Application Domain Managers

If you're writing an application involving multiple application domains, you'll almost certainly want to take advantage of a concept called an application domain manager. An application domain manager makes it easy to provide much of the infrastructure your application will need to manage multiple domains in a process. In particular, an application domain manager helps you do the following:

- **Implement a host runtime** When you provide an application domain manager, the CLR takes care of loading an instance of your domain manager into each application domain that gets created in the process. This is exactly the behavior I talked about needing in a host runtime. In essence, your application domain manager serves as your host runtime.

- **Customize individual application domains** An application domain manager enables you to intercept all calls that create application domains in the process. Each time a new application domain is being created, your domain manager is called to give you a chance to configure the new domains as you see fit. An application domain manager even enables you to reuse an existing domain instead of creating a new one when requested. In this way, you can control how many application domains exist in your process and what code runs in each of them. This role of an application domain manager is covered in detail in Chapter 6.

■ **Call into managed code from your CLR host**   As described in Chapters 2 and 3, all CLR hosts contain some unmanaged code that is used to initialize and start the CLR. After the CLR is loaded into the process, the host needs to transition into managed code to run the application extensions the host supports. This is done by calling methods on your application domain manager through the CLR COM Interoperability layer from the unmanaged portion of your host.

Providing an application domain manager requires two steps. First you must implement a managed class that derives from *System.AppDomainManager*. Once your class is written, you must direct the CLR to use your domain manager for all application domains created in your process. The next few sections describe these steps in detail.

Creating an Application Domain Manager

The *System.AppDomainManager* class provides the framework you need to write an application domain manager. The implementation of *System.AppDomainManager* doesn't provide much functionality, but rather is intended to be used as a base class for writing application domain managers for different scenarios. Application domain managers play a key role in many aspects of multidomain applications. In addition to the introduction provided in this chapter, I use an application domain manager in Chapter 10 to customize the security settings for application domains and in Chapter 6 to customize how application domains are created. Table 5-1 describes the methods on *System.AppDomainManager* and where in the book they are discussed.

Table 5-1   The Methods of *System.AppDomainManager*

Method	Purpose
CreateDomain	As you'll see later in this chapter, application domains are created by calls to the static method *System.AppDomain.CreateDomain*. Each time this method is called, the CLR calls your application domain manager to enable you to customize the creation of the new application domain. I discuss this method in more detail in Chapter 6.
InitializeNewDomain	After a new application domain is created, the CLR calls *InitializeNewDomain* from within the newly created application domain. This method gives you a chance to set up any infrastructure you need within the domain. If you're writing a CLR host, you can use *InitializeNewDomain* to pass a pointer to your domain manager out to the unmanaged portion of your host. I show you how to do this later in this chapter when I describe how to associate a domain manager with a process using the CLR hosting APIs.

Table 5-1   The Methods of *System.AppDomainManager*

Method	Purpose
InitializationFlags	Each application domain manager has a set of flags that are used to control various aspects of how the domain manager is initialized. In the "Associating an Application Domain Manager with a Process" section later this chapter, I discuss how *InitializationFlags* is used to enable communication with a domain manager from unmanaged code
ApplicationActivator	The *ApplicationActivator* property is part of the new CLR infrastructure in .NET Framework version 2.0 that is used for activating application add-ins defined by a formal manifest. I don't cover activation using a manifest in this book. Details can be found in the .NET Framework SDK.
HostSecurityManager	This property enables you to return an instance of a *HostSecurityManager* class that the CLR will use to configure security for application domains as they are created. This property is covered in Chapter 10.
HostExecutionContextManager	This property enables you to return an instance of a *HostExecutionContextManager* class that the CLR will call when determining how context information flows across thread transitions. This property is not discussed further in this book. Refer to the .NET Framework SDK for more information on this property.
CreateDomainHelper	*CreateDomainHelper* is a protected static method that application domain managers can call to create new application domains. This method is typically called from a domain manager's implementation of *CreateDomain*. *CreateDomainHelper* is discussed in more detail in Chapter 6.

Now that I've discussed the role of an application domain manager, I want to dig into the details by writing one. Throughout the remainder of this chapter and into the next (Chapter 6), we'll build an application domain manager for a game application that simulates a sailboat race. The application will be a CLR host that enables third parties to write assemblies that represent individual sailboats in the race. These assemblies are the add-ins to the application. In particular, the application and its domain manager will have the following characteristics:

- Each boat in the race will be loaded into its own application domain. We'll use application domains to ensure that individual boats are isolated from each other.

- Our application domain manager will be the sole means used to communicate between application domains. Therefore, our domain manager will have more methods than just the ones defined in its base class, *System.AppDomainManager*. We'll add our own methods that enable us to interact with boats loaded in other application domains.

- Our application domain manager will serve as the means for calling from the unmanaged portion of our host into managed code. So our domain manager will derive from an interface that we can call from unmanaged code using the CLR's COM Interoperability layer.

- Only our domain manager will be loaded into the default application domain. The add-ins (the boats) will be loaded into application domains we create. I've chosen this design because the default application domain cannot be unloaded. Were we to load a boat into the default domain, we'd never be able to unload it without shutting down the process. The practice of loading only your host runtime into the default domain is very common among CLR hosts for exactly the reason we've chosen to use it in this example.

These characteristics of our boat race host can be seen in the architecture diagram shown in Figure 5-6.

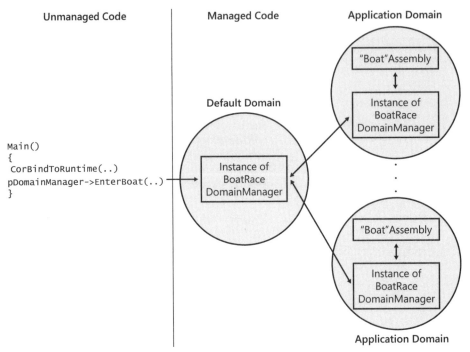

Figure 5-6   BoatRace game architecture

The code for our application domain manager consists of one interface and one class. The interface contains a method we'll use to communicate between domain managers in different application domains and to communicate with the domain manager in the default domain from the unmanaged portion of our host. I created a separate interface rather than just adding additional methods directly to our domain manager class because we need to call through the interface from COM.[3] As expected, our application domain manager class derives both from this interface and from *System.AppDomainManager*. The initial interface and a skeletal class definition are shown here:

---

3. The CLR's COM Interoperability layer can generate an interface automatically for you based on the class definition, but it's generally considered a better practice to define the interface explicitly. Automatically generated interfaces can result in versioning problems later when you add methods to a class.

```
namespace BoatRaceHostRuntime
{
   public interface IBoatRaceDomainManager
   {
      Int32 EnterBoat(string assemblyFileName, string boatTypeName);
   }

   public class BoatRaceDomainManager : AppDomainManager,
                                        IBoatRaceDomainManager
   {
      // Implementation of EnterBoat and other methods omitted for now.
   }
}
```

Associating an Application Domain Manager with a Process

Now that I've sketched out what a simple application domain manager looks like, we need to associate our application domain manager class with the process we're hosting. In this way, the CLR will create an instance of our domain manager in each new application domain for us. In the .NET Framework version 2.0 release of the CLR, all application domains in the process contain the same application domain manager type. In future releases it might be possible to have different application domain managers for different application domains.

You can use either of two approaches to associate your domain manager type with a process: you can specify the name of your type using either the CLR hosting APIs or a set of environment variables. The next two sections describe these two approaches.

The CLR Hosting APIs

CLR hosts use the *ICLRControl::SetAppDomainManagerType* method to associate an application domain manager with a process. Recall from Chapter 2 that you get a pointer to the *ICLR-Control* interface by calling the *GetCLRControl* method on the *ICLRRuntimeHost* pointer returned from *CorBindToRuntimeEx*. *SetAppDomainManagerType* takes two string parameters: one that gives the identity of the assembly containing the application domain manager type and one that gives the name of the type itself. Here's the signature of *ICLRControl::SetApp-DomainManagerType* from mscoree.idl:

```
interface ICLRControl: IUnknown
{
   HRESULT SetAppDomainManagerType(
         [in] LPCWSTR pwzAppDomainManagerAssembly,
         [in] LPCWSTR pwzAppDomainManagerType);
}
```

If we compiled our domain manager into an assembly with the identity

```
BoatRaceHostRuntime, Version=1.0.0.0, PublicKeyToken=5cf360b40180107c, culture=neutral
```

the following code snippet would initialize the CLR and establish our *BoatRaceHostRuntime.BoatRaceDomainManager* class as the application domain manager for the process:

```
int main(int argc, wchar_t* argv[])
{
    // Initialize the CLR using CorBindToRuntimeEx. This gets us
    // the ICLRRuntimeHost pointer we'll need to call Start.
    ICLRRuntimeHost *pCLR = NULL;
    HRESULT hr = CorBindToRuntimeEx(

        L"v2.0.41013,
        L"wks",
        STARTUP_CONCURRENT_GC,
        CLSID_CLRRuntimeHost,
        IID_ICLRRuntimeHost,
        (PVOID*) &pCLR);

    // Start the CLR.
    hr = pCLR->Start();

    // Get a pointer to the ICLRControl interface.
    ICLRControl *pCLRControl = NULL;
    hr = pCLR->GetCLRControl(&pCLRControl);

    // Call SetAppDomainManagerType to associate our domain manager with
    // the process.
    pCLRControl->SetAppDomainManagerType(
                    L BoatRaceHostRuntime, Version=1.0.0.0,
                       PublicKeyToken=5cf360b40180107c, culture=neutral ,
                    L"BoatRaceHostRuntime.BoatRaceDomainManager"
                                      );
    // rest of main() omitted...
}
```

Calling an Application Domain Manager from Unmanaged Code

One of the roles of an application domain manager is to serve as the entry point into managed code for CLR hosts. To make this initial transition into managed code, the unmanaged portion of the host must have an interface pointer to the instance of the application domain manager that has been loaded into the default application domain. Given this pointer, we can then call from unmanaged code to managed code using COM interoperability. Obtaining a pointer to an instance of an application domain manager in unmanaged code requires two steps. First, the application domain manager must notify the CLR that it would like a pointer to a domain manager sent out to unmanaged code. This is done by setting the *InitializationFlags* property on *System.AppDomainManager* to *DomainManagerInitializationFlags.RegisterWithHost*. Next, the unmanaged portion of the host must provide an implementation of *IHostControl::SetAppDomainManager* to receive the pointer. The relationship between these two steps is shown in Figure 5-7.

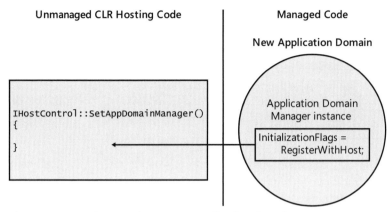

Figure 5-7   Passing a pointer to an application domain manager to unmanaged code

***Step 1: Setting* InitializationFlags *to* RegisterWithHost**   By setting *InitializationFlags* to *RegisterWithHost*, you make the unmanaged hosting code in the process aware of the new instance of your application domain manager, and thus that a new application domain has been created. A convenient place to set *InitializationFlags* is from your domain manager's implementation of *InitializeNewDomain*. When a new application domain is created, the CLR creates a new instance of your application domain manager in the new domain and calls its *InitializeNewDomain* method. This gives your domain manager a chance to initialize any state in the new domain as discussed in Chapter 6. Our *BoatRaceDomainManager* sets *Initialization-Flags* from *InitializeNewDomain* as shown in the following code snippet:

```
public class BoatRaceDomainManager : AppDomainManager,
                                IBoatRaceDomainManager
{
   public override void InitializeNewDomain(AppDomainSetup
                                      appDomainInfo)
   {
      InitializationFlags = DomainManagerInitializationFlags.RegisterWithHost;
   }
}
```

***Step 2: Implement* IHostControl::SetAppDomainManager**   When you set *InitializationFlags* to *RegisterWithHost*, the CLR calls the *SetAppDomainManager* method on your implementation of *IHostControl* to pass information about the instance of your application domain manager out to the unmanaged portion of your host. Recall from Chapter 2 that *IHostControl* is one of the CLR hosting interfaces implemented by the host. Here's the signature for *IHostControl::SetAppDomainManager* from mscoree.idl:

```
interface IHostControl : IUnknown
{
   // other methods omitted...

   HRESULT SetAppDomainManager(
         [in] DWORD dwAppDomainID,
         [in] IUnknown* pUnkAppDomainManager);

}
```

SetAppDomainManager has two parameters. The first is a numerical identifier for the application domain that has just been created. Whenever a new domain is created, the CLR generates a unique identifier and assigns it to the domain. This identifier is used to interact with the application domain in various places throughout the CLR hosting interfaces. For example, you can use the unique identifier passed to *SetAppDomainManager* to later call *ICLRRuntime-Host::UnloadAppDomain* to unload the application domain from the process. You can determine an application domain's unique identifier in managed code using the *Id* property on the *System.AppDomain* class.

The second parameter to *SetAppDomainManager* is a COM interface pointer to the new instance of your application domain manager. The type of this pointer is *IUnknown*. Clearly, we'll need a pointer to a more specific interface to get real work done. Recall that our application domain manager (*BoatRaceDomainManager*) is derived from an interface we defined in C# called *IBoatRaceDomainManager*. This interface has the specific methods we need to interact with the host runtime we implemented in managed code. To call these methods we need to obtain this interface from the *IUnknown* that was passed to *SetAppDomainManager*. We do this using the standard COM *QueryInterface* mechanism. Before we can call *QueryInterface*, however, we must have a definition of *IBoatRaceDomainManager* in unmanaged code. The easiest way to get an unmanaged definition of an interface you've defined in managed code is to use the tlbexp.exe tool that ships in the .NET Framework SDK. This tool takes a managed assembly as input and generates a COM type library that can be used to interact with managed classes through COM. Running tlbexp.exe on our *BoatRaceHostRuntime* assembly (the assembly containing our application domain manager) generates a type library called BoatRaceHostRuntime.tlb. We can use the *#import* directive in C++ to import our type library so we have access to the COM definition of *IBoatRaceDomainManager*:

```
#import <BoatRaceHostRuntime.tlb>
using namespace BoatRaceHostRuntime;
```

Now we have all we need to use *QueryInterface* to get a pointer of type *IBoatRaceDomainManager* as shown in the following sample implementation of *SetAppDomainManager*:

```
HRESULT STDMETHODCALLTYPE CHostControl::SetAppDomainManager(
                                    DWORD dwAppDomainID,
                                    IUnknown *pUnkAppDomainManager)
{
    HRESULT hr = S_OK;
    IBoatRaceDomainManager *pDomainManager = NULL;

    hr = pUnkAppDomainManager->QueryInterface(__uuidof(IBoatRaceDomainManager),
                                    (PVOID*) &pDomainManager);
    // pDomainManager can now be used to access the new instance of
    // BoatRaceDomainManager.
    return hr;
}
```

In hosts involving multiple application domains, the CLR calls *IHostControl::SetAppDomain-Manager* multiple times—once for every domain that is created in the process. Most hosts find it useful to save the data needed to access the application domain that the CLR passes to *Set-AppDomainManager*. As I mentioned earlier, the application domain's unique identifier is used to interact with the domain in various places throughout the hosting APIs. In addition, no APIs provided enable you to enumerate the application domains in the process other than the CLR debugging APIs that were described earlier in the chapter as part of the AppDomain-Viewer sample. So, the most convenient way to get a list of all application domains in the process is to build up the list yourself by saving the identifiers and interface pointers you obtain from *SetAppDomainManager*.

You might also find it useful to explicitly save the interface pointer to the instance of the application domain manager that exists in the default application domain. It is likely that the unmanaged portion of your CLR host will interact mostly with the instance of your application domain manager that is loaded in the default application domain. That application domain manager will then do most of the work needed to create other domains and run the application's add-ins in those domains. This is the approach taken with our boat race example, as shown in Figure 5-7.

The following class is a sample implementation of *IHostControl* that both maintains a list of all application domain managers (and hence application domains) created in the process and explicitly identifies the application domain manager for the default domain. The list of application domain managers is stored in a Standard Template Library (STL) map that relates the unique identifier for an application domain to the interface pointer used to interact with its application domain manager. Here's the class definition for our sample implementation of *IHostControl*:

```
typedef map<DWORD, IBoatRaceDomainManager *> DomainMap;

class CHostControl : public IHostControl
{
    public
    // IHostControl
    HRESULT STDMETHODCALLTYPE GetHostManager(REFIID riid,
                                             void **ppObject);

    HRESULT STDMETHODCALLTYPE SetAppDomainManager(DWORD dwAppDomainID,
                                             IUnknown *pUnkAppDomainManager);

    HRESULT STDMETHODCALLTYPE GetDomainNeutralAssemblies(
            ICLRAssemblyReferenceList **ppReferenceList);

    // IUnknown
    virtual HRESULT STDMETHODCALLTYPE QueryInterface(const IID &iid,
                                             void **ppv);
    virtual ULONG STDMETHODCALLTYPE    AddRef();
    virtual ULONG STDMETHODCALLTYPE    Release();

    CHostControl();
    virtual ~CHostControl();
```

```
    IBoatRaceDomainManager *GetDomainManagerForDefaultDomain();
    DomainMap &GetAllDomainManagers();

    private:
    long m_cRef;
    IBoatRaceDomainManager *m_pDefaultDomainDomainManager;
    DomainMap              m_Domains;
};
```

As you can see from the class definition, *CHostControl* stores both the pointer to the domain manager in the default application domain and the map of application domain identifiers to interface pointers in the private member variables *m_pDefaultDomainDomainManager* and *m_Domains*. The class also provides the public methods *GetDomainManagerForDefaultDomain* and *GetAllDomainManagers* that enable the rest of the host to access the data stored in the class.

The following implementations of *SetAppDomainManager*, *GetDomainManagerForDefaultDomain*, and *GetAllDomainManagers* show how both the map and the variable holding the pointer to the default application domain are populated and returned.

```
HRESULT STDMETHODCALLTYPE CHostControl::SetAppDomainManager(
                                        DWORD dwAppDomainID,
                                        IUnknown *pUnkAppDomainManager)
{
    HRESULT hr = S_OK;

    // Each time a domain gets created in the process, this method is
    // called. We keep a mapping of domainIDs to pointers to application
    // domain managers for each domain in the process. This map is handy for
    // enumerating the domains and so on.
    IBoatRaceDomainManager *pDomainManager = NULL;
    hr = pUnkAppDomainManager->QueryInterface(
                            __uuidof(IBoatRaceDomainManager),
                            (PVOID*) &pDomainManager);
    assert(pDomainManager);

    m_Domains[dwAppDomainID] = pDomainManager;

    // Save the pointer to the default domain for convenience. We
    // initialize m_pDefaultDomainDomainManager to NULL in the
    // class's constructor. The first time this method is called
    // is for the default application domain.
    if (!m_pDefaultDomainDomainManager)
    {
        m_pDefaultDomainDomainManager = pDomainManager;
    }
    return hr;
}

IBoatRaceDomainManager* CHostControl::GetDomainManagerForDefaultDomain()
{
    // AddRef the pointer before returning it.
    if (m_pDefaultDomainDomainManager) m_pDefaultDomainDomainManager->AddRef();
```

```
    return m_pDefaultDomainDomainManager;
}

DomainMap& CHostControl::GetAllDomainManagers()
{
    return m_Domains;
}
```

Now that we've built a host control object that enables us to get interface pointers to instances of our application domain manager, let's take a look at a small sample that shows how to call through those pointers into managed code from a CLR host. Recall that the interface we use to interact with our domain managers, *IBoatRaceDomainManager*, has a method called *Enter-Boat* that takes the name of the assembly and the type that implement one of our application's add-ins. The following sample CLR host uses the host control object to get a pointer to the instance of our application domain manager in the default application domain. It then calls the *EnterBoat* method to add a boat to our simulated boat race.

```
#include "stdafx.h"
#include "CHostControl.h"

int main(int argc, wchar_t* argv[])
{
    // Start the CLR.  Make sure .NET Framework version 2.0 is used.
    ICLRRuntimeHost *pCLR = NULL;
    HRESULT hr = CorBindToRuntimeEx
        L"v2.0.41013,
        L"wks",
        STARTUP_CONCURRENT_GC,
        CLSID_CLRRuntimeHost,
        IID_ICLRRuntimeHost,
        (PVOID*) &pCLR);

    assert(SUCCEEDED(hr));

    // Create an instance of our host control object and "register"
    // it with the CLR.
    CHostControl *pHostControl = new CHostControl();
    pCLR->SetHostControl((IHostControl *)pHostControl);

    // Start the CLR in the process.
    hr = pCLR->Start();
    assert(SUCCEEDED(hr));

    // Get a pointer to our AppDomainManager running in the default domain.
    IBoatRaceDomainManager *pDomainManagerForDefaultDomain =
                pHostControl->GetDomainManagerForDefaultDomain();
    assert(pDomainManagerForDefaultDomain);

    // Call into the default application domain to enter a boat in the race.
    pDomainManagerForDefaultDomain->EnterBoat("StevensBoat",
                                        "J29.ParthianShot");

    // Clean up.
```

```
        pDomainManagerForDefaultDomain->Release();
        pHostControl->Release();
        return 0;
    }
```

Environment Variables

You can associate your application domain manager with a process using a set of environment variables instead of through the CLR hosting APIs. Setting the environment variables requires less code, but you lose the ability to interact with your domain manager from unmanaged code. Specifically, if you haven't implemented the *IHostControl* interface, the CLR cannot call out to your unmanaged code to give you a pointer to the domain manager. As a result, specifying an application domain manager using a configuration file is useful only if your extensible application is written completely in managed code or if you're writing a CLR host but don't need to interact with your domain manager from unmanaged code.

The environment variables you need to set to associate your application domain manager with a process are called *APPDOMAIN_MANAGER_ASM* and *APPDOMAIN_MANAGER_TYPE*. *APPDOMAIN_MANAGER_ASM* must be set to the fully qualified name of the assembly containing your application domain manager type, whereas *APPDOMAIN_MANAGER_TYPE* must be set to the name of the type within that assembly that implements your domain manager. For example, if we were to associate our *BoatRaceDomainManager* type with a process, the two environment variables would have the following values:

```
APPDOMAIN_MANAGER_ASM=BoatRaceHostRuntime, Version=1.0.0.0, PublicKeyToken=5cf360b40180107c,
 culture=neutral
```

```
APPDOMAIN_MANAGER_TYPE= BoatRaceHostRuntime.BoatRaceDomainManager
```

Setting these values in an unmanaged CLR host is straightforward—just call the Win32 API *SetEnvironmentVariable* any time before you start the CLR using *ICLRRuntimeHost::Start*. The following example uses *SetEnvironmentVariable* to set *APPDOMAIN_MANAGER_ASM* and *APPDOMAIN_MANAGER_TYPE* to the values described previously:

```
int main(int argc, wchar_t* argv[])
{
    // Start the CLR.  Make sure .NET Framework 2.0 is used.
    ICLRRuntimeHost *pCLR = NULL;
    HRESULT hr = CorBindToRuntimeEx
        L"v2.0.41013
        L"wks",
        STARTUP_CONCURRENT_GC,
        CLSID_CLRRuntimeHost,
        IID_ICLRRuntimeHost,
        (PVOID*) &pCLR);

    assert(SUCCEEDED(hr));
```

```
    // Use Win32's SetEnvironmentVariable to set up the domain manager.
    SetEnvironmentVariable(L"APPDOMAIN_MANAGER_TYPE",
                            L"BoatRaceHostRuntime.BoatRaceDomainManager");
    SetEnvironmentVariable(L"APPDOMAIN_MANAGER_ASM",
                            L"BoatRaceHostRuntime, Version=1.0.0.0,
                              PublicKeyToken=5cf360b40180107c,
                              culture=neutral");
    // Start the CLR.
    hr = pCLR->Start();
    assert(SUCCEEDED(hr));

    // The rest of the host's code is omitted.
}
```

If your application is written entirely in managed code, setting *APPDOMAIN_MANAGER_ASM*
and *APPDOMAIN_MANAGER_TYPE* isn't as straightforward. You can't set these environment
variables from within your process as we did in the earlier unmanaged example because by
the time your managed code is running, it's too late. The CLR honors the environment variables only if they are set before the default application domain is created. So you must write a
small bootstrap application that creates a process to run your real application. Values for
APPDOMAIN_MANAGER_ASM and *APPDOMAIN_MANAGER_TYPE* can be passed into the
new process as it's created. The following example shows how you might accomplish this
using the *Process* and *ProcessStartInfo* classes from *System.Diagnostics*:

```
using System;
using System.Diagnostics;

namespace AppDomainManagerProcess
{
    class Launch
    {
        [STAThread]
        static void Main(string[] args)
        {
            ProcessStartInfo mdProcessInfo = new
                ProcessStartInfo("BoatRaceHost.exe");

            mdProcessInfo.EnvironmentVariables["APPDOMAIN_MANAGER_ASM"] =
                        "BoatRaceHostRuntime, Version=1.0.0.0,
                         PublicKeyToken=5cf360b40180107c, culture=neutral";

            mdProcessInfo.EnvironmentVariables["APPDOMAIN_MANAGER_TYPE"] =
                        "BoatRaceHostRuntime.BoatRaceDomainManager";

            mdProcessInfo.UseShellExecute = false;
            Process.Start(mdProcessInfo);
        }
    }
}
```

Creating Application Domains

Application domains are exposed in the .NET Framework programming model through the *System.AppDomain* class. *System.AppDomain* has a static method called *CreateDomain* you can use to create a new application domain. There are several different flavors of *AppDomain.CreateDomain*, ranging from a simple method that creates a domain with just a friendly name to methods that create domains with custom security evidence or configuration properties. The signatures for *CreateDomain* are as follows:

```
public static AppDomain CreateDomain(String friendlyName)

public static AppDomain CreateDomain(String    friendlyName,
                                     Evidence securityInfo)

public static AppDomain CreateDomain(String friendlyName,
                                     Evidence securityInfo,
                                     AppDomainSetup info)
```

The parameters to *CreateDomain* are described in Table 5-2.

Table 5-2   The Parameters to *AppDomain.CreateDomain*

Parameter	Description
friendlyName	A textual name to associate with the domain.
	The contents of this string are completely up to the creator of the domain—the CLR doesn't require specific formats or conventions to be followed.
	This name is typically used to display information about application domains in user interfaces. For example, AppDomainViewer uses a domain's friendly name in its tree view. Similarly, some debuggers use friendly names to display application domains when attached to a process.
	A domain's friendly name can be accessed using the *friendlyName* property. Once an application domain is created, its name cannot be changed.
securityInfo	Security evidence to be associated with the domain. This parameter is optional in that you can pass null, causing the CLR not to set any evidence.
	Earlier in the chapter, I talked about two ways to customize the Code Access Security for an application domain—provide a domain-level policy tree and limit the permissions granted to an assembly using application domain evidence. This parameter is the way you set that evidence.
	Much more information about domain evidence is provided in Chapter 10.
info	An object of type *System.AppDomainSetup* that contains all the configuration properties for the domain. Using this object to configure an application domain is a broad subject in and of itself. A complete description of how to use *AppDomainSetup* is provided in Chapter 6.

Choosing which flavor of *CreateDomain* to call is dictated by how much you need to configure the domain upfront. For example, several configuration properties are exposed by *AppDomainSetup* that can be specified only when the domain is created (more on this in Chapter 6).

I typically find that the *CreateDomain* that takes a friendly name, security evidence, and an *AppDomainSetup* object is the most useful. When a high degree of application domain configuration is required, this is the only flavor of *CreateDomain* that gives you full access to all the configuration options. For scenarios in which such customization is not required, any of its three parameters can be set to null.

Calling *CreateDomain* returns a new instance of *System.AppDomain* that you use to start interacting with the domain. The following code snippet shows a typical call to *CreateDomain*. Note that for now I'm passing null for both the security evidence and *AppDomainSetup* parameters. As described, I cover the details of those parameters in upcoming chapters.

```
using System;
AppDomain ad = AppDomain.CreateDomain("Stevenpr Domain", null, null);
```

> **Note**   For completeness, it's worth noting that there is a fourth flavor of *CreateDomain* that takes just a few of the configuration properties exposed through *AppDomainSetup*:
>
> ```
> public static AppDomain CreateDomain(String friendlyName,
>                                      Evidence securityInfo,
>                                      String appBasePath,
>                                      String appRelativeSearchPath,
>                                      bool shadowCopyFiles)
> ```
>
> This flavor of *CreateDomain* is not all that useful in my opinion. It was implemented before the *AppDomainSetup* object was and is kept in place for backward-compatibility reasons. As described, using *AppDomainSetup* is the preferred way to configure an application domain as it is being created.

Typically, one of the first things you'll want to do after creating a new domain is load an assembly into it. If you're writing an extensible application, it's likely that the assembly you load into the new domain will be an add-in. Recall from earlier discussions about application domain isolation that you typically want the code that loads your add-ins to be running in the domain in which the add-in is to be loaded. Otherwise, a proxy to the new extension would have to be returned across the application domain boundary, thereby requiring the assembly containing the extension to be loaded into multiple domains. The simplest, most efficient way to load an assembly from within its target domain is to take advantage of the host runtime, or application domain managers, discussed in the previous section. Because the CLR automatically creates an instance of an application domain manager in each new application domain, you must simply pass information about which assembly to load into the new domain manager and let it take care of the loading. Remember, too, that this practice also results in a clean design because all communication between application domains is done through the domain managers.

System.AppDomain has a property called *DomainManager* that returns the instance of the application domain manager for the given application domain. After a new domain is created, you can use this property to get its domain manager with which you can start interacting with the new domain. To see how this works, let's return to our boat race example and look at the implementation of the *EnterBoat* method. *EnterBoat* is responsible for creating a new application domain and loading the new boat into that domain. The implementation of *BoatRaceDomainManager.EnterBoat* is as follows:

```
public class BoatRaceDomainManager : AppDomainManager,
                               IBoatRaceDomainManager
{
   // Other methods omitted…

   public Int32 EnterBoat(string assemblyFileName, string boatTypeName)
   {
      // Create a new domain in which to load the boat.
      AppDomain ad = AppDomain.CreateDomain(boatTypeName, null, null);

      // Get the instance of BoatRaceDomainManager running in the
      // new domain.
      BoatRaceDomainManager adManager =
                 (BoatRaceDomainManager)ad.DomainManager;

      // Pass the assembly and type names to the new domain so the
      // assembly can be loaded.
      adManager.InitializeNewBoat(assemblyFileName, boatTypeName);

      return ad.Id;
   }
}
```

EnterBoat first creates a new application domain for the boat by calling *AppDomain.Create-Domain*. After the domain is created, *AppDomain.DomainManager* is used to get the instance of the domain manager in the new domain. Finally, *EnterBoat* calls a method on *BoatRace-DomainManager* called *InitializeNewBoat*, passing the name of the assembly containing the boat and the name of the type that represents the boat. *InitializeNewBoat* then takes this information and uses the methods on the *System.Reflection.Assembly* class to load the assembly into the new domain. The discussion of how to load assemblies is broad enough to warrant an entire chapter. I cover this topic in detail in Chapter 7.

Note You might recall from looking at Table 5-1 that *System.AppDomainManager* also has a method called *CreateDomain*. This method is not intended to be called explicitly. Instead, as you'll see in Chapter 6, the CLR calls *AppDomainManager.CreateDomain* (or its overrides) whenever a new application domain is created using *AppDomain.CreateDomain*. This gives the domain manager a chance to configure the new domain as it is being created.

> **Note** If you're familiar with the CLR hosting APIs that were provided in the first two versions of the CLR (.NET Framework version 1.0 and .NET Framework version 1.1), you might recall that the *ICorRuntimeHost* interface includes methods that enable you to create application domains directly from unmanaged code. These methods returned an interface pointer through which you could interact directly with the new domain using COM interoperability. The ability to create an application domain from unmanaged code was occasionally useful, but in practice most hosts created their domains in managed code because the programming model was simpler and tended to perform better because the amount of communication between unmanaged and managed code was less. To encourage this model, and to reduce the number of duplicate ways to do the same thing, Microsoft has removed the ability to create application domains directly from unmanaged code in .NET Framework version 2.0.

Application Domains and Threads

One aspect of how the isolation provided by an application domain differs from that provided by a process is in the treatment of operating system threads. You must consider two primary differences when designing your application to use domains most effectively. First, threads are not confined to a particular application domain. In the Windows process model, all threads are specific to a process. A given thread cannot begin execution in one process and continue execution in another process. This is not true in the application domain model. Threads are free to wander between domains as necessary. The CLR does the proper checks and data structure adjustments at the domain boundaries to ensure that information associated with the thread that is intended for use only within a single domain doesn't leak into the other domain, thereby affecting its behavior. For example, you can store data on a thread using the *Alloc(Named)DataSlot* methods on the *System.Threading.Thread* object. These methods and the related methods to retrieve the data provide a managed implementation of thread local storage (TLS). Whenever a domain boundary is crossed, the CLR ensures the managed TLS is removed from the thread and saved in the application domain data structures so that the thread appears "clean" when it enters the new domain. In contrast, some thread-related state should flow between domains. The primary example of this type of state is the data that describes the call that is being made across domains. This data is held in the CLR's execution context and includes everything from the call stack, to the current Windows token, to synchronization information. For more information on the execution context, see the .NET Framework 2.0 SDK.

The fact that threads wander between application domains does not mean, however, that a given domain can have only one thread running in it at a given time. Just as with a Win32 process, several threads can be running in a single application domain simultaneously.

The second difference in the way threads are treated in the application domain model is that, unlike when you create a new process, creating a new application domain does not result in the creation of a new thread. When you create a new domain and transfer control into it by calling a method on a type in that domain, execution continues on the same thread on which the domain was created. To see how this works, let's return to the implementation of *BoatRaceDomainManager.EnterBoat* that we discussed in the previous section. As shown in the following code, the thread on which we're running switches into the new domain when we invoke the *InitializeNewBoat* method on the domain manager running in that domain.

```
public class BoatRaceDomainManager : AppDomainManager,
                                     IBoatRaceDomainManager
{
    // Other methods omitted...

    public Int32 EnterBoat(string assemblyFileName,
                           string boatTypeName)
    {
        // Create a new domain in which to load the boat.
        AppDomain ad = AppDomain.CreateDomain(boatTypeName,
                                              null, null);

        // Get the instance of BoatRaceDomainManager
        // running in the new domain.
        BoatRaceDomainManager adManager =
            (BoatRaceDomainManager)ad.DomainManager;

        // Pass⁴ the assembly and type names to the new
        // domain so the assembly can be loaded.
        adManager.InitializeNewBoat(assemblyFileName,
                                    boatTypeName);

        return ad.Id;
    }
}
```

The high-level relationship between threads and application domains is shown in Figure 5-8.

The .NET Framework provides some static members you can use to obtain the current relationship between threads and application domains running in a process. For example, *System.AppDomain.CurrentDomain* and *System.Threading.Thread.GetDomain* both return the application domain in which the thread from the calling domain is executing as shown in the following code snippet:

```
using System;
using System.Threading;
// Both return the domain in which the current thread is executing.
AppDomain currentDomain1 = AppDomain.CurrentDomain();
AppDomain currentDomain2 = Thread.GetDomain();
```

---

4. When *InitializeNewBoat* is called, the thread transfers into the new domain. It then returns to the default domain when the call completes.

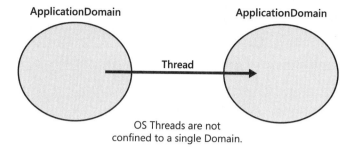

OS Threads are not
confined to a single Domain.

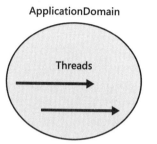

Multiple OS Threads may be executing
in the same Domain.

Figure 5-8   The relationship between threads and application domains

If you need to obtain the object that represents the current thread running in a domain, use the *System.Threading.Thread.CurrentThread* method. The *System.AppDomain* class also has a method called *GetCurrentThreadId* that returns an identifier for the current thread running in the calling domain. The relationship of this value to the thread identifiers provided in Win32 is undefined and can vary between different versions of the CLR. As a result, it's not safe to assume a direct mapping between these two concepts of thread identification.

The CLR Thread Pool

If you're writing a multithreaded managed application, it's much easier to achieve high performance and scalability by using the CLR thread pool instead of creating, managing, and destroying threads yourself. There are a few reasons why this is the case. First, creating and destroying threads are expensive. By reusing the threads in the pool, you're able to minimize drastically the number of times a new thread is created. Second, creating the ideal numbers of threads needed to accomplish a given workload requires a significant amount of tuning to get right. If too many threads are created, time is wasted in excessive context switches between threads. If too few threads are created, the amount of time spent waiting for an available thread can adversely affect performance. The CLR thread pool has been tuned over several years of experience building scalable managed applications. The number of threads in the CLR thread pool is optimized on a case-by-case basis based on the performance characteristics of the hardware on which you're running and the workload in the process. The thread pool injects new threads into the process when it determines that doing so increases the overall throughput of the work items currently queued to the pool. Experience has shown that most applications can achieve better throughput by leveraging the existing thread pool mechanism instead of dealing with thread management themselves.

The CLR thread pool is represented by the *System.Threading.ThreadPool* class. The managed thread pool is similar in spirit and functionality to the thread pool provided by Win32. In fact, if you're familiar with the Win32 thread pool APIs, you'll feel comfortable with the members of the *ThreadPool* class in no time.

There is one managed thread pool per process. Because threads aren't confined to a particular application domain, the thread pool doesn't need to be either. This enables the CLR to optimize work across the entire process for greater overall performance. It's very common for a given thread pool thread to service requests for multiple application domains. Whenever a thread is returned to the pool, its state is reset to avoid unintended leaks between domains. Dispatching requests to the thread pool is easy. *System.Threading.ThreadPool* includes a member called *QueueUserWorkItem* that takes a delegate. This delegate is queued to the thread pool and executed when a thread becomes available.

Multithread applications that use several application domains often follow a common pattern: first, a request comes in to execute some code. This request varies completely by scenario. For example, in SQL Server the request might result from building a plan to execute a query containing managed code. In the Internet Explorer case, the request might take the form of creating a new instance of a managed control on a Web page. Second, the application determines in which domain the request should be serviced. Depending on how your process is partitioned into multiple application domains, you can choose to execute your new request in an existing domain, or you can choose to create a new one. Next, an instance of the object representing the new request is created in the chosen domain. Finally, a delegate is queued to the thread that calls a method on the object to execute the request.

To illustrate this technique, let's return again to our implementation of *BoatRaceDomainManager.EnterBoat*. This time, let's use the CLR thread pool to initialize our new boat asynchronously:

```
using System;
using System.Threading;

namespace BoatRaceHostRuntime
{
    // Some code omitted for clarity.

    // This struct is used to pass request data to the delegate that
    // will be executed by the thread pool.
    struct ThreadData
    {
        public BoatRaceDomainManager domainManager;
        public string assemblyFileName;
```

```
        public string boatTypeName;
    };

    public class BoatRaceDomainManager : AppDomainManager,
                              IBoatRaceDomainManager
    {
        // This is the method that gets queued to the thread pool.
        static void RunAsync(Object state)
        {
            ThreadData td = (ThreadData)state;

            // Get the domain manager object out of the thread state
            // object and call its InitializeNewBoat method.
            td.domainManager.InitializeNewBoat(td.assemblyFileName,
                                          td.boatTypeName);
        }

        public Int32 EnterBoat(string assemblyFileName, string boatTypeName)
        {
            // Create a new domain in which to load the boat.
            AppDomain ad = AppDomain.CreateDomain(boatTypeName, null,
                                         null);

            BoatRaceDomainManager adManager =
                        (BoatRaceDomainManager)ad.DomainManager;

            // Gather the domain manager and the name of the assembly
            // and type into an object to pass to thread pool.
            ThreadData threadData = new ThreadData();

            threadData.domainManager = adManager;
            threadData.assemblyFileName = assemblyFileName;
            threadData.boatTypeName = boatTypeName;

            // Queue a work item to the thread pool.
            ThreadPool.QueueUserWorkItem(new WaitCallback(RunAsync),
                                      threadData);
            return ad.Id;
        }
    }
}
```

In this version of the implementation, we begin by declaring a structure called *ThreadData* that we'll use to pass the data to the new thread that we'll need to make the call. This data includes the application domain manager for the new domain and the name of the assembly and type containing the implementation of the boat. Next, we need to define a delegate to act as our thread proc. The *RunAsync* delegate takes a *ThreadData* structure, pulls out the application domain manager, and calls its *InitializeNewBoat* method. Now, after we create the new domain for the boat, we get its domain manager as before, but this time instead of calling *InitializeNewBoat* directly, we save the data needed to make the call into an instance of the *ThreadData* structure and invoke *RunAsync* asynchronously by queuing a request to the thread pool using *ThreadPool.QueueUserWorkItem*.

Clearly, there is much more to the CLR thread pool than I've described here. For a more complete description, see the .NET Framework SDK reference material for *System.Threading.ThreadPool.*

Unloading Application Domains

As described, unloading code from a process requires you to unload the application domain in which the code is running. The CLR currently doesn't support unloading individual assemblies or types. There are several scenarios in which an application might want to unload a domain. One of the most common reasons for wanting to unload an application domain is to reduce the working set of a process. This is especially important if your application has high scalability requirements or operates in a constrained memory environment. Another common reason to unload an application domain is to enable code running in your process to be updated on the fly. The ASP.NET host is a great example of using application domains to achieve this effect. As you might know, ASP.NET enables you to update a Web application dynamically by simply copying a new version of one or more of the application's DLLs into the bin directory. When ASP.NET detects a new file, it begins routing requests for that application to a new domain. When it determines that all requests in the old application domain have completed, it unloads the domain. In this way, applications can be updated without restarting the Web server. In many cases, this update is completely transparent to the end user. I show you how to implement this feature in your own applications when I talk about the family of shadow copy properties in Chapter 6.

Application domains can be unloaded by calling a static method on *System.AppDomain* called *Unload. AppDomain.Unload* takes one parameter—an instance of *System.AppDomain* representing the domain you want to unload. Application domains can also be unloaded from unmanaged code using the CLR hosting interfaces. *ICLRRuntimeHost* includes a method called *UnloadAppDomain* that takes the unique numerical identifier of the application domain you want to unload.

Calls to *AppDomain.Unload* or *ICLRRuntimeHost::UnloadAppDomain* cause the CLR to unload the application domain gracefully. By *gracefully*, I mean that the CLR unloads the domain in an orderly fashion that lets the application code currently running in the domain reach a natural, predictable endpoint. Specifically, the following sequence of events occurs during a graceful shutdown of an application domain:

1. The threads running in the domain are aborted.

2. An event is raised to indicate the domain is being unloaded.

3. Finalizers are run for objects in the application domain.

4. The CLR cleans up its internal data structures associated with the domain.

These steps are described in the following sections.

Step 1: Aborting the Threads Running in the Domain

The CLR begins the process of unloading an application domain by stopping all code that is currently executing in the domain. Threads running in the domain are given the opportunity to complete gracefully rather than being abruptly terminated. This is accomplished by sending a *ThreadAbortException* to all threads in the domains. Although a *ThreadAbortException* signals to the application that the thread is going away, it does not provide a mechanism for the application to catch the exception and stop the thread from aborting. A *ThreadAbortException* is persistent in that although it can be caught, it always gets rethrown by the CLR if an application catches it.

Code that is running on a thread destined to be aborted has two opportunities to clean up. First, the CLR runs code in all *finally* blocks as part of thread termination. Also, the finalizers for all objects are run (see the "Step 3: Running Finalizers" section).

Be aware that a *ThreadAbortException* can be thrown on threads that are currently not even executing in the partially unloaded application domain. If a thread executed in that domain at one point and must return to that domain as the call stack is being unwound, that thread receives a *ThreadAbortException*. For example, consider the case in which a thread is executing some code in Domain 1. At some later point in time, the thread leaves Domain 1 and begins executing in Domain 2. If *AppDomain.Unload* is called on Domain 1 at this point, the thread's stack would look something like the stack shown in Figure 5-9.

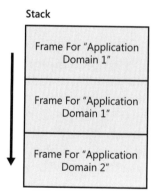

AppDomain.Unload called on "Application
Domain 1" while executing in "Application
                Domain 2"

Figure 5-9   A thread's stack on a cross-domain call

Clearly, aborting this thread is necessary because the stack contains addresses of calls that will be invalid after the domain is completely unloaded.

Step 2: Raising an Unload Event

After the *ThreadAbortExceptions* have been thrown and the *finally* blocks have been run, the CLR raises an event to indicate the domain is unloading. This event can be received in either managed code or unmanaged code. I talk more about how to catch this event later in the chapter.

Step 3: Running Finalizers

Earlier in the unloading process, the CLR ran all *finally* clauses as one way to enable the threads running in the domain to clean up before being aborted. In addition to running *finallys*, the CLR finalizes all objects that live in the domain. This gives the objects a final opportunity to free all resources allocated while the domain was active.

Typically, finalizers are run as a part of a garbage collection. When an object is being collected, all unused objects that reference it are likely being finalized and collected as well. However, the order in which objects are finalized is less well defined when the application domain in which an object lives is being unloaded. As a result, it might be necessary for an object's finalizer to behave differently depending on whether the object is being finalized because the domain is unloaded or as part of a collection. A finalizer can tell the difference between these two cases by calling the *IsFinalizingForUnload* method on *System.AppDomain*. As its name implies, *IsFinalizingForUnload* returns true if the finalizer from which it is called is being run during application domain unload.

Clearly, running finalizers and *finallys* during unload enables code contained in add-ins to be run. By default, the CLR makes no guarantees that this code will actually ever terminate. For example, a finalizer could get stuck in an infinite loop, causing the object to stay alive forever. Without customization, the CLR does not impose any timeouts on thread abort or application domain unload. As a result, an attempt to unload an application domain might never actually finish. Fortunately, the CLR hosting interfaces provide an extensible set of customizations related to the way errors are handled and the way attempts to abort threads and unload domains are handled. For example, a host can use these interfaces to specify timeouts for various actions and to cause the CLR to terminate a thread more forcefully when the timeout expires. A host specifies its policy around error handling and unloading using the *ICLRPolicyManager* interface. I cover the details of how to specify policy using this interface in Chapter 11.

As you've seen, the CLR does its best to enable cleanup code to be run as part of unloading an application domain. Although this helps provide for a clean shutdown, the application's logic is terminated the instant the *ThreadAbortException* is thrown. As a result, the work the application was doing might be halted prematurely. In the best case, this simply results in a program that safely stops running early. However, it's easy to imagine scenarios in which the premature termination of the application leaves the system in an inconsistent state. As the author of an application that initiates application domain unloads, it's in your best interest to unload a domain only when no active threads are running in the domain. This helps you minimize the times when unloading a domain adversely affects the application. The CLR provides no APIs or other mechanisms to help you determine when a domain is empty. You must build additional logic into your application to determine when requests you've dispatched to different threads have been completed. When they all complete successfully, you know the domain is safe to unload.

Step 4: Freeing the Internal CLR Data Structures

After all finalizers have run and no more threads are executing in the domain, the CLR is ready to unload all the in-memory data structures used in the internal implementation. Before this happens, however, the objects that resided in the domain must be collected. After the next garbage collection occurs, the application domain data structures are unloaded from the process address space and the domain is considered unloaded.

Exceptions Related to Unloading Application Domains

You should be aware of a few exceptions that might get thrown as a result of unloading an application domain. First, once a domain is unloaded, access to objects that used to live in that domain is illegal. When an attempt to access such an object occurs, the CLR will throw an *ApplicationDomainUnloadedException*. Second, there are a few cases in which unloading an application domain is invalid. For example, *AppDomain.Unload* cannot be called on the default domain (remember, it must live as long as the process) or on an application domain that has already been unloaded. In these cases, the CLR throws a *CannotUnloadAppDomainException*.

Receiving Application Domain Unload Events

The CLR raises an event to notify the hosting application that an application domain is being unloaded. This event can be received in either managed or unmanaged code. In managed code, domain unload notifications are raised through the *System.AppDomain.DomainUnload* event. In unmanaged code, the CLR sends application domain unload notifications to hosts through the *IActionOnCLREvent* interface. I show you how to use *IActionOnCLREvent* to catch these notifications in the next section.

The *AppDomain.DomainUnload* event takes the standard event delegate that includes arguments for the object that originated the event (the *sender*) and any additional data that is specific to that event (the *EventArgs*). The instance of *System.AppDomain* representing the application domain that is being unloaded is passed as the *sender* parameter. The *EventArgs* are null. The following code snippet shows a simple event handler that prints the name of the application domain that is being unloaded:

```
public static void DomainUnloadHandler(Object sender, EventArgs e)
{
    AppDomain ad = (AppDomain)sender;
    Console.WriteLine("Domain Unloaded Event fired: " + ad.FriendlyName);
}
```

This event is hooked up to the domain using the standard event syntax:

```
AppDomain ad1 = AppDomain.CreateDomain("Application Domain 1");
ad1.DomainUnload += new EventHandler(DomainUnloadHandler);
```

Because information about the unloaded domain is passed as a parameter, it's convenient to register the same delegate for all application domains you create. When the event is raised you simply use the *sender* parameter to tell which domain has been unloaded.

Receiving Domain Unload Events Using the *IActionOnCLREvent* Interface

Listening to domain unload events in managed code is much easier to program and therefore is the approach you're likely to use most. However, you can also receive these events in unmanaged code by providing an object that implements the *IActionOnCLREvent* interface. *IActionOnCLREvent* contains one method (*OnEvent*) that the CLR calls to send an event to a CLR host. Here's the definition of *IActionOnCLREvent* from mscoree.idl:

```
interface IActionOnCLREvent: IUnknown
{
    HRESULT OnEvent(
        [in] EClrEvent    event,
        [in] PVOID        data
        );
}
```

The CLR passes two parameters to *OnEvent*. The first parameter, *event*, is a value from the *EClrEvent* enumeration that identifies the event being fired. The second parameter is the data associated with the event. For application domain unloads, the *data* parameter is the unique numerical identifier representing the unloaded domain.

You register your intent to receive events by passing your implementation of *IActionOnCLREvent* to the CLR through the *ICLROnEventManager* interface. As with all CLR-implemented hosting managers, you obtain this interface from *ICLRControl* as shown in the following code snippet:

```
// Get an ICLRRuntimeHost by calling CorBindToRuntimeEx.
ICLRRuntimeHost *pCLR = NULL;
hr = CorBindToRuntimeEx(......,(PVOID*) &pCLR);

// Get the CLR Control object.
ICLRControl *pCLRControl = NULL;
pCLR->GetCLRControl(&pCLRControl);

// Ask for the Event Manager.
ICLROnEventManager *pEventManager = NULL;
pCLRControl->GetCLRManager(IID_ICLROnEventManager,
                           (void **)&pEventManager);
```

ICLROnEventManager contains two methods. *RegisterActionOnEvent* enables you to register your object that implements *IActionOnCLREvent* with the CLR. When you are no longer interested in receiving events, you can unregister your event handler using *UnregisterActionOn-Event*. Here's the interface definition for *ICLROnEventManager* from mscoree.idl:

```
interface ICLROnEventManager: IUnknown
{
   HRESULT RegisterActionOnEvent(
      [in] EClrEvent        event,
      [in] IActionOnCLREvent *pAction
      );
   HRESULT UnregisterActionOnEvent(
      [in] EClrEvent        event,
      [in] IActionOnCLREvent *pAction
      );
}
```

Notice that both methods take a parameter of type *EClrEvent*. This enables you to register to receive only those events you are interested in.

To demonstrate how to receive application domain events using *IActionOnCLREvent*, I've modified our boat race host sample to unload an application domain that was created for one of the add-ins. Listing 5-2 shows the updated sample.

Listing 5-2 BoatRaceHost.cpp
```
#include "stdafx.h"
#include "CHostControl.h"

// This class implements IActionOnCLREvent. An instance of this class
// is passed as a "callback" to the CLR's ICLROnEventManager to receive
// a notification when an application domain is unloaded.
class CActionOnCLREvent : public IActionOnCLREvent
{
   public:

   // IActionOnCLREvent
   HRESULT __stdcall OnEvent(EClrEvent event, PVOID data);

   // IUnknown
   virtual HRESULT __stdcall QueryInterface(const IID &iid, void **ppv);
   virtual ULONG __stdcall AddRef();
   virtual ULONG __stdcall Release();

   // constructor and destructor
   CActionOnCLREvent()
   {
      m_cRef=0;
   }
   virtual ~CActionOnCLREvent()
   {
   }

   private:
   long m_cRef; // member variable for ref counting
};
```

```cpp
// IActionOnCLREvent methods
HRESULT __stdcall CActionOnCLREvent::OnEvent(EClrEvent event, PVOID data)
{

    wprintf(L"AppDomain %d Unloaded\n", (int) data);
    return S_OK;

}


// IUnknown methods
HRESULT __stdcall CActionOnCLREvent::QueryInterface(const IID &iid,void **ppv)
{
    if (!ppv) return E_POINTER;
    *ppv=this;
    AddRef();
    return S_OK;
}

ULONG __stdcall CActionOnCLREvent::AddRef()
{
    return InterlockedIncrement(&m_cRef);
}

ULONG __stdcall CActionOnCLREvent::Release()
{
    if(InterlockedDecrement(&m_cRef) == 0){
        delete this;
        return 0;
    }
    return m_cRef;
}

int main(int argc, wchar_t* argv[])
{
    // Start the CLR.  Make sure .NET Framework version 2.0 is used.
    ICLRRuntimeHost *pCLR = NULL;
    HRESULT hr = CorBindToRuntimeEx(
        L"v2.0.41013 ,
        L"wks",
        STARTUP_CONCURRENT_GC,
        CLSID_CLRRuntimeHost,
        IID_ICLRRuntimeHost,
        (PVOID*) &pCLR);
    assert(SUCCEEDED(hr));

    // Create an instance of our host control object and  register
    // it with the CLR.
    CHostControl *pHostControl = new CHostControl();
    pCLR->SetHostControl((IHostControl *)pHostControl);

    // Get the CLRControl object. This object enables us to get the
    // CLR's OnEventManager interface and hook up an instance of
    // CActionOnCLREvent.
    ICLRControl *pCLRControl = NULL;
    hr = pCLR->GetCLRControl(&pCLRControl);
    assert(SUCCEEDED(hr));
```

```
      ICLROnEventManager *pEventManager = NULL;
      hr = pCLRControl->GetCLRManager(IID_ICLROnEventManager,
                                    (void **)&pEventManager);
      assert(SUCCEEDED(hr));

      // Create a new object that implements IActionOnCLREvent and
      // register it with the CLR. We're only registering to receive
      // notifications on app domain unload.
      CActionOnCLREvent *pEventHandler = new CActionOnCLREvent();
      hr = pEventManager->RegisterActionOnEvent(Event_DomainUnload,
                         (IActionOnCLREvent *)pEventHandler);
      assert(SUCCEEDED(hr));

      hr = pCLR->Start();
      assert(SUCCEEDED(hr));

      // Get a pointer to our AppDomainManager running in the default domain.
      IBoatRaceDomainManager *pDomainManagerForDefaultDomain =
                      pHostControl->GetDomainManagerForDefaultDomain();
      assert(pDomainManagerForDefaultDomain);

      // Enter a new boat in the race. This creates a new application domain
      // whose id is returned.
      int domainID = pDomainManagerForDefaultDomain->EnterBoat(L"Boats",
                             L"J29.ParthianShot");


      // Unload the domain the boat was just created in. This will
      // cause the CLR to call the OnEvent method in our implementation of
      // IActionOnCLREvent.
      pCLR->UnloadAppDomain(domainID);

      // Clean up.
      pDomainManagerForDefaultDomain->Release();
      pHostControl->Release();
      return 0;
   }
```

In this sample, the implementation of *IActionOnCLREvent* is provided by the *CActionOnCLR-Event* class. Notice the implementation of the *OnEvent* method is very simple—it just prints out the identifier of the application domain that is being unloaded. In the main program an instance of *CActionOnCLREvent* is created and registered with the CLR by calling the *Register-ActionOnEvent* method on the *ICLROnEventManager* pointer obtained from *ICLRControl*. To trigger the event handler to be called, an application domain is unloaded using *ICLRRuntime-Host::UnloadAppDomain*.

Summary

Application domains are often described as subprocesses because they provide an isolation boundary around a grouping of assemblies in a process. If the code running in the application domain is verifiably type safe, the isolation provided by the domain is roughly equivalent to that provided by a process in Win32. Application domains also provide the ability to unload code from a running process dynamically. As the author of an extensible application, one of the key decisions you'll make is how to partition your process into multiple application domains. The key is to use application domains to achieve the isolation you want while minimizing the amount of communication between domains because of the cost associated with remote calls.

When writing an extensible application, you'll likely want to take advantage of a new concept in .NET Framework version 2.0 called an application domain manager. Providing an application domain manager is an easy way to implement the host runtime design pattern because the CLR automatically creates an instance of your domain manager in every application domain. Also, if you're writing a CLR host, an application domain manager is the mechanism you use to call into managed code from the unmanaged portion of your host.

Chapter 6

Configuring Application Domains

In Chapter 5, I describe application domains as a construct used to isolate groups of assemblies that are loaded into the same process. An important aspect of this isolation is the ability for the creator of an application domain to be able to constrain various aspects of how the domain operates. For example, a domain's creator must be able to limit the locations from which unsigned assemblies can be loaded into the domain. Other examples include the ability to control how version policy applies to assemblies in the domain and to specify the configuration file where application-specific settings can be stored. These aspects of application domain behavior, along with many others, can be customized through various settings specified when the domain is created. In this chapter, I describe how you can use these settings to customize the behavior of application domains to fit your particular scenario.

Application domain managers also play a key role in your ability to customize how application domains are created in the process. Recall from the previous chapter that an instance of your application domain manager is created by the CLR in every application domain. As part of this process, the CLR calls your application domain manager both before and after a new domain has been created to give you a chance to configure it. This detail is important because it gives you, the author of an extensible application, the ability to decide how all domains are created in the process, including those created by any add-ins you have loaded, not just the ones you create yourself. After I describe the full set of application domain configuration settings, I explain your domain manager's role in customizing how application domains are created in a process.

Application Domain Configuration Settings

The complete list of application domain configuration settings is shown here. These settings are manipulated programmatically through public properties on the *System.AppDomainSetup* object.

ApplicationBase
PrivateBinPath
DisallowApplicationBaseProbing
PrivateBinPathProbe
DisallowPublisherPolicy
DisallowBindingRedirects
ConfigurationFile
LicenseFile
AppDomainInitializer
ConfigurationBytes

ShadowCopyFiles
ShadowCopyDirectories
CachePath
DynamicBase
ApplicationName
LoaderOptimization
DisallowCodeDownload
ActivationArguments
AppDomainInitializerArguments

The *ConfigurationBytes* "property" is actually implemented by two methods: *GetConfiguration-Bytes* and *SetConfigurationBytes*.

Before discussing how to use *AppDomainSetup*, take a look at the general categories of settings you can apply to an application domain:

- **Private assembly location settings**   These settings are used to specify the root directory (and the structure of its subdirectories) in which the CLR will look for assemblies considered private to a particular application domain. The settings in this category are represented by the *ApplicationBase*, *PrivateBinPath*, *DisallowApplicationBaseProbing*, and *PrivateBinPathProbe* properties on *System.AppDomainSetup*.

- **Application-specific configuration settings**   Applications written in managed code use configuration files to store their settings. These settings can be custom settings defined by the application, or they can be settings that are known to the CLR, such as version policy statements and remote call configuration. Configuration files are associated with an application domain using either the *ConfigurationFile* or the *ConfigurationBytes* property on *System.AppDomainSetup*. The ability to scope an application's configuration data to the domain in which it is running is an essential part of the isolation provided by application domains.

- **Shadow copy settings**   The CLR includes a feature called *shadow copy* that you can use to build applications that can be updated dynamically. Shadow copy works by leaving an assembly's files unlocked when they are loaded from disk. In this way, the files can be replaced and reloaded without having to shut down and restart the process. The properties used to set up the shadow copy feature are *ShadowCopyFiles*, *ShadowCopyDirectories*, *CachePath*, and *ApplicationName*.

- **Assembly version binding settings**   This group of settings enables you to customize how different aspects of the version policy system apply to code running in an application domain. Specifically, you can prevent from having any effect the version policy statements made either by the application or the publisher of a shared assembly. These customizations are specified using the *DisallowPublisherPolicy* and *DisallowBindingRedirects* properties on *System.AppDomainSetup*.

- **Miscellaneous settings**   There are a few settings that don't fit directly into the preceding categories. These settings are used to indicate whether code should be loaded into the application domain as domain neutral, to specify whether code running in the domain can dynamically download other code, and so on. The settings in this category are *LicenseFile*, *LoaderOptimization*, *DynamicBase*, *DisallowCodeDownload*, *ActivationArguments*, *AppDomainInitializer*, and *AppDomainInitializerArguments*.

Typically, the settings used to configure an application domain are specified when the domain is created. This is done by creating a new instance of *System.AppDomainSetup*, providing values for the properties you're interested in, and passing the new instance to the *System.AppDomain.CreateDomain* method. For example, the following code specifies the base directory in which the CLR will search for private assemblies for the new domain:

```
using System;

AppDomainSetup adSetup = new AppDomainSetup();
adSetup.ApplicationBase = @"c:\Program Files\MyApp";
AppDomain ad = AppDomain.CreateDomain("New Domain", null, adSetup);
```

Any time after the domain has been created, you can retrieve the current settings by obtaining an instance of *AppDomainSetup* using the *SetupInformation* property of *System.AppDomain*. For example, the following code prints the application root directory for the application domain running on the current thread:

```
using System;

AppDomainSetup adSetup = Thread.GetDomain().SetupInformation;

Console.WriteLine("The application base directory for the current
                    Domain is: " + adSetup.ApplicationBase);
```

Accessing Configuration Properties Using *System.AppDomain*

Using *AppDomain.SetupInformation* is the preferred way of accessing the application domain configuration settings. However, a few of the individual settings can also be obtained directly from properties on *System.AppDomain*. The following table describes these properties and their *AppDomainSetup* equivalents.

System.AppDomain Property	*System.AppDomainSetup* Equivalent
BaseDirectory	*ApplicationBase*
RelativeSearchPath	*PrivateBinPath*
ShadowCopyFiles	*ShadowCopyFiles*

It might seem odd that only a few of the configuration settings are exposed directly on *System.AppDomain*. The reason for this situation is primarily historical. The first several iterations of the *AppDomain* class contained just a few configurable settings, so it made perfect sense to expose them directly as properties on *AppDomain*. However, as time passed and the number of settings grew, it became convenient to wrap them all in the *AppDomainSetup* class. Unfortunately, by that time a few of the initial public betas had been released, and the CLR team decided to keep the original properties on *System.App-Domain* for compatibility reasons.

As I explained earlier, you typically specify the configuration settings for an application domain when you create the domain. However, *System.AppDomain* exposes public methods that enable you to change the value of a small number of these settings after the domain has been created. If you use these methods to change domain settings, you must do so before any assemblies are loaded into the domain. Calling them later will have no effect. The settings that can be changed through properties on *AppDomain*, along with the corresponding properties on *AppDomainSetup* they affect, are shown in Table 6-1.

Table 6-1 Application Domain Settings Exposed by *System.AppDomain*

System.AppDomain Property	*System.AppDomainSetup* Equivalent
AppendPrivatePath	*PrivateBinPath*
ClearPrivatePath	*PrivateBinPath*
ClearShadowCopyPath	*ShadowCopyDirectories*
SetCachePath	*CachePath*
SetDynamicBase	*DynamicBase*
SetShadowCopyFiles	*ShadowCopyFiles*
SetShadowCopyPath	*ShadowCopyDirectories*

I describe how to use these methods in the following sections, where their matching *AppDomainSetup* property is described.

Now that I've provided an overview of each of the settings, let's dig into the details of how you can use the *AppDomainSetup* properties to customize the application domains you create.

Private Assembly Directory Settings

If you've written and deployed a managed executable, you've probably deployed that executable and many of the assemblies it depends on to the same directory on disk. Similarly, if you've written a Microsoft ASP.NET application, you've probably deployed the code needed for your application to the bin directory under the site's virtual directory on the Web server. By deploying applications in this way, you're taking advantage of one of the key features of the Microsoft .NET Framework deployment model: the ability to deploy (almost) everything needed to run an application into the same directory. This deployment model has several benefits. It makes your application easier to install, uninstall, or replicate between machines. Furthermore, it enables you as an application developer to have tighter control over the dependencies that your application loads.

The key to providing this private deployment model is the *ApplicationBase* property on *AppDomainSetup*. When a host creates an application domain, this property is set to the root directory under which all dependent assemblies will be deployed. For example, the ASP.NET host sets *ApplicationBase* to the virtual root for the Web site. Similarly, the default CLR host sets the *ApplicationBase* for an executable to the directory on disk where the executable file is located. The following example sets the *ApplicationBase* for a new domain to a location in the Program Files directory:

```
using System;
AppDomainSetup adSetup = new AppDomainSetup();
adSetup.ApplicationBase = @"c:\Program Files\MyApp";
AppDomain ad = AppDomain.CreateDomain("MyApp", null, adSetup);
```

Typically, the value of *ApplicationBase* is set to a fully qualified directory on the same machine on which the host is running. However, because an *ApplicationBase* can be any directory, you can also set it to a directory on a remote Web or file server. For example, you could set the *ApplicationBase* for a domain to *http://www.cohowinery.com* or \\cohowinery\myapp. When doing so, however, keep in mind that the security requirements for code running in the application domain are greater. Specifically, code loaded from a remote location obtains a lower level of trust by default than code running from the local machine.

If you don't provide a value for *ApplicationBase* when creating a new domain, the CLR will set *ApplicationBase* to the directory containing the executable file that caused the process to be created. For example, if you launch an executable file from c:\program files\myapp, that directory will be the default *ApplicationBase* for all domains created in the process.

Customizing the *ApplicationBase* Directory Structure

Once you've established the root directory for your new application domain, you can customize the subdirectories under the root in which the CLR will look for private assemblies by using the *PrivateBinPath*, *PrivateBinPathProbe*, and *DisallowApplicationBaseProbing* properties on *AppDomainSetup*.

By default, the CLR will look for dependencies directly in the *ApplicationBase* and in a subdirectory of the *ApplicationBase* that matches the simple name of the assembly you are looking for. For example, consider an application myapp.exe that depends on an assembly in the file utils.dll. Myapp.exe is deployed to c:\program files\myapp. When resolving the reference from myapp to utils, the CLR will look for the file utils.dll in the following two directories (in the order shown):

- c:\program files\myapp
- c:\program files\myapp\utils

> **Note**   The CLR looks in different subdirectories for satellite resource assemblies. Satellite assemblies have a culture as part of their name. In these cases, the CLR looks for the assembly in subdirectories of the *ApplicationBase* named by culture instead of in the subdirectories in the preceding example. For example, if utils were a satellite resource assembly, requests for the German satellite would cause the CLR to look for utils.dll in the following subdirectories of the *ApplicationBase*:
>
> ❑   c:\program files\myapp\de
> ❑   c:\program files\myapp\de\utils

You can change the set of subdirectories the CLR looks in for dependencies by using the *PrivateBinPath* property on *AppDomainSetup*. *PrivateBinPath* is a semicolon-delimited list of subdirectories under the *ApplicationBase* in which you'd like the CLR to search for dependencies. Keep in mind that all directories specified using *PrivateBinPath* must be subdirectories of the *ApplicationBase*. You cannot use this property to cause assemblies to be loaded from outside of the *ApplicationBase*. Any subdirectories you supply using this property are searched in addition to the subdirectories the CLR would search by default. For example, the following code creates an application domain with an *ApplicationBase* of c:\program files\myapp and uses *PrivateBinPath* to add a subdirectory named bin to the list of subdirectories searched:

```
AppDomainSetup adSetup = new AppDomainSetup();
adSetup.ApplicationBase = @"c:\Program Files\MyApp";
adSetup.PrivateBinPath = "bin";

AppDomain ad = AppDomain.CreateDomain("one", null, adSetup);
```

Not only does this code cause the bin subdirectory to be searched, it also causes the CLR to look in subdirectories under bin named by assembly name. That is, the CLR applies the same searching rules to the new bin subdirectory that it applies to the *ApplicationBase* itself. If myapp.exe were to be run in this domain, the CLR would now look in the following directories for utils.dll (assuming no culture is involved):

- c:\program files\myapp

- c:\program files\myapp\utils

- c:\program files\myapp\bin

- c:\program files\myapp\bin\utils

There are two other techniques you can use to customize the layout of the directory structure under the *ApplicationBase*. First, you can specify additional directories to search using settings in an application configuration file. Configuration files are associated with domains by using the *ConfigurationFile* property on *AppDomainSetup* as described later in the chapter. You use the *<probing/>* element with the *privatePath* attribute to specify additional search directories. The directories you add using the configuration file are searched in addition to the directories specified using the *AppDomainSetup.PrivateBinPath* property. Here's a simple example of a configuration file that uses *privatePath* to add the bin directory to the search list:

```
<configuration>
    <runtime>
        <assemblyBinding xmlns="urn:schemas-microsoft-com:asm.v1">
            <probing privatePath="bin" />
        </assemblyBinding>
    </runtime>
</configuration>
```

For simple configuration files such as this one, editing the Extensible Markup Language (XML) directly using a text editor works great, but in more complex scenarios you might find it more convenient to enter your values for *privatePath* using the .NET Framework Configuration tool. This tool is available under the Administrative Tools group in the Microsoft Windows control panel. After adding an application to the tool, simply use its Properties dialog box to specify additional search directories. An example of an application's Properties dialog box is shown in Figure 6-1. See the .NET Framework SDK documentation for a complete description of application configuration files and the .NET Framework Configuration tool.

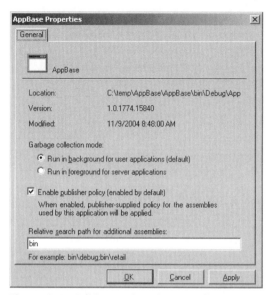

Figure 6-1   Editing settings in an application's Properties dialog box using the .NET Framework Configuration tool

The second alternative to using the *PrivateBinPath* property to customize the private assembly search list is to use the *AppendPrivatePath* and *ClearPrivatePath* methods on *System.AppDomain*. As their names imply, *AppendPrivatePath* is used to add additional search directories and *ClearPrivatePath* sets the search list back to the empty string.

Turning Off *ApplicationBase* Searching

In some scenarios, you might not want the CLR to look for assemblies in the *ApplicationBase* directory structure at all. For example, as I discuss in Chapter 8, the CLR hosting APIs enable you to customize the assembly loading process to such an extent that you can define your own assembly storage formats and locations. CLR hosts such as Microsoft SQL Server 2005 use this capability to store and load assemblies out of a relational database instead of from the file system, for example. Because SQL Server 2005 ensures that all application assemblies are loaded out of the database, it doesn't make sense to have the CLR look for assemblies in a directory specified by *ApplicationBase*. Even if you do rely on the standard file system–based assembly storage, you might have a deployment model in which you want to prevent assemblies from being loaded directly out of your *ApplicationBase*. ASP.NET is an example of a CLR host that uses such a deployment model. If you've built a Web application using ASP.NET, you probably noticed that you must place the private assemblies for your application in the bin directory under the *ApplicationBase*—the *ApplicationBase* itself is never searched.

AppDomainSetup has two properties to support scenarios such as these: *DisallowApplication-BaseProbing* and *PrivateBinPathProbe* (easily the most poorly named setting of the bunch). *DisallowApplicationBaseProbing* is a *boolean* property you can use to prevent the CLR from looking for assemblies anywhere in the *ApplicationBase* directory structure. By setting this property to *true*, the CLR will not look in the *ApplicationBase* or in any of its subdirectories. The *PrivateBinPathProbe* property is similar in spirit to *DisallowApplicationBaseProbing*, but there is one key difference. When *PrivateBinPathProbe* is set, the *ApplicationBase* directory is never searched, but all subdirectories are. This is the property that ASP.NET uses to force you to put your private assemblies in the bin subdirectory under the *ApplicationBase*. *PrivateBinPathProbe* is not a *boolean* property, as you'd probably expect. (I know I did.) Instead, *PrivateBinPathProbe* is a string. By supplying any string whatsoever for this property, you are indicating that only the subdirectories of *ApplicationBase* should be searched—not the *ApplicationBase* itself. The following example enables this behavior by setting *PrivateBinPathProbe* to the string *:

```
AppDomainSetup adSetup = new AppDomainSetup();
adSetup.PrivateBinPathProbe = "*";

AppDomain ad = AppDomain.CreateDomain("No AppBase Domain", null, adSetup);
```

Configuration File Settings

The .NET Framework allows applications to store settings in XML configuration files. In many cases, these settings are known only to the applications themselves. For example, an application might wish to store a connection string that is used to connect to a database. However, as I've shown, these configuration files can also contain settings used to customize how the CLR behaves while running that application. In the previous section, I demonstrated how these configuration files can be used to specify an assembly search path, for example. It's likely that you've run across these configuration files already as you've built .NET Framework applications. For example, you've probably edited the web.config file to customize the way your ASP.NET application works.

An application's settings can be specified in one of a number of XML configuration files arranged in a hierarchy. At a minimum, settings can be supplied in either a configuration file that affects all applications on a machine or in a file specific to a particular application. Some scenarios support more extensive configuration systems. For example, ASP.NET allows a developer or administrator to provide settings at any level in the directory structure.

All application scenarios supported by the CLR include the notion of machine-wide configuration settings. These settings are stored in a file with a fixed name (*machine.config*) and location (%windir%\microsoft.net\framework*versionnumber*Config) so the CLR knows exactly where to find the file. In contrast, the name and location of an application-level configuration file (if one exists) must be specified when an application domain in which to run the application is created. The association between the configuration file and the application is made using the *ConfigurationFile* or *ConfigurationBytes* properties of *AppDomainSetup*. For example, the default CLR host supports configuration files for executable files. These configuration files must be in the same directory as the executable and must be named *exe name.exe.config*, where *exe name* is the name of the executable being launched. When the default CLR host creates the domain in which to run the executable, it sets the *ConfigurationFile* property to the *exe name.exe.config* file as shown in the following example:

```
AppDomainSetup adSetup = new AppDomainSetup();
adSetup.ApplicationBase = @"c:\MyApp";
adSetup.ConfigurationFile = @"c:\MyApp\MyApp.exe.config";

AppDomain ad = AppDomain.CreateDomain("MyApp", null, adSetup);
```

Other application scenarios work the same way. ASP.NET uses the same technique to associate a web.config file with a domain, for example.

The *ConfigurationBytes* property enables you to specify your configuration file as an array of bytes instead of by supplying the name of a configuration file on disk. The byte array you pass to *ConfigurationBytes* is simply the contents of your XML configuration file laid out in memory. Specifying a configuration file with *ConfigurationBytes* is convenient for scenarios in which you generate configuration information dynamically instead of storing the data ahead of time in a disk file.

Shadow Copy Settings

One reason ASP.NET applications are easier to deploy and manage than their Active Server Pages (ASP) counterparts is because of a feature called shadow copy. Using shadow copy enables ASP.NET Web applications to be updated dynamically without shutting down and restarting the Web server. Because the application can be updated without affecting the status of the Web server, ASP.NET can support sites that must be continuously available. In this section, I describe how to configure your application domains to take advantage of shadow copy. After describing how to implement shadow copy, I walk through a sample application so you can see it in action.

Shadow copy works by making copies of the files it is requested to load. The copy is then loaded, leaving the original file untouched. By default, when an assembly file is loaded from disk, it is locked by the CLR and the Windows file system. The file cannot be replaced with a new version until the file is unloaded. The only way to unload a file in the CLR is to unload the application domain into which the file has been loaded. Unloading a domain just to unlock a file is rarely feasible in applications that must be highly available and that support a constant stream of users. As described, the shadow copy feature solves this problem by making a copy of the requested file and loading the copy, thereby leaving the original file unlocked. As a result, the original file can be replaced on the fly. It's important to note, however, that shadow copy applies only to assemblies privately deployed with the application. Assemblies stored in the global assembly cache (GAC) are never copied using shadow copy.

Four properties on *AppDomainSetup* enable you to configure the shadow copy feature when creating a new domain: *ShadowCopyFiles*, *CachePath*, *ApplicationName*, and *ShadowCopyDirectories*. At a minimum, you must use *ShadowCopyFiles*. The other three properties are used to customize the way shadow copy works. To enable shadow copy for an application domain, complete the following steps:

1. Turn on the shadow copy feature.

2. Specify where the CLR should store the copied files.

3. Specify which files are copied.

4. Clean up the copied files if necessary.

These steps are described in detail in the sections that follow.

Turning on Shadow Copy

Shadow copy is off by default. To turn it on, you must set the value of the *ShadowCopyFiles* property on *AppDomainSetup* to any non-null string. *ShadowCopyFiles* is a string value and not a *boolean* as you'd probably expect. As a result, setting the value to any string enables shadow copy, although most implementations set the value to *"true"* for clarity. You can turn shadow copy on after a domain has been created by calling the *AppDomain.SetShadowCopyFiles()* method. The following code snippet demonstrates how to enable shadow copy using the *AppDomainSetup* object.

```
using System;
AppDomainSetup setup = new AppDomainSetup();
setup.ShadowCopyFiles = "true";
AppDomain newAD = AppDomain.CreateDomain("Shadow Copy Domain",), null, setup);
```

Specifying the Location for the Copied Files

As described, shadow copy works by making a copy of each file it is asked to load. As a result, after you've enabled shadow copy, you need to decide where you'd like the CLR to store the copied files. By default, the CLR will copy the files to a location in the *downloaded files cache*. This is the same cache that is used to store files that have been downloaded from another machine while running an application. If you'd rather not use the downloaded files cache, you can specify a directory in which the CLR will place the copied files by using the *CachePath* and *ApplicationName* properties on *AppDomainSetup*.

> **Note** The downloaded files cache is a CLR-specific cache. It is not the same cache used by Microsoft Internet Explorer to cache Web pages, controls, and other content downloaded from Web sites.

Whether you choose to use the downloaded files cache or to specify a custom location depends on your scenario. The primary advantage of storing the copied files in the downloaded files cache is that you don't have to worry about cleanup. The cache has a size limit that, when reached, causes the files used least recently to be deleted. As a result, you're free to cause files to be copied into the cache and they will eventually get deleted automatically. If you specify a custom directory in which to store the files, you're responsible for deleting them when they're no longer used. Using the downloaded files cache does have its disadvantages, however. First, because the CLR cleans up the cache based on size quotas, you can't control the lifetime of the copied files. If your application generates a lot of copies, you might find that the CLR tries to remove a file from the cache before you are ready for it to be removed. Second, your application must have the correct security permissions to write to the directory in which the CLR will copy the files. Specifically, the user account that your application is running under must have Write access to its user profile directory. If it doesn't, the CLR will not be able to copy files into the downloaded files cache.

If you decide that a custom location works better for your scenario, you must set both the *CachePath* and *ApplicationName* properties on *AppDomainSetup* when you create a new domain. The CLR concatenates the values of these two properties to obtain the directory into which the copied files will be placed. A common way to use these two properties is to keep the value of *CachePath* consistent throughout your application, but provide a new value for *ApplicationName* for each application domain you create. In this way, all shadow copy files you create are stored under the same root directory, but subdirectories identify from which domain the files come. This makes it easy to delete the files for a particular domain when the time comes. It's also worth noting that because you can set *CachePath* and *ApplicationName* separately for each domain, files for more than one domain can be copied by shadow copy to the same location. This is useful to reduce the number of copies made if you create multiple application domains that run the same code. For example, ASP.NET might create multiple application domains (maybe even in separate processes) to run the same Web application based on a number of scalability factors, including the number of users accessing the application. In this case, ASP.NET logically uses the name of the Web application as the value of *ApplicationName* so all running instances of that application share the same location for files copied by shadow copy, thereby reducing the number of copies that must be made.

Always remember that if you use *CachePath* and *ApplicationName* to specify a custom shadow copy location, you're responsible for deleting those directories when they are no longer needed. In part because shadow copy target directories don't map one-to-one with application domains, the CLR has no idea when it's OK to clean up the copied files. So it's up to you to decide when no running domains rely on a particular shadow copy location so you can delete the directory.

Specifying Which Files Are Copied

By default, all assemblies the CLR loads out of a domain's *ApplicationBase* directory structure are shadow copied. This includes assemblies found by the CLR's default loading rules (that is, those in the *ApplicationBase* and those in subdirectories named by version and culture) as well as any assemblies located in subdirectories specified using the *PrivateBinPath* property of *AppDomainSetup*. If you don't want all privately located assemblies shadow copied, you can use the *ShadowCopyDirectories* property of *AppDomainSetup* to customize this behavior. *ShadowCopyDirectories* takes a semicolon-delimited set of subdirectories containing files that you *do* want to leave unlocked through shadow copy. If you specify a list of subdirectories using *ShadowCopyDirectories*, all files loaded out of directories not on the list, including the *ApplicationBase* itself, will *not* be copied before being loaded. For example, the following code creates an application domain such that only those files in the bin subdirectory of *ApplicationBase* are shadow copied:

```
using System;
AppDomainSetup setup = new AppDomainSetup();
setup.ShadowCopyFiles = "true";
setup.ShadowCopyDirectories = "bin";
AppDomain newAD = AppDomain.CreateDomain("Shadow Copy Domain", null, setup);
```

The *System.AppDomain* class also has a method called *SetShadowCopyPath* that you can use to set the list of directories copied by shadow copy after the application domain has been created.

The Shadow Copy Sample

The shadowcopy.exe sample included with this book is a Windows Forms application that shows how to use the *ShadowCopyFiles*, *CachePath*, and *ApplicationName* properties of *App-DomainSetup* to configure the shadow copy feature. Shadowcopy.exe creates secondary application domains configured for shadow copy based on the options you pick in the user interface. For example, shadowcopy.exe allows you to select either the default or a custom location in which the CLR will place the copied files. The shadowcopy.exe application is shown in Figure 6-2.

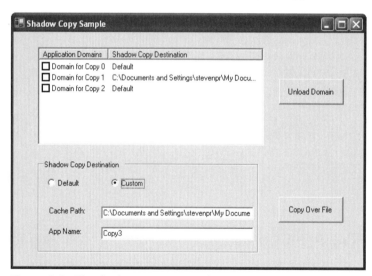

Figure 6-2   The shadowcopy.exe sample

Shadowcopy.exe determines when to create a new application domain by using the *System.IO.FileSystemWatcher* class to monitor changes made to a particular assembly. Each time the file is changed, a new domain is created in which to load the new file. As domains are created, their friendly names and target copy locations are added to the table in the user interface. After you build the shadowcopy project in Microsoft Visual Studio 2005, you'll end up with the following directory structure:

```
C:\<project directory>\bin\Debug\
                ShadowCopy.exe
                CopySampleAppBase\
                        CopiedFile.dll
```

Note that under the location into which shadowcopy.exe is built is a subdirectory called *Copy-SampleAppBase*. This directory serves as the *ApplicationBase* for all new domains created by shadowcopy.exe. In the *CopySampleAppBase* directory is a file called copiedfile.dll. This is the file containing the assembly that the *FileSystemWatcher* class is configured to monitor. Copied-file.dll can be replaced in a few different ways. First, you can open a command window or use Windows Explorer simply to copy a new version of copiedfile.dll over the existing one. Remember, the existing file is left unlocked because the application domains in which it is loaded are configured for shadow copy. Alternatively, you can click the Copy Over File button in the user interface. This button is just a convenience that replaces copiedfile.dll for you so you don't have to do it manually.

When a new domain is created based on a change to copiedfile.dll, shadowcopy.exe sets the target location for the copied files based on the values of the controls in the Shadow Copy Destination group box in the user interface. If the Default radio button is selected, the shadow-copied files will end up in the downloaded files cache. If you select the Custom radio button, you must supply values for the *CachePath* and *ApplicationName* properties by filling in the appropriate text boxes. When you run shadowcopy.exe in the Visual Studio debugger, you can use the Output window to verify that the files are being copied to the location you expect. You can tell by reading the debug output that shows the directory from which the CLR loaded copiedfile.dll. For example, if copiedfile.dll is loaded from the downloaded files cache, the Output window in the debugger will include a line such as the following:

```
'Domain for Copy 0': Loaded 'c:\documents and settings\stevenpr\
local settings\application data\assembly\dl2\78kokvbt.qmq\m96q78ev.m4o\
7c177d03\20791c6f_4a37c301\copiedfile.dll', Symbols loaded.
```

A few interesting characteristics about this path are worth pointing out. First, the path points to a location under your user profile. As described earlier, the downloaded files cache is stored per user, so saving the files in your profile directory is a natural choice. Second, the file that has been copied (copiedfile.dll) is "hidden" several levels down in your profile's directory structure. These extra directories are just part of the layout of the downloaded files cache. Most of this indirection is done to make the location of the files in the cache unpredictable so that files downloaded from other machines cannot easily be found on your machine.

In contrast, if you specify a custom copy location, the CLR will load copiedfile.dll from that directory. Assuming that you've told the CLR to save the copied files to c:\program files\extapp\shadow\401k, the debugger's Output window will include the following line:

```
'Domain for Copy 0': Loaded 'c:\program files\extapp\shadow\401k\assembly\dl2\
7c177d03\20791c6f_4a37c301\copiedfile.dll', Symbols loaded.
```

As described, each new application domain created by shadowcopy.exe is displayed in the user interface. Next to the table containing the list of domains is a button you can use to unload a particular domain from the process. When a domain is unloaded, shadowcopy.exe looks to see if a custom copy location was specified by looking at the *CachePath* and *ApplicationName* properties on the *AppDomainSetup* object associated with the domain. If a custom location was specified, the directory containing the copied files is deleted after the application domain has been unloaded.

To summarize, the shadowcopy.exe sample works as follows:

1. Upon startup, shadowcopy.exe creates an instance of the *System.IO.FileSystemWatcher* class and initializes it to monitor changes to copiedfile.dll, which resides in the *CopySampleAppBase* directory under the directory from which you launch shadowcopy.exe.

2. When copiedfile.dll is replaced, a new application domain is created in which to load the new file. The location of the copied files is determined based on the controls you've selected in the user interface (UI). Note that copiedfile.dll can be replaced either through the command line or shell or by using the Copy Over File button in the user interface. Once the new domain is created, and the new copiedfile.dll has been loaded into it, the friendly name of the domain is added to a list displayed in the user interface.

3. When an application domain is unloaded by clicking the Unload Domain button, shadowcopy.exe determines whether a custom directory was specified as the location for the copied files. If so, that directory is deleted.

The code for shadowcopy.exe is shown in the following listing. I've deleted much of the Windows Forms boilerplate code that has more to do with laying out the user interface than with the actual functionality of the application.

Listing 6-1   shadowcopy.exe Source Code

```
using System;
using System.Drawing;
using System.Collections;
using System.ComponentModel;
using System.Windows.Forms;
using System.Data;
using System.IO;
using System.Diagnostics;
using System.Threading;
using System.Reflection;
using CopiedFile;

namespace ShadowCopy
{

    public class frmShadowCopy : System.Windows.Forms.Form
    {
        // Windows Forms locals omitted…
```

```csharp
private FileSystemWatcher m_watcher;
private String m_copyAppBase;
private int m_numCopies;

public static frmShadowCopy ShadowCopyAppForm ;
public static DateTime eventTime;

// This event handler receives the "File Changed" event generated by
// FileSystemWatcher when copiedfile.dll gets overwritten. Three events
// get raised for every file copy so I use time to make sure I don't
// process the "extra" events.
private static void OnFileChanged(object source, FileSystemEventArgs e)
{
    TimeSpan t = DateTime.Now - frmShadowCopy.eventTime;

    if (t > (new TimeSpan(TimeSpan.TicksPerSecond)))
    {
        frmShadowCopy.ShadowCopyAppForm.CreateDomainForNewFile();
    }

    frmShadowCopy.eventTime = DateTime.Now;
}

public frmShadowCopy()
{
    // Required for Windows Forms Designer support
    InitializeComponent();

    // Initialize a private string to hold the name of the ApplicationBase
    // for all new domains I create.
    m_copyAppBase = AppDomain.CurrentDomain.BaseDirectory +
                            "CopySampleAppBase";

    // Initialize the event time so we handle only one FileChange event from
    // the FileSystemWatcher.
    frmShadowCopy.eventTime = DateTime.Now;

    // I keep track of the number of copies made just as a convenience for
    // assigning friendly names to application domains and to initialize the
    // the "Application Name" field in the UI with a reasonable
    // value for the next copy.
    m_numCopies = 0;
}

[STAThread]
static void Main()
{
    frmShadowCopy frm = new frmShadowCopy();
    frmShadowCopy.ShadowCopyAppForm = frm;

    Application.Run(frm);
}

private void frmShadowCopy_Load(object sender, System.EventArgs e)
{
```

```
    // Initialize the FileSystemWatcher so OnFileChanged is called each time
    // copiedfile.dll is overwritten.
    m_watcher = new FileSystemWatcher();
    m_watcher.Path = m_copyAppBase;
    m_watcher.Filter = "CopiedFile.dll";
    m_watcher.NotifyFilter = NotifyFilters.LastWrite;
    m_watcher.Changed += new FileSystemEventHandler(OnFileChanged);
    m_watcher.EnableRaisingEvents = true;

    // Initialize the CachePath and ApplicationName text boxes to point to a
    // directory under the AppBase.
    txtCachePath.Text = m_copyAppBase;
    txtAppName.Text = "Copy" + m_numCopies.ToString();
}

private void btnCopy_Click(object sender, System.EventArgs e)
{
    // Copy over copiedfile.dll. This causes the FileSystemWatcher
    // to raise an event that we'll catch to begin the process
    // of creating a new application domain.
    File.Copy(AppDomain.CurrentDomain.BaseDirectory + "CopiedFile.dll",
                     m_copyAppBase + "\\CopiedFile.dll", true);
}

// This method gets called from the OnFileChanged event handler. It
// contains all the logic to create a new application domain
// configured for shadow copy.
public void CreateDomainForNewFile()
{

    String copyLocation;

    // Create a new instance of AppDomainSetup and turn shadow copy on by
    // setting ShadowCopyFiles.
    AppDomainSetup setup = new AppDomainSetup();
    setup.ApplicationBase = m_copyAppBase;
    setup.ShadowCopyFiles = "true";

    // Determine where the files should be copied to. Initialize CachePath
    // and ApplicationName appropriately.
    if (rbCustom.Checked)
    {
        if ((txtCachePath.TextLength == 0) || (txtAppName.TextLength == 0))
        {
            MessageBox.Show("You must enter values for Cache Path
                            and Application Name when specifying
                            a custom copy location");
            return;
        }

        setup.CachePath = txtCachePath.Text;
        setup.ApplicationName = txtAppName.Text;

        copyLocation = setup.CachePath + "\\" + setup.ApplicationName;
    }
```

```
            else
            {
               copyLocation = "Default";
            }

            // Create a new domain.
            AppDomain newAD = AppDomain.CreateDomain("Domain for Copy " +
                              m_numCopies.ToString(), null, setup);

            // Load the assembly into the domain. As a side effect of this
            // call to Load, copiedfile.dll will be copied to the "copied files
            // location" and will be loaded from there, thereby leaving the
            // original unlocked so it can be overwritten.
            Assembly asm = newAD.Load("CopiedFile", null);

            // Add the new domain to the list displayed in the UI.
            ListViewItem newLVI = new ListViewItem(new string[] {
                        newAD.FriendlyName , copyLocation}, -1);
            newLVI.Tag = newAD;
            listView1.Items.Add(newLVI);

            m_numCopies++;

            // Update the AppName text box so we copy to a new location next time.
            txtAppName.Text = "Copy" + m_numCopies.ToString();
        }

        private void btnUnload_Click(object sender, System.EventArgs e)
        {
            if (listView1.CheckedItems.Count == 0)
            {
                MessageBox.Show("Please select one or more Domains to unload
                              by selecting the check boxes");
                return;
            }

            foreach (ListViewItem i in listView1.CheckedItems)
            {
                AppDomain ad = (AppDomain)i.Tag;

                // If a custom shadow copy location was specified, we need to
                // delete the contents of the directory after the domain is
                // unloaded. Remember the name of the custom directory here
                // (if one was specified).
                String delDirectory = ad.SetupInformation.CachePath + "\\" +
                                    ad.SetupInformation.ApplicationName;

                // Unload the domain and remove the entry from the UI.
                AppDomain.Unload(ad);
                listView1.Items.Remove(i);

                // Delete the shadow copy directory if any. We check to see
                // if it's greater than one because above we added "\".
                if (delDirectory.Length > 1)
                {
```

```
            Directory.Delete(delDirectory, true);
        }
      }
   }

   }
}
```

Assembly Binding Settings

When a strong-named assembly is loaded into an application domain, the default versioning rules provided by the CLR make sure that the exact version of the assembly being referenced is the one that gets loaded. This default behavior lets you enjoy the highest degree of confidence that the application as a whole will run properly because only the set of assemblies that were built and tested together will be loaded. However, there are some cases in which you might want more flexibility. So the CLR provides a version policy system that allows the application consuming the assembly, the author, or the assembly or machine administrator to change which version of an assembly gets loaded given a particular reference. By default, the version policy system is enabled in the sense that if any of these versioning rules (termed binding redirects) are in place, the CLR will use them when determining which version of an assembly to load.

Although the version policy system is beneficial for the vast majority of application scenarios, I could imagine cases in which the creator of an application domain might want to disable one or more of the available policy levels. The *AppDomainSetup* object includes two properties that enable you to specify such customizations. The first of these properties, *DisallowBindingRedirects*, causes all version policy statements made in the application configuration file to be ignored. You might find this property useful to ensure that a consistent set of assemblies is always running in your domain, for example. The second property, *DisallowPublisherPolicy*, causes all publisher policy statements to be ignored for shared assemblies loaded into the application domain. This property is also used in environments where the creator of the application domain wants very tight control over the versions of the assemblies that are loaded. For example, by using *DisallowBindingRedirects* and *DisallowPublisherPolicy* together, the creator of a domain can ensure that only the administrator of the machine is allowed to alter which versions of shared assemblies are loaded into the domain.

Miscellaneous Settings

There are seven properties of *AppDomainSetup* left to cover. These properties don't fit directly into any of the categories described earlier and are typically used only in very specialized scenarios. It is worth describing them briefly so you know they exist should a situation arise in which you could use them.

These miscellaneous properties are *LicenseFile*, *LoaderOptimization*, *DynamicBase*, *Disallow-CodeDownload*, *ActivationArguments*, *AppDomainInitializer*, and *AppDomainInitializerArguments*.

LicenseFile

The *LicenseFile* property was part of an early design for a licensing model for .NET Framework components. At this time, it seems this property is obsolete. However, the CLR team cannot change existing APIs for compatibility reasons, so this obsolete property is likely to stay.

LoaderOptimization

The *LoaderOptimization* property is used to configure whether code loaded into an application domain is done so in a domain-neutral fashion. I defer further discussion of this property to Chapter 9, where I describe the details of domain-neutral code and the various ways the CLR provides to let you configure it.

DynamicBase

Some applications generate assemblies dynamically using the classes from the *System.Reflection.Emit* namespace or by other means such as simply writing code out to a text file and compiling it. If the dynamically generated assemblies are private to a particular application (that is, they aren't sharable and thus don't have a strong name), they must be written to the domain's *ApplicationBase* or a subdirectory thereof as discussed earlier in this chapter. There are scenarios, however, in which this deployment model is too restrictive. The primary reason is that the *ApplicationBase* directory structure must be left writable so the files can be saved there. This is not always acceptable because it allows other portions of the application to be overwritten unintentionally. An excellent example of this scenario is the ASP.NET host, which emits assemblies on the fly by compiling the code written into the Web pages that make up the application. If they were forced to write to the *ApplicationBase*, Web site administrators would have to leave that directory unprotected, which clearly isn't acceptable in scenarios when an admin wants to control the contents of the application folders tightly.

The CLR solves this problem by letting the host specify an additional directory, outside of the *ApplicationBase*, in which dynamically generated assemblies can be stored. This directory is treated as a logical extension of the *ApplicationBase* in that it is searched in the same manner that the *ApplicationBase* directory structure is. This additional directory is specified using a combination of the *DynamicBase* and *ApplicationName* properties on *AppDomainSetup*. Note, however, that the CLR does not create the directory specified with *DynamicBase* for you. You must create it yourself before attempting to store any assemblies there.

> **Note**   If you want, you can also set the dynamic base using the *SetDynamicBase* method on the *System.AppDomain* class. If you do this, however, make sure you call *SetDynamicBase* before any assemblies are loaded into the application domain.

When the *DynamicBase* and *ApplicationName* properties are set, the CLR adds a directory of the form

```
<DynamicBase>\<random number>\<ApplicationName>
```

to the list of directories that are searched when resolving references to private assemblies. Notice that the name of the directory contains a random number. This random number is used to obfuscate the location of the dynamic base a bit so it's not predictable. As a result, the host cannot determine the location in which it can write dynamic assemblies just by remembering the values it specified for *DynamicBase* and *ApplicationName*. Instead, a host must use the *DynamicDirectory* property on *System.AppDomain* after the application domain has been created to determine where to write its assemblies.

If your application is using the shadow copy feature, the CLR automatically adds the dynamic directory to the list of directories in which files are left unlocked when they are loaded. This feature is convenient in that it enables you to write over previous versions of the assemblies you generate dynamically without shutting down and restarting an application domain.

DisallowCodeDownload

The ability to download code dynamically from Web servers onto a client machine is sometimes used to provide a richer user interface for users browsing Web sites. Furthermore, code download enables new capabilities that otherwise wouldn't be available to rich client applications, including the ability to download updates when they become available. The fact that code might get downloaded to a machine as a side effect of running an application has been popular for years. This technique lends itself quite well to client applications, but the nature of server environments makes code download less appealing for server applications. Oftentimes, servers are much more tightly controlled than client machines in part because they often support applications and services that are critical to the day-to-day running of an organization. Bringing code onto a server machine without the administrator's knowledge goes against the preference to keep the server machine as static as possible.

The CLR supports this locked-down scenario with respect to downloaded code by allowing the creator of an application domain to disable code download completely for a particular domain. This is accomplished by setting the *boolean DisallowCodeDownload* property to *true* on the instance of *AppDomainSetup* that is passed to *AppDomain.CreateDomain*. When set, *DisallowCodeDownload* shuts down all avenues through which code can be downloaded onto the machine by code running in that domain. These include both the ability to download code programmatically using such methods as *System.Reflection.Assembly.LoadFrom* as well as using code base locations that point to Web servers in configuration files.

ActivationArguments

The .NET Framework 2.0 version of the CLR introduces a new activation model based on applications and components that are defined by an application manifest. This new activation model was initially built to support the ClickOnce deployment model. In ClickOnce, an application manifest provides enough information about the contents and security requirements of the application that the CLR deployment infrastructure can safely download and execute a rich client application over the Web without explicitly installing the application on the client machine. It's likely that application manifests will be used in other scenarios in future versions of the Windows operating system as well. The topic of activation by a manifest is outside the scope of this book. The best place to look for information is in the .NET Framework SDK.

AppDomainInitializer and AppDomainInitializerArguments

Recall from the discussion of application domain boundaries in Chapter 5 that a good goal to have when designing an application that uses multiple application domains is to keep the communication between the various domains to a minimum. Reducing the amount of cross-domain communication helps improve performance by reducing the number of remote calls that must be made. In addition, applications that limit the number of calls between application domains often have a simpler deployment model because fewer assemblies must be deployed to a location that is visible to all application domains. The *AppDomainInitializer* and *AppDomainInitializerArguments* properties on *AppDomainSetup* help you build applications that minimize cross-domain communication. Oftentimes, the first thing you want to do after creating a new application domain is load an assembly into that domain, instantiate a type from that assembly, and call one of its methods. The *AppDomainInitializer* property enables you to implement this common design pattern with much better performance by eliminating the need for cross-domain calls. Let's look at an example to see how this works. Say we have a human resources application that creates separate application domains in which to load objects that represent employees. Each time we create a new domain, we want to load the assembly representing the employee into that domain and initialize it. Without using the *App-DomainInitializer* property, we'd probably write code something like the following:

```
using System;
using System.Reflection;
using HumanResources;
using System.Runtime.Remoting;

namespace AppDomainInit
{
    class ADInit
    {
        [STAThread]
        static void Main(string[] args)
```

```
            {
                AppDomain ad = AppDomain.CreateDomain(
                                    "AppDomainInitializer", null, null);

                ObjectHandle objHandle = ad.CreateInstance("HumanResources",
                                                "HumanResources.Employee");

                Employee e = (Employee) objHandle.Unwrap();
                e.Setup();
            }
        }
    }
```

In this code we create a new application domain and then use the *CreateInstance* method on *System.AppDomain* to create a new instance of the *Employee* type. *CreateInstance* returns an *ObjectHandle* that we then unwrap and cast to a local variable of type *Employee*. Given an object of type *Employee*, we then call its *Setup* method to initialize the data for the employee. This code accomplishes what we want it to do—it loads a new instance of *Employee* into the new application domain. However, we pay the cost of several remote calls to accomplish this. Remote calls are involved both in creating the *Employee* instance and calling it.

The *AppDomainInitializer* and *AppDomainInitializerArguments* properties can be used to accomplish the same end result without the cost of any cross-domain calls. As part of its initialization, *AppDomainInitializer* takes a delegate you supply that the CLR calls from within the new application domain. *AppDomainInitializerArguments* is an array of strings that the CLR passes to the delegate stored in *AppDomainInitializer*. The preceding sample passed the name of the assembly containing the *Employee* type and the name of the type itself to *AppDomain.CreateInstance*. We can make the sample more efficient by passing these same parameters as arguments to our *AppDomainInitializer*. Our *AppDomainInitializer* can then create the *Employee* type from within the new application domain. The following code shows the modified sample:

```
using System;
using System.Reflection;
using HumanResources;
using System.Runtime.Remoting;

namespace AppDomainInit
{
    class ADInit
    {
        static void Initializer(string[] args)
        {
            Assembly hrAssembly = Assembly.Load(args[0]);
            Employee e = (Employee) hrAssembly.CreateInstance(args[1]);
            e.Setup();
        }
```

```
[STAThread]
static void Main(string[] args)
{
    AppDomainSetup adSetup = new AppDomainSetup();
    adSetup.AppDomainInitializer = new
            AppDomainInitializer(ADInit.Initializer);

    string[] initializerArgs = new string[2];
    initializerArgs[0] = "HumanResources";
    initializerArgs[1] = "HumanResources.Employee";
    adSetup.AppDomainInitializerArguments = initializerArgs;

    AppDomain ad = AppDomain.CreateDomain("AppDomainInitializer",
                                      null, adSetup);

}
}
}
```

In this example, we create a new application domain, as before, but this time we set the *App-DomainInitializer* property on *AppDomainSetup* to the method called *ADInit.Initializer* and set the *AppDomainInitializerArguments* to the assembly and the type representing an *Employee*. As it's setting up the new domain, the CLR calls *ADInit.Initializer*, passing in the arguments we specified using *AppDomainInitializerArguments*. *ADInit.Initializer* then loads the assembly, creates the instance of *Employee*, and calls its *Setup* method. Again, the key difference in this second example is that the interaction with the *Employee* type is all happening from within the new application domain. In this way, no remote calls are needed to set up the *Employee* type in the new domain.

In some ways, the functionality provided by *AppDomainInitializer* and *AppDomainInitializer-Arguments* is similar to what can be accomplished using an application domain manager. As discussed in Chapter 5, an application domain manager enables you to initialize new application domains as they are created in the process. I cover this in more detail in the next section of this chapter. However, a few distinctions between these two similar approaches are worth keeping in mind. First, the application domain manager implementation doesn't provide a way to pass arguments into the new application domain unless you are using *ActivationArguments* and participating in activations defined by a formal manifest. In simple scenarios such as the preceding *Employee* example, the mechanism for passing arguments using *AppDomain-Initializer* is probably more straightforward. The second point to consider is that typically the implementer of the extensible application provides the application domain manager type for the process. If you are writing one of the extensions that plugs into the extensible application, you won't be able to provide a domain manager, so the only technique available to you is the *AppDomainInitializer* property. As mentioned, in the next section we look in more detail at how application domain managers can be used to initialize new application domains.

Customizing Application Domain Creation Using *System.AppDomainManager*

Recall from Chapter 5 that an application domain manager has three primary roles. First, an application domain manager makes it easy to implement the host runtime design pattern for multidomain applications. Second, a domain manager is the means used to communicate between the managed and unmanaged portions of a CLR host. And, finally, application domain managers provide a central point from which you can customize all application domains that are created in a process. It is this last role that I discuss in this section.

Earlier in this chapter, I showed how an instance of *AppDomainSetup* can be passed to *AppDomain.CreateDomain* to customize application domains as they are being created. This approach to customizing application domains works great for the domains you create yourself, but sometimes you might want to have a say in how application domains created by others are customized. A common example of this scenario is that of an extensible application. As the author of an extensible application, you'll likely create several application domains in which to run the add-ins authored by others. Obviously, you can customize the domains you create, but what if the add-ins create application domains of their own? There is no way to influence how those domains are created with the techniques described so far. This can be a problem if your application has the requirement to keep at least some characteristics of all domains in the process the same. For example, typically you want to enforce the same security policy on all domains in the process regardless of who created them. As the author of an extensible application, you don't want other code in the process to be able to create application domains with more liberal security policy than you are willing to grant. Application domain managers help you solve this problem by essentially letting you intercept all calls to create an application domain within a process. The CLR calls your application domain manager at strategic points when a new application domain is being created. (See Chapter 5 for details on how to create an application domain manager.) These interception points enable you to configure all domains as you see fit, regardless of who initially called *AppDomain.CreateDomain*.

To understand how this works, take a look at the steps the CLR uses to involve your domain manager when a new domain is requested by a call to *AppDomain.CreateDomain* (see Figure 6-3):

1. The *CreateDomain* method is called on your *AppDomainManager* to give you a chance to control the settings for the new application domain.

2. A new instance of your *AppDomainManager* class is created by the CLR and loaded into the new domain.

3. The *InitializeNewDomain* method is called on the new instance of *AppDomainManager*.

4. The new domain manager's *ApplicationActivator* property is retrieved. Providing an *ApplicationActivator* gives you a chance to customize how applications are activated by an application manifest.

5. The new domain manager's *HostExecutionContextManager* property is retrieved. Providing a *HostExecutionContextManager* enables you to configure how various context information flows across threads that run in the new application domain.

6. The new domain manager's *HostSecurityManager* property is retrieved. Providing a *HostSecurityManager* gives you a chance to configure security for the new application domain.

Existing Application Domain   **New Application Domain**

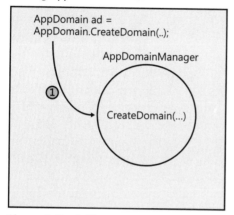
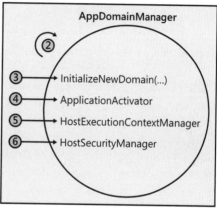

Figure 6-3 Calling an *AppDomainManager* when a new application domain is created

These steps are described in more detail in the following sections.

Step 1: Call *AppDomainManager.CreateDomain*

The *System.AppDomainManager* base class contains a virtual *CreateDomain* method that you can override in your application domain manager to hook all calls to *AppDomain.CreateDomain*. Whenever *AppDomain.CreateDomain* is called within a process, the CLR delegates the call to the application domain manager of that process by taking the parameters passed to *AppDomain.CreateDomain* and passing them to the *CreateDomain* method on the application domain manager. If you've associated an application domain manager with a process, as discussed in Chapter 5, your domain manager's *CreateDomain* method is called. If there is no domain manager associated with the process, the implementation of *CreateDomain* from *System.AppDomainManager* itself is called.

AppDomainManager.CreateDomain has the same method signature as the most commonly used variety of *AppDomain.CreateDomain* as shown in the following abbreviated class definition:

```
public class AppDomainManager : MarshalByRefObject
{
    public virtual AppDomain CreateDomain (string friendlyName,
                                           Evidence securityInfo,
                                           AppDomainSetup appDomainInfo)
```

```
        return CreateDomainHelper(friendlyName, securityInfo,
                                  appDomainInfo);
    }
```

By delegating all calls to create an application domain to your domain manager, the CLR provides you with a hook you can use to change any of the parameters passed to *AppDomain.CreateDomain* before the domain is actually created. In this way, you can customize any of the properties on *AppDomainSetup* or change the security evidence or the friendly name to enforce the rule that all application domains are created with properties that meet your requirements.

You might have noticed that the implementation of *CreateDomain* from the *AppDomainManager* class calls a method named *CreateDomainHelper*. *CreateDomainHelper* is a protected static method on *AppDomainManager* that creates an application domain. It, too, has the same parameters as *AppDomain.CreateDomain*. Typically, the implementation of *CreateDomain* in classes derived from *AppDomainManager* follow a two-step pattern: (1) edit any of the properties on *AppDomainSetup*, the security evidence, or the friendly name to fit your scenario; (2) call *CreateDomainHelper*, passing in your edited values. For example, in Chapter 5 I introduced a fictional CLR host that simulated a sailboat race. This application implemented an application domain manager called *BoatRaceDomainManager*. The add-ins to this host are boats written by third parties. Each boat is loaded into its own application domain. To illustrate how a domain manager can be used to control how domains are created, let's impose the following constraints on all boats that are added to our application:

1. Boats must be installed in a specific directory to be loaded.

2. A boat cannot turn on the shadow copy feature—this could result in extra files being placed on the disk that we're not aware of.

3. A boat cannot specify any versioning rules that would cause the CLR to load a different version of a .NET Framework assembly than it would under the default rules.

We can meet these three requirements by changing some of the properties on the instance of *AppDomainSetup* that we pass on to *CreateDomainHelper*. We can enforce that a boat must be installed to a specific directory by setting that directory as the new domain's *ApplicationBase*. If a boat is not installed in that directory, the CLR will not find the assembly containing the boat when we attempt to load it. We can enforce our last two requirements simply by setting *ShadowCopyFiles* to *false* and *DisallowBindingRedirects* to *true*. The implementation of *CreateDomain* from *BoatRaceDomainManager* is shown in the following code. As discussed, this implementation follows the typical pattern of modifying properties on the *AppDomainSetup* object before creating the new application domain with *CreateDomainHelper*.

```
public class BoatRaceDomainManager : AppDomainManager, IBoatRaceDomainManager
{
    public virtual AppDomain CreateDomain (string friendlyName,
                                           Evidence securityInfo,
                                           AppDomainSetup appDomainInfo)
```

```
// Modify the ApplicationBase, ShadowCopyFiles, and
// DisallowBindingRedirects properties.
appDomainInfo.ApplicationBase = @"c:\Program Files\BoatRace\boats";
appDomainInfo.ShadowCopyFiles = "false";
appDomainInfo.DisallowBindingRedirects = true;

return CreateDomainHelper(friendlyName, securityInfo,
                          appDomainInfo);  }
```

Up until now, we've been assuming that a domain manager's implementation of *CreateDomain* always creates and returns a new application domain. This is not required, however. Instead of customizing and creating a new application domain, we could take other approaches in *CreateDomain*. First, we could prevent the domain from being created altogether just by returning *null*. More commonly, we could return an application domain that already exists. In this way, we could control the number of application domains that are created and reuse them instead of creating a new application domain every time *AppDomain.CreateDomain* is called. This enables us to implement a load-balancing scheme for application domains, which can be useful if you'd like to restrict the number of application domains that are created for performance reasons, for example.

Step 2: Create a New Instance of the Application Domain Manager

If a new application domain is returned from your application domain manager's implementation of *CreateDomain*, the CLR creates a new instance of your application domain manager and loads it into the new domain.

Step 3: Call *AppDomainManager.InitializeNewDomain*

After loading an instance of the application domain manager into the new domain, the CLR calls its *InitializeNewDomain* method. *InitializeNewDomain* gives you a chance to do any further application domain configuration while running within the new domain. By implementing an application domain manager, you are given two chances to customize a new application domain: one from outside the domain, and one from inside the new domain. The opportunity to customize the domain from the outside is provided when the CLR calls your application domain manager's *CreateDomain* method. The opportunity to customize the new domain from inside is provided by the *InitializeNewDomain* method. It's important to remember that *CreateDomain* and *InitializeNewDomain* are called on different instances of your application domain manager. (This distinction is shown in Figure 6-3.)

At first glance it might seem that *CreateDomain* and *InitializeNewDomain* are just two different ways of doing exactly the same thing. Although it is true that both enable you to customize the new domain, a few subtleties justify having both methods. First, as discussed in the previous section, an application domain manager enables you to circumvent the process of creating a new domain entirely. Instead of creating a new application domain each time, you can simply reuse an existing domain. The decision of whether to create a new domain or use an existing one obviously must be made from the outside or before the creation of the new domain begins. As a result, this type of customization can be done only within your implementation of *CreateDomain*.

In contrast, *InitializeNewDomain* is useful for doing the type of initializations that can be accomplished more efficiently from within the application domain. The classic example is loading assemblies. As discussed in Chapter 5 and earlier in this chapter, loading an assembly from within the destination domain helps you avoid the performance cost of cross-domain calls. Another important scenario in which *InitializeNewDomain* is useful is in the customization of the default application domain. The CLR creates the default domain internally when the process starts, so *CreateDomain* is not called. In this case, your only chance to customize the default domain is from within *InitializeNewDomain*.

InitializeNewDomain takes an instance of *AppDomainSetup* as shown in the following definition from the *AppDomainManager* base class:

```
public class AppDomainManager : MarshalByRefObject
{
    public virtual void InitializeNewDomain (AppDomainSetup appDomainInfo)
    {
    }
}
```

Although the application domain is partially constructed at the time *InitializeNewDomain* is called, any changes you make to the properties of the *AppDomainSetup* object have an effect. As described, this is the only way you can change the properties for the *AppDomainSetup* object belonging to the default application domain. For example, the following sample implementation of *InitializeNewDomain* modifies the *ApplicationBase* property for the default domain:

```
public class BoatRaceDomainManager : AppDomainManager, IBoatRaceDomainManager
{
    public virtual void InitializeNewDomain (AppDomainSetup appDomainInfo)
    {
        if (IsDefaultAppDomain())
            appDomainInfo.ApplicationBase = @"c:\Program Files\BoatRace";
    }
}
```

Step 4: Get the *ApplicationActivator*

After *CreateDomain* and *InitializeNewDomain* are called, the CLR takes three objects from your application domain manager that you can provide to customize other aspects of how the new application domain will work. The CLR obtains these objects through public properties on your application domain manager class. The first of these three properties is *ApplicationActivator*. The *ApplicationActivator* property returns an object of type *ApplicationActivator* that you can use to customize how applications defined by manifests are activated. I don't cover the generic topic of manifest-based activation in this book. Information about how to use a custom *ApplicationActivator* can be found in the .NET Framework SDK.

Step 5: Get the *HostExecutionContextManager*

The next object the CLR gets from your application domain manager is an object of type *HostExecutionContextManager* (from a property of the same name). An instance of *HostExecutionContextManager* enables you to control how the state related to security and call contexts flows across threads running in the application domain. Information about how to use a custom *HostExecutionContextManager* can be found in the .NET Framework SDK.

Step 6: Get the *HostSecurityManager*

The last object the CLR gets from your application domain manager is of type *HostSecurityManager*. The CLR accesses this object through the *HostSecurityManager* property. Providing an implementation of *HostSecurityManager* enables you to supply security evidence and to customize the code access security policy for code running in the application domain. See Chapter 10 for a discussion of *HostSecurityManager*.

Summary

The *System.AppDomainSetup* class has several properties you can use to customize the behavior of the application domains you create. Some of these properties you'll use almost every time you create an application domain, whereas some of the properties are for situations esoteric enough that you'll likely never use them. The most common *AppDomainSetup* property used is the *ApplicationBase*. *ApplicationBase* specifies a root directory that is used to find all assemblies that are private to your application domain. Application domains are customized by setting the properties on an instance of *AppDomainSetup* and passing that instance to *AppDomain.CreateDomain*.

Application domain managers also play a key role in application domain customization. The CLR calls your application domain manager implementation at various points during the creation of an application domain. These interception points give you an opportunity to set the *AppDomainSetup* parameters, load assemblies into the new application domain, and perform other customizations specific to your application.

Chapter 7

Loading Assemblies in Extensible Applications

You've seen how application domains can be used to isolate groups of assemblies within a process and have taken a look at the techniques available to customize domains for various scenarios. In this chapter, I discuss what's involved in loading assemblies into the application domains you create as part of your extensible application. Much has been written in various books, magazines, and product documentation about the general topic of assembly loading. Rather than repeating it, I focus on those aspects of assembly loading that are of specific interest to writers of extensible applications.

By their nature, extensible applications don't have upfront knowledge of which assemblies will be loaded while the application is running. Instead, the set of add-ins to be loaded is typically specified either interactively by the end user or through some sort of dynamic configuration system. For example, the user of a productivity application can have the option to choose an add-in to run using a menu command. Similarly, a Microsoft SQL Server administrator has the option of adding new assemblies to a database at any time. In addition, it's often the case that the assemblies loaded into an extensible application are written by a variety of different vendors.

The dynamic nature of extensible applications makes assembly loading more complicated for two primary reasons. First, assemblies are typically loaded in a late-bound fashion. In more static applications, the majority of assembly references are recorded in an application's metadata when the application is compiled. The CLR reads these references as the application is running and follows a well-defined set of rules for locating and loading the assembly. In contrast, the add-in assemblies in extensible applications are loaded using a variety of APIs, some of which are managed and some of which are unmanaged. Not only can you use numerous APIs, you can use different basic techniques to identify the assembly you'd like to load. You can specify a reference to an assembly dynamically either by supplying the assembly's identity (or even just part of its identity) or by providing the fully qualified name of a disk file that contains the assembly's manifest. The second reason that assembly loading is more complicated in dynamic applications is CLR and Microsoft .NET Framework versioning. Because the origin of the assemblies you'll load into an extensible application varies, there's a good chance that not all assemblies will be built using the same version of the CLR and the .NET Framework. As times goes on and the number of publicly available versions of the .NET Framework increases, it will become more and more likely that you'll load assemblies with varying version dependencies into the same process. Understanding the implications of loading assemblies built with different versions of the .NET Framework is necessary not only to ensure that add-ins work predictably, but also to ensure that the stability of your overall application isn't compromised.

Concepts and Terminology

Before I get into the details of how to load assemblies into extensible applications, let me take a step back and outline some basic concepts and terminology. The topic of assembly loading is laden with new terms that are sometimes overloaded when they shouldn't be. To describe how to reference and load assemblies, it's best to agree on a consistent set of terminology. In the next few sections I describe the concepts and terminology that I use throughout the rest of this chapter. In particular, I define the following:

- Strong versus weak assembly names
- Early-bound versus late-bound references
- Fully specified versus partially specified references
- Version policy

Strong and Weak Assembly Names

A .NET Framework assembly is said to have either a *weak name* or a *strong name*. Throughout this chapter, I demonstrate how the factors you must consider when loading an assembly are different based on whether the assembly has a strong name or a weak name. For example, I'll show that the CLR uses different rules for locating an assembly when referring to it by its strong name rather than its weak name.

An assembly has a strong name if it has been signed with a cryptographic key pair using either a compiler or the sn.exe SDK tool. If an assembly has not been signed, it has a weak name. Structurally, assemblies with strong names are different from assemblies with weak names in two key ways:

1. Assemblies with strong names have a digital signature embedded in the file containing the manifest.

2. The name of strong-named assemblies contains the public key used to generate the signature.

This second characteristic is particularly important to the process of referencing and loading an assembly.

An assembly's identity consists of four parts:

- Friendly name
- Version
- Public key
- Culture

Assemblies with weak names have a friendly name, a version, and an optional culture. Assemblies with a strong name have a friendly name, a version, a public key, and a culture. You can see this difference in the portion of an assembly's metadata that records its name. In the following listing, I've used the ildasm.exe SDK tool to display a portion of the metadata for an assembly with a strong name. Note the presence of a public key in the name.

```
.assembly BoatRaceHostRuntime
{
  .publickey = (00 24 00 00 04 80 00 00 94 00 00 00 06 02 00 00
                00 24 00 00 52 53 41 31 00 04 00 00 01 00 01 00
                07 D1 FA 57 C4 AE D9 F0 A3 2E 84 AA 0F AE FD 0D
                E9 E8 FD 6A EC 8F 87 FB 03 76 6C 83 4C 99 92 1E
                B2 3B E7 9A D9 D5 DC C1 DD 9A D2 36 13 21 02 90
                0B 72 3C F9 80 95 7F C4 E1 77 10 8F C6 07 77 4F
                29 E8 32 0E 92 EA 05 EC E4 E8 21 C0 A5 EF E8 F1
                64 5C 4C 0C 93 C1 AB 99 28 5D 62 2C AA 65 2C 1D
                FA D6 3D 74 5D 6F 2D E5 F1 7E 5E AF 0F C4 96 3D
                26 1C 8A 12 43 65 18 20 6D C0 93 34 4D 5A D2 93 )
  .hash algorithm 0x00008004
  .ver 1:0:0:0
}
```

In contrast, the following listing shows the metadata stored for an assembly with a weak name:

```
.assembly Utilities
{
.ver 1:0:0:0
}
```

Assemblies are given strong names when you intend them to be shared among several applications on the system. Shared code has much more stringent requirements than code that is private to only one application. These additional requirements are primarily related to security and versioning. For example, assemblies used by many applications require a robust approach to versioning to avoid the versioning conflicts associated with Win32 DLLs. New versions of the shared assembly must be able to be added to the system without breaking applications that depend on previous versions. A cryptographically strong name is required to ensure that a given assembly can't be altered by anyone other than the original assembly author.

For a more thorough description of assembly names, including more discussion on the motivation behind using strong names, see Chapters 2 and 3 in *Applied Microsoft .NET Framework Programming* (Microsoft Press, 2002) by Jeffrey Richter.

Early-Bound and Late-Bound References

Assemblies can be referenced in either an early-bound or a late-bound fashion. Early-bound references are recorded in metadata when an assembly is compiled. Late-bound references are specified on the fly using the APIs on such classes as *System.Reflection.Assembly*, *System.Activator*, or *System.AppDomain*.

Extensible applications are likely to use both early- and late-bound references. Assemblies that are part of the implementation of the extensible application are likely to be referenced using early binding. In contrast, the add-ins that are dynamically added to the application to extend it are loaded using late binding because the application doesn't know which add-ins it will load (and, hence, can't reference them) when the application is compiled.

Let's return to the boat race example introduced in Chapter 5 to illustrate more concretely how these two types of references are likely to be used in an extensible application. Assume that our boat race application is written entirely in managed code and consists of a main executable called boatracehost.exe and three utility DLLs called boatracehostruntime.dll, weather.dll, and sailconfigurations.dll. When boatracehost.exe is compiled, it statically references the utility DLLs using the /r compiler switch, like so:

```
C:\temp\BoatRaceHost>csc /target:winexe /
r:BoatRaceHostRuntime.dll, SailConfigurations.dll,Weather.dll BoatRaceHost.cs
```

After compiling boatracehost.cs using this command line, the manifest for boatracehost.exe looks like this (produced with ildasm.exe):

```
.assembly BoatRaceHost
{
  .ver 1:0:0:0
}
.assembly extern BoatRaceHostRuntime
{
  .publickeytoken = (4B 7D 48 01 D8 95 67 95)
  .ver 1:0:0:0
}
.assembly extern SailConfigurations
{
  .publickeytoken = (4B 7D 48 01 D8 95 67 95)
  .ver 1:0:0:0
}
.assembly extern Weather
{
  .publickeytoken = (4B 7D 48 01 D8 95 67 95)
  .ver 1:0:0:0
}
.assembly extern System.Windows.Forms
{
  .publickeytoken = (B7 7A 5C 56 19 34 E0 89)
  .ver 1:0:5000:0
}
.assembly extern System
{
  .publickeytoken = (B7 7A 5C 56 19 34 E0 89)
  .ver 1:0:5000:0
}
.assembly extern mscorlib
{
  .publickeytoken = (B7 7A 5C 56 19 34 E0 89)
  .ver 1:0:5000:0
}
```

```
.assembly extern System.Drawing
{
  .publickeytoken = (B0 3F 5F 7F 11 D5 0A 3A)
  .ver 1:0:5000:0
}
```

Each *.assembly extern* statement in the previous listing represents an early-bound reference to an assembly. Notice that in addition to the references to *SailConfigurations*, *Weather*, and *BoatRaceHostRuntime*, our application has early-bound references to the .NET Framework assemblies it uses, including *System.Drawing* and *System.Windows.Forms*.

To illustrate when late-bound references are used, let's assume our boatracehost application includes a menu command that enables users to add boats to the race dynamically. During a particular run of the application, the end user adds two boats to the race. These two boats are contained in the assemblies *Alingi* and *TeamNZ*. Both *Alingi* and *TeamNZ* are loaded dynamically; hence, late binding is used as shown in Figure 7-1.

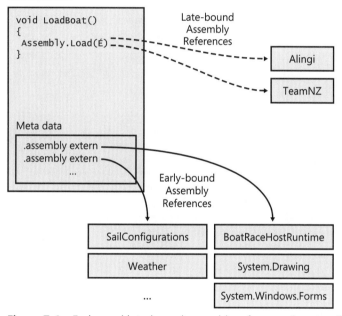

Figure 7-1   Early- and late-bound assembly references in extensible applications

This chapter focuses primarily on late binding because the flexibility introduced by loading assemblies on the fly introduces several considerations unique to extensible applications. In particular, the fact that late-bound references can be partially specified introduces complexities you don't run into when all assembly references are early bound.

Fully Specified and Partially Specified References

As described, assemblies in .NET Framework are identified by a friendly name, a public key, a version number, and a culture. When referencing an assembly, you can specify all four of these fields or you can specify just the friendly name—the public key, version number, and culture are all optional. When all four fields are specified, the assembly reference is said to be fully specified. If anything less than all four fields is included, the reference is partially specified.

Partially specified references are unique to late binding. When a compiler records an early-bound reference to an assembly in metadata, it stores values for all four fields. These values can be null (as the value for the public key is when an assembly has a weak name), but they are values nonetheless. In contrast, the APIs that enable you to load an assembly dynamically allow you to omit values for the public key, version number, and culture fields. Referencing an assembly by only a portion of its name results in looser binding semantics than a fully speci-fied reference does. For example, if you want to load an assembly by its friendly name only, without regard to version, you can simply omit a version number from your reference. If the CLR finds an assembly whose friendly name matches, it loads it regardless of which version it is. These looser binding semantics are useful in some scenarios. Microsoft ASP.NET, for exam-ple, uses partial binding and weakly named assemblies to implement loose version binding for assemblies stored in the bin subdirectory under the application's root directory. You might have noticed you can place any assembly in the bin directory and, as long as its name matches, it is loaded, regardless of version.

Although the flexibility allowed by partially specified assembly references is useful in scenar-ios like these, you should also be aware of its complexities. For example, the rules for which of the four fields must match are different depending on whether the assembly that matches the friendly name has a strong name or a weak name. I discuss these complexities in the section "Partially Specified Assembly References" later in this chapter.

Version Policy

As described, strong names are part of the infrastructure the CLR uses to provide a system that employs strict version checking to minimize inadvertent conflicts between different ver-sions of an assembly. By default, the CLR loads the exact version of the assembly you specify in your reference. However, this version can be redirected to a different version through a series of statements called *version policy*. Version policy is useful in several scenarios. For example, a machine administrator can specify version policy that would prevent anyone on the machine from using a version of an assembly that is known to have security vulnerabilities or other serious bugs. In addition, an application can use version policy to load a version of a .NET Framework assembly different from the default.

These version policy statements are specified in Extensible Markup Language (XML) files and are most easily created with the .NET Framework Configuration tool. The following is an example of a version policy statement that causes version 6.0.0.0 of an assembly whose friendly name is Alingi to be loaded, regardless of which version was specified:

```
<assemblyBinding xmlns="urn:schemas-microsoft-com:asm.v1">
  <dependentAssembly>
    <assemblyIdentity name="Alingi" publicKeyToken="ae4cc5eda5032777" />
      <bindingRedirect oldVersion="0.0.0.0-65535.65535.65535.65535"
        newVersion="6.0.0.0" />
  </dependentAssembly>
</assemblyBinding>
```

Version policy can be specified at three different levels. First, the author of an application that uses shared assemblies can specify version policy in the application configuration file. Second, the publisher of a shared assembly can provide version policy in what is called a *publisher policy assembly*. Finally, the machine administrator can specify version policy through entries in the machine.config file. When the CLR resolves a reference to a strong-named assembly, it begins by looking in these three locations for version policy statements that might redirect the assembly reference to a different version. The three policy levels also form a hierarchy in that they are evaluated in sequence with the output of one level feeding into the next. For example, say an application configuration file contains a policy statement that redirects all references to an assembly from version 1.0.0.0 to version 2.0.0.0. If the policy statement in the application configuration file applies to the reference being resolved, the CLR next evaluates publisher policy looking for any policy statements that redirect version 2.0.0.0 of the assembly. Likewise, administrator policy is evaluated based on the outcome of the publisher policy phase.

This brief description of version policy gives you what you need to understand the concepts presented in this chapter. For more details on how version policy is specified and resolved, see Chapters 2 and 3 in *Applied Microsoft .NET Framework Programming* (Microsoft Press, 2002) by Jeffrey Richter.

Loading Assemblies by Assembly Identity

The .NET Framework class libraries provide several APIs you can use to load an assembly dynamically by assembly identity. Throughout this chapter, I refer to these APIs, as well as the APIs that enable you to load an assembly given a filename, as the *assembly loading APIs*. The assembly loading APIs that take an assembly identity enable you to specify an assembly's identity in one of two ways. First, you can supply the identity as a string that follows a well-defined format. Or you can supply an instance of the *System.Reflection.AssemblyName* class. This class contains properties for the textual name, public key, culture, and version components of the assembly identity. In this section I describe how to use the assembly loading APIs to load add-ins into an extensible application dynamically.

Before I get into the details of how to call these APIs, however, it's worth taking a step back and revisiting the extensible application architecture introduced in Chapter 1. Making the most effective use of the assembly loading APIs involves more than just knowing the details of how to call the APIs. Your extensible application will have a much cleaner design and will perform much better if you think through how your use of application domains relates to assembly loading. This involves understanding your application domain boundaries and taking advantage of the application domain manager infrastructure discussed in Chapter 5. By looking back at the basic architecture, you can see how best to take advantage of the assembly loading APIs without introducing unintended side effects such as assemblies loaded into the wrong application domain.

After I've discussed how the assembly loading APIs fit into the overall architecture of an extensible application, I cover the details involved in calling these APIs. In addition to looking at the APIs themselves, I discuss briefly the CLR's rules for locating assemblies and the impact of partially specified references.

Architecture of an Extensible Application Revisited

In Chapter 1, I introduced the typical architecture of an extensible application. In the last few chapters, I've made this architecture more concrete by describing the role that application domains play in applications that are extensible. Application domains exist for one purpose: as containers for assemblies. The main goal of this architecture is to provide the infrastructure in which to load assemblies dynamically. Let me review this architecture now and highlight the key design points that affect how the add-in assemblies are loaded (see Figure 7-2). The key points include the following:

- **Multiple application domains are used**   Extensible applications typically create multiple application domains to isolate add-ins (or groups of add-ins) from others loaded in the same process. It's important to call the assembly loading APIs from the domain in which an add-in is to be loaded. This results in the cleanest design and the best overall performance.

- **An application domain manager is created for each domain**   In Chapter 5 I introduced the notion of an application domain manager. An application domain manager is a convenient place from which to call the assembly loading APIs because the CLR automatically creates an instance of your application domain manager in each new application domain rather than requiring you to write code to load your domain manager explicitly into each new domain you create.

- **Add-in assemblies are not loaded in the default application domain**   Most extensible applications avoid loading add-in assemblies into the default application domain primarily because the default domain cannot be unloaded without shutting down the entire process. As a result, you typically see just the application domain manager class loaded into the default domain. From there, other domains are created to contain the add-ins.

- **Communication between application domains is limited to the application domain managers**   In Chapter 5 I discuss how to design your application to make the most effective use of application domains. One design goal is to limit communication between application domains as much as possible. This includes two aspects. First, the volume of communication should be limited both in terms of the number of calls made and the amount of data exchanged by those calls. Limiting the volume of communication helps your application perform better because less cross-domain marshaling is required. The other aspect of cross-domain communication that you aim to limit is the number of assemblies involved in calls across application domains. If an assembly is to participate in a call between two application domains, that assembly must be loaded into both application domains. To be loaded into two application domains, an assembly must be deployed in such a way as to be visible to both domains. Furthermore, both domains must be unloaded to remove the assembly from the process completely. In short, the fewer assemblies that are involved in cross-domain communication, the better, from the perspective of both performance and ease of deployment. Because an application domain manager is automatically loaded into each new domain for you, it must already be deployed in such a way that it is visible to multiple application domains. So it's natural to use application domain managers to communicate across application domains.

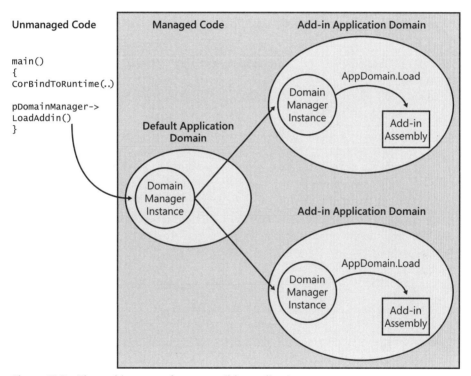

Figure 7-2   The architecture of an extensible application

As described, the primary goal to keep in mind when designing your assembly loading infrastructure is always to call the assembly loading APIs from the application domain in which you intend the add-in assembly to be loaded. This design is shown in Figure 7-2 by the calls to *AppDomain.Load* originating in the application domain manager and resulting in the add-in assembly being loaded into the same domain. To get a clear picture of why this design goal is desirable, take a look at how assemblies are represented in the .NET Framework class libraries and how that representation relates to the CLR's infrastructure for calling methods on a class in a different application domain.

System.Reflection.Assembly and CLR Remote Calls

Recall from Chapter 5 that calling a method on a type in another application domain is a remote call. The mechanics for a remote call are different depending on the marshaling characteristics of the type you are calling. Generally speaking, types are either considered *marshaled by value* or *marshaled by reference* in CLR remoting terminology. Types that are marshaled by reference are those types that derive from the *System.MarshalByRefObject* base class. When you call a method on a type derived from *MarshalByRef* in a different application domain, the CLR creates a proxy for that type in the calling application domain. All calls are made through the proxy to the actual type as shown in Figure 7-3.

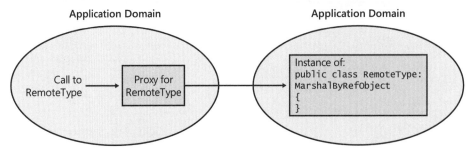

Figure 7-3   Calling a *MarshalByRefObject* in a different application domain

In contrast, when a call is made to an object in another application domain that is marshaled by value, a copy of the instance is made in the calling domain. All objects that are marshaled by value must be marked with the *[Serializable]* custom attribute so the CLR knows how to transfer the object into the new domain. All calls on the type are made to the copy instead of through a proxy to the original as shown in Figure 7-4.

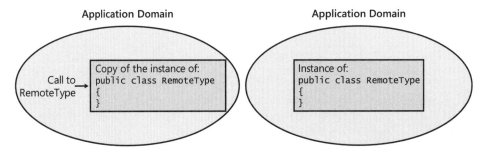

Figure 7-4   Calling a type in a different application domain that is marshaled by value

At this point, you might be wondering what this discussion about CLR remoting has to do with loading assemblies. This matters because the type used to represent assemblies in the .NET Framework class libraries, *System.Reflection.Assembly*, is marshaled by value, not by reference. Because instances of *System.Reflection.Assembly* are copied between application domains, it's easy to inadvertently end up loading an assembly into an application domain unintentionally. Look at a concrete example to see how easy it is to make this mistake.

In Chapters 5 and 6, we used a CLR host called boatracehost.exe as an example of how to make effective use of application domains in an extensible application. We continue that example in this chapter as we discuss how to use the assembly loading APIs in conjunction with application domains. As described, you can use several APIs in the .NET Framework class libraries to load assemblies dynamically. *AppDomain.Load* is one of these methods that enables you to load an assembly into an application domain. Let's say for purposes of example that a new boat is entering a race hosted by boatracehost. We'd like to load this add-in into a new application domain, so we use *AppDomain.CreateDomain* to create the new domain. We then call *AppDomain.Load* to load the boat add-in in the new domain as shown in the following code:

```
static void Main(string[] args)
{
   AppDomainSetup adSetup = new AppDomainSetup();
   adSetup.ApplicationBase = @"c:\Program Files\BoatRaceHost\Addins";

   AppDomain ad = AppDomain.CreateDomain("Alingi Domain",
                                        null,
                                        adSetup);

   Assembly alingiAssembly = ad.Load("Alingi, Version=5.0.0.0,
                                     PublicKeyToken=5cf360b40180107c,
                                     culture=neutral");
}
```

The call to *AppDomain.Load* in the preceding code is a remote call from the default application domain (in which *main()* is running) to the new domain held in the variable of type *AppDomain* named *ad*. *AppDomain.Load* takes as input the name of the assembly we'd like to load and returns an instance of *System.Reflection.Assembly*. Because *Assembly* is marshaled by value, a copy of the instance of the *Assembly* type is made in the default domain when the call to *AppDomain.Load* returns as shown in Figure 7-5.

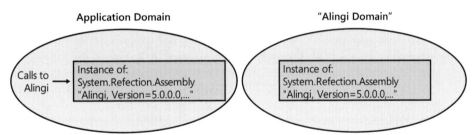

Figure 7-5   An assembly inadvertently loaded into two application domains

Instances of *Assembly* contain data describing the underlying assembly they represent. For example, given an instance of *Assembly*, you can determine the assembly's name, the assemblies it depends on, and so on. The underlying assembly represented by an instance of *Assembly* must be loaded into the application domain where the instance resides. In this example, this means that the *Alingi* assembly must be loaded into both the default application domain and the Alingi Domain. This side effect of calling *AppDomain.Load* affects our application design in a few key ways. First, the fact that the add-in assembly has been loaded into our default application domain means we can't unload that assembly from our application without terminating the entire process. This is clearly undesirable from both the perspectives of memory usage and type visibility. Because we can never unload the assembly, we might be stuck dealing with the additional memory it consumes even when we no longer need the assembly within the application. Also, once an assembly is loaded into a given application domain, it can discover all other assemblies in that same domain using the *GetAssemblies* method on the *AppDomain* type. Once another assembly is discovered, it can be reflected upon using the types in the *System.Reflection* namespace. If the code access security policy for that domain isn't configured to disallow it, code in an add-in assembly could even invoke methods on any other assembly loaded in the same domain.

The other reason loading an add-in into the default application domain affects our design is that it complicates the deployment of the add-in. Recall from Chapter 6 that each application domain has an *ApplicationBase* that establishes a root directory in which assemblies for that domain can be deployed. In the preceding code sample, the *ApplicationBase* for Alingi Domain has been set to c:\program files\boatracehost\addins. By deploying the *Alingi* assembly to that directory, it is found by the CLR when we call *AppDomain.Load*. However, because we've also inadvertently added *Alingi* to the default application domain, the add-in must be deployed to a location where the CLR will find it for that domain as well. This means deploying the add-in to another *ApplicationBase* or adding it to a global location such as the global assembly cache (GAC). This subtlety often results in unexpected failures to load an assembly. For example, in looking at the previous code, it's obvious that we need to deploy our add-in to c:\program files\boatracehost\addins. However, if we did just that, we'd get a *FileNotFound-Exception* telling us that the assembly we're loading cannot be found. When I see these errors, I typically look in the directory in which I expect the assembly to be found, and, seeing it there, I'm at a loss for a few minutes before I realize that the CLR is trying to load my assembly into an application domain I never intended. Because of all this, it is far better to call the assembly loading APIs from within the domain in which you intend the add-in to be loaded.

Recommendations for Loading Assemblies in Extensible Applications

Most extensible applications leverage the application domain manager concept introduced in Chapter 5 to load add-ins from within the desired application domain. As described, the application domain manager is a natural place from which to initiate assembly loads because the CLR takes care of creating an instance of the application domain manager in each new application domain you create. In leveraging this design, most extensible applications follow a series of steps similar to the following when loading a new add-in to the application:

1. The extensible application is made aware of the new add-in.

2. An application domain is chosen in which to load the new add-in.

3. The application domain manager in the target domain is called to load the add-in.

4. The application domain manager in the target domain loads the add-in.

These steps are described in the following sections.

Step 1: The Extensible Application Is Made Aware of the New Add-In   The means by which add-ins are introduced to an extensible application are completely up to the application. So there is no general approach to recommend. Instead, I discuss some common examples.

Typically, an extensible application either presents a user interface or provides a configuration system that enables a user to add a new add-in to the application. For example, new managed types, procedures, and so on are added to SQL Server by editing the SQL catalog, whereas some graphical applications include dialog boxes that enable users interactively to specify the add-ins they'd like to load. In other examples, add-ins are specified in code that the application interprets and runs. For example, add-ins are included in client-side Web pages using the <*object*> tag in a Hypertext Markup Language (HTML) source file.

Step 2: An Application Domain Is Chosen in Which to Load the New Add-In   In Chapter 5 I discuss the criteria to consider when partitioning a process into multiple application domains. These criteria include the need to isolate assemblies from others that are loaded in the same process, to unload code dynamically from a running process, and to limit the amount of communication that occurs between objects loaded in different application domains. When a new add-in is introduced to your extensible application, you must examine the add-in and load it into an application domain that meets your requirements for partitioning. Depending on your scenario, you might load the add-in into an existing application domain, or you might create a new one in which to load the add-in. For example, in Chapter 5 I describe how the Microsoft Internet Explorer host partitions a process into application domains based on Web sites. That is, all controls that are downloaded from the same site are loaded into the same application domain. As a result, when Internet Explorer comes across a reference to a control while parsing a Web page, it looks to see if it has already created an application domain corresponding to the site from which the control originates. If it has, the control is loaded into that domain. If not, a new application domain is created in which to load the control. Your application will likely follow similar logic when deciding how to load a new add-in. Most extensible applications keep an internal data structure that holds the list of application domains in the process along with some descriptive data for each domain that is used to determine the appropriate domain for new add-ins (in the Internet Explorer case, this extra piece of data is the name of a Web site).

Step 3: The Application Domain Manager in the Target Domain Is Called to Load the Add-In   After you've chosen an application domain in which to load the new add-in, you must transfer control into that target domain so the actual loading of the assembly can take place. As described, calling the assembly loading APIs from within the domain in which you'd like the add-in to run makes for a cleaner design. The easiest way to transition into a different application domain is to call a method on the application domain manager in the target domain. Look at some code from our boatracehost to see how this is done. Recall from Chapter 5 that the application domain manager for boatracehost is implemented in a class called *BoatRaceDomainManager*. *BoatRaceDomainManager* derives from an interface called *IBoatRaceDomainManager*,

which includes a method called *EnterBoat* that we'll use to load a new add-in into the application. Here's a portion of *BoatRaceDomainManager* and the interface it derives from:

```
public interface IBoatRaceDomainManager
{
    // loads the boat identified by boatTypeName from the
    // assembly in assemblyName into the application domain
    // in which this instance of the domain manager is
    // running.
    void EnterBoat(string assemblyName, string boatTypeName);
}

public class BoatRaceDomainManager : AppDomainManager,
                                     IBoatRaceDomainManager
{
    void EnterBoat(string assemblyName, string boatTypeName)
    {
        // load the boat into this application domain…
    }
}
```

The following code uses the *BoatRaceDomainManager* class to load an assembly into a new application domain:

```
AppDomainSetup adSetup = new AppDomainSetup();
adSetup.ApplicationBase = @"c:\Program Files\BoatRaceHost\Addins";

AppDomain ad = AppDomain.CreateDomain("Alingi Domain",
                                      null,
                                      adSetup);

BoatRaceDomainManager adManager = (BoatRaceDomainManager)ad.DomainManager;

adManager.EnterBoat("AlingiBoat", "Alingi, Version=5.0.0.0,
                    PublicKeyToken=5cf360b40180107c,
                    culture=neutral);
```

In this example, we use the *DomainManager* property on *System.AppDomain* to get the instance of *BoatRaceDomainManager* that the CLR has created for us in the new domain. Given our domain manager instance, we simply call the *EnterBoat* method to transition into the new application domain.

Step 4: The Application Domain Manager in the Target Domain Loads the Add-In

Once inside the new application domain, using the assembly loading APIs to load the add-in is easy. Just as we used the *AppDomain.Load* method earlier in the chapter to load an assembly into a different application domain, you can use it now to load an assembly in the domain in which you're running. The application domain manager from boatracehost does just this. The implementation of *BoatRaceDomainManager.EnterBoat* determines the current application domain using the static *CurrentDomain* property on *System.AppDomain*. It then calls the *AppDomain.Load* method, passing in the name of the assembly to load as shown in the following code:

```
public class BoatRaceDomainManager : AppDomainManager,
                              IBoatRaceDomainManager
{
    void EnterBoat(string assemblyName, string boatTypeName)
    {
        // load the assembly containing boat into this
        // application domain…
        Assembly alingiAssembly = AppDomain.CurrentDomain.Load(assemblyName);

        // load the type from the new assembly...
    }
}
```

Using *Assembly.Load* and Related Methods

Now that I've shown how best to make use of the assembly loading APIs within your application, let's dig into the details of the APIs themselves. As described, several methods in the .NET Framework provide the ability to load an assembly dynamically given an assembly identity—the *AppDomain.Load* method used in the previous section is just one such API. In some cases, multiple APIs provide the same functionality and are therefore redundant, but in other cases the APIs offer different capabilities. For example, some APIs enable you to load an assembly into a different application domain, whereas some load an assembly only into the current domain. Following are the methods in the .NET Framework that enable you to load an assembly and brief descriptions of each method's capabilities. Keep in mind that these are the APIs that enable you to load an assembly given an assembly name. Several APIs enable you to load an assembly by providing the name of the file containing the manifest. I cover these APIs later on in the section, "Loading Assemblies by Filename."

- **AppDomain.Load**   This is the only method that enables you to load an assembly into an application domain other than the one in which you're currently running. As discussed earlier in this chapter, it's easy to load an assembly into the current application domain inadvertently if you're not careful.

   The overloads for *AppDomain.Load* are as follows:

   ```
   public Assembly Load (AssemblyName assemblyRef)
   ```

   ```
   public Assembly Load(AssemblyName assemblyRef, Evidence assemblySecurity)
   ```

   ```
   public Assembly Load(String assemblyString)
   ```

- **AppDomain.ExecuteAssemblyByName**   This is the only method in the group that causes code to be executed when it is called. *ExecuteAssemblyByName* is used to launch managed executable files programmatically. You provide the pathname to the executable, and the CLR runs its *main()* method. This method doesn't return until the executable has finished running.

The overloads for *AppDomain.ExecuteAssemblyByName* are as follows:

```
public int ExecuteAssemblyByName(String assemblyName)

public int ExecuteAssemblyByName(String assemblyName,
    Evidence assemblySecurity)

public int ExecuteAssemblyByName(String assemblyName,
    Evidence assemblySecurity,
    String[] args)

public int ExecuteAssemblyByName(AssemblyName assemblyName,
    Evidence assemblySecurity,
    String[] args)
```

■ **Assembly.Load**   This is the most commonly used API for loading an assembly into the current application domain. Because it is static, there's no way to use this method to load an assembly in an application domain other than the one in which you're currently running.

The overloads for *Assembly.Load* are as follows:

```
public static Assembly Load(String assemblyString)

public static Assembly Load(String assemblyString, Evidence assemblySecurity)

static public Assembly Load(AssemblyName assemblyRef)

static public Assembly Load(AssemblyName assemblyRef,
    Evidence assemblySecurity)
```

■ **Assembly.LoadWithPartialName**   This method has been deprecated in .NET Framework 2.0 and will be removed in a future version of the .NET Framework. *Assembly.LoadWith-PartialName* enables you to load a strongly named assembly from the GAC using a partial reference. This was commonly used to implement a use latest version policy, whereby the caller would omit a version number from the reference and would load the latest version of the assembly from the GAC that matched the name and public key. Blindly loading the latest version of a shared assembly brings back the world of DLL Hell by exposing you to versioning conflicts between different releases of an assembly. For that reason, this method is being removed from the .NET Framework.

The overloads for *Assembly.LoadWithPartialName* are as follows:

```
static public Assembly LoadWithPartialName(String partialName)

static public Assembly LoadWithPartialName(String partialName,
    Evidence securityEvidence)

static public Assembly LoadWithPartialName(String partialName,
    Evidence securityEvidence, bool oldBehavior)
```

As you can see from the preceding list, the assembly loading APIs enable you to specify the assembly to load either by supplying its identity as a string or by providing an instance of *System.Reflection.AssemblyName*. In addition, each API has an overload that lets you associate security evidence with the assembly you are loading. I cover the details of using this parameter in Chapter 10.

> **Note** It's often the case that the first thing you'd like to do after loading an assembly is create a type from that assembly. To support this scenario, the .NET Framework provides several APIs that enable you to load an assembly and create a type with a single method call. When using these APIs, you pass the name of the type you'd like to create in addition to the name of the assembly you'd like to load. These convenience methods eliminate a lot of boilerplate code you'd find yourself writing over and over again. The methods that enable you to load an assembly and create a type are these:
>
> - *System.AppDomain.CreateInstance*
> - *System.AppDomain.CreateInstanceAndUnwrap*
> - *System.Activator.CreateInstance*
>
> With respect to assembly loading, these methods work just like the ones in the preceding list, so I don't talk about them explicitly in this chapter. Documentation of these methods can be found in the .NET Framework SDK.

Specifying Assembly Identities as Strings

When specifying an assembly identity by string, you must follow a well-defined format that the CLR understands. This format enables you to specify all four parts of an assembly's name: the friendly name, version number, culture, and information about the public portion of the cryptographic key pair used to give the assembly a strong name. The string form of an assembly is as follows:

```
"<friendlyName>, Version=<version number>, PublicKeyToken=<publicKeyToken>,
    Culture=<culture>"
```

When specifying identities in this format, the *<friendlyName>* portion of the identity must come first. The *PublicKeyToken*, *Version*, and *Culture* elements can be specified in any order. Strings that follow this format are passed directly to the assembly loading APIs as shown in the following simple example:

```
public class BoatRaceDomainManager : AppDomainManager,
                                     IBoatRaceDomainManager
{
    void EnterAlingi()
    {
        // load the assembly into this application domain...
        Assembly a = Assembly.Load("Alingi, Version=5.0.0.1,
                            PublicKeyToken=3026a3146c675483,
                            Culture=neutral");
```

```
        // load the type from the new assembly...
    }
}
```

As I explained earlier, it is possible to reference an assembly by supplying less than the full identity. I cover the details of how such references work in the section "Partially Specified Assembly References" later in the chapter.

Specifying assembly identities using the string format is generally straightforward as long as the CLR can correctly parse the string you supply. Any extra characters in the string (such as duplicate commas) or misspelled element names will cause a *FileLoadException* exception to be raised and your assembly will not be loaded.

> **Note** The CLR error checking process when parsing assembly identities in .NET Framework 2.0 is much stricter than it was in previous versions of the CLR. For example, any extra characters or unrecognized element names (such as those caused by misspellings) were simply ignored instead of flagged as errors in previous versions. As always, make sure you thoroughly test your application on all versions of the CLR you intend to support to catch subtle differences like this.

Failures to load an assembly because of errors in parsing the assembly identity are easy to diagnose because the instance of *FileLoadException* that is thrown contains a specific message and *HRESULT*. The *HRESULT* indicating a parsing error is *0x80131047* (this error code is defined as *FUSION_E_INVALID_NAME* in the file corerror.h from the include directory in the .NET Framework SDK). The message property of the exception will say, "Unknown error - HRESULT 0x80131047."

In addition to forming the string correctly, it's important that the values you supply for each element are valid. The following points summarize the valid values for friendly name, culture, and version.

- **Friendly name** Friendly names can contain any characters that are valid for naming files in the file system. Friendly names are not case sensitive.

- **Version** Assembly version numbers consist of four parts as specified in the following format:

  `Major.minor.build.revision`

  When specifying a version number, it's best to include all four parts because the CLR will make sure that the version number of the loaded assembly exactly matches the version number you specify. You can omit values for some portions of the version number, but doing so results in a partial reference. When resolving an assembly based on a partial version number reference, the CLR matches only those portions of the version number you provide. This looseness in binding semantics can cause you to load an assembly inadvertently. For example, given the following reference:

```
"Alingi, Version=5, PublicKeyToken=3026a3146c675483, Culture=neutral"
```

the CLR only makes sure that the major number of the assembly you load is 5—none of the other portions of the version number are checked. In other words, the first assembly found in the application directory (the global assembly cache is not searched when resolving a partial reference) whose major number is 5 will be loaded regardless of the values for the other three portions of the version number. I cover partial references in more detail later in the chapter.

■ **Culture**   Values for the culture element of the assembly name follow a format described by RFC 1766. This format includes both a code for the language and a more specific code for the region. For example, "de-AT" is the culture value for German-Austria, whereas "de-CH" represents German-Switzerland. See the documentation for the *System.Globalization.CultureInfo* class in the .NET Framework SDK for more details.

The public key token portion of an assembly name requires a bit more explanation. Typing an entire 1024-bit (or larger) cryptographic key when referencing an assembly would be overly cumbersome. To make referencing strong-named assemblies easier, the CLR enables you to provide a shortened form of the key called a *public key token*. A public key token is an 8-byte value derived by taking a portion of a hash of the entire public key. Fortunately, the .NET Framework SDK provides a tool called the Strong Name utility (sn.exe) so you don't have to be a cryptography wizard to obtain a public key token. The easiest way to obtain the public key token from an assembly is to use the –T option of sn.exe. For example, issuing the following command at a command prompt:

```
C:\Projects\Alingi> sn -T Alingi.dll
```

yields the following output:

```
Microsoft (R) .NET Framework Strong Name Utility Version 2.0.40301.9
Copyright (C) Microsoft Corporation 1998-2004. All rights reserved.

Public key token is 3026a3146c675483
```

From here, you can paste the public key token value into your source code.

Specifying Assembly Identities Using *System.Reflection.AssemblyName*

Calling the assembly loading APIs by passing the assembly identity as a string is the most common approach because it's so easy to use. However, as shown earlier, most of the assembly loading APIs also allow you to pass an instance of *System.Reflection.AssemblyName* to identify the assembly you want to load. *AssemblyName* has properties and methods that enable you to specify those elements of the assembly identity you wish to load in your assembly. Table 7-1 describes these members.

Table 7-1 Members of *System.Reflection.AssemblyName* Used to Load Assemblies

AssemblyName Member	Description
Name	A string used to specify the assembly's friendly name
Version	An instance of *System.Version* that identifies the version of the assembly you'd like to load
CultureInfo	An instance of *System.Globalization.CultureInfo* that describes the assembly's culture
SetPublicKey *SetPublicKeyToken*	Methods that accept an array of *System.Byte* and that hold either the public key or the public key token of the assembly you wish to load

The following example shows how to call the assembly loading APIs by passing an instance of *AssemblyName*. In this example, I specify a partial reference using the friendly name only by constructing a new instance of *AssemblyName*, setting its *Name* property, and passing it to *Assembly.Load*:

```
public class BoatRaceDomainManager : AppDomainManager,
                               IBoatRaceDomainManager
  {
     void EnterBoat()
     {
        // load the assembly into this
        // application domain…
        AssemblyName name = new AssemblyName();
        name.Name = "Alingi";

           Assembly a = Assembly.Load(name);

        // load the type from the new assembly

     }
  }
```

How the CLR Locates Assemblies

The CLR follows a consistent, well-defined set of steps to locate the assembly you've specified when calling one of the assembly-loading APIs. These steps are different based on whether you are referencing a strong-named assembly or a weakly named one.

> **Note** All aspects of the CLR's behavior for loading assemblies can be customized by you as the author of an extensible application. In Chapter 8, I write a CLR host that shows the extent of customization possible.

Understanding the steps the CLR follows to load an assembly is essential when building an extensible application that can work well in a variety of add-in deployment scenarios. Several factors influence both the version and the location of the assembly the CLR loads given your reference. Some factors are aspects of the deployment environment that you can control, such as the base directories for the application domains you create. Other factors, such as the specification of version policy by an administrator or the author of a shared assembly, are beyond your control. Fortunately, great tools are available for you to understand how the CLR locates assemblies and diagnose any problems you might encounter. I cover how to use these tools after describing the steps the CLR uses to locate assemblies.

The factors the CLR considers when resolving an assembly reference include deployment locations and the presence of any version policy or assembly codebase locations as shown in Figure 7-6 and described in the following points.

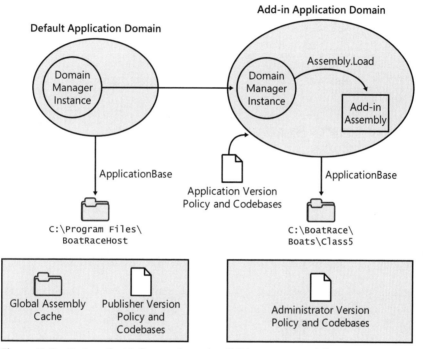

Figure 7-6   Factors that influence how the CLR locates assemblies

- **ApplicationBase**   As described in Chapter 6, an application domain's *ApplicationBase* establishes a root directory in which the CLR looks for assemblies intended to be private to that domain. You'll almost always want to set this property when creating a new application domain.

- **Global assembly cache**   The GAC is a repository for assemblies that are meant to be shared by several applications. The CLR looks in the GAC first when resolving a reference to a strong-named assembly, as I discuss in a bit.

- **Version policy**   As described, version binding redirects can be specified either in an application configuration file, by the publisher of a strong-named assembly, or by the administrator of the machine. As the creator of an application domain, you can completely control whether application-level version redirects exist—you can turn off such version redirects either by not specifying a *ConfigurationFile* for your application domain or by setting the *DisallowBindingRedirects* property described in Chapter 6. However, there is no way for you to control whether binding redirects specified by the machine administrator are applied. It is possible that the CLR will load a version of an assembly other than the one you specify.

■ **Codebases**   The same configuration files used to specify version policy can also be used to provide a codebase location at which a given version of an assembly can be found. This is done using the *<codebase>* XML element (for more information on using *<codebase>* to supply an assembly location, see the .NET Framework SDK documentation). As with version redirects, you can control whether an application configuration file can be used to supply a codebase, but you can't prevent a codebase location from being supplied by an administrator. Therefore, it is possible that the CLR will load a given assembly from a location other than what you expect. Later in the chapter, I show you how to determine where an assembly was loaded by using the properties and methods of the *Assembly* class.

How the CLR Locates Assemblies with Weak Names

Weakly named assemblies can be loaded only from an application domain's *ApplicationBase* or a subdirectory thereof. As a result, the CLR's rules for finding such an assembly are relatively straightforward. The CLR follows two steps when resolving a reference to an assembly with a simple name:

1. Look for a codebase in the application configuration file.

2. Probe for the assembly in the *ApplicationBase* and its subdirectories.

Step 1 rarely applies when loading add-ins into extensible applications. This is primarily because authoring a configuration file to specify a location for an assembly requires up-front knowledge that such an assembly will be loaded. As I mentioned, this isn't the case with extensible applications because the add-ins are typically loaded dynamically. So the only way to use a configuration file to specify a codebase in this case is if somehow the configuration file was shipped along with the add-in and you set the *ConfigurationFile* property of your application to use it. Although possible, this scenario is unlikely to occur in practice.

Given that step 1 isn't likely to apply, loading weakly named add-ins into extensible applications typically involves looking for the assembly in the *ApplicationBase* and its subdirectories. This process, termed *probing*, is described in detail in Chapter 6. Remember, too, that weakly named assemblies are loaded by name only—no other elements of the assembly name, such as the assembly's version, are checked.

Note It is possible to end up loading a strongly named assembly given a reference that appears to be to a weakly named assembly. This happens if you have a strong-named assembly deployed somewhere in your *ApplicationBase* directory structure whose friendly name matches the name you are referencing using one of the assembly loading APIs. For example, given the following reference:

```
Assembly a = Assembly.Load("Alingi");
```

The CLR will load the first file it finds named alingi.dll, regardless of whether it has a strong name or a weak name. If the assembly it loads has a strong name, the CLR essentially starts over by taking the identity of the assembly and loading and treating that as a strong-name reference to resolve. In the next section I describe the steps involved in loading a strong-named assembly. A strong-named assembly could get loaded given the preceding reference because that reference is partial—no value is supplied for the public key token. This situation would not occur in scenarios in which the reference is fully specified, such as when an assembly is referenced in an early-bound fashion. If you want to be sure that only a weakly named assembly is loaded in this case, you must specify a *null* public key token like this:

```
Assembly a = Assembly.Load("Alingi, PublicKeyToken=null");
```

How the CLR Locates Assemblies with Strong Names

The process of loading a strongly named assembly is much more involved because of the potential for version policy and the existence of the GAC. The CLR takes the following steps to resolve a reference to a strong-named assembly:

1. Determine which version of the assembly to load.

2. Look for the assembly in the GAC.

3. Look in the configuration files for any codebase locations.

4. Probe for the assembly in the *ApplicationBase* and its subdirectories.

When loading a strongly named assembly, by default the CLR loads the version you specify in your reference. However, as described earlier in the chapter, that version can be redirected to another version of the same assembly by one of the three levels of version policy—application, publisher, or administrator. The first step the CLR takes in resolving a reference to a strongly named assembly is to compare the identity specified in the reference to the binding redirect statements in the three version policy files to determine whether an alternative version of the assembly should be loaded.

Next, the CLR looks for the assembly in the GAC. The CLR always prefers to load strong-named assemblies from the GAC primarily for performance reasons. There are a few different reasons why loading from the GAC is better for overall system performance. First, if several applications are using the same strong-named assembly, loading the assembly from the same location on disk uses less memory than if each application were to load the same DLL from private locations. When a DLL is loaded from the same location multiple times, the operating system loads the DLL's read-only pages only once and shares them among all instances. The second reason is related to how an assembly's strong name is verified. Recall that a strong name involves a cryptographic signature. This signature must be verified to guarantee that the assembly hasn't been altered since it was built. Verifying a cryptographic signature involves computing a hash of the entire contents of the file and other mathematically intense operations. As a result, it's best to verify the signature at a time when its cost will be noticed the least (without compromising security, of course). An assembly's strong name is verified during installation into the GAC. The cache is considered secure, so once the assembly has been successfully installed, its signature doesn't have to be reverified. In contrast, because assemblies placed elsewhere in the file system (such as in an *ApplicationBase* directory) aren't explicitly installed into a secure location, their strong-name signatures must be verified every time the assembly is loaded. By loading from the GAC, the CLR attempts to reduce the number of times these cryptographic signatures must be verified.

If an assembly cannot be found in the GAC, the CLR next looks to see whether a codebase location for the assembly has been provided in any of the configuration files. If such a location is found, the CLR uses it. If not, the CLR probes in the *ApplicationBase* directory just as it does for simply named assemblies.

Using *System.Reflection.Assembly* to Determine an Assembly's Location on Disk

Once an assembly has been loaded, you can use the *CodeBase*, *Location*, and *GlobalAssembly-Cache* properties of the *Assembly* class to determine information about where the CLR found it.

The *Location* and *CodeBase* properties are very similar in that they both provide information about the physical file from which the assembly was loaded. In fact, these two properties have the same value when an assembly is loaded from the local computer's disk into an application domain that does not have shadow copy enabled. In this scenario, these two properties simply give you the name of the physical file on the local disk from which the assembly was loaded. The *CodeBase* and *Location* properties differ in two scenarios, however. First, if the assembly was downloaded from an HTTP server, the *CodeBase* property gives the location of the file on the remote server, whereas the *Location* property gives the location of the file in the downloaded files cache on the local machine. These properties also have different values if an assembly is loaded into an application domain in which shadow copy is enabled. In this scenario, *CodeBase* gives you the original location of the file, whereas *Location* tells you the location to which the file was shadow copied. See Chapter 6 for more information about how to enable shadow copy for the application domains you create.

> **Note** The *Assembly* class also has a property called *EscapedCodeBase* that gives you the same pathname as *CodeBase*, except the value returned has the original escape characters.

The *GlobalAssemblyCache* property is a *boolean* value that tells you whether the CLR loaded the assembly from the GAC.

Using Fuslogvw.exe to Understand How Assemblies Are Located

The .NET Framework SDK includes a tool called the Assembly Binding Log Viewer (fuslogvw.exe) that is great not only for diagnosing errors encountered when loading assemblies, but also to help understand the assembly loading process in general. Fuslogvw.exe works by logging each step the CLR completes when resolving a reference to an assembly. These logs are written to .html files that can be viewed using the fuslogvw.exe user interface. The logging is turned off by default because of the expense involved in generating the log files. You can turn on logging in one of two modes: you can choose to log every attempt to load an assembly or log only those attempts that fail. Logging is enabled using the Settings dialog box from the fuslogvw.exe user interface as shown in Figure 7-7.

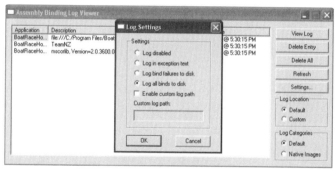

Figure 7-7   Enabling logging using fuslogvw.exe

Take a look at how the output generated by fuslogvw.exe helps you understand how the CLR locates assemblies. After turning logging on, I ran boatracehost.exe and had it load an add-in from an assembly called TeamNZ. In this simple example, fuslogvw.exe logged that we attempted to load three assemblies as shown in Figure 7-8.

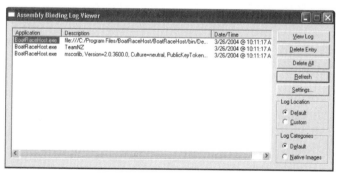

Figure 7-8   Fuslogvw.exe after running boatracehost.exe

Double-clicking the row labeled TeamNZ displays the log generated while the CLR resolved the reference to that assembly. The log text is as follows:

```
0| *** Assembly Binder Log Entry  (4/2/2004 @ 4:30:15 PM) ***
1| The operation was successful.
2| Bind result: hr = 0x0. The operation completed successfully.
3| Assembly manager loaded from:
   C:\WINDOWS\Microsoft.NET\Framework\v2.0.40301\mscorwks.dll
4| Running under executable
   C:\Program Files\BoatRaceHost\BoatRaceHost\bin\Debug\BoatRaceHost.exe
5| --- A detailed error log follows.
6| === Pre-bind state information ===
7| LOG: DisplayName = TeamNZ
 (Partial)
8| LOG: Appbase = file:///C:/Program Files/BoatRaceHost/BoatRaceHost/bin/Debug/
9| LOG: Initial PrivatePath = NULL
10| LOG: Dynamic Base = NULL
11| LOG: Cache Base = NULL
12| LOG: AppName = BoatRaceHost.exe
13| Calling assembly : BoatRaceHost, Version=1.0.1553.29684, Culture=neutral,
    PublicKeyToken=null.
===
14| LOG: Attempting application configuration file download.
15| LOG: Download of application configuration file was attempted from
    file:///C:/Program Files/BoatRaceHost/BoatRaceHost/bin/
    Debug/BoatRaceHost.exe.config.
16| LOG: Application configuration file does not exist.
17| LOG: Using machine configuration file from
    C:\WINDOWS\Microsoft.NET\Framework\v2.0.40301\config\machine.config.
18| LOG: Policy not being applied to reference at this time (private, custom,
    partial, or location-based assembly bind).
19| LOG: Attempting download of new URL
    file:///C:/Program Files/BoatRaceHost/BoatRaceHost/bin/Debug/TeamNZ.dll.
20| LOG: Attempting download of new URL
    file:///C:/Program Files/BoatRaceHost/BoatRaceHost/bin/
    Debug/TeamNZ/TeamNZ.dll.
21| LOG: Assembly download was successful. Attempting setup of file:
    C:\Program Files\BoatRaceHost\BoatRaceHost\bin\Debug\TeamNZ\TeamNZ.dll
22| LOG: Entering run-from-source setup phase. 23| LOG: A partially-
specified assembly bind succeeded from the application
    directory. Need to re-apply policy.
24| LOG: Policy not being applied to reference at this time (private, custom,
    partial, or location-based assembly bind).
```

I annotated the log text with line numbers so we can step through this in detail.

Lines 1–2 show whether the attempt to load the assembly succeeded. In error conditions, you can look up the *HRESULT* in the corerror.h file in the .NET Framework SDK to help determine what went wrong. However, the rest of the log explains the failure in detail.

Line 3 shows the directory from which the CLR was loaded. You can use this to determine which version of the CLR was running when this assembly bind was attempted.

Line 4 displays the name of the executable that initiated the assembly load. In our case, the executable is boatracehost.exe.

Line 7 shows the identity of the assembly we are trying to load. In late-bound cases such as this, this is the assembly identity that was passed to the assembly loading APIs. In addition to providing the identity, line 7 tells you whether the reference is partial or fully specified. This particular reference is partial. It was initiated with a simple call to *Assembly.Load* such as this:

```
Assembly a = Assembly.Load("TeamNZ");
```

Line 8 displays the *ApplicationBase* directory for the application domain in which the assembly load was initiated.

Lines 9–12 show some of the application domain properties that can affect how assemblies are loaded. These properties are covered in Chapter 6.

Line 13 gives the name of the assembly from which this assembly load was made. This information is useful for debugging in cases in which you might make the same attempt to load an assembly in several places throughout your application.

Lines 14–16 show the CLR attempting to find the configuration file associated with the application domain making the request. As described, this configuration file is consulted both for version policy information and for codebase locations.

Line 17 gives the location of the administrator configuration file. Again, this file can contain either version policy or codebase information.

Line 18 states that version policy is not being applied to this reference. In our case, version policy isn't being applied because we have a partial reference. I discuss the output generated when resolving a fully qualified reference to a strong-named assembly in a bit. Version policy gets applied in that example.

Lines 19–22 show how the CLR probes for the assembly in the *ApplicationBase* directory. In this example, you can see that the first attempt to find the assembly failed, but the second one succeeded. The statement "Entering run-from-source setup phase" means that the CLR is loading the assembly directly from its location on disk. In contrast, if the assembly were located on an HTTP server, it would have to be downloaded first before it could be loaded.

Lines 23–24 state that the assembly was loaded from the *ApplicationBase* and that version policy is not being applied. In our case, version policy isn't being applied because the assembly that was found has a weak name. If we had happened to load a strong-named assembly from the *ApplicationBase*, the CLR would look at the identity of the assembly that was loaded and go back and reapply version policy to determine whether a different version of the assembly should be loaded. If so, it would start the process of finding the assembly over again with the new reference.

You will see two primary differences in the log when you load a strong-named assembly—version policy is applied to the reference, and the CLR looks in the GAC as shown in the following output from fuslogvw.exe:

```
0| *** Assembly Binder Log Entry  (4/4/2004 @ 12:27:26 PM) ***
1| The operation was successful.
2| Bind result: hr = 0x0. The operation completed successfully.
3| Assembly manager loaded from:
   C:\WINDOWS\Microsoft.NET\Framework\v2.0.40301\mscorwks.dll
4| Running under executable
   C:\Program Files\BoatRaceHost\BoatRaceHost\bin\Debug\BoatRaceHost.exe
5| --- A detailed error log follows.
6| === Pre-bind state information ===
7| LOG: DisplayName = Alingi, Version=5.0.0.0, Culture=neutral,
   PublicKeyToken=ae4cc5eda5032777
   (Fully specified)
8| LOG: Appbase = file:///C:/Program Files/BoatRaceHost/BoatRaceHost/bin/Debug/
9| LOG: Initial PrivatePath = NULL
10| LOG: Dynamic Base = NULL
11| LOG: Cache Base = NULL
12| LOG: AppName = BoatRaceHost.exe
13| Calling assembly : BoatRaceHost, Version=1.0.1555.20566, Culture=neutral,
   PublicKeyToken=null.
===
14| LOG: Attempting application configuration file download.
15| LOG: Download of application configuration file was attempted from
    file:///C:/Program Files/BoatRaceHost/BoatRaceHost/bin/
    Debug/BoatRaceHost.exe.config.
16| LOG: Application configuration file does not exist.
17| LOG: Using machine configuration file from
    C:\WINDOWS\Microsoft.NET\Framework\v2.0.40301\config\machine.config.
18| LOG: No redirect found in host configuration file.
19| LOG: Machine configuration policy file redirect found: 5.0.0.0 redirected
    to 6.0.0.0.
20| LOG: Post-policy reference: Alingi, Version=6.0.0.0, Culture=neutral,
    PublicKeyToken=ae4cc5eda5032777
21| LOG: Found assembly by looking in the GAC.
```

In this example, I used the .NET Framework Configuration tool to specify machine-level version policy to redirect the version of the assembly I'm referencing from 5.0.0.0 to 6.0.0.0. The differences between this assembly load and the previous one are shown in lines 7, 19, 20, and 21.

Line 7 shows that the reference is fully specified. Values are supplied for all four parts of the assembly's name.

Line 19 shows that the CLR found my version policy statement in the machine configuration file.

Line 20 shows my reference after policy has been applied. Notice that the CLR is now looking for version 6.0.0.0 of Alingi.

Line 21 shows that the assembly was found in the GAC.

As you can see, stepping through the logs generated by fuslogvw.exe removes the mystery behind how the CLR locates assemblies. Fuslogvw.exe has several other options I haven't discussed here. See the .NET Framework SDK documentation for more details.

Common Assembly Loading Exceptions

Failures to load assemblies typically show up in your application as one of three types of exceptions:

- **System.IO.FileNotFoundException**   The *FileNotFoundException* is thrown when the assembly you specify in your reference cannot be found by the CLR.

- **System.IO.FileLoadException**   As discussed earlier in this chapter, the *FileLoadException* is thrown when the CLR encounters an error while parsing the assembly name string you passed to one of the assembly loading APIs. This exception is also thrown when the CLR finds an assembly to load, but the assembly it finds doesn't match all of the criteria specified in the reference. This scenario occurs most often when resolving partial references to strong-named assemblies located in the *ApplicatonBase* directory structure. For example, given the following reference:

```
Assembly a = Assembly.Load( Alingi, PublicKeyToken=45d39a21bc3ff098 );
```

the CLR will load the first file named alingi.dll it finds in the *ApplicationBase* directory structure. If the assembly it loads has a public key other than the one specified by the *PublicKeyToken* value in the reference, the CLR will throw a *FileLoadException* stating that the assembly it found doesn't match the reference.

> **Note**   The GAC is not searched in this case because the reference is partial. I explain more about how the CLR resolves partial references such as this later in the chapter (see "Partially Specified Assembly References").

- **System.BadImageFormatException**   If the CLR finds a file to load, but the file is not a managed code assembly, a *BadImageFormatException* is thrown. This doesn't happen often, but could occur if you have a native code file in your *ApplicationBase* directory structure with a filename matching that of an assembly you are referencing. More commonly, this exception occurs when loading an assembly by a filename as discussed later in the "Loading Assemblies by Filename" section.

All three exceptions have a string property called *FusionLog* that contains the text of a log file like those you viewed earlier in the discussion of fuslogvw.exe. In this way, you get the diagnostic information about why your call to the assembly loading APIs failed without having to enable logging using the fuslogvw.exe user interface.

Partially Specified Assembly References

As described, only the assembly's friendly name is required when you're using late-bound references. Values for the public key token, version, and culture can be omitted. Such partially specified assembly references are convenient to use, especially when your intent is to load weakly named assemblies, regardless of version, from your application directory. To do so, all you need to do is called *Assembly.Load* with the assembly's friendly name as I've done several times throughout this chapter:

```
Assembly a = Assembly.Load( TeamNZ );
```

However, a few complexities might cause you to load an assembly unintentionally. As always, you can use the fuslogvw.exe tool to find out exactly what's going on.

The following points summarize how the CLR treats a partially specified reference:

- A partially specified reference always causes the *ApplicationBase* directory structure to be searched first. Searching never starts with the GAC. However, if a strong-named assembly is found in the *ApplicationBase* as a result of a partial reference, the CLR opens the file and extracts the strong-named assembly's full identity. That identity then essentially is treated as a fully specified reference in that the CLR follows all the steps described earlier when looking for a strongly named assembly. Specifically, the CLR will evaluate version policy, look back in the GAC, and so on. If no policy is found, and the assembly is not found in the GAC, the file from the *ApplicationBase* is loaded. This is another example of how the CLR prefers to load an assembly from the GAC if possible.

- If a public key token is specified in addition to the assembly's friendly name, the value you specify is checked against any assemblies found in the *ApplicationBase* directory structure. If the keys don't match, the CLR throws a *FileLoadException* stating that the identity of the assembly found didn't match the reference.

- If a version is specified in addition to the assembly's friendly name, the behavior is different depending on whether the assembly found in the *ApplicationBase* has a strong name or a weak name. If the assembly has a strong name, the version number in the reference must match that of the assembly that is loaded. If not, a *FileLoadException* is thrown. If the assembly that is found has a weak name, the version number is not checked—the assembly is loaded regardless of version.

Loading Assemblies by Filename

At first glance, you might expect that loading an assembly by providing a filename would be much more straightforward than loading by assembly name. After all, instead of going through the steps to resolve the reference described earlier, the CLR could just directly load the file you supply. Unfortunately, things aren't as simple as they seem. Although several APIs in the .NET Framework allow you to load an assembly by filename, none are guaranteed to load exactly the file you specify. There are two reasons for this. First, all strong-named assemblies loaded by filename are subject to version policy. This means that once the file is loaded, the CLR extracts its identity, looks to see whether any version policy applies to that identity, and if so, tries to load the new redirected version. The second reason you might get a different file than the one you specified is because the CLR has a set of binding rules it uses to force an application's behavior to be deterministic regardless of the order in which its early-bound references are loaded. It's not obvious how this requirement relates to loading assemblies dynamically by filename, so I describe this in detail.

You can use several APIs to load an assembly by filename dynamically, including the following:

- *System.Reflection.Assembly.LoadFrom*
- *System.AppDomain.CreateInstanceFrom*
- *System.AppDomain.CreateInstanceFromAndUnwrap*
- *System.Activator.CreateInstanceFrom*
- *System.Reflection.Assembly.LoadFile*

These APIs can be grouped into two categories. *Assembly.LoadFrom*, *AppDomain.CreateInstanceFrom(AndUnwrap)*, and *Activator.CreateInstanceFrom* all behave the same with respect to how assemblies are loaded. However, *Assembly.LoadFile* works differently. Historically speaking, *Assembly.LoadFrom* and its relatives were created first and shipped in the initial version of the .NET Framework (1.0). *Assembly.LoadFile* was introduced in .NET Framework 1.1 in an attempt to make loading by filename easier. However, the behavior of this API has now changed in .NET Framework 2.0, and its use is being discouraged. For that reason, this section focuses primarily on the *Assembly.LoadFrom* APIs.

> **Note** From here on, all descriptions of *Assembly.LoadFrom* also apply to *AppDomain.CreateInstanceFrom(AndUnwrap)* and *Activator.CreateInstanceFrom*.

Subtleties of *Assembly.LoadFrom*

I mentioned earlier that the CLR makes sure applications behave deterministically regardless of the order in which their dependencies are loaded. To provide this guarantee, the CLR must ensure that assemblies loaded dynamically by filename do not conflict with the assemblies the application has referenced statically. Take a look at an example to better understand how these rules work and how they might affect you as the author of an extensible application.

The .NET Framework SDK contains a tool called regasm.exe. Regasm.exe takes an assembly as input and creates a set of registry keys that allow the public types in that assembly to be created from COM. What makes regasm.exe interesting for our example is not this core functionality, but rather the fact that it takes the filename of an assembly and loads it dynamically using *Assembly.LoadFrom*. You can expect to encounter this same sort of scenario in an extensible application—it's entirely possible that your extensibility model involves obtaining the filenames of the add-in assemblies you'd like to load into your application domains.

Regasm.exe depends on a utility assembly called regcode.dll, which, for the purposes of this example, has a weak name and is installed in the same directory as regasm.exe.

```
c:\regasm
   \Regasm.exe
   \Regcode.dll
```

The dependency between these two assemblies is specified at compile time, so regasm.exe has an early-bound reference to regcode.dll recorded in its assembly manifest. Now say that a user invokes regasm.exe and passes in the filename to a completely different assembly that is coincidentally also called regcode.dll:

```
c:\regasm\regasm.exe c:\temp\regcode.dll
```

If the regcode.dll in c:\temp were substituted for the "real" regcode.dll in the application directory, regasm.exe wouldn't run if for no other reason than the types it expects to find in regcode.dll wouldn't exist.

To solve this problem, the CLR isolates assemblies loaded using *Assembly*.LoadFrom from those that are referenced statically by the application by using a concept called *binding contexts*. Every application domain maintains two load contexts, or lists of loaded assemblies. One context, called the *load context*, contains those assemblies referenced statically by the application. The other context, the *loadfrom context*, contains those assemblies loaded dynamically given a filename. In our case, the regcode.dll from the *ApplicationBase* is loaded into the load context, and the regcode.dll that was loaded dynamically from c:\temp is placed in the loadfrom context as shown in Figure 7-9. Notice also that the application also has some static dependencies on the .NET Framework assemblies; thus, they are loaded in the load context as well.

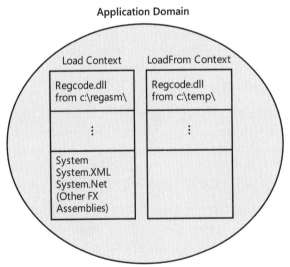

Figure 7-9 The CLR maintains a load context and a loadfrom context in every application domain.

LoadFrom's Second Bind

So far, I've said that all assemblies referenced statically by the application are placed in the load context and all assemblies loaded dynamically by filename are placed in the loadfrom context. There is one exception to this rule: if the assembly you are loading by filename would have been found were it referenced statically, that assembly is placed in the load context instead of the loadfrom context. For an assembly to be placed in the load context in this scenario, not only must it have the same identity as the assembly you are loading by filename, but it must be at the same location on disk. In other words, it must be *exactly* the same file.

This behavior is implemented by the CLR with what is known as *LoadFrom's second bind*. It works like this: when you load a file using *LoadFrom*, the CLR opens the file, extracts its identity, and attempts to find an assembly that matches that identity through using the normal assembly resolution steps. If it finds a file, and the pathname matches the assembly loaded using *LoadFrom*, the CLR places that assembly in the load context instead of the loadfrom context. If the filenames are different, or if an assembly of that identity cannot be found, the assembly you loaded using *LoadFrom* is placed in the loadfrom context. You can see this behavior by looking at the output generated by fuslogvw.exe when *LoadFrom* is called. Let's look at a specific example. Consider a scenario in which our boatracehost.exe loads add-in assemblies by filename using *Assembly.LoadFrom*. We can see both how the CLR treats filename-based loads in general and the second bind specifically by looking at the following log that was generated after calling *Assembly.Load* with a filename of c:\temp\alingi.dll:

```
0| *** Assembly Binder Log Entry  (4/8/2004 @ 8:46:58 AM) ***
1| The operation was successful.
2| Bind result: hr = 0x0. The operation completed successfully.
3| Assembly manager loaded from:
    C:\WINDOWS\Microsoft.NET\Framework\v2.0.40301\mscorwks.dll
4| Running under executable
    C:\Program Files\BoatRaceHost\BoatRaceHost\bin\Debug\BoatRaceHost.exe
--- A detailed error log follows.

=== Pre-bind state information ===
5| LOG: Where-ref bind. Location = c:\temp\Alingi.dll
6| LOG: Appbase = file:///C:/Program Files/BoatRaceHost/BoatRaceHost/bin/Debug/
7| LOG: Initial PrivatePath = NULL
8| LOG: Dynamic Base = NULL
9| LOG: Cache Base = NULL
10| LOG: AppName = BoatRaceHost.exe
11| Calling assembly : (Unknown).
===
12| WRN: Native image will not be probed in LoadFrom context. Native image will
    only be probed in default load context, like with Assembly.Load().
13| LOG: Attempting application configuration file download.
14| LOG: Download of application configuration file was attempted from
    file:///C:/Program Files/BoatRaceHost/BoatRaceHost/bin/
    Debug/BoatRaceHost.exe.config.
15| LOG: Application configuration file does not exist.
16| LOG: Using machine configuration file from
    C:\WINDOWS\Microsoft.NET\Framework\v2.0.40301\config\machine.config.
17| LOG: Attempting download of new URL file:///c:/temp/Alingi.dll.
```

```
18| LOG: Assembly download was successful. Attempting setup of file:
    c:\temp\Alingi.dll
19| LOG: Entering run-from-source setup phase.
20| LOG: Re-apply policy for where-ref bind.
21| LOG: No redirect found in host configuration file.
22| LOG: Post-policy reference: Alingi, Version=5.0.0.0, Culture=neutral,
    PublicKeyToken=ae4cc5eda5032777
23| LOG: GAC Lookup was unsuccessful.
24| LOG: Where-ref bind Codebase does not match what is found in default
    context.
```

The following lines show us what we're looking for:

- *Line 5* indicates the assembly reference was made by filename, not by assembly name. The term *where-ref* comes from the fact that the bind was initiated by telling the CLR where the assembly is. You see this term from time to time throughout these logs.

- *Lines 17–19* show that the CLR succeeded in finding the file at c:\temp\alingi.dll.

- *Lines 21–22* show the beginning of the second bind. In these lines, the CLR extracts the identity from the file just loaded and evaluates version policy. Because no policy was found, the identity of the assembly it looks for is that of the file just loaded. In this case, that's *Alingi, Version=5.0.0.0, Culture=neutral, PublicKeyToken=ae4cc5eda5032777*.

- *Line 23* shows the CLR trying to find the assembly through its normal means. Because the assembly loaded by filename has a strong name, the CLR looks for it in the GAC.

- *Line 24* states that either the second bind didn't find the assembly or, if it did, the assembly it found was at a different location than the one loaded by filename. As a result, the assembly at c:\temp\alingi.dll is placed in the loadfrom context.

In practice, it's not too likely that *LoadFrom*'s second bind will cause you trouble, although I've definitely seen people run into this. When it does happen, the result is usually confusion over type identity as I explain in the next section.

Binding Contexts and Type Identity

I've discussed how the CLR uses binding contexts to separate an application's early-bound dependencies from those loaded dynamically by filename. However, to make this isolation complete, the CLR must also make sure that types of the same name from the different binding contexts are not mistaken for each other. The enforcement of this isolation effectively means that you cannot perform certain operations, such as casting, between types originating in different binding contexts. In some cases, this can lead to errors when you really expect that an operation involving two types should work. As an example, consider what would happen if regasm.exe attempted to cast an instance of a type in the loadfrom context to an instance in the load context as shown in the following code:

```
Assembly loadFromAssembly = Assembly.LoadFrom(@"c:\temp\Regcode.dll");
Object loadFromInstance =
    loadFromAssembly.CreateInstance("Regcode.UtilClass");
  Regcode.UtilClass loadInstance = (Regcode.UtilClass)loadFromInstance; //FAIL!
```

In this case, the type cast from the variable *loadFromInstance* to the variable *loadInstance* would fail. The variable *loadFromInstance* holds an instance of an object from the loadfrom context because the instance is created from an assembly loaded using *LoadFrom*. The variable *loadInstance* comes from the early-bound reference to regcode.dll because its declaration relies on the compiler being able to find the definition of *Regcode.UtilClass* at compile time.

If you see errors such as these in cases where you think it should work based on the source code, be suspicious of different type identities caused by assemblies in different binding contexts.

Loading Multiple Files with the Same Name

At this point, you should be getting a feel for the subtle complexities of the *Assembly.LoadFrom* API. You've seen cases in which the assembly you loaded can end up in the wrong binding context, causing errors in type operations, and how *LoadFrom's* second bind can cause you to load an assembly with a completely different identity than the one you pointed to using a filename. In addition, in one more scenario you might end up loading an assembly other than the one you intend: if you load two assemblies with the same weak name from different locations, only one of them is loaded. This happens because the CLR allows only one assembly with a given weak name in the loadfrom context. Take a look at the following code, which loads two assemblies with the same weak name using *LoadFrom*:

```
Assembly alingiA = Assembly.LoadFrom(@ c:\addins\Alingi.dll );
Assembly alingiB = Assembly.LoadFrom(
   @ c:\program files\boatracehost\common\Alingi.dll");
```

When the first line is executed, the CLR loads the assembly at c:\addins\alingi.dll into the loadfrom context. When executing the second line, the CLR looks in the loadfrom context and sees that an assembly with the simple name *Alingi* is already loaded. Instead of loading the assembly at c:\program files\boatracehost\common\alingi.dll, the CLR simply returns the existing assembly. As a result, the variables *alingiA* and *alingiB* will both contain the assembly from c:\temp\alingi–the assembly at c:\program files\boatracehost\common\alingi will never be loaded.

The Loadfrom Context and Dependencies

Earlier in this chapter and in Chapter 6, I describe how the CLR looks for weakly named assemblies only within the *ApplicationBase* directory structure of the referencing application. As with many things, there is an exception to this rule. When you load an assembly with *LoadFrom*, the CLR adds the directory from which that assembly came to the list of directories in which it probes for static dependencies. For example, say that alingi.dll has an early-bound dependency on an assembly in spars.dll. Furthermore, boatracehost.exe loads alingi.dll from c:\temp using *Assembly.LoadFrom*. In this case, you can deploy spars.dll to c:\temp, and the CLR will find it, even though it is not located in boatracehost.exe's *ApplicationBase* directory. This feature makes it convenient to deploy an add-in and all of its dependencies to the same directory. However, be aware that this directory is searched last. Specifically, the CLR looks in the GAC (if the assembly has a strong name) and in the *ApplicationBase* directory before consulting the directory from which the referring assembly was loaded. As a result, if the CLR happens to find an assembly that satisfies the reference to spars.dll (in this case) in any other location, that DLL would be loaded instead of the one in c:\temp.

> **Note**   In an effort to reduce some of the confusion around using *Assembly.LoadFrom*, the CLR introduced a new API called *Assembly.LoadFile* in .NET Framework 1.1. The intent of this API was to load the exact file specified as opposed to issuing a second bind and doing identity checks that can cause an assembly other than the intended one to be loaded. Although *Load-File* did work this way in .NET Framework 1.1, its behavior has been changed in .NET Framework 2.0 to be subject to version policy and rebinding just as *LoadFrom* is. As a result, the CLR team is discouraging its use. I expect *LoadFile* to be removed in a future version of the .NET Framework.

The *ReflectionOnly* APIs

The 2.0 version of the .NET Framework introduces a new set of APIs called the *ReflectionOnly* APIs. I mention them here only because the *ReflectionOnly* APIs provide a way to load an assembly by filename without any of the subtleties inherent in *Assembly.LoadFrom*. That is, you can use the *ReflectionOnly* APIs to load exactly the file you want—no policy is applied, no second bind occurs, and so on. Although this might sound like exactly what you're looking for, the scenarios for which the *ReflectionOnly* APIs were built do not include the ability to load and execute assemblies dynamically. Specifically, the *ReflectionOnly* APIs enable you only to discover information about an assembly, they do not enable you to execute any code in that assembly. For this reason, they will not help you if you need to load and execute add-ins in an extensible application. For this reason, I don't discuss them here. For more information, see the documentation for the following methods in the .NET Framework SDK guide:

- *Assembly.ReflectionOnly*
- *Assembly.ReflectionOnlyLoad*
- *Assembly.ReflectionOnlyLoadFrom*
- *AppDomain.ReflectionOnlyGetAssemblies*
- *AppDomain.ApplyPolicy*
- *Type.ReflectionOnlyGetType*

Loading Assemblies Using *ICLRRuntimeHost*

In addition to the managed assembly loading APIs discussed so far, the CLR provides a method that enables you to load an assembly and execute one of its methods using the unmanaged CLR hosting interfaces. This method, named *ICLRRuntimeHost::ExecuteInDefaultAppDomain*, is useful when you need to use the hosting interfaces to customize some aspect of the CLR, but don't have a need to write any managed code as part of your host. These scenarios aren't very common, but I could imagine needing to write a host that customizes how the CLR loads domain-neutral code using *IHostControl* or that enforces specific programming model constraints using *ICLRHostProtectionManager*, for example. In these scenarios, the customizations are available only through the CLR hosting interfaces. If these are the only customizations you need to make, and if your only other requirement is to be able to execute a managed method in the default application domain, *ExecuteInDefaultAppDomain* can satisfy your needs.

ExecuteInDefaultAppDomain loads an assembly given a filename. In addition to supplying the path to the assembly you want to load, you must supply the name of the method you want to execute and the name of the type that method is in. The method you supply must have a specific signature—it must be static, return an *int*, and have one string argument:

```
static int MethodName(string argument)
```

If you attempt to call a method with a signature other this, *ExecuteInDefaultAppDomain* returns with an *HRESULT* of 0x80131513 (*COR_E_MISSINGMETHOD*). The parameters to *ExecuteInDefaultAppDomain* are shown in Table 7-2.

Table 7-2   Parameters to *ICLRRuntimeHost::ExecuteInDefaultAppDomain*

Parameter	Description
pwzAssemblyPath	[in] The fully qualified path to the file containing the manifest of the assembly you'd like to load.
pwzTypeName	[in] The name of the type containing the method to execute. Remember to fully qualify the type name with the namespace the type is in.
pwzMethodName	[in] The name of the method to execute. Remember, this method must be static, return an *int*, and take a single string argument.
pwzArgument	[in] The argument to the method. The CLR imposes no format on this argument—it is completely up to you as the writer of the host.
pReturnValue	[out] The value returned from the method that was executed.

Listing 7-1 shows a simple CLR host that uses *ExecuteInDefaultAppDomain* to execute a method in an assembly. In this example, I call *CorBindToRuntimeEx* to initialize the CLR and to get a pointer to the *ICLRRuntimeHost* interface. Given that pointer, I call *ExecuteInDefault-AppDomain*, passing in the path of the assembly to load along with the name of the method to execute.

Listing 7-1   ExecApp.cpp

```
#include "stdafx.h"
#include <mscoree.h>

int main(int argc, wchar_t* argv[])
{
   ICLRRuntimeHost *pCLR = NULL;
   // initialize the CLR
   HRESULT hr = CorBindToRuntimeEx(
      L"v2.0.41013",
      L"wks",
      NULL,
```

```
        CLSID_CLRRuntimeHost,
        IID_ICLRRuntimeHost,
        (PVOID*) &pCLR);

   assert(SUCCEEDED(hr));

   // Any specific CLR customizations would be done here.

   // Start the CLR
   hr = pCLR->Start();
   assert(SUCCEEDED(hr));

   // Execute the application.
   DWORD retVal = 0;
   hr = pCLR->ExecuteInDefaultAppDomain(L"RealEstate.exe",
                                        L"RealEstate.Program",
                                        L"Start",
                                        NULL,
                                        &retVal);
   assert(SUCCEEDED(hr));

   return retVal; }
```

Capturing Assembly Load Events

The *System.AppDomain* class has an event called *AssemblyLoad* that is raised whenever an assembly is loaded into an application domain. *AssemblyLoad* provides notification when an assembly is loaded, but it doesn't allow you to affect how the assembly is loaded in any way.

> **Note**   Several events do let you change how the assembly is loaded. These events, including *AppDomain.AssemblyResolve*, are discussed in detail in Chapter 8.

One scenario in which I find the *AssemblyLoad* event useful is in debugging. Earlier in the chapter I presented some examples that show how easy it is to load an assembly inadvertently into a different application domain than the one you intended. I've often used the *AssemblyLoadEvent* to trace all assemblies that get loaded into a process to help diagnose such problems.

To register for the *AssemblyLoad* event, you supply a delegate of type *AssemblyLoadEvent-Handler*. Instances of *AssemblyLoadEventHandler* have the *sender* and *args* parameters required by the .NET Framework event model as shown in the following declaration:

```
public delegate void AssemblyLoadEventHandler(Object sender,
                    AssemblyLoadEventArgs args);
```

The arguments passed to handlers of *AssemblyLoad* are of type *AssemblyLoadEventArgs*. The *LoadedAssembly* property of *AssemblyLoadEventArgs* identifies the assembly that has just been loaded.

The *InitializeNewDomain* method of your *AppDomainManager* class is a convenient place to register your event handler for the *AssemblyLoad* event. Recall from Chapter 6 that the CLR calls *InitializeNewDomain* from within each new application domain that is created. Placing your registration code here is a more foolproof way to make sure your handler is attached to all application domains than searching through your code looking for each call to *AppDomain.CreateDomain* is. The following example creates a new instance of *AssemblyLoadEventHandler* and registers it for the *AssemblyLoad* event within *InitializeNewDomain*. The event handler traces both the identity of the assembly and the friendly name of the application domain into which the assembly was loaded:

```
public class BoatRaceDomainManager : AppDomainManager, IBoatRaceDomainManager
{

// The event handler for AssemblyLoad
static void BoatRaceAssemblyLoadEventHandler(object sender,
 AssemblyLoadEventArgs args)
{   Trace.WriteLine("Assembly " + args.LoadedAssembly.FullName +
      " was loaded into " + AppDomain.CurrentDomain.FriendlyName);
}


public override void InitializeNewDomain(AppDomainSetup appDomainInfo)
{
   // Register a new instance of AssemblyLoadEventHandler to receive the
   // AssemblyLoad event.   AppDomain.CurrentDomain.AssemblyLoad += new
     AssemblyLoadEventHandler(BoatRaceAssemblyLoadEventHandler);
   }
}
```

Versioning Considerations for Extensible Applications

At the time of this writing, three major versions of the .NET Framework have been released: versions 1.0, 1.1, and 2.0. If you're writing an extensible application that dynamically loads add-ins, it's likely you'll encounter an add-in built with a different version of the .NET Framework than your application is. If the add-in was built with an older version of the .NET Framework than your application was, it's likely that everything will work fine because of the CLR's commitment to backward compatibility. However, we all know that backward compatibility cannot be completely guaranteed. As a result, it's useful to know how the CLR behaves in a process containing assemblies built with multiple versions of the .NET Framework. As with the other topics discussed in this chapter, dynamic, extensible applications are likely to encounter a greater range of versioning scenarios than applications in which all dependencies are known when the application is compiled. There are five main points to keep in mind when considering how add-ins built with various versions of the CLR will affect your extensible application:

- In general, it's not a good idea to try to load an add-in built with a newer version of the CLR than the version used to build your application. In fact, the CLR prevents you from loading an assembly built with .NET Framework 2.0 into a process that is running either .NET Framework 1.0 or .NET Framework 1.1. You can, however, load an assembly built with .NET Framework 1.1 into a process running .NET Framework 1.0, although it is not recommended.

■ Loading an add-in built with a version of the CLR older than the version used to build your application is generally OK. As described, the CLR's commitment to backward compatibility means the add-in has a pretty good chance of working. If a particular add-in doesn't work in this scenario, it is sometimes possible to fix the problem by including version policy statements in your application's configuration file. I describe this in more detail later in the chapter when I discuss overriding .NET Framework unification in the section "Overriding Unification."

■ As the author of the extensible application, you get to pick which version of the CLR is loaded into your process. The add-ins do not have a say in which version of the CLR is selected.

■ Once you've selected a version of the CLR to load into the process, the CLR automatically enforces that a matching set of .NET Framework assemblies comes with it. This concept, called .NET Framework unification, ensures that a consistent set of .NET Framework assemblies is loaded into the process. I talk about .NET Framework unification later in this chapter in the section "Microsoft .NET Framework Unification."

■ If .NET Framework unification introduces an assembly into your process that causes something to stop working, you can use your application configuration file to override the CLR's choice of assembly version.

The rest of this section expands on these five points. Before I go on, however, look at a few .NET Framework APIs that are useful when dealing with versioning in extensible applications.

Determining Which Version of the CLR Was Used to Build an Assembly

As described in Chapter 4, every assembly contains information about the version of the .NET Framework it was compiled with. Being able to determine which version of the .NET Framework was used to build a particular add-in can be useful, especially if you begin to see problems in your application that you believe are version related. The version of the .NET Framework used to build an assembly can be obtained using the *ImageRuntimeVersion* property on *System.Reflection.Assembly*. Keep in mind, however, that the version number this property returns is the CLR version number, not the version number of the .NET Framework itself. For example, *Assembly.ImageRuntimeVersion* returns the string "v1.1.4322" for an assembly built with .NET Framework 1.1. Table 7-3 shows the CLR versions and the corresponding versions of the .NET Framework. Refer to Chapter 4 for a more complete description of how these version numbers relate.

Table 7-3   How CLR Version Numbers Map to .NET Framework Versions

CLR Version	.NET Framework Version
v1.0.3705	.NET Framework 1.0
v1.1.4322	.NET Framework 1.1
v2.0.41013	.NET Framework 2.0

There is one caveat when using the *ImageRuntimeVersion* property. The fact that *ImageRuntime-Version* is a member of the *Assembly* class means that the CLR must load the assembly for which you'd like version information into the process before you can access the property. If you then decide that you don't want to use the assembly, you can't unload it without unloading the application domain containing the assembly. If you need to be able to determine which version of the CLR was used to build an assembly without having to load it, you need to use an unmanaged API. The CLR startup shim, mscoree.dll, provides an unmanaged API for exactly this purpose. This API, called *GetFileVersion*, takes an assembly's filename and returns the version number used to build that assembly in a buffer. Here's the signature for *GetFileVersion* from mscoree.idl in the .NET Framework SDK:

```
STDAPI GetFileVersion(LPCWSTR szFilename,
                      LPWSTR  szBuffer,
                      DWORD   cchBuffer,
                      DWORD*  dwLength)
```

The Extensible Application Chooses the Version

As discussed in Chapter 3, only one version of the CLR can be loaded into a given process. It's up to you, as the author of the extensible application, to decide which version to load. The add-ins that you dynamically load into your process have no say in which version of the CLR is loaded. Furthermore, no infrastructure currently available allows an add-in to express a dependency on a particular version of the CLR.

As discussed in Chapters 3 and 4, it's typically best to load the same version of the CLR that you used to build your application. Refer to those chapters for both the strategies to consider and the mechanics involved in loading the CLR.

At any point you can determine which version of the CLR is loaded into your process using the *Version* property on the *System.Environment* class. This property returns the CLR version, not the .NET Framework version. For example, the value of *System.Environment.Version* for a process running .NET Framework 2.0 is "2.0.41013." Table 7-3 contains the mapping between CLR version numbers and the corresponding versions of the .NET Framework.

Microsoft .NET Framework Unification

When you load an add-in assembly into your process, that assembly contains static references to the versions of the .NET Framework assemblies it was built against. For example, an assembly built with .NET Framework 1.1 has references to the 1.1 versions of *System*, *System.XML*, *System.Data*, and so on. If you load several add-ins into your process, some of which are built with different versions, you'll have references to multiple versions of the .NET Framework assemblies. Figure 7-10 shows a scenario in which an extensible application built against .NET Framework 2.0 has loaded add-ins built against all three versions of the .NET Framework.

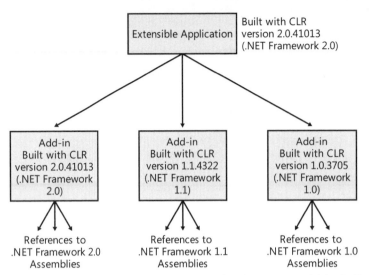

Figure 7-10   An extensible application with references to add-ins built with multiple versions of the .NET Framework

Given this scenario, the question arises as to whether it is preferable to load multiple versions of the .NET Framework assemblies into the same process or redirect the various references to a single version of the .NET Framework assemblies. Clearly, there are arguments for doing it either way. On the one hand, it might be desirable to load the exact version of the .NET Framework assemblies that a given add-in has requested. After all, presumably the add-in was tested against this version; therefore, it has the best chance to work. On the other hand, loading multiple versions of the .NET Framework assemblies into the same process has two complications: one is technical, whereas the other is a matter of logistics. Although it is technically feasible to load multiple versions of the same assembly into a given application domain or process, complications arise if two add-ins built against different versions of the .NET Framework need to communicate by exchanging types. Because the identity of the assembly in which a type is contained is part of that type's identity, a given type from two different versions of the same assembly is considered a different type by the CLR. For example, an *XMLDocument* type from version 2.0.3600 of *System.XML* is a different type than the *XMLDocument* type from version 1.0.3705 of *System.XML*. As a result, the CLR throws an exception if an assembly tries to pass an instance of the 1.0.3705 version of *XMLDocument* to a method on a type expecting a 2.0.3600 version of *XMLDocument*. The amount different add-ins need to communicate with each other clearly varies by scenario, so it might be possible that this particular restriction isn't an issue for you. However, the other complication that arises when multiple versions of the .NET Framework assemblies are loaded simultaneously is related to the consistency between assemblies. From the beginning, the .NET Framework assemblies were built to work as a matched set. Several interdependencies between these assemblies must remain consistent. Also, because mixing and matching these assemblies hasn't been a priority yet, the amount of testing done by Microsoft to support these scenarios has been limited.

As a result of the complexities involved in loading multiple versions of the .NET Framework assemblies into a process or application domain, the default behavior of the CLR is to redirect all references to .NET Framework assemblies to the version of those assemblies that matches the CLR that is loaded into the process. The process of redirecting all references to this matched set is termed .*NET Framework unification*. The result of this unification is shown in Figure 7-11.

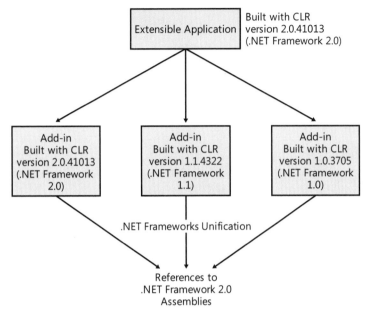

Figure 7-11   The CLR unifies all references to .NET Framework assemblies.

It's important to remember that only references to the .NET Framework assemblies are unified. All other assembly references are resolved as is (subject to version policy, of course). For example, say you load two add-in assemblies that reference different versions of the same shared assembly called *AcmeGridControl*. Because *AcmeGridControl* is not a .NET Framework assembly, references to it will not be unified. Instead, both versions are loaded. The following is a list of those assemblies that are unified by the CLR:

- *mscorlib*
- *System*
- *System.Xml*
- *System.Data*
- *System.Data.OracleClient*
- *System.Runtime.Remoting*
- *System.Windows.Forms*
- *System.Web*

- *System.Drawing*
- *System.Design*
- *System.Runtime.Serialization.Formatters.Soap*
- *System.Drawing.Design*
- *System.EnterpriseServices*
- *System.DirectoryServices*
- *System.Management*
- *System.Messaging*
- *System.Security*
- *System.ServiceProcess*
- *System.Web.Mobile*
- *System.Web.RegularExpressions*
- *System.Web.Services*
- *System.Configuration.Install*
- *Accessibility*
- *CustomMarshalers*
- *cscompmgd*
- *IEExecRemote*
- *IEHost*
- *IIEHost*
- *ISymWrapper*
- *Microsoft.JScript*
- *Microsoft.VisualBasic*
- *Microsoft.VisualBasic.Vsa*
- *Microsoft.VisualC*
- *Microsoft.Vsa*
- *Microsoft.Vsa.Vb.CodeDOMProcessor*
- *Microsoft_VsaVb*
- *mscorcfg*
- *vjswfchtml*
- *vjswfccw*

- *VJSWfcBrowserStubLib*

- *vjswfc*

- *vjslibcw*

- *vjslib*

- *vjscor*

- *VJSharpCodeProvider*

Overriding Unification

If the unification of .NET Framework assembly references causes problems in your scenario, you can override the unification using version policy statements. You shouldn't have to resort to this too often because the CLR's backward compatibility has been pretty good so far. However, it's not inconceivable for you to encounter a compatibility issue that will cause you to want to load a different version of a .NET Framework assembly than the one the CLR selects by default. The best way to override unification is by issuing version policy statements in the configuration file for a particular application domain. This approach is preferable to using machine-wide policy because it affects only your application domain(s), not every process on the machine (also, it's often the case that the machine configuration file is secured, so you can't write to it anyway unless you're an administrator).

To see how this works, consider an example in which a particular add-in that you must load has a strict dependency on the version of *System.XML* that shipped with version 1.1 of the .NET Framework, but you are running .NET Framework 2.0 in your process. To redirect the reference to *System.XML* from .NET Framework 2.0 back down to .NET Framework 1.1, you'd author a configuration file that looks like this:

```xml
<?xml version="1.0"?>
<configuration>
  <runtime>
    <assemblyBinding xmlns="urn:schemas-microsoft-com:asm.v1">
      <dependentAssembly>
        <assemblyIdentity name="System.Xml"
          publicKeyToken="b77a5c561934e089" />
        <bindingRedirect oldVersion="0.0.0.0-2.0.3600"
          newVersion="1.1.5000" />
      </dependentAssembly>
    </assemblyBinding>
  </runtime>
</configuration>
```

This configuration file causes version 1.1.5000 of *System.XML* (the version that shipped in .NET Framework 1.1) to be loaded regardless of which version is referenced. Given this configuration file, you have the choice of how widely you'd like to apply this redirection. It can be that you want 1.1.5000 to be the only version of *System.XML* that is loaded in your process. In this case, you'd assign your configuration file to every application domain you create using the

ConfigurationFile property of *AppDomainSetup* as described in Chapter 6. You might also choose to load *System.XML* version 1.1.5000 only into the application domain in which the add-in that requires it is running. If so, add-ins in other application domains that reference *System.XML* will get the unified version (the version that ships with .NET Framework 2.0).

Note that it is also possible to use version policy statements to cause all references to the .NET Framework assemblies to be redirected for a particular application domain. If you start by redirecting one reference, you might find inconsistencies that cause you to want to redirect the entire set of references to .NET Framework assemblies. In this way, you can cause two parallel stacks of .NET Framework assemblies to be loaded into the same process, yet be isolated from each other using application domain boundaries as shown in Figure 7-12.

> **Note** Even though *mscorlib* is in the set of unified assemblies, you cannot use a *bindingRedirect* statement (or any other mechanism) to override the unification of *mscorlib*. The version of *mscorlib* to load is chosen by the CLR when the process starts and cannot be changed.

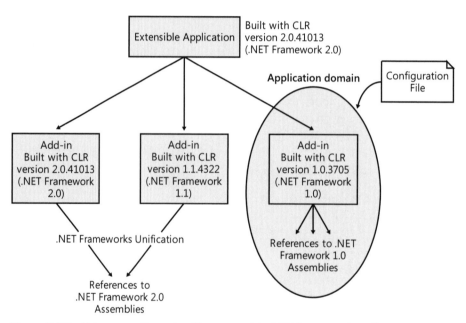

Figure 7-12 Using a configuration file to override .NET Framework unification

Summary

The dynamic nature of extensible applications makes loading assemblies more complicated than for applications in which all dependencies are statically referenced when the application is compiled. There are two reasons for this. First, the add-in assemblies that are added to the application must be loaded in a late-bound fashion. Loading assemblies on the fly like this requires the use of a set of methods in the .NET Framework called the assembly loading APIs. These APIs let you reference an assembly by providing either its name or the name of the file on disk that contains the assembly's manifest. When using the assembly loading APIs, take care to make sure you are calling them from the application domain in which you'd like the assembly to be loaded. Otherwise, you often end up loading an assembly into an application domain that you didn't intend to. The fuslogvw.exe utility from the .NET Framework SDK is a great tool not only to track down assembly loading failures, but also to understand how the process of loading assemblies works in general.

The other reason that loading assemblies in extensible applications can get complicated is the need to understand how assemblies built with different versions of the CLR interact in the same process. As the author of the extensible application, you get to decide which version of the CLR is loaded in your process. Given that, the CLR will automatically make sure that the versions of the .NET Framework assemblies that are loaded are the ones that were built and tested along with the CLR running in the process. If, for some reason, this default behavior doesn't work in your scenario, you can always override it using a configuration file associated with your application domain.

Chapter 8
Customizing How Assemblies Are Loaded

In Chapter 7, I describe the CLR default behavior for locating and loading assemblies. This default deployment model works well for common application scenarios ranging from rich client executables to Web applications to controls embedded in Web pages. Part of the reason the default deployment model has gained such broad acceptance is that it promotes concepts that address problems (most notably DLL Hell) that were prevalent in the native Microsoft Windows programming model. The CLR encourages a private deployment model that helps keep applications isolated and makes them easier to install, uninstall, and replicate. In addition, the CLR provides a hierarchical version policy system that gives application developers, administrators, and component vendors a say in which version of an assembly is loaded.

Although the characteristics of the default deployment model are positive, the CLR implementation of this model has three fundamental assumptions that sometimes make it difficult to realize these benefits in other application scenarios. First, the CLR assumes that all assemblies are contained in files stored on disk. Assumptions are even made about the extensions of these files in some cases. For example, all dependent assemblies stored in an application's directory must have a .dll extension. Second, the CLR assumes that all assemblies for an application are stored either in the application's base directory, in the global assembly cache (GAC), or at locations identified in the application's configuration file. Finally, the CLR assumes that the hierarchy of version policies applies equally in all scenarios. A prime example of how these built-in assumptions make it hard to adapt the CLR deployment model to a new application environment is Microsoft SQL Server 2005. SQL Server 2005 has some deployment requirements that are at odds with how the CLR works by default. For example, SQL Server stores all assemblies directly in the database—not as individual files in the file system. Second, the level of control over which versions of assemblies get loaded as part of a SQL Server application differs quite dramatically from other scenarios, such as rich client or Web applications. Specifically, SQL Server would like to disable the ability to run a different version of an assembly than the one that was originally installed with the application. This requirement arises from the fact that SQL Server can persist instances of managed objects as data stored in the database. This occurs, for example, if a user defines a database column whose type is a class written in managed code (that is, a user-defined database type, in SQL Server terminology). In these cases, the data is persisted by serializing the object instance directly into the table. If, later, a different version of the type were used to deserialize the object, a mismatch of fields might occur and the type would not load. Similar issues occur if managed objects are used as part of the definition of a database index. If one version of a type is used to create the index and another version is used to read it, there's a chance that the index might be invalid, resulting in dramatically decreased performance. In a production environment that requires a nearly perfect degree of reliability and consistent performance, the chance of failure introduced by loading a new version of an assembly cannot be tolerated. So SQL Server requires that the assemblies defined as part of the application are exactly the ones used when the application is run.

I can imagine many other scenarios in which you'd like to store assemblies somewhere other than in a standard portable executable file (PE file) on disk, search for them in a location the CLR normally wouldn't look, or customize the way the default version policy system works. For example, instead of storing assemblies on disk, you might need to generate assemblies dynamically using the classes in the *System.Reflection.Emit* namespace. You might also want to load assemblies out of a "container" file such as a .cab or a .jar file. Furthermore, you might need to implement a new mechanism for locating assemblies. You can find this useful if you're moving an existing application model from a different platform to Microsoft .NET Framework, for example.

You can take two approaches to customize the CLR default deployment model to accommodate the scenarios I've described. First, you can use some of the events and methods on the *System.AppDomain* and *System.Reflection.Assembly* classes (namely, the *AppDomain.Load(byte[]...), Assembly.Load(byte[]...)* methods, and the *AppDomain.AssemblyResolve()* event). Although this approach enables you to customize the CLR entirely from within managed code, you can control only certain aspects of the assembly loading process. The second way you can customize the default deployment model is to use the CLR hosting APIs to write a host that implements an assembly loading manager. This approach requires you to write unmanaged code and requires more effort, but you can customize the CLR to a much greater extent because you are integrating with the CLR at a much lower level. In fact, the amount of customization available when writing an assembly loading manager is so extensive that you can completely replace the CLR assembly loading implementation. This is the approach that SQL Server has taken to implement its custom deployment model.

The goal of this chapter is to describe these two approaches in enough detail that you can decide which approach best fits your scenario.

The Cocoon Deployment Model

To demonstrate how to customize the CLR default behavior for locating and loading assemblies, I need to introduce a new deployment model in which you change all three of the built-in assumptions discussed earlier. Specifically, you need a model in which the assemblies are stored in a format other than the standard PE file format on disk, are found in places other than in the application's base directory or the global assembly cache, and have different versioning rules. To this end, I introduce a new deployment model called a *cocoon*.[1]

---

1. Thanks to my colleague Jim Hogg for the term *cocoon*.

A cocoon is a new packaging format for applications. A single cocoon file contains all the assemblies needed to run an application (minus the assemblies shipped as part of the .NET Framework). Packaging all of an application's files into one single file simplifies deployment because the application is more self-contained: it can be installed, removed, or copied simply by moving a single file around. Cocoon files are very similar in concept to .cab files. After I describe how cocoon files are structured and built, I'll walk through the steps needed to write a CLR host that runs applications contained in cocoons. In going through this exercise, I discuss the details of how to write an assembly loading manager. Toward the end of the chapter, I write a program that runs cocoons completely in managed code using the events and methods of *System.AppDomain* and *System.Reflection.Assembly*. This second program won't provide the same level of customization as the CLR host does, but it will serve to demonstrate the different capabilities offered by the two approaches.

My implementation of the cocoon deployment model is based on object linking and embedding (OLE) structured storage files. The structured storage technology lends itself particularly well to this scenario because it includes concepts that map directly to directories and files on disk (namely, storages and streams). If you're not familiar with structured storage, or your knowledge is a bit rusty, you can find plenty of documentation on the Microsoft Developer Network (MSDN) or in the platform SDK.

Cocoons are built by a utility I wrote called makecocoon.exe. This utility packages all executable files in the directory from which it's run into a structured storage file with a .cocoon extension. Each file in the directory ends up as a stream in the .cocoon file. The name of the stream is set to the name of the file on disk, minus its file extension.

Makecocoon.exe takes as input the executable containing the entry point for the application and the name of the type within that executable that contains the *main* method. The name of the .cocoon file created by makecocoon.exe is based on the name of the main executable for the application. For example, consider an application called hrtracker that is contained in the directory shown in the following listing:

```
Volume in drive C has no label.
 Volume Serial Number is 18EE-14D2

 Directory of C:\HRTracker

10/03/2003  10:30 AM    <DIR>          .
10/03/2003  10:30 AM    <DIR>          ..
10/01/2003  04:37 PM            50,688 HRTracker.exe
10/01/2003  04:36 PM           122,880 Benefits.dll
09/24/2003  01:56 PM            16,384 Employee.dll
10/01/2003  04:36 PM           453,348 Payroll.dll
               5 File(s)        643,300 bytes
               2 Dir(s)  45,701,091,328 bytes free
```

The following command would create a cocoon file named hrtracker.cocoon:

```
MakeCocoon HRTracker.exe HRTracker.Application
```

Hrtracker.cocoon contains a stream for each assembly as shown in Figure 8-1.

OLE Structured Storage File (.cocoon)

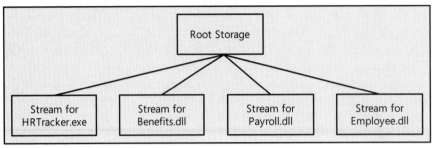

Figure 8-1   A .cocoon file for the HRTracker application

In addition to the streams containing the main executable and its dependent assemblies, each .cocoon file also contains three additional streams. These extra streams contain data that is needed by the programs I write later in the chapter to run executables contained in .cocoon files. The first of these streams contains the name of the type in the main executable that contains the main method. This stream, called _entryPoint, is needed so you know which type to instantiate to run the application contained in the .cocoon file. The need for the other two streams isn't quite as obvious. To understand the role these streams play, I need to introduce the notion of CLR binding identities.

CLR Binding Identities

Recall from Chapter 7 that assemblies can be referenced by strings consisting of the assembly's friendly name and optional values for the public key used to sign the assembly, the assembly's version, and the culture for any resources that the assembly contains. Working with these string-based identities can be problematic for three reasons:

- Parsing these strings can be error prone. As I've shown, these strings must adhere to a specific format to be understood by the CLR. To parse them correctly, you must understand all the rules the CLR enforces on format of the strings.

- Assembly identities evolve over time. For example, .NET Framework version 2.0 of the CLR introduces support for 64-bit processors. As part of this support, the string that identifies an assembly can now specify a dependency on a particular processor architecture. Assemblies can contain native code that depends on either a 64- or 32-bit processor, or the assembly can consist entirely of Microsoft intermediate language (MSIL) code, which is processor independent.

- Determining equality between string-based identities is nearly impossible to get right. As discussed in Chapter 7, the steps taken by the CLR to resolve a reference to an assembly are quite involved. Given a reference to a specific assembly, the CLR can choose to load a different assembly depending on whether you are referencing an assembly with a strong name or a weak name, whether version policy is present, and so on. Attempting to duplicate these rules yourself would be prohibitively difficult. Later in this chapter I write a CLR host that implements an assembly loading manager to customize how the CLR loads assemblies. As you'll see, an assembly loading manager can completely take over the process of loading an assembly–including the steps needed to determine which assembly to load given a reference.

To help alleviate these problems, the CLR hosting interfaces provide a set of methods that make it easy to work with string-based identities. These methods are part of an interface called *ICLRAssemblyIdentityManager*. Given an assembly, *ICLRAssemblyIdentityManager* gives you back a fully qualified string identity in the correct format. These canonical textual strings are what I was referring to earlier as binding identities. The nice thing about binding identities is that you can (and should) treat them as opaque identifiers for assemblies. So, you don't need to parse them or interpret their contents in any way. The methods on *ICLRAssemblyIdentity-Manager* and the methods provided by the interfaces you use as part of an assembly loading manager handle all that for you. In fact, if you ever find yourself looking inside a binding identity, it's likely you're doing something wrong.

The extra streams included in each .cocoon file are needed because the assembly loading manager I write later in the chapter requires the use of binding identities. I use them in two specific places, hence the need for two additional binding identity–related streams in the .cocoon files. The first place I use a binding identity is to load the executable containing the entry point for the application in the cocoon. Remember that one of the goals of writing an assembly loading manager is to force the CLR to call the host to resolve references to assemblies contained in cocoon files. For this to work properly, all assemblies must be referenced by a full identity–the CLR will not call the assembly loading manager for partial references. I've added a stream to the .cocoon file that contains the binding identity (remember, these are fully qualified) for the assembly containing the application's entry point. This stream is called *_exeBindingIdentity*.

I also need to use binding identities when the CLR calls the assembly loading manager to resolve a reference to an assembly. As you'll see, the CLR passes the assembly reference to resolve in the form of a binding identity. You must know which stream in the .cocoon file contains the assembly with the given binding identity. The easiest way to implement this would have been simply to name the streams in the cocoon based on the binding identity of the assembly the stream contains. Unfortunately, OLE structured storage places constraints on how streams can be named, and binding identities violate those constraints. To work around this limitation, I name the assembly streams based on the assembly's friendly name and create an index stream that maps binding identities to the names of the streams containing the assemblies. The name of this mapping stream is called *_index*. The format of the *_index* stream is shown in Figure 8-2.

_index Stream

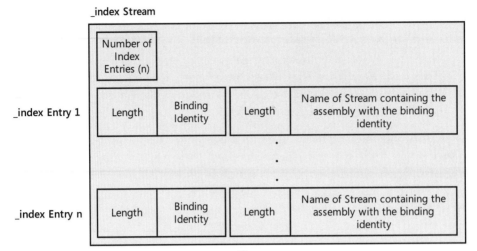

Figure 8-2   The _index stream in a .cocoon file

Now that you understand the need for the additional streams I had to create, take a look at the overall structure of a .cocoon file. To summarize, each .cocoon file has the following streams:

- One stream for each assembly in the directory from which makecocoon.exe is run. These streams are named based on the simple name of the assembly they contain.

- A stream named _entryPoint that identifies the type that contains the application's *main* routine.

- A stream named _exeBindingIdentity that contains the binding identity for the application's .exe file.

- A stream named _index that contains entries that map a given binding identity to the stream within the .cocoon that contains that assembly.

The platform SDK contains a utility called DocFile Viewer that you can use to look at the contents of structured storage files. Figure 8-3 shows the contents of the HRTracker cocoon file using DocFile Viewer.

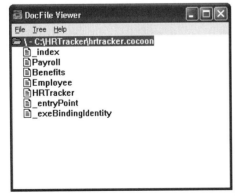

Figure 8-3   A .cocoon file as shown in DocFile Viewer

Obtaining Binding Identities

Now that you've seen the role that binding identities will play in the cocoon scenario, take a look at the steps involved in obtaining these identities. As I mentioned, the *ICLRAssembly-IdentityManager* interface includes methods that return binding identities for a given assembly. In addition to returning binding identities, *ICLRAssemblyIdentityManager* also has methods that help determine the list of an assembly's references, the list of files the CLR will look for when attempting to resolve a reference to an assembly, and so on. The complete list of methods on *ICLRAssemblyIdentityManager* is shown in Table 8-1.

Table 8-1   The Methods on *ICLRAssemblyIdentityManager*

Method Name	Description
GetBindingIdentityFromFile	Returns a binding identity for an assembly given a path to its manifest.
GetBindingIdentityFromStream	Returns a binding identity for an assembly given a stream that contains the assembly.
GetCLRAssemblyReferenceList	Translates string-based assembly references to binding identities. The list of binding identities returned from *GetCLRAssemblyReferenceList* is used in several places throughout the CLR hosting interfaces. For example, you use *GetCLRAssemblyReferenceList* later in this chapter as part of the assembly loading manager implementation. In addition, *GetCLRAssemblyReferenceList* is used in Chapter 9 when I talk about how to load assemblies domain neutral.
GetReferencedAssembliesFromFile	Given the filename of an assembly manifest, this method returns the list of that assembly's references.
GetReferencedAssembliesFromStream	Given a stream containing an assembly, this method returns the list of that assembly's references.
GetProbingAssembliesFromReference	Recall from Chapter 6 that one of the steps the CLR follows to resolve an assembly reference is to probe for that assembly in the *ApplicationBase* directory structure. *GetProbingAssembliesFromReference* returns the list of the files the CLR would look for when attempting to resolve a reference to a given assembly.

As shown in the table, *ICLRAssemblyIdentityManager* enables you to supply the assembly for which you'd like a binding identity by either providing a pathname to the file containing that assembly's manifest or by supplying a pointer to an *IStream* that contains the assembly's contents. Given these methods, two steps are involved in obtaining a binding identity for an assembly:

1. Obtain a pointer to *ICLRAssemblyIdentityManager*.

2. Call *GetBindingIdentityFromFile* (or *Stream*) to get a binding identity.

Step 1: Obtaining a Pointer to *ICLRAssemblyIdentityManager*

Unfortunately, obtaining a pointer to an *ICLRAssemblyIdentityManager* is more involved than obtaining pointers to the rest of the hosting interfaces implemented by the CLR. You may recall from Chapter 2 that a host typically uses the *ICLRControl* interface to request pointers to the hosting interfaces implemented by the CLR. *ICLRAssemblyIdentityManager* doesn't follow this pattern. Instead, you must call a function named *GetCLRIdentityManager* to get a pointer of type *ICLRAssemblyIdentityManager*. Here's the definition of *GetCLRIdentityManager* from mscoree.idl:

```
STDAPI GetCLRIdentityManager(REFIID riid, IUnknown **ppManager);
```

To make matters more complicated, *GetCLRIdentityManager* is implemented in the main CLR runtime DLL, mscorwks.dll, not from the startup shim (mscoree.dll) like the other functions we've used, such as *CorBindToRuntimeEx*. Even though *GetCLRIdentityManager* is implemented in mscorwks.dll, you must still go through mscoree.dll to access it. Recall from Chapter 3 that all accesses to the CLR from unmanaged code must go through mscoree.dll to make sure the proper CLR runtime DLLs are loaded when multiple versions are installed on the machine. The end result of this is that you must access *GetCLRIdentityManager* dynamically through a function pointer obtained from the *GetRealProcAddress* function exported from mscoree.dll. *GetRealProcAddress* redirects the request for a particular function to the proper version of mscorwks.dll. The following sample code uses *GetRealProcAddress* to get a pointer to the *GetCLRIdentityManager* function and calls through that function pointer to get an interface of type *ICLRAssemblyIdentityManager*:

```
// Declare a type for our pointer to GetCLRIdentityManager.
typedef HRESULT (__stdcall *CLRIdentityManagerProc)(REFIID, IUnknown **);

// Declare variables to hold both the function pointer and the
// interface of type ICLRAssemblyIdentityManager.
CLRIdentityManagerProc pIdentityManagerProc = NULL;
ICLRAssemblyIdentityManager *pIdentityManager = NULL;
// Use GetRealProcAddress to get a pointer to GetCLRIdentityManager.
HRESULT hr = GetRealProcAddress("GetCLRIdentityManager",
    (void **)&pIdentityManagerProc);

// Call GetCLRIdentityManager to get a pointer to ICLRAssemblyIdentityManager.
hr = (pIdentityManagerProc)(IID_ICLRAssemblyIdentityManager,
    (IUnknown **)&pIdentityManager);
```

Step 2: Calling *GetBindingIdentityFromFile* (or *Stream*)

Now that you've got a pointer of type *ICLRAssemblyIdentityManager*, you can call either *GetBindingIdentityFromFile* or *GetBindingIdentityFromStream* to obtain a binding identity for an assembly. Mscoree.idl defines these two methods as follows:

```
interface ICLRAssemblyIdentityManager : IUnknown
{
    HRESULT GetBindingIdentityFromFile(
        [in]    LPCWSTR     pwzFilePath,
```

```
    [in]      DWORD        dwFlags,
    [out, size_is(*pcchBufferSize)]   LPWSTR  pwzBuffer,
    [in, out]  DWORD       *pcchBufferSize
);

HRESULT GetBindingIdentityFromStream(
    [in]      IStream      *pStream,
    [in]      DWORD        dwFlags,
    [out, size_is(*pcchBufferSize)]   LPWSTR  pwzBuffer,
    [in, out]  DWORD               *pcchBufferSize
);

// other methods omitted
}
```

Makecocoon.exe deals with files, so it uses *GetBindingIdentityFromFile* exclusively. As discussed, the *_index* stream requires a binding identity for every file in the cocoon. So, *GetBindingIdentityFromFile* is called by makecocoon as it iterates through the files in the directory in preparation to add them to a cocoon. *GetBindingIdentityFromFile* takes as input a buffer in which it will store the binding identity for the assembly you request. However, binding identities vary in size based on certain factors, including the assembly's friendly name, whether it has a strong name, and so on. Given this, there's no way to know how much buffer space to allocate beforehand. As a result, the *GetBindingIdentityFromFile* method is designed to be called twice in succession. On the first call to *GetBindingIdentityFromFile*, you pass NULL for the buffer in which the binding identity is to be stored and *0* for the *pcchBufferSize* parameter. The CLR determines how much buffer space is required for the binding identity you are asking for and returns the required size in *pcchBufferSize*. Next, you allocate a buffer of the requested size and call *GetBindingIdentityFromFile* again, passing it the allocated buffer. After this second call returns, *pwzBuffer* contains the binding identity. The following code shows how you call *GetBindingIdentityFromFile* twice to obtain a binding identity for a given assembly:

```
// Call once to get the required buffer size. pszFileName
// contains the path to the manifest of the assembly for which you'd like
// a binding identity.
DWORD cbBuffer = 0;
HRESULT hr = m_pIdentityManager->GetTextualIdentityFromFile(
                pszFileName,
                0,
                NULL,
                &cbBuffer);

// Allocate a buffer is size cbBuffer. This example uses UNICODE strings,
// hence the multiplication by sizeof(wchar_t).
wchar_t *pBindingIdentity = (wchar_t *)malloc(cbBuffer*sizeof(wchar_t));

// Call again to actually get the binding identity.
hr = m_pIdentityManager->GetTextualIdentityFromFile(
                pszFileName,
                0,
                pBindingIdentity,
                &cbBuffer);
```

```
// pBindingIdentity now contains the binding identity.

// ...

// Remember to free the string containing the binding identity.
free(pBindingIdentity);
```

The Makecocoon.exe Program

Now that you've looked at all the pieces required to build makecocoon.exe, take a closer look at how the program works. Makecocoon.exe begins by creating a structured storage file based on the name of the executable file passed in. It then enumerates the contents of the directory looking for files with a .dll extension. For each .dll file, makecocoon.exe maps a view of the file's contents into memory using the Win32 memory-mapped file APIs. Given the view of the file in memory, makecocoon.exe creates a new stream in the structure storage file and writes the contents of the mapped memory to that stream. As each stream is created, I build up a data structure that contains the name of the stream and the binding identity of the assembly contained in that stream. This data structure is eventually written to the _index_ stream I described earlier.

The source code for makecocoon.exe's primary source file is given in Listing 8-1. The program includes a few other files that contain helper classes for obtaining an *ICLRAssemblyIdentity-Manager* and for maintaining the index data structure. The complete source code can be found at this book's companion Web site.

Listing 8-1   Makecocoon.cpp

```
//
// MakeCocoon.cpp
//
// Takes a directory of files and makes a "cocoon." MakeCocoon.exe takes
// as input the main executable to wrap in the cocoon. It streams that
// executable, plus all DLLs in the same directory into an OLE structured
// storage file.

#include "stdafx.h"
#include "CStreamIndex.h"
#include "CCLRIdentityManager.h"


// Given an assembly file on disk, this function creates a stream under
// pRootStorage and writes the bytes of the assembly to that stream. It also
// creates an entry in the index that maps the name of the new stream to the
// binding identity of the file it contains.
HRESULT CreateStreamForAssembly(IStorage *pRootStorage,
                                CStreamIndex *pStreamIndex,
                                LPWSTR pAssemblyFileName)
{
    // Make sure you can open the file.
    HANDLE hFile = CreateFile(pAssemblyFileName, GENERIC_READ, 0, NULL,
        OPEN_EXISTING, FILE_ATTRIBUTE_NORMAL, NULL);
```

```
  if (hFile == INVALID_HANDLE_VALUE)
  {
     printf("Error opening file: %s\n", pAssemblyFileName);
     return E_FAIL;
  }

  wprintf(L"Creating Stream for Assembly in file: %s\n", pAssemblyFileName);

  // Get the file size so you know how many bytes to write to the OLE
  // structured storage file.
  DWORD dwSize = GetFileSize(hFile, NULL);

  // Map the file into memory.
  HANDLE hFileMapping = CreateFileMapping(hFile, NULL, PAGE_READONLY, 0,
                                  dwSize, NULL);
  PVOID pFile = MapViewOfFile(hFileMapping, FILE_MAP_READ, 0, 0, 0);

  // Pull the file extension off the name so you're left with just the
  // simple assembly name.
  wchar_t wszSimpleAsmName[MAX_PATH];
  ZeroMemory(wszSimpleAsmName, MAX_PATH*2);
  wcsncpy(wszSimpleAsmName, pAssemblyFileName, wcslen(pAssemblyFileName)-4);

  // Create a stream in which to store the assembly.
  IStream *pMainStream = NULL;
  HRESULT hr = pRootStorage->CreateStream(wszSimpleAsmName,
           STGM_DIRECT | STGM_CREATE | STGM_WRITE | STGM_SHARE_EXCLUSIVE,
           0, 0, &pMainStream);
  assert(SUCCEEDED(hr));

  // Write the assembly into the stream.
  ULONG ulSizeWritten = 0;
  hr = pMainStream->Write(pFile, dwSize, &ulSizeWritten);
  assert(SUCCEEDED(hr));
  assert(ulSizeWritten == dwSize);

  // Clean up - release the Stream, Unmap the file, and close handles.
  pMainStream->Release();
  UnmapViewOfFile(pFile);
  CloseHandle(hFileMapping);
  CloseHandle(hFile);

  // Add an entry to the index for this stream.
  CCLRIdentityManager *pIdentityManager = new CCLRIdentityManager();

  wchar_t *pBindingIdentity = pIdentityManager
     ->GetBindingIdentityForFile(pAssemblyFileName);
  assert(pBindingIdentity);

  hr = pStreamIndex->AddIndexEntry(wszSimpleAsmName, pBindingIdentity);
  assert(SUCCEEDED(hr));

  free(pBindingIdentity);
  delete pIdentityManager;

  return hr;
}
```

```
// Create a stream that holds a string. Use this to write entry point data
// into the storage and to record the binding identity of the assembly
// containing the application's executable.
HRESULT CreateStreamForString(IStorage *pRootStorage, wchar_t *pszStreamName, wchar_t *pszSt
ring)
{
    wprintf(L"Creating String Stream containing: %s\n", pszString);

    // Create a stream in which to store the string.
    IStream *pStringStream = NULL;
    HRESULT hr = pRootStorage->CreateStream(pszStreamName,
        STGM_DIRECT | STGM_CREATE | STGM_WRITE | STGM_SHARE_EXCLUSIVE,
        0, 0, &pStringStream);
    assert(SUCCEEDED(hr));

    // Write the string to the stream.
    ULONG ulSizeWritten = 0;
    DWORD dwSize = wcslen(pszString)*sizeof(wchar_t);
    hr = pStringStream->Write(pszString, dwSize, &ulSizeWritten);
    assert(SUCCEEDED(hr));
    assert(ulSizeWritten == dwSize);

    pStringStream->Release();

    return S_OK;
}


int wmain(int argc, wchar_t* argv[])
{
    // Make sure the correct number of arguments was passed.
    if (argc != 3)
    {
        wprintf(L"Usage: MakeCocoon <exe file name> <name of type containing
            Main()>\n");
        return 0;
    }

    // Construct the filename for the cocoon. I use the name of the exe
    // minus ".exe" + the ".cocoon" extension.
    wchar_t wszCocoonName[MAX_PATH];
    ZeroMemory(wszCocoonName, MAX_PATH*2);
    wcsncpy(wszCocoonName, argv[1], wcslen(argv[1])-4);
    wcscat(wszCocoonName, L".cocoon");

    // Create the structured storage file in which to store the assemblies.
    wprintf(L"Creating Cocoon: %s\n", wszCocoonName);
    IStorage *pRootStorage = NULL;
    HRESULT hr = StgCreateDocfile(wszCocoonName,
        STGM_DIRECT | STGM_READWRITE | STGM_CREATE | STGM_SHARE_EXCLUSIVE,
        0, &pRootStorage);
    assert(SUCCEEDED(hr));

    // Create the index you'll use to map stream names to binding identities.
    CStreamIndex *pStreamIndex = new CStreamIndex(pRootStorage);
```

```
// Initialize and start the CLR.
ICLRRuntimeHost *pCLR = NULL;
 hr = CorBindToRuntimeEx(
    L"v2.0.41013",
    L"wks",
    STARTUP_CONCURRENT_GC,
    CLSID_CLRRuntimeHost,
    IID_ICLRRuntimeHost,
     (PVOID*) &pCLR);

 assert(SUCCEEDED(hr));

 pCLR->Start();

 // Obtain an identity manager. This is a helper class that wraps the
 // methods provided by ICLRAssemblyIdentityManager.
 CCLRIdentityManager *pIdentityManager = new CCLRIdentityManager();

 // Get the binding identity for the application's executable.
 wchar_t *pExeIdentity = pIdentityManager
    ->GetBindingIdentityForFile(argv[1]);
 assert(pExeIdentity);

 // Create a stream to hold the binding identity of the exe file.
 hr = CreateStreamForString(pRootStorage, L"_exeBindingIdentity",
    pExeIdentity);
 assert(SUCCEEDED(hr));

 free(pExeIdentity);
 delete pIdentityManager;

 // Create a stream that contains the name of the type containing the
 // application's main() method.
 hr = CreateStreamForString(pRootStorage, L"_entryPoint", argv[2]);
 assert(SUCCEEDED(hr));

 // Create a stream for the exe file.
 hr = CreateStreamForAssembly(pRootStorage, pStreamIndex, argv[1]);
 assert(SUCCEEDED(hr));

 // Loop through the current directory creating streams for all
 // dependent assemblies.
 wchar_t bCurrentDir[MAX_PATH];
 GetCurrentDirectory(MAX_PATH, bCurrentDir);
 wcsncat(bCurrentDir, L"\\*",2);

 WIN32_FIND_DATA fileData;
 HANDLE hFind = FindFirstFile(bCurrentDir, &fileData);

 while (FindNextFile(hFind, &fileData) != 0)
 {
    // Determine if the file is a DLL - ignore everything else.
    wchar_t *pDllExtension = wcsstr(fileData.cFileName, L".dll");
    if (pDllExtension)
    {
```

```
        // Create a stream in the Compound File for the assembly.
        hr = CreateStreamForAssembly(pRootStorage, pStreamIndex,
            fileData.cFileName);
        assert(SUCCEEDED(hr));
    }
  }

  // Write the index to the structured storage file. This creates the
  // _index stream.
  pStreamIndex->WriteStream();

  // Clean up.
  delete pStreamIndex;
  FindClose(hFind);
  pRootStorage->Release();

  return 0;
}
```

Implementing an Assembly Loading Manager

As described, writing a host using the CLR hosting APIs offers you the most control over how assemblies are loaded into an application domain. To demonstrate the range of customizations available, I write a host that runs applications encased in the cocoons described earlier. The host, runcocoon.exe, takes the name of the cocoon to run as input and uses the methods in the *System.Reflection* namespace to invoke the application's main entry point to start it running. As the application runs, you'll load its assemblies out of the .cocoon file instead of letting the CLR follow its default rules.

You'll also implement different versioning rules than the ones the CLR would normally enforce. Specifically, you always use the assemblies that are contained in the cocoon as you're running the application. If a different version of one of the assemblies is placed on disk somewhere, and version policy has been set that would normally cause that version to be used, you can generally ignore it. This keeps the cocoon static and isolated—changes made to the system by other applications won't affect it. However, there is one scenario in which you would consider version policy. (This is why I said you would only generally ignore policy earlier.) The CLR default version policy system comprises three levels as discussed in Chapter 7: application, publisher, and administrator. In this versioning scheme, you ignore application and publisher policy, but pay attention to administrator policy. A primary purpose of this policy level is to give an administrator a way to specify that a particular version of an assembly should not be used on the system because of a security vulnerability, a consistent crash, or some other fatal flaw. So if a banned assembly is contained in a cocoon you are trying to run, you'll fail to load it. Instead, you can print an error message and stop running the application. This new policy system is reasonable behavior and gives me a good chance to demonstrate how the hosting API can be used to implement a custom version policy scheme.

Recall from Chapter 2 that the COM interfaces in the hosting API are grouped into a set of managers. All of the interfaces in a given manager work together to provide a coherent set of functionality. One of these managers, the assembly loading manager, contains the two COM interfaces the host must implement to satisfy the requirements of the cocoon scenario: *IHostAssemblyManager* and *IHostAssemblyStore*. In addition to the implementations of these two interfaces, the runcocoon.exe host also contains an application domain manager, a host control object, and the main program logic that ties it all together (see Figure 8-4). In the next several sections, I describe each of these primary components of the host.

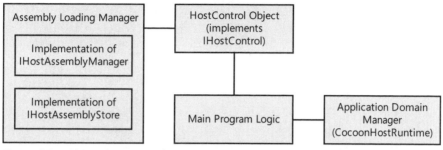

Figure 8-4   The architecture of the runcocoon.exe host

Implementing the *IHostAssemblyManager* Interface

IHostAssemblyManager is the primary interface in the assembly loading manager. That is, it is the interface the CLR asks for through the host control mechanism to determine whether you'd like to customize how the CLR loads assemblies. (Recall from Chapter 2 that the CLR calls the host's implementation of *IHostControl::GetHostManager* at startup once for every primary interface to determine which managers a host supports.) The methods on *IHostAssemblyManager* are described in Table 8-2.

Table 8-2   The Methods on *IHostAssemblyManager*

Method	Description
GetNonHostStoreAssemblies	Returns a list of assemblies that should be loaded by the CLR rather than by the host.
GetAssemblyStore	Returns the host's implementation of the *IHostAssemblyStore* interface. The CLR calls methods on *IHostAssemblyStore* to enable the host to load an assembly.
GetHostApplicationPolicy	In Chapter 6, I discuss how application-level policy can be specified for an application domain using the *Configuration-File* property on *AppDomainSetup*. *GetHostApplicationPolicy* provides an alternate way to specify application-level policy.

In addition to its role as the primary interface in the assembly loading manager, *IHostAssembly-Manager* provides two key capabilities. First, it allows the host to specify the list of assemblies that should be loaded by the CLR instead of being redirected to the host. Second, *IHostAssembly-Manager* allows the host to return its implementation of the other interface in this manager—*IHostAssemblyStore*. I discuss these capabilities in the next two sections.

Specifying Non-Host-Loaded Assemblies

When a host provides an implementation of the assembly loading manager, the CLR calls the host directly to load an assembly instead of going through its normal resolution and loading process. Although this is exactly what is needed for the assemblies you've stored in the cocoon, or for the assemblies users have stored in the database in the SQL Server scenario (for example), it's almost always the case that the host does not want to take over the responsibility for loading some assemblies, namely, those assemblies that are shipped by Microsoft as part of the .NET Framework platform. These include assemblies such as *System*, *System.Windows.Forms*, and *System.Web*. Although it's possible for a host to load these assemblies, doing so leads to complications downstream. To imagine the issues you can run into, consider what would happen if the cocoons you are running contained the .NET Framework assemblies in addition to the assemblies that make up the application. Although this would make the cocoons even more self-contained, it causes some additional implementation concerns that you, as the writer of the host, might not be willing to tackle. For example, recall from Chapter 3 that the CLR automatically enforces that the .NET Framework assemblies loaded into a process are the versions that were built and tested with the CLR that has been loaded. If a host were to load the .NET Framework itself, this benefit would be lost. In theory, you could figure out which assemblies to load based on a list of published version numbers, but even so, the host would just be guessing—only Microsoft as the builder of the .NET Framework knows the exact set of assemblies that are meant to work together.

The second complication involves handling servicing releases to the .NET Framework assemblies. Occasionally, Microsoft releases updates to the .NET Framework assemblies in the form of single bug fix releases, service packs, and so on. These updates are made directly to the .NET Framework assemblies stored in the global assembly cache. If a host were to package these assemblies in a custom format and load them from that format as I discussed doing with cocoons, the applications run by the host would not pick up these bug fix releases because the versions of those assemblies stored in the global assembly cache would not be used. Although you could argue this extra isolation is desired, there are clearly cases when the host would want the applications it runs to use the updated .NET Framework assemblies. The classic case when this behavior is desired is to pick up a bug fix that closes a security vulnerability, for example. If a host did want to be responsible for loading the .NET Framework assemblies, it could work around the servicing issue by loading the assemblies directly out of the global assembly cache itself. However, the process of doing so is not straightforward and, therefore, the benefits aren't likely worth the extra work. The .NET Framework SDK does include a set of APIs that enables you to enumerate the contents of the global assembly cache (see fusion.h in the Include directory of the SDK), but there are no APIs that enable you to load an assembly directly from the cache. It might be tempting to think that a managed API such as *System.Reflection.Assembly.Load* could be used to load the .NET Framework assembly, but because you've hooked the loading process by implementing an assembly loading manager, that call would just get redirected back to your host anyway!

Because of the complexities of dealing with service releases and of guaranteeing the .NET Framework assemblies match the CLR that is loaded, most hosts choose to load only those assemblies that their users have built as part of the applications they are hosting and let the CLR load the .NET Framework assemblies.

In the cocoon scenario, it's now clear that you'll load the assemblies built as part of the application out of the cocoon, but you'll let the CLR load the .NET Framework assemblies out of the global assembly cache. However, there is one more assembly I haven't considered yet: the *CocoonHostRuntime* assembly that contains the application domain manager. This assembly is neither a .NET Framework assembly, nor is it written by the user as part of the application. Rather, it is part of the host. You must decide whether you should load it yourself or leave it up to the CLR. In this case, there is no clear-cut answer. On one hand, you could include a copy of *CocoonHostRuntime* with each cocoon and load it yourself, or you could carry it along with the runcocoon.exe host and have the CLR load it. For this sample, choose the latter. The *CocoonHostRuntime* assembly will be deployed to the same directory as runcocoon.exe and loaded by the CLR from there. Figure 8-5 gives a summary of the various assemblies involved in running a cocoon, including from where and by whom they are loaded.

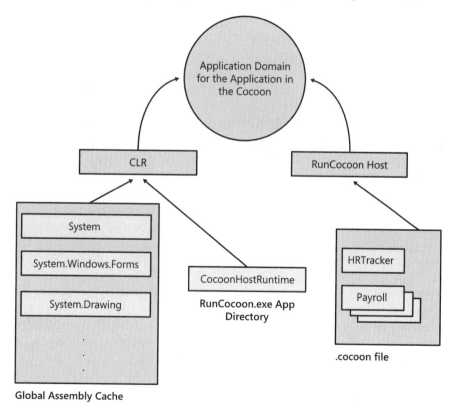

Figure 8-5   Assembly loading in the cocoon scenario

The CLR determines which assemblies it should load as opposed to which assemblies it should ask the host to load by calling the host's implementation of *IHostAssemblyManager::Get-NonHostStoreAssemblies*. As the host, you have two choices for specifying how the CLR should behave regarding assemblies you'd like it to load. First, you can provide an exact list of assemblies you'd like the CLR to load. In this scenario, the CLR will load all assemblies in the list you provide and will call your implementation of *IHostAssemblyStore* for all others. Your other option is to let the CLR try to load all assemblies first by looking in the global assembly cache. If an assembly is found in the cache, it is loaded–the host is never asked. On the other hand, if the assembly could not be found in the global assembly cache, the host is asked to resolve the reference. In this case, if the host doesn't successfully resolve the reference, the CLR continues to look for the assembly by probing in the *ApplicationBase* directory structure.

These options both have their pros and cons. The advantage of telling the CLR exactly which assemblies you'd like it to load ensures that you as the host will always have complete control over the assemblies that you'd like to load. For example, in the cocoon scenario, this means that the CLR will never load an assembly from the global assembly cache that is also contained in the cocoon file. This preserves the isolation in that you always know that the assemblies encased in the cocoon files are the ones that are loaded.

On the other hand, the disadvantage of providing an exact list of assemblies for the CLR to load is that this list can become stale as the deployment environment changes around you. For example, say you've asked the CLR to load version 2.0.5000 of *System.XML*. Later, a version policy statement is issued (either by the publisher or the administrator) that redirects all references to *System.XML* from version 2.0.5000 to 2.0.6000. The CLR will apply this version policy and look to see whether the resulting reference is to an assembly you've asked it to load. In this case, the resulting reference will not be in the list of assemblies you've asked the CLR to load (because the version is different), so the CLR will call your implementation of *IHost-AssemblyStore* to load the assembly. In this particular case, you can work around this by not providing a version number when you tell the CLR to load *System.XML*. Doing so, however, results in looser binding semantics than you might want. Either way, you can see how the installation of new assemblies and the presence of version policy can invalidate the list you provide.

As discussed, the alternative is to let the CLR look for all assemblies in the global assembly cache before giving the host the opportunity to load the assembly. Although this approach gets around the fragility problems you might see when you're providing a full list, it can result in the CLR loading some assemblies you wish it wouldn't. For example, say that an application in a cocoon file uses a statistical package in an assembly named *AcmeStatistics*. *AcmeStatistics* has a strong name and is packaged in the cocoon file along with the application that uses it. Furthermore, assume that another, completely unrelated application installed the *AcmeStatistics* assembly in the global assembly cache. If the CLR is given the first chance to load all assemblies, it's possible that the copy of *AcmeStatistics* in the global assembly cache will be loaded instead of the copy contained in the cocoon file. If the *AcmeStatistics* assembly in the global assembly cache is *exactly* the same as the copy in the cocoon file, it really doesn't matter from where it is loaded. However, because you are allowing the CLR to load *AcmeStatistics* from a location other than the cocoon, it is possible that the assembly that is loaded differs from the one contained in the cocoon file. For example, it could be that the copy of *AcmeStatistics* in the global assembly cache is a service release that just happens to have the same version number as the one in the cocoon. It's also possible that a version policy statement is present that redirects all references to the version of *AcmeStatistics* contained in the cocoon to the version in the global assembly cache.

GetNonHostStoreAssemblies returns a list of the assemblies you'd like the CLR to load. The list of assemblies is in the form of a pointer to an interface called *ICLRAssemblyReferenceList*, as you can see in the following definition from mscoree.idl:

```
interface IHostAssemblyManager: IUnknown
{
    HRESULT GetNonHostStoreAssemblies
            (
            [out] ICLRAssemblyReferenceList **ppReferenceList
            );
    // Other methods omitted.
}
```

Telling the CLR to attempt to load all assemblies first is straightforward—you just return NULL for **ppReferenceList* as shown in the following example:

```
HRESULT STDMETHODCALLTYPE CCocoonAssemblyManager::GetNonHostStoreAssemblies(
                ICLRAssemblyReferenceList **ppReferenceList)
{
    *ppReferenceList = NULL;
    return S_OK;
}
```

If, on the other hand, you'd like to supply the CLR with an exact list of assemblies to load, you must obtain a pointer to an *ICLRAssemblyReferenceList* that describes your list. Obtaining such an interface is done using the *GetCLRAssemblyReferenceList* method from *ICLRAssemblyIdentity-Manager* discussed earlier. Here's the definition of *GetCLRAssemblyReferenceList* from mscoree.idl:

```
interface ICLRAssemblyIdentityManager : IUnknown
{
    HRESULT  GetCLRAssemblyReferenceList(
        [in]    LPCWSTR  *ppwzAssemblyReferences,
        [in]    DWORD    dwNumOfReferences,
        [out]   ICLRAssemblyReferenceList    **ppReferenceList
    );
    // Other methods omitted.
}
```

GetCLRAssemblyReferenceList takes an array of string-based identities describing the assemblies you'd like the CLR to load. These identities are in the standard string-based form used in Chapter 7; that is:

```
"<assemblyName, Version=<version>, PublicKeyToken=<token>,
  culture=<culture>"
```

Given an array of assembly identities, along with a count of the number of items in the array, *GetCLRAssemblyReferenceList* returns an interface of type *ICLRAssemblyReferenceList* that you can pass to *GetNonHostStoreAssemblies*.

The string-based identities you pass to *GetCLRAssemblyReferenceList* can be either fully qualified (that is, they contain values for the public key token, version, and culture in addition to the required friendly name) or partial. The ability to specify partial identities in this case comes in handy, especially when referring to the .NET Framework assemblies. Recall from Chapter 3 that the CLR ensures that the .NET Framework assemblies that are loaded match the CLR that is running in the process. As a result, there's really no need to specify a version number when referring to an assembly that is part of the .NET Framework. In this case, it's much better to leave it to the CLR to determine which version to load.

Runcocoon.exe's implementation of *GetNonHostStoreAssemblies* tells the CLR to load the *mscorlib*, *System*, and *CocoonHostRuntime* assemblies as shown in the following code snippet. References to all other assemblies are redirected to the implementation of *IHostAssemblyStore*.

```
// The names of the assemblies you'd like the CLR to load
const wchar_t *wszNonHostAssemblies[] =
{
    L"CocoonHostRuntime, PublicKeyToken=38c3b24e4a6ee45e",
    L"mscorlib, PublicKeyToken=b77a5c561934e089",
    L"System, PublicKeyToken=b77a5c561934e089",
};

// RunCocoon's implementation of GetNonHostStoreAssemblies
HRESULT STDMETHODCALLTYPE CCocoonAssemblyManager::GetNonHostStoreAssemblies(
            ICLRAssemblyReferenceList **ppReferenceList)
{
    // GetIdentityManager is a private method that uses GetRealProcAddress to
    // call GetCLRIdentityManager to get the ICLRAssemblyIdentityManager
    // interface.
    ICLRAssemblyIdentityManager *pIdentityManager = GetIdentityManager();

    DWORD dwCount =
        sizeof(wszNonHostAssemblies)/sizeof(wszNonHostAssemblies[0]);



    HRESULT hr = pIdentityManager->GetCLRAssemblyReferenceList(
                            wszNonHostAssemblies,
                            dwCount,
                            ppReferenceList);
    assert(SUCCEEDED(hr));

    pIdentityManager->Release();
    return S_OK;
}
```

Another, less obvious use for *GetNonHostStoreAssemblies* is to enable a host to prevent a particular assembly from ever being loaded into a process. I discuss some of the motivation for this in Chapter 12, but for now, suffice it to say that some .NET Framework assemblies just don't make sense in certain hosting environments. For example, it probably doesn't make sense for the *System.Windows.Forms* assembly ever to be loaded in a server environment such as Microsoft ASP.NET or SQL Server. By not including such an assembly in the list returned from *GetNonHostStoreAssemblies*, and then refusing to load it yourself when your implementation of *IHostAssemblyStore* is called, you can prevent particular assemblies from ever being loaded.

Returning an Assembly Store

GetAssemblyStore, the final method to discuss on *IHostAssemblyManager*, is used to return an implementation of the *IHostAssemblyStore* interface. *IHostAssemblyStore* is the interface you implement to load assemblies out of the cocoon file as described in the next section. All hosts that implement *GetCLRLoadedAssemblies* will likely want to implement *GetAssemblyStore*, too. After all, without an implementation of *IHostAssemblyStore*, there would be no way to load any assembly other than those returned from *GetNonHostStoreAssemblies*. *GetAssemblyStore*'s only parameter is a pointer into which you'll return the implementation of *IHostAssemblyStore* as shown in the following method signature:

```
interface IHostAssemblyManager: IUnknown
{
    // Other methods omitted …
    HRESULT GetAssemblyStore([out] IHostAssemblyStore **ppAssemblyStore);
};
```

Runcocoon.exe's implementation of *IHostAssemblyStore* is contained in a class called *CCocoonAssemblyStore*. The implementation of *GetAssemblyStore* is straightforward: simply create a new instance of *CCocoonAssemblyStore*, cast it to a pointer to the *IHostAssemblyStore* interface, and return it through the out parameter as shown in the following code:

```
HRESULT STDMETHODCALLTYPE CCocoonAssemblyManager::GetAssemblyStore(
            IHostAssemblyStore **ppAssemblyStore)
{
    m_pAssemblyStore = new CCocoonAssemblyStore(m_pRootStorage);

    *ppAssemblyStore = (IHostAssemblyStore *)m_pAssemblyStore;
    return S_OK;
}
```

Implementing the *IHostAssemblyStore* Interface

The *IHostAssemblyStore* interface contains methods that hosts can use to load assemblies from formats other than standard PE files stored in the file system. It is this interface that enables SQL Server to load assemblies directly out of the database and the runcocoon.exe host to load assemblies directly from OLE structured storage files. Instead of returning the assembly as a filename on disk, implementers of *IHostAssemblyStore* return assemblies in the form of a pointer to an *IStream* interface. This enables you to load assemblies from literally anywhere that you can store or construct a contiguous set of bytes. It is *IHostAssemblyStore* that also enables you to customize how the default CLR version policy system works.

As you've seen, the CLR determines whether a host wishes to implement a custom assembly store using a two-step process. First, it calls the host implementation of *IHostControl*, passing in the IID for *IHostAssemblyManager*. This tells the CLR that the host implements the assembly loading manager. Next, the CLR calls *IHostAssemblyManager::GetAssemblyStore* to get a pointer to the *IHostAssemblyStore* interface representing the custom store.

IHostAssemblyStore contains two methods: one the CLR calls to resolve references to assemblies (*ProvideAssembly*), and another that is called to resolve references to individual files within an assembly (*ProvideModule*). This latter method is called only for assemblies that consist of more than one file.

Take a look at how to implement these two methods. As before, I describe them in the context of the runcocoon.exe host.

Resolving Assembly References

If a host provides an implementation of *IHostAssemblyStore*, the CLR will call the *ProvideAssembly* method to resolve all references to assemblies not contained in the non-host-store assemblies list. The input to *ProvideAssembly* is a structure called *AssemblyBindInfo* that contains not only the identity of the assembly to load, but also information about how the default CLR version policy system would affect the reference to that assembly. Assemblies resolved out of a custom store are returned to the CLR in the form of a pointer to an *IStream* interface. If you're not familiar with how *IStream* works, there's plenty of information on MSDN or in the platform SDK.

In addition to the *AssemblyBindInfo* structure and the stream through which the assembly is returned, *ProvideAssembly* also contains parameters that enable you to return debugging information, to associate any host-specific context data with a particular assembly bind, and to specify a unique identity for the assembly you are returning (more on this later). Here's the definition for *ProvideAssembly* from mscoree.idl:

```
interface IHostAssemblyStore: IUnknown
{
    HRESULT ProvideAssembly
            (
            [in] AssemblyBindInfo *pBindInfo,
            [out] UINT64           *pAssemblyId,
            [out] UINT64           *pContext,
            [out] IStream          **ppStmAssemblyImage,
            [out] IStream          **ppStmPDB);
// Other method definitions omitted…
}
```

The *AssemblyBindInfo* Structure   The *AssemblyBindInfo* structure has four fields:

```
typedef struct _AssemblyBindInfo
{
    DWORD          dwAppDomainId;
    LPCWSTR        lpReferencedIdentity;
    LPCWSTR        lpPostPolicyIdentity;
    DWORD          ePolicyLevel;
} AssemblyBindInfo;
```

The first field, *dwAppDomainId*, identifies the application domain into which the assembly will be loaded. This field isn't particularly useful in the runcocoon.exe host because there is only one application domain. To understand why this field is needed, consider what would happen if the host were capable of running multiple cocoons simultaneously in the same process. In this case, you'd probably choose to load each cocoon into its own application domain. Given the fact that there is only one implementation of *IHostAssemblyStore* per process, you'd have no way of identifying which cocoon file to load the requested assembly from without the *dwAppDomainId* field. The way you'd likely implement this is to keep a table that maps application domain IDs to .cocoon files. Then when *ProvideAssembly* was called, you'd use the *dwApp-DomainId* you're passed to find the appropriate cocoon file in the table. The unique identifier for an application domain can be obtained using the *Id* property on *System.AppDomain*.

The rest of the fields in the *AssemblyBindInfo* structure identify the assembly that the host needs to load. This information is contained in three fields: *lpReferencedIdentity*, *ePolicyLevel*, and *lpPostPolicyIdentity*. The first field, *lpReferencedIdentity*, contains the identity of the original assembly as referenced by its caller. The *ePolicyLevel* field indicates whether that original reference would be redirected by any version policy were the CLR to load that assembly. (The values for *ePolicyLevel* are defined by the *EBindPolicyLevels* enumeration discussed later in the chapter.) That is, the *ePolicyLevel* field tells you whether any version policy that would affect the reference is present on the system. Finally, the *lpPostPolicyIdentity* field contains the assembly that would be referenced if the policy identified in *ePolicyLevel* were actually applied. Look at the following example to see how the values of these fields work together. Consider the case in which code is running in one of the cocoons that loads an assembly like so:

```
Assembly a = Assembly.Load("Customers, Version=1.1.0.0,
    PublicKeyToken=865931ab473067d1, culture=neutral");
```

Furthermore, say the administrator of the machine has used the .NET Configuration tool to specify some version policy for the *Customers* assembly. Specifically, the administrator has specified policy that redirects all references to version 1.1 of *Customers* to version 2.0. In XML, that policy would look like the following:

```
<configuration>
  <runtime>
    <assemblyBinding xmlns="urn:schemas-microsoft-com:asm.v1">
      <dependentAssembly>
        <assemblyIdentity name="Customers"
          publicKeyToken="865931ab473067d1" />
          <bindingRedirect oldVersion="1.1.0.0" newVersion="2.0.0.0" />
      </dependentAssembly>
    </assemblyBinding>
  </runtime>
</configuration>
```

In this situation, the relevant fields in the *AssemblyBindInfo* structure would have the following values when *ProvideAssembly* is called:

```
lpReferencedIdentity = "Customers, Version=1.1.0.0,
    PublicKeyToken=865931ab473067d1, Culture=neutral";

lpPostPolicyIdentity = "Customers, version=2.0.0.0, culture=neutral
    publickeytoken=865931ab473067d1,  processorarchitecture=msil";

ePolicyLevel = ePolicyLevelAdmin
```

> **Note**   You might notice that the format of *lpPostPolicyIdentity* is slightly different from the format of *lpReferencedIdentity*. Specifically, the keywords *version*, *publickeytoken*, and *culture* have a different case, and a new element called *processorarchitecture* appears. *lpPostPolicy-Identity* looks a bit different because it is a binding identity, whereas *lpReferencedIdentity* is the literal string from the assembly reference (the call to *Assembly.Load* in the example).

Implementers of *ProvideAssembly* can use the information in *lpReferencedIdentity*, *lpPostPolicyIdentity*, and *ePolicyLevel* for informational purposes only. That is, the CLR will enforce that the assembly you return from *ProvideAssembly* has a binding identity that matches *lpPostPolicyIdentity*—you are not free to return an assembly with any identity you want. In some ways this restriction is unfortunate because it limits the flexibility of what you can do with an assembly loading manager. Nevertheless, a host still has control over version policy because you control how policy is applied within your application domain .

Even though the implementation of *ProvideAssembly* cannot return an assembly the CLR doesn't expect, you can still implement some versioning rules quite easily. To demonstrate what you can do, let's implement some versioning rules to ensure that the assemblies stored in the cocoon file are the exact ones you load at run time. Specifically, you won't load a different version of an assembly based on the existence of version policy. You can avoid application-level policy easily because you control that for your application domain. As for publisher policy, there are a few ways to keep that from affecting you. As discussed in Chapter 6, the *AppDomainSetup* object has a property called *DisallowPublisherPolicy* you can set to cause all publisher policy statements to be ignored for code running in a particular application domain. Alternatively, you can specify the same setting using the *<publisherPolicy>* element of your application configuration file. This is the approach I've taken with runcocoon.exe. If you download the samples for this book, you'll find a file called runcocoon.exe.config in the same directory as runcocoon.exe. This file uses the *<publisherPolicy>* element to turn off publisher policy for the applications contained in cocoon files:

```
<?xml version="1.0"?>
<configuration>
  <runtime>
    <assemblyBinding xmlns="urn:schemas-microsoft-com:asm.v1">
      <publisherPolicy apply="no" />
    </assemblyBinding>
  </runtime>
</configuration>
```

Now that I've discussed how to prevent application and publisher policy from affecting your host, turn your attention to policy specified by the administrator. The primary use of administrator-specified version policy is to provide a mechanism that administrators can use to prevent a particular version of an assembly from being used. Administrators use this policy to prevent any application from using an assembly that has a known security vulnerability, causes a fatal crash, and so on. It's generally good practice to honor any policy set by an administrator. To that end, runcocoon.exe host will not load any assembly that an administrator has explicitly disallowed through version policy. However, instead of loading the alternate version the administrator calls for, you can simply print an error message and discontinue execution. In a way, you're taking the middle ground here: you are honoring what the administrator says by not loading the referenced assembly, but you're not opening yourself up to the possibility of unintended behavior by executing an assembly that wasn't originally tested as part of the application contained in the cocoon.

Testing to see whether the administrator has issued a version policy statement for an assembly in the cocoon is easy. Simply check for the appropriate value in the *AssemblyBindInfo* structure and return a "file not found" *HRESULT* to tell the CLR you can't find the assembly (that is, you won't load it). At this point, execution of the cocoon would stop with an exception. The following snippet from runcocoon's implementation of *ProvideAssembly* shows how to do this:

```
HRESULT STDMETHODCALLTYPE CCocoonAssemblyStore::ProvideAssembly(
                AssemblyBindInfo *pBindInfo,
                UINT64           *pAssemblyId,
                UINT64           *pContext,
                IStream          **ppStmAssemblyImage,
                IStream          **ppStmPDB)
{
    // Check to see if administrator policy was applied. If so, print an error
    // to the command line and return "file not found." This will cause the
    // execution of the cocoon to stop with an exception.
    if (pBindInfo->ePolicyLevel == ePolicyLevelAdmin)
    {
        wprintf(L"Administrator Version Policy is present that redirects:
            %s to %s .  Stopping execution\n",
            pBindInfo->lpReferencedIdentity, pBindInfo->lpPostPolicyIdentity);
        return HRESULT_FROM_WIN32(ERROR_FILE_NOT_FOUND);
    }

// Rest of the function omitted for brevity... }
```

The EBindPolicyLevels Enumeration   Most of the values in the *EBindPolicyLevels* enumeration are self-explanatory because they map directly to the levels of the default version policy scheme, such as application, publisher, or administrator. A few, however, don't fit that pattern and require additional explanation. Here's the definition of the enumeration from mscoree.idl:

```
typedef enum
{
    ePolicyLevelNone = 0x0,
    ePolicyLevelRetargetable = 0x1,
    ePolicyUnifiedToCLR = 0x2,
```

```
        ePolicyLevelApp = 0x4,
        ePolicyLevelPublisher = 0x8,
        ePolicyLevelHost = 0x10,
        ePolicyLevelAdmin = 0x20
} EBindPolicyLevels;
```

The first value that might not look familiar is *ePolicyLevelRetargetable*. Although it's not likely you'll ever see this value in your implementation of *ProvideAssembly*, it's worth spending a few minutes understanding for what it could be used. *ePolicyLevelRetargetable* is related to a feature in the CLR to support the different implementations of the CLR as described in the European Computer Manufacturers Association (ECMA) standard. Because the CLR is part of an international standard, anyone can produce an implementation of it on any platform. The *ePolicyLevelRetargetable* value shows up if an implementation of the CLR other than the version shipped as part of the full .NET Framework chose to reference a different assembly than the one the application originally referenced. This is useful, for example, in alternate implementations that have different names for the .NET Framework assemblies.

The second value of *EBindPolicyLevels* that doesn't fit the pattern of the familiar policy levels is *ePolicyUnifiedToCLR*. This value relates to the feature I discuss in Chapters 3 and 7 whereby a given CLR will load the matching versions of the .NET Framework assemblies. The term *Unified* comes from the sense that the CLR is unifying all references to the .NET Framework assemblies such that the set of assemblies that were shipped together are always used together. Two things would have to be true before you'd see this value passed to *ProvideAssembly*. First, your host would have to run an application that contains assemblies built with an older version of the CLR than the one running in the process (and hence would have references to the older .NET Framework assemblies). Second, your host would have to be responsible for loading some of the .NET Framework assemblies. In most scenarios, hosts don't load the .NET Framework assemblies as I concluded during the discussion of the *IHostAssemblyManager::GetNonHostStoreAssemblies* method earlier in the chapter.

Associating Host-Specific Data with an Assembly   The *pContext* parameter to *ProvideAssembly* enables you to communicate any host-specific data about an assembly from the unmanaged portion of your host to the managed portion. *pContext* is a pointer to a 64-bit unsigned integer in which you can store any host-specific data to associate with the assembly you return from *ProvideAssembly*. This data can be retrieved in managed code using the *HostContext* property on *System.Reflection.Assembly*.

The SQL Server host provides a good example of how host-specific data for an assembly can be used. When an administrator registers an assembly in the SQL Server catalog, she indicates which predefined set of security permissions that assembly should be granted when it is run. SQL Server records this information in its catalog along with the contents of the assembly. When an assembly is returned from *ProvideAssembly*, SQL Server reads the data describing the requested permission set from the catalog and returns it in **pContext*. On the managed side, this information is obtained from the *HostContext* property on *Assembly* and is used as input into the security policy system to make sure the proper permission set is granted to the assembly. More details about how to associate permissions with an assembly are provided in Chapter 10.

Assigning Assembly Identity   Before you look at runcocoon's implementation of *ProvideAssembly*, I have one more topic to discuss: how assemblies are uniquely identified within the CLR data structures at run time. When the CLR loads an assembly from disk, it uses the fully qualified pathname of the file, in addition to the assembly's name, to uniquely identify the assembly. The pathname is used as part of the internal identity of an assembly partly to ensure application correctness, but also as a performance optimization. If the CLR is asked to load the same physical file from disk multiple times, it can reuse the memory and data structures it has already set up for the assembly instead of loading the assembly multiple times.

When hosts take over the assembly loading process and return pointers to streams from *ProvideAssembly*, there is nothing (at least that can be computed cheaply) to uniquely identify the bytes pointed to by that stream within the CLR. It's up to the host to associate a unique piece of data with each stream that serves the same purpose that the filename does for an assembly loaded from the file system. That is, it enables the CLR to uniquely identify the assembly internally so performance can be increased by preventing multiple loads of the same assembly. The ability for the host to provide this unique identity is the purpose of the *pAssemblyId* parameter to *ProvideAssembly*.

Upon return from *ProvideAssembly*, *pAssemblyId* is intended to hold a 64-bit number that uniquely identifies the assembly. If multiple calls to *ProvideAssembly* result in the same number being returned in *pAssemblyId*, the CLR assumes the assemblies are the same and reuses the bytes and data structures it already has instead of mapping the contents of the stream again. The CLR treats the unique number assigned by the host as an opaque identity—it never interprets the number in any way. Therefore, the semantics of this unique identifier are completely up to the host. The host can choose to use a value from an internal data structure, it can generate a unique value based on the assembly (such as a hash of the name), and so on.

The implementation of *ProvideAssembly* in runcocoon.exe uses a value from one of its internal data structures to uniquely identify assemblies to the CLR. Recall that each cocoon file has a stream named *_index* that contains a mapping of binding identities to the names of the streams containing the assemblies. When the CLR calls the implementation of *ProvideAssembly*, you would look through the index to find the name of the stream containing the assembly corresponding to the binding identity specified in *pBindInfo->lpPostPolicyIdentity*. When you find the appropriate index entry, remember its place in the index and use that as the assembly's unique identifier. Given that each binding identity is unique within the index, the position makes a perfect unique identifier for an assembly. As an example, consider the contents of the *_index* stream shown in Figure 8-6.

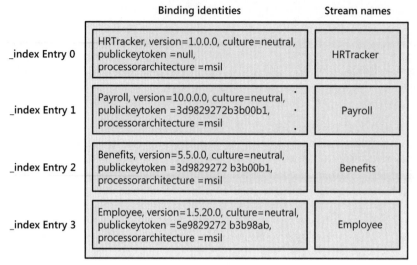

Figure 8-6   The *_index* stream for the HRTracker application

When the CLR calls *ProvideAssembly* with a binding identity of

```
Payroll, version=10.0.0.0, culture=neutral, publickeytoken=3d9829272b3b00b1,
    processorarchitecture=msil
```

look in the index and find the requested identity in entry number 1. Return the number 1 in **pbAssemblyId*. Subsequent requests for the same binding identity will cause you to find the same entry in the index and therefore to return a pointer to the same stream within the cocoon file.

Again, the value you return in **pbAssemblyId* can be any number that serves to uniquely identify a given assembly in your host. The assembly's position within the *_index* stream makes a perfect unique identifier in the cocoon scenario.

Loading Assemblies from a Cocoon   Now that I've covered the concepts needed to implement *ProvideAssembly*, look at the implementation in runcocoon.exe. The facts that assemblies are returned from *ProvideAssembly* in the form of pointers to streams and the cocoons are constructed of streams named after the assemblies they contain make the implementation pretty straightforward. After all, OLE structured storage files support streams directly, so there's no need for you to provide a custom implementation of *IStream*. All you need to do is use the structured storage APIs to open streams based on assembly name and return those streams directly from *ProvideAssembly*.

To recap, the implementation of *ProvideAssembly* in runcocoon.exe contains the following logic:

1. Check to see whether administrator policy is set for the referenced assembly. If so, display an error message, set the appropriate error code, and return.

2. Extract the binding identity of the requested assembly from the *AssemblyBindInfo.lpPostPolicyIdentity* field. Given this binding identity, look in the *_index* stream to find the

name of the stream in the cocoon that contains the assembly corresponding to the requested binding identity. The implementation of *ProvideAssembly* does this using a helper class called *CStreamIndex*.

3. Set a unique identifier for the assembly to the position of the requested assembly in the index.

4. Open the stream that contains the assembly you're looking for using the *IStorage::Open* stream structured storage API.

The implementation of *ProvideAssembly* from runcocoon.exe is shown in the following code. As described, *ProvideAssembly* uses some helper classes to get its job done. The source for these helper classes, along with the full source for runcocoon, can be found on this book's companion Web site.

```
HRESULT STDMETHODCALLTYPE CCocoonAssemblyStore::ProvideAssembly(
                AssemblyBindInfo *pBindInfo,
                UINT64           *pAssemblyId,
                UINT64           *pContext,
                IStream          **ppStmAssemblyImage,
                IStream          **ppStmPDB)
{
    assert(m_pCocoonStorage);
    wprintf(L"ProvideAssembly called for binding identity: %s\n",
    pBindInfo->lpPostPolicyIdentity);

    // Check to see if administrator policy was applied. If so, print an error
    // to the command line and return "file not found." This will cause the
    // execution of the cocoon to stop with an exception.
    if (pBindInfo->ePolicyLevel == ePolicyLevelAdmin)
    {
        wprintf(L"Administrator Version Policy is present that redirects:
            %s to %s . Stopping execution\n", pBindInfo->lpReferencedIdentity,
            pBindInfo->lpPostPolicyIdentity);
        return HRESULT_FROM_WIN32(ERROR_FILE_NOT_FOUND);
    }


    // The CStreamIndex class contains the contents of the _index stream.
    // Call this class to find and open the stream containing the
    // assembly described by AssemblyBindInfo.lpPostPolicyIdentity.
    HRESULT hr = m_pStreamIndex->GetStreamForBindingIdentity(
                                    pBindInfo->lpPostPolicyIdentity,
                                    pAssemblyId,
                                    ppStmAssemblyImage);

    // Don't use pContext for any host-specific data - set it to 0.
    // Also, don't return a stream containing debugging information
    // for this assembly.
    *pContext   = 0;
    *ppStmPDB   = NULL;

    return hr;
}
```

Resolving Module References

The *ProvideModule* method on *IHostAssemblyStore* exists to support assemblies that consist of multiple files. Before I get into the details of how *ProvideModule* works, some clarification of the terms *assembly* and *module* would be useful. Strictly speaking, an assembly is a collection of types and resources that act as a consistent unit in terms of versioning, deployment, security, and type visibility, among other characteristics. Nothing in the formal definition of an assembly says anything about how its contents are physically packaged. That is, the definition of an assembly does not dictate that all of an assembly's contents must be contained in a single file. In practice, though, this is almost always the case. The primary reason for this is that most development tools present assemblies as single physical files. Nevertheless, the capability does exist using some tools to build assemblies consisting of multiple files. For example, both the C# .NET and Visual Basic .NET compilers support a command-line option called *addmodule* that enables you to construct an assembly from multiple stand-alone files. In addition, you can use the SDK tool al.exe to build multi-file assemblies.

When an assembly consists of multiple files, one of those files contains an *assembly manifest*. A manifest is metadata that describes various aspects of the assembly, including its name and the files that make up the assembly. For example, consider the case of an assembly called *Statistics* that consists of three files: a file called statistics.dll, which contains the manifest, and two other code files called curves.dll and probability.dll. A high-level view of the contents of each of the files in this assembly is shown in Figure 8-7.

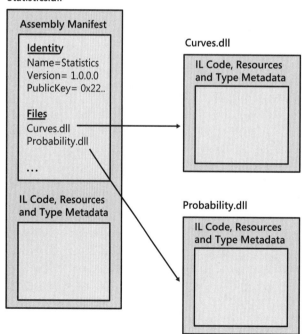

Figure 8-7 The contents of the files in the Statistics assembly

For purposes of the discussion of the *IHostAssemblyStore* interface, the file containing the assembly manifest (statistics.dll in the example) is called the *assembly*, whereas the other files in the assembly are called *modules*. When the *Statistics* assembly is initially referenced in code, the CLR calls the *ProvideAssembly* method to get the stream that contains the contents of statistics.dll. Then, if code contained in either curves.dll or probability.dll is referenced, the CLR calls *ProvideModule* to get the contents of those files.

Now that you understand when *ProvideModule* would be used, look at how to implement it. Many of the concepts I cover in the discussion of *ProvideAssembly* apply to *ProvideModule* as well. For example, the contents of modules are returned as pointers to *IStream* interfaces just as they are for assemblies. Also, the concept of assigning a unique identity to the stream that is returned applies here as well. So, many of the parameters to *ProvideModule* should look familiar. Here's its definition from mscoree.idl:

```
interface IHostAssemblyStore: IUnknown
{
// Other method definitions omitted…

    HRESULT ProvideModule
            (
            [in]  ModuleBindInfo *pBindInfo,
            [out] DWORD           *pdwModuleId,
            [out] IStream        **ppStmModuleImage,
            [out] IStream        **ppStmPDB);
}
```

As you can probably guess, the *pdwModuleId* parameter is used to assign a unique identity to the stream, the *ppStmModuleImage* parameter is used to return the *IStream* pointer representing the module, and *ppStmPDB* is an *IStream* pointer to the debugging information. The parameter that's new is the *ModuleBindInfo* parameter. This parameter serves the same logical purpose as does the *AssemblyBindInfo* parameter to *ProvideAssembly*—it identifies the module to be loaded. The *ModuleBindInfo* structure has three fields as shown in the following definition:

```
typedef struct _ModuleBindInfo
{
    DWORD                       dwAppDomainId;
    LPCWSTR                     lpAssemblyIdentity;
    LPCWSTR                     lpModuleName;
} ModuleBindInfo;
```

The first field, *dwAppDomainId*, identifies the application domain into which the module will be loaded. This field serves the same purpose as does the *dwAppDomainId* field in the *AssemblyBindInfo* structure. Because modules are always contained in part of an assembly, the implementer of *ProvideModule* must know which assembly contains the module being requested. The *lpAssemblyIdentity* field provides this information in the form of the string name of the containing assembly. The final field, *lpModuleName*, is the name of the module to load.

Not all CLR hosts support multi-file assemblies. As the creator of a new host, it's up to you to decide how important multi-file assemblies are to your scenario. As I said earlier, the tools support for creating multi-file assemblies isn't great, so in practice you don't see many of these assemblies. If you look at the popular hosts that exist today, you'll see a mixed bag of support: the ASP.NET, Microsoft Internet Explorer, and Default Host all support multi-file assemblies, but the SQL Server host doesn't. For purposes of this example, I've chosen not to support multi-file assemblies in runcocoon.exe. Opting not to support this scenario is easy from a coding perspective. All you need to do is return the *HRESULT* corresponding to *ERROR_FILE_NOT_FOUND* from *IHostAssemblyStore::ProvideModule* as shown in the following example:

```
HRESULT STDMETHODCALLTYPE CCocoonAssemblyStore::ProvideModule(
                ModuleBindInfo *pBindInfo,
                DWORD          *pdwModuleId,
                IStream        **ppStmModuleImage,
                IStream        **ppStmPDB)
{
    return HRESULT_FROM_WIN32(ERROR_FILE_NOT_FOUND);
}
```

Bringing It All Together

The bulk of the implementation of the runcocoon.exe host is contained in the assembly loading manager I've been discussing in the last several sections. Let me now take that implementation and show what else is needed to make a fully functional runcocoon.exe. You need to take the following steps to complete the host:

1. Open the .cocoon file passed as a command-line argument to runcocoon.exe.

2. Initialize the CLR using *CorBindToRuntimeEx*.

3. Create the objects that contain the implementation of the assembly loading manager and notify the CLR of their existence using a host control object.

4. Use the application domain manager from the *CocoonHostRuntime* assembly to invoke the application contained in the cocoon. As the application runs, assemblies will be referenced and the implementation of *IHostAssemblyStore* will be called to load them from the cocoon.

The next several sections describe each step in detail.

Opening the Cocoon File

Because cocoons are OLE structured storage files, you can use the *StgOpenStorage* API from the platform SDK to open them. *StgOpenStorage* returns an *IStorage* pointer that you'll save and use later to open the streams corresponding to the application's assemblies. The following code from the main routine of runcocoon.exe uses *StgOpenStorage* to open the cocoon:

```
int wmain(int argc, wchar_t* argv[])
{
   HRESULT hr = S_OK;

   // Make sure a cocoon file was passed as a command-line argument.
   if (argc != 2)
   {
      wprintf(L"Usage: RunCocoon <cocoon file name>\n");
      return 0;
   }

   // Open the cocoon using the structured storage APIs.
   IStorage *pRootStorage = NULL;
   hr = StgOpenStorage(argv[1], NULL,
      STGM_READ | STGM_DIRECT | STGM_SHARE_EXCLUSIVE,
      NULL, 0, &pRootStorage);

   if (!SUCCEEDED(hr))
   {
      wprintf(L"Error opening cocoon file: %s\n", argv[1]);
      return 0;
   }
   // The rest of main omitted for brevity…
}
```

Initializing the CLR

After you've verified that you can open the cocoon, it's time to initialize the CLR using *Cor-BindToRuntimeEx*. Your use of this API is straightforward: make sure .NET Framework version 2.0 of the CLR gets loaded, then save the pointer to *ICLRRuntimeHost* so you can use it later to start the CLR, set the host control object, and access the *ICLRControl* interface to register your application domain manager with the CLR:

```
// Start the CLR. Make sure .NET Framework 2.0 build is used.
   ICLRRuntimeHost *pCLR = NULL;
   hr = CorBindToRuntimeEx(
      L"v2.0.41013",
      L"wks",
      STARTUP_CONCURRENT_GC,
      CLSID_CLRRuntimeHost,
      IID_ICLRRuntimeHost,
      (PVOID*) &pCLR);
```

Creating the Assembly Loading Manager and Host Control Object

It's now time to hook your implementation of the assembly loading manager into the CLR so you get called to load assemblies out of the cocoon. Do this in three steps:

1. Create an instance of the *CCocoonAssemblyManager* class. This class provides your implementation of *IHostAssemblyManager*. Recall from earlier in the chapter that this interface contains the *GetNonHostStoreAssemblies* method and also provides the CLR with your custom assembly store implementation through the *GetAssemblyStore* method.

2. Create an instance of your host control object that provides the CLR with the implementation of your assembly loading manager. Runcocoon's host control object is contained in the class *CHostControl*. This class implements the *IHostControl* interface that the CLR uses to discover which managers a host supports. When the CLR calls *IHostControl::GetHostManager* with the IID for *IHostAssemblyManager*, *CHostControl* returns your instance of *CCocoonAssemblyManager* (casted to a pointer to an *IHostAssemblyStore* interface, of course).

3. The final step in hooking your assembly loading manager implementation into the CLR is to register your host control object with the CLR. Do this by passing an instance of *CHostControl* to *ICLRRuntimeHost::SetHostControl*.

The following code snippet from runcocoon's *main* routine demonstrates these three steps:

```
int wmain(int argc, wchar_t* argv[])
{
    // The first part of main omitted...

    // Create an instance of CCocoonAssemblyManager. This class contains your
    // implementation of the assembly loading manager, specifically the
    // IHostAssemblyStore interface. Pass the IStorage for the cocoon's
    // root storage object to the constructor. CCocoonAssemblyManager saves
    // this pointer and uses it later to load assemblies from the cocoon using
    // IHostAssemblyStore.
    CCocoonAssemblyManager *pAsmManager = new
    CCocoonAssemblyManager(pRootStorage);
    assert(pAsmManager);

    // Create a host control that takes the new assembly loading manager. The
    // CHostControl class implements IHostControl, which the CLR calls at
    // startup to determine which managers you support. In this case,
    // support just the assembly loading manager.
    CHostControl *pHostControl = new CHostControl(NULL,
                    NULL,
                    NULL,
                    NULL,
                    NULL,
                    (IHostAssemblyManager *)pAsmManager,
                    NULL,
                    NULL,
                    NULL);

    // Tell the CLR about your host control object. Remember that you must do
    // this before calling ICLRRuntimeHost::Start.
    pCLR->SetHostControl((IHostControl *)pHostControl);
```

Invoking the Hosted Application

The application contained in the cocoon is invoked from runcocoon's application domain manager. Your application domain manager is implemented by a class called *CocoonDomainManager* in the *CocoonHostRuntime* assembly. *CocoonDomainManager* has a *Run* method that takes the name of the assembly containing the application's executable and the name of the type within that assembly that contains the *main* method. *Run* loads the assembly containing the executable using the *Assembly.Load* method. After the assembly is loaded, *Run* uses other methods in the *System.Reflection* namespace to launch the application. The code for the *CocoonHostRuntime* assembly is shown in Listing 8-2.

Listing 8-2   CocoonHostRuntime.cs

```
using System;
using System.Text;
using System.Reflection;

namespace CocoonHostRuntime
{
    public interface ICocoonDomainManager
    {
        void Run(string assemblyName, string typeName);
    }

    public class CocoonDomainManager : AppDomainManager, ICocoonDomainManager
    {
        public override void InitializeNewDomain(          AppDomainSetup appDomainInfo)
        {
            // Set the flags so that the unmanaged portion of your
            // host gets notified of your domain manager via
            // IHostControl::SetAppDomainManager.
            InitializationFlags =
                DomainManagerInitializationFlags.RegisterWithHost;
        }

        // Run the "main" method from <assemblyName>.<typeName>.
        public void Run(string assemblyName, string typeName)
        {
            try
            {
                Assembly asm = Assembly.Load(assemblyName);
                Type t = asm.GetType(typeName, true, true);
                MethodInfo m = t.GetMethod("Main");
                m.Invoke(null, null);
            }
            catch (Exception e)
            {
                Console.WriteLine("Exception executing entry point: "
                    + e.Message);
            }
        }
    }
}
```

Before you can use *CocoonDomainManager* to execute your hosted application, you need to get the name of the assembly and the type containing the application's *main* from the cocoon.

Recall that these names are contained in the *_exeBindingIdentity* and *_entryPoint* streams, respectively. The complete code for runcocoon's *main* program is shown in Listing 8-3.

Listing 8-3   Runcocoon.cpp

```cpp
//
// Runcocoon.cpp : The main program for the runcocoon host.
//

#include "stdafx.h"
#include "CHostControl.h"
#include "CStreamIndex.h"
#include "CCocoonAssemblyStore.h"
#include "CCocoonAssemblyManager.h"

// Returns the contents of pszStreamName and returns it in pszString.
// This method is used to read the _exeBindingIdentity and _entryPoint
// streams, which contain the binding identity of the assembly and the name of
// the type containing the application's entry point.
HRESULT GetStringFromStream(IStorage *pStorage, wchar_t *pszStreamName,
 wchar_t *pszString)
{

    IStream *pStream = NULL;
    HRESULT hr = pStorage->OpenStream(pszStreamName, 0,
                        STGM_READ | STGM_DIRECT | STGM_SHARE_EXCLUSIVE,
                        0, &pStream);
    assert(SUCCEEDED(hr));

    // Determine how many bytes to read based on the size of the stream.
    STATSTG stats;
    pStream->Stat(&stats, STATFLAG_DEFAULT);

    // Read the bytes into pszString.
    DWORD dwBytesRead = 0;
    hr = pStream->Read(pszString, stats.cbSize.LowPart, &dwBytesRead);
    assert(stats.cbSize.LowPart == dwBytesRead);
    assert(SUCCEEDED(hr));

    pStream->Release();

    return S_OK;
}

int wmain(int argc, wchar_t* argv[])
{
    HRESULT hr = S_OK;

    // Make sure a cocoon file was passed as a command-line argument.
    if (argc != 2)
    {
        wprintf(L"Usage: RunCocoon <cocoon file name>\n");
        return 0;
    }
```

```
// Open the cocoon using the structured storage APIs.
IStorage *pRootStorage = NULL;
hr = StgOpenStorage(argv[1], NULL,
   STGM_READ | STGM_DIRECT | STGM_SHARE_EXCLUSIVE,
   NULL, 0, &pRootStorage);

if (!SUCCEEDED(hr))
{
   wprintf(L"Error opening cocoon file: %s\n", argv[1]);
   return 0;
}

// Start .NET Framework 2.0 version of the CLR.
ICLRRuntimeHost *pCLR = NULL;
 hr = CorBindToRuntimeEx(
   L"v2.0.41013 ,
  L"wks",
   STARTUP_CONCURRENT_GC,
   CLSID_CLRRuntimeHost,
   IID_ICLRRuntimeHost,
   (PVOID*) &pCLR);

assert(SUCCEEDED(hr));

// Create an instance of CCocoonAssemblyManager. This class contains your
// implementation of the assembly loading manager, specifically the
// IHostAssemblyStore interface. Pass the IStorage for the cocoon's
// root storage object to the constructor. CCocoonAssemblyManager saves
// this pointer and uses it later to load assemblies from the cocoon using
// IHostAssemblyStore.
CCocoonAssemblyManager *pAsmManager = new
   CCocoonAssemblyManager(pRootStorage);
assert(pAsmManager);

// Create a host control object that takes the new assembly loading
// manager. The CHostControl class implements IHostControl, which
// the CLR calls at startup to determine which managers you support.
// In this case, support just the assembly loading manager.
CHostControl *pHostControl = new CHostControl(NULL,
                NULL,
                NULL,
                NULL,
                (IHostAssemblyManager *)pAsmManager,
                NULL,
                NULL,
                NULL);

// Tell the CLR about your host control object. Remember that you
// must do this before calling ICLRRuntimeHost::Start.
hr = pCLR->SetHostControl((IHostControl *)pHostControl);
assert(SUCCEEDED(hr));

// Get the CLRControl object. Use this to set your AppDomainManager.
ICLRControl *pCLRControl = NULL;
```

```
    hr = pCLR->GetCLRControl(&pCLRControl);
    assert(SUCCEEDED(hr));

    hr = pCLRControl->SetAppDomainManagerType(L"CocoonHostRuntime,
        Version=5.0.0.0, PublicKeyToken=38c3b24e4a6ee45e, Culture=neutral",
        L"CocoonHostRuntime.CocoonDomainManager");
    assert(SUCCEEDED(hr));

    // Start the CLR.
    hr = pCLR->Start();

    // Get the binding identity for the exe contained in the cocoon.
    wchar_t wszExeIdentity[MAX_PATH];
    ZeroMemory(wszExeIdentity, MAX_PATH*sizeof(wchar_t));
    hr = GetStringFromStream(pRootStorage, L"_exeBindingIdentity",
        wszExeIdentity);

    // Get the name of the type containing the application's main method.
    wchar_t wszEntryType[MAX_PATH];
    ZeroMemory(wszEntryType, MAX_PATH*sizeof(wchar_t));
    hr = GetStringFromStream(pRootStorage, L"_entryPoint", wszEntryType);

    // Launch the application using your domain manager.
    ICocoonDomainManager *pDomainManager =
    pHostControl->GetDomainManagerForDefaultDomain();
    assert(pDomainManager);

    hr = pDomainManager->Run(wszExeIdentity, wszEntryType);
    assert(SUCCEEDED(hr));

    pDomainManager->Release();
    pCLRControl->Release();
    pHostControl->Release();
    return 0;
}
```

The complete source code for the runcocoon host can be found on this book's companion Web site.

Customizing How Assemblies Are Loaded Using Only Managed Code

By writing the runcocoon.exe host in unmanaged code, you were able to implement an assembly loading manager that enabled you to customize completely how the CLR loads assemblies. However, as you've seen, there were several new concepts to learn and a considerable amount of code to write. You can also customize the CLR assembly loading process to some degree by writing completely in managed code. The amount of customization available is less than what you can achieve by writing an assembly loading manager, but if what you need to accomplish can be done from within managed code, this approach can save you some time and effort.

In this section, you'll rewrite the runcocoon.exe host in managed code. Doing so gives you a good chance to contrast the amount of customization available between an unmanaged CLR host and a managed extensible application. The extensible application, called runcocoonm.exe, will provide the same basic functionality that the unmanaged host did. That is, it will run applications encased in .cocoon files. You'll invoke the application's entry point just as you did in runcocoon.exe and load the application's assemblies out of the cocoon file instead of having the CLR find them. Although on the surface the functionality you'll be providing is the same, there are several subtle differences in the way the two programs work. Understanding these differences can help you decide which approach best meets your needs.

Before I describe how runcocoonm.exe is implemented, take a look at the pieces you need to build it. To start with, let me revisit the requirements I set for the cocoon deployment model:

1. Assemblies must be loaded from formats other than standard executable files on disk. In this case, the assemblies must be loaded out of your custom deployment format, an OLE structured storage file.

2. Assemblies must be loaded from a location other than the application's base directory, the global assembly cache, or from locations described by codebases.

3. The assemblies contained in the cocoon are the exact assemblies to be loaded when the application is run. The presence of external version policy won't cause you to load a different assembly.

In the unmanaged implementation, these requirements were satisfied by writing an assembly loading manager. In managed code, you achieve a similar effect by using some of the managed methods and events on the *System.AppDomain* and the *System.Reflection.Assembly* classes. Specifically, the ability to load assemblies from alternate formats is provided by the versions of *Assembly.Load* and *AppDomain.Load* that enable you to specify an array of bytes containing the assembly you'd like to load. The ability to load assemblies from locations in which the CLR wouldn't normally find them is provided by an event on *System.AppDomain* called *AssemblyResolve*. The third requirement—to be able to circumvent default version policy—isn't directly provided in managed code. This is one of the primary limitations in what a managed program can do, as you'll see in a bit.

The next few sections describe how the *Assembly.Load(byte[]...)* and *AppDomain.Load(byte[]...)* methods and the *AppDomain.AssemblyResolve* event work. Once you see how to implement the pieces, you bring them together in writing the runcocoonm.exe sample.

The *Load(byte[]...)* Methods

In runcocoon.exe, you returned assemblies from the cocoon to the CLR by returning a pointer to an *IStream* interface from *IHostAssemblyStore::ProvideAssembly*. You can achieve the same effect from within managed code by passing the assembly you'd like to load as a managed byte array to *AppDomain.Load* and *Assembly.Load*. The following partial class definitions show the versions of *Load* that accept a byte array as input:

```
public sealed class AppDomain : MarshalByRefObject, _AppDomain,
    IEvidenceFactory
```

```
    {
        //...
        public Assembly Load(byte[] rawAssembly)

        public Assembly Load(byte[] rawAssembly,
                             byte[] rawSymbolStore)

        public Assembly Load(byte[] rawAssembly,
                             byte[] rawSymbolStore,
                             Evidence securityEvidence)
        // ...
    }

    public class Assembly : IEvidenceFactory, ICustomAttributeProvider,
        ISerializable
    {
        // ...
        static public Assembly Load(byte[] rawAssembly)
        static public Assembly Load(byte[] rawAssembly,
                                    byte[] rawSymbolStore)
        static public Assembly Load(byte[] rawAssembly,
                                    byte[] rawSymbolStore,
                                    Evidence securityEvidence)
        // ...
    }
```

As you can see by these definitions, both *Assembly.Load* and *AppDomain.Load* also enable you to pass a byte array containing the debugging file. In the unmanaged implementation, you accomplished this by returning an *IStream* pointer to the debugging file from *IHostAssembly-Store::ProvideAssembly*. I'm going to skip the *Evidence* parameter for now and leave it for the discussion of security in Chapter 10.

On the surface, the forms of *Load* that accept a byte array and *IHostAssemblyStore::Provide-Assembly* provide the same functionality—they both enable you to load an assembly from any store you choose. However, using the managed *Load* method to achieve this is much less efficient. To understand why, you need to take a high-level look at how memory is used by the CLR when it loads an assembly for execution. Before the CLR can run the code in an assembly, it reads the contents of the assembly into memory, verifies that it is well formed, and builds several internal data structures. All of this is done in a heap allocated by a component of the CLR called the class loader. Because these heaps hold only native CLR data structures and not managed objects, I refer to them as *unmanaged heaps*. In contrast, every process in which managed code is run has a heap where the managed objects are stored. This is the heap that is managed by the CLR garbage collector. I call this heap the *managed heap*. When an assembly is loaded from an *IStream**, the CLR calls *IStream::Read* to pull the contents of the assembly into an unmanaged heap where it can be verified and then executed. Because the contents of the assembly can be directly loaded into an unmanaged heap, loading from an *IStream** is very efficient, as shown in Figure 8-8.

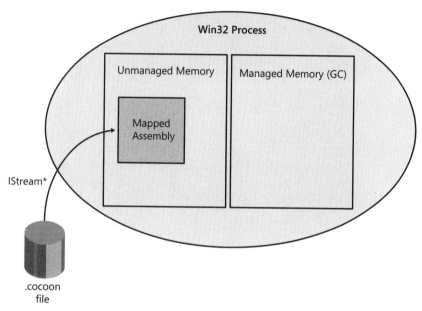

Figure 8-8   Assembly loading from *IStream**

Loading an assembly with the managed *Load* method is less efficient because extra copies of the assembly must be made in memory before the CLR can execute it. The *Load* method takes an array of managed byte objects. Because these objects are managed, they must live in the managed heap. However, the CLR ultimately needs a copy of the bytes in an unmanaged heap to run them. As a result, an extra copy is made by the CLR to move the assembly's contents from the managed heap to an unmanaged heap. In the cocoon scenario, the case is even worse. You start by reading the contents of a stream into unmanaged memory. From there, you marshal those bytes to the managed heap so *Load* can be called. The CLR implementation of *Load* then copies the bytes back to unmanaged memory again! So, you've made two full copies of the assembly before it can be executed. This situation is shown in Figure 8-9.

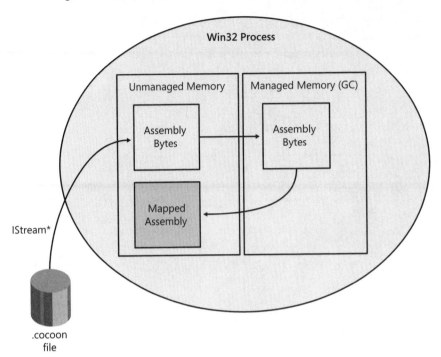

Figure 8-9 Assembly loaded from managed byte array (byte[ ])

In addition to the fact that multiple memory copies must be made to prepare an assembly for execution, the *Load* method is also less efficient because it doesn't provide a way for the caller to assign a unique identifier to the assembly. Recall that the CLR uses a unique identifier internally to prevent loading the same assembly multiple times. When loading an assembly from a file, the fully qualified filename is used as this unique identifier. When loading an assembly returned from *IHostAssemblyStore::ProvideAssembly*, the host creates a unique identity and returns it in the *pAssemblyId* parameter. Because there is no way to specify a unique identifier for an assembly loaded from a managed byte array, the CLR has no way to tell whether the same assembly is being loaded multiple times, so it must treat each call to *Load* as a separate assembly. As a result, much more memory is used than would be in scenarios when one assembly is loaded multiple times.

Despite its limitations, *Load* is still commonly used to load assemblies from custom formats. The reason, of course, is that it's far easier to use than implementing an entire assembly loading manager. If you need to load an assembly from something other than a standard PE file, try using *Load* first. If you find that the performance is inadequate for your scenario, you can always go back and reimplement part of your application in unmanaged code to take advantage of an assembly loading manager.

The *AssemblyResolve* Event

The CLR raises the *AppDomain.AssemblyResolve* event when it cannot resolve a reference to an assembly. Managed programs can load assemblies from locations in which the CLR wouldn't normally find them by providing a handler for this event.

The key difference between resolving assemblies by handling the *AssemblyResolve* event and by implementing an assembly loading manager is that the *AssemblyResolve* event is raised *after* the CLR has failed to locate an assembly where the assembly loading manager (specifically *IHostAssemblyStore::ProvideAssembly*) is called, before the CLR even starts looking. This difference has huge implications in that it prevents you from building an application model that is completely isolated from the way the CLR applies version policy and loads assemblies by default. As an example, consider how the cocoon deployment model is affected by this difference in behavior. Consider the case in which one of the assemblies contained in the cocoon file is also present in the global assembly cache. Because the CLR would look in the GAC first, the assembly would be found there and the event would never be raised, so you'd never have the chance to load the assembly out of the cocoon. Furthermore, consider the case in which version policy is present on the system for an assembly contained in the cocoon. Because policy is evaluated as part of the CLR normal resolution process, this could cause a different version of the assembly to be loaded–again without you ever getting the chance to affect this. So, as you can see, although the *AssemblyResolve* event does enable you to load an assembly from a location in which the CLR wouldn't normally look, it doesn't provide the same level of customization that you can achieve by writing an assembly loading manager in unmanaged code.

To use the *AppDomain.AssemblyResolve* event, you simply create a delegate of type *System.ResolveEventHandler* and add it to the application domain's list of handlers for the event as shown in the following code snippet:

```
class ResolveClass
{
    static Assembly AssemblyResolveHandler(Object sender, ResolveEventArgs e)
    {
        // Locate or create an assembly depending on your scenario and return
        // it.
        Assembly asm = ...
        return asm;
    }
    static void Main(string[] args)
    {
        // ...

        // Set up the delegate for the assembly resolve event.
        Thread.GetDomain().AssemblyResolve +=new
        ResolveEventHandler(ResolveClass.AssemblyResolveHandler);

        //...
    }
}
```

As you can see, the *AssemblyResolve* event takes as input an object of type *ResolveEventArgs* and returns an instance of an *Assembly*. *ResolveEventArgs* has a public property called *Name* that contains the string name of the assembly the CLR could not locate. Upon return from the event handler, the CLR checks the assembly it has been given to make sure it has the identity given in the *Name* property. As long as the assembly you return has the correct identity, you're free to take whatever steps you need in your event handler to find the assembly.

The Runcocoonm Sample

Now that you've seen how the *AssemblyResolve* event and the *Load(byte[]...)* methods work, it's easy to put them together to implement the managed version of the cocoon host. You'll create a delegate to handle the *AssemblyResolve* event and add it to the default application domain's list of handlers. Then, just as you did in the unmanaged implementation, you'll use the *CocoonHostRuntime* assembly to invoke the main entry point for the application contained in the cocoon. The CLR will fail to find the assemblies in the cocoon, so it will raise the *Assembly-Resolve* event and your handler will get called. In your handler, you'll use the *ResolveEventArgs.Name* property to determine which assembly you need to load. You pull that assembly out of the cocoon file as a managed array of bytes and call *Assembly.Load*.

Because the cocoon files are OLE structured storage files, you need some intermediate layer that reads the assembly using the structured storage interfaces (specifically *IStorage* and *IStream*) and then returns the contents as a series of bytes. I've written an unmanaged helper DLL called cocoonreader.dll that performs this task. The code in the runcocoonm.exe program uses the CLR Platform Invoke services to call cocoonreader.dll. The architecture of runcocoonm.exe is shown in Figure 8-10.

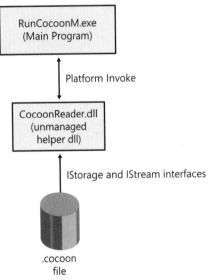

Figure 8-10 Runcocoonm architecture

The code for the complete program is shown in following listings. Listing 8-4 contains the code for cocoonreader.dll, and Listing 8-5 shows the code for runcocoonm.exe.

Listing 8-4   Cocoonreader.dll

```
//
// Cocoonreader.cpp: Contains utilities used by runcocoonm.exe to read
// assemblies out of OLE structured storage cocoon files.
//

#include "stdafx.h"

// Opens a cocoon file given a name. Each call to CocoonOpenCocoon must
// be matched by a call to CocoonCloseCocoon.
extern "C" __declspec(dllexport) HRESULT CocoonOpenCocoon(
LPWSTR pszCocoonName, IStorage **pRootStorage)
{
    return StgOpenStorage(pszCocoonName, NULL, STGM_READ | STGM_DIRECT |
        STGM_SHARE_EXCLUSIVE, NULL, 0, pRootStorage);
}


// Closes the cocoon file by releasing the cocoon's root storage.
extern "C" __declspec(dllexport) HRESULT CocoonCloseCocoon(
IStorage *pRootStorage)
{
    if (pRootStorage) pRootStorage->Release();
    return S_OK;
}


// Opens a stream within a cocoon given a name. Each call to CocoonOpenStream
// must be matched by a call to CocoonCloseStream.
extern "C" __declspec(dllexport) HRESULT CocoonOpenStream(
IStorage *pRootStorage, LPWSTR pszStreamName, IStream **pStream)
{
    return pRootStorage->OpenStream(pszStreamName, 0, STGM_READ | STGM_DIRECT |
        STGM_SHARE_EXCLUSIVE, 0, pStream);
}


// Closes a stream.
extern "C" __declspec(dllexport) HRESULT CocoonCloseStream(IStream *pStream)
{
    if (pStream) pStream->Release();
    return S_OK;
}


// Returns the size of a stream in bytes.
extern "C" __declspec(dllexport) HRESULT CocoonGetStreamSize(IStream *pStream,
DWORD *pSize)
{
    assert(pStream);

    // Get the statistics for the stream - which includes the size.
    STATSTG stats;
    pStream->Stat(&stats, STATFLAG_DEFAULT);

    // Return the size.
    *pSize = stats.cbSize.LowPart;
```

```
    return S_OK;
}

// Returns the contents of the stream. The caller is responsible
// for allocating and freeing the memory pointed to by pBytes.
extern "C" __declspec(dllexport) HRESULT CocoonGetStreamBytes(
IStream *pStream, BYTE *pBytes)
{
    assert (pStream);

    // Get the number of bytes to read.
    STATSTG stats;
    pStream->Stat(&stats, STATFLAG_DEFAULT);
    DWORD dwSize = stats.cbSize.LowPart;

    // Read from the stream.
    DWORD dwBytesRead = 0;
    pStream->Read(pBytes, dwSize, &dwBytesRead);
    assert (dwSize == dwBytesRead);
    return S_OK; }
```

Listing 8-5   Runcocoonm.exe

```
using System;
using System.Runtime.InteropServices;
using System.Reflection;
using System.Threading;
using CocoonRuntime;

namespace RunCocoonM
{

    class CCocoonHost
    {
      // Import the definitions for the helper routines from
      // cocoonreader.dll.
      [ DllImport( "CocoonReader.dll",CharSet=CharSet.Unicode)]
      public static extern int CocoonOpenCocoon(string cocoonName,
          ref IntPtr pCocoon);

      [ DllImport( "CocoonReader.dll",CharSet=CharSet.Unicode)]
      public static extern int CocoonCloseCocoon(IntPtr pCocoon);

      [ DllImport( "CocoonReader.dll",CharSet=CharSet.Unicode)]
      public static extern int CocoonOpenStream(IntPtr pCocoon,
          string streamName, ref IntPtr pStream);

      [ DllImport( "CocoonReader.dll",CharSet=CharSet.Unicode)]
      public static extern int CocoonCloseStream(IntPtr pStream);

      [ DllImport( "CocoonReader.dll",CharSet=CharSet.Unicode)]
      public static extern int CocoonGetStreamSize(IntPtr pStream,
          ref int size);

      [ DllImport( "CocoonReader.dll",CharSet=CharSet.Unicode)]
      public static extern int CocoonGetStreamBytes(IntPtr pStream,
          IntPtr streamBytes);
```

```csharp
static Assembly AssemblyResolveHandler(Object sender,
ResolveEventArgs e)
{
    // Get the name of the assembly you need to resolve from the
    // event args. You want just the simple text name. If the name
    // is fully qualified, you want just the portion before the
    // comma.
    string simpleAssemblyName;
    int commaIndex = e.Name.IndexOf('.');

    if (commaIndex == -1)
        simpleAssemblyName = e.Name;
    else
        simpleAssemblyName = e.Name.Substring(0, commaIndex);

    // Retrieve the cocoon from the application domain property.
    IntPtr pCocoon = (IntPtr) Thread.GetDomain().GetData("Cocoon");

    // Open the stream for the assembly.
    IntPtr pStream = IntPtr.Zero;
    CocoonOpenStream(pCocoon, simpleAssemblyName, ref pStream);

    // Call the helper DLL to get the number of bytes in the stream
    // you're about to read. You need the size so you can allocate
    // the correct number of bytes in the managed array.
    int size = 0;
    CocoonGetStreamSize(pStream, ref size);

    // Allocate enough memory to hold the contents of the entire
    // stream.
    IntPtr pBytes = Marshal.AllocHGlobal(size);

    // Read the assembly from the cocoon.
    CocoonGetStreamBytes(pStream, pBytes);

    // Copy the bytes from unmanaged memory into your managed byte
    // array. You need the bytes in this format to call
    // Assembly.Load.
    byte[] assemblyBytes = new byte[size];
    Marshal.Copy(pBytes, assemblyBytes, 0 , size);

    // Free the unmanaged memory.
    Marshal.FreeHGlobal(pBytes);

    // Close the stream.
    CocoonCloseStream(pStream);

    // Load the assembly from the byte array and return it.
    return Assembly.Load(assemblyBytes, null, null);
}

static string GetTypeNameString()
{
    // Retrieve the cocoon from the application domain property.
    IntPtr pCocoon = (IntPtr) Thread.GetDomain().GetData("Cocoon");
```

```
    // Open the "_entryPoint" stream.
    IntPtr pStream = IntPtr.Zero;
    CocoonOpenStream(pCocoon, "_entryPoint", ref pStream);

    // Get the size of the stream containing the main type name.
    // You need to know the size so you can allocate the correct
    // amount of space to hold the name.
    int size = 0;
    CocoonGetStreamSize(pStream, ref size);

    // Allocate enough space to hold the main type name.
    IntPtr pBytes = Marshal.AllocHGlobal(size);

    // Read the main type name from the cocoon.
    CocoonGetStreamBytes(pStream, pBytes);

    // Copy the stream's contents from unmanaged memory into a
    // managed character array - then create a string from the
    // character array.
    char[] typeNameChars = new char[size];
    Marshal.Copy(pBytes, typeNameChars, 0 , size);
    string typeName = new string(typeNameChars, 0, size/2);

    // Free the unmanaged memory.
    Marshal.FreeHGlobal(pBytes);

    // Close the "MainTypeName" stream.
    CocoonCloseStream(pStream);

    return typeName;
}

[STAThread]
static void Main(string[] args)
{
    // Make sure the name of a cocoon file was passed on the
    // command line.
    if (args.Length != 1)
    {
        Console.WriteLine("Usage: RunCocoonM <cocoon file>");
        return;
    }

    // Open the cocoon file and store a pointer to it in
    // an application domain property. You need this value in
    // your AssemblyResolve event handler.
    IntPtr pCocoon = IntPtr.Zero;
    CocoonOpenCocoon(args[0], ref pCocoon);

    Thread.GetDomain().SetData("Cocoon", pCocoon);

    // Strip off the .cocoon from the command-line argument to get
    // the name of the assembly within the cocoon that contains the
    // Main method.
    int dotIndex = args[0].IndexOf('.');
    string assemblyName = args[0].Substring(0, dotIndex);
```

```
        // Get name of type containing the application's Main method
        // from the cocoon.
        string typeName = CCocoonHost.GetTypeNameString();

        // Set up the delegate for the assembly resolve event.
        Thread.GetDomain().AssemblyResolve +=new
            ResolveEventHandler(CCocoonHost.AssemblyResolveHandler);

        // Use CocoonHostRuntime to invoke Main.
        CocoonDomainManager cdm = new CocoonDomainManager();
        cdm.Run(assemblyName, typeName);

        // Close the cocoon file.
        CocoonCloseCocoon(pCocoon);
    }
  }
}
```

Supporting Multifile Assemblies

Managed programs can support multifile assemblies by handling the *Assembly.ResolveModule* event. This event is raised by the CLR if it cannot find one of an assembly's modules at run time, just as the *AssemblyResolve* event is raised if the file containing the assembly's manifest cannot be found.

Because modules are always part of an assembly, handlers for the *ModuleResolve* event are always associated with a particular assembly, not with the application domain as the *AssemblyResolve* event is. To register for the *ModuleResolve* event, create a delegate of type *ModuleResolveEvent-Handler* and add it to the appropriate assembly's list of handlers. The following code shows a handler for the *ModuleResolve* event being registered for the currently executing assembly:

```
class ResolveClass
{
    static Module ModuleResolveHandler(Object sender, ResolveEventArgs e)
    {
        // Locate or create the module depending on your scenario and
        // return it.
        Module m = ...
        return m;
    }
    static void Main(string[] args)
    {
        // ...

        // Set up the delegate for the module resolve event.
        Assembly currentAssembly = Assembly.GetExecutingAssembly();
        currentAssembly.ModuleResolve += new
            ModuleResolveEventHandler(ResolveClass.ModuleResolveHandler);

        //...
    }
}
```

The *ModuleResolve* event takes as input an object of type *ResolveEventArgs* and returns an instance of a *System.Reflection.Module*. *ResolveEventArgs* is the same type of class that was passed to the *AssemblyResolve* event. In this case, the *Name* property contains the string name of the module the CLR could not locate.

The most common way to get an instance of *Module* to return from the *ModuleResolve* event is to load one from an array of bytes using the *LoadModule* method on *System.Reflection.Assembly*. (The other way to get a module is to create one dynamically using the classes in *System.Reflection.Emit*.) *LoadModule* has two overloads, one that enables you to specify debugging information in addition to the module itself and one that does not:

```
public Module LoadModule(String moduleName,
                         byte[] rawModule)

public Module LoadModule(String moduleName,
                         byte[] rawModule,
                         byte[] rawSymbolStore)
```

When calling *LoadModule*, you must pass the name of the module in the *moduleName* parameter. The CLR uses this string to identify which module is being loaded by checking the name against the list of modules stored in the assembly's manifest. If you pass a *moduleName* that cannot be found in the manifest, the CLR throws an exception of type *System.ArgumentException*.

Summary

The CLR is incredibly flexible in its ability to be adapted to a variety of application environments and deployment scenarios. In this chapter, I discussed how you can completely replace the way the CLR locates and loads assemblies if you need that amount of customization. In general, you can use two different techniques to customize the CLR default deployment model. The approach you pick will depend directly on the amount of customization you require. The CLR hosting APIs provide the hooks necessary to load assemblies from virtually any format or storage mechanism imaginable. Although this approach provides the greatest degree of flexibility, it also requires the most effort in terms of implementation. As an alternative to writing an unmanaged host, you can achieve some level of customization from completely within managed code. The primary capability you lose with this approach is the ability to change the way the version policy system works. You also see slightly poorer performance than you would if you were to write a full CLR host. If neither issue is of concern, you can save yourself some time and effort by taking advantage of the productive gains you'll realize by sticking with managed code.

Chapter 9

Domain-Neutral Assemblies

In Chapter 5, I discuss how application domains act as subprocesses by providing an isolation boundary around a logical application running in an operating system process. To guarantee this isolation, the CLR must make sure that all assemblies are scoped to a particular application domain. That is, all assemblies are loaded within the context of an application domain, and, once loaded, an assembly is not visible to code running in a different application domain. However, I've shown that applications that create multiple application domains often end up loading many of the same assemblies into each domain. For example, it's often the case that many of the Microsoft .NET Framework libraries are loaded into every application domain created by an extensible application. Also, the host runtime assembly that contains the application's application domain manager must be loaded into every application domain. In scenarios such as these, it's unfortunate to load multiple copies of the same assembly into the same process, especially because much of the runtime information the CLR requires to run a statically compiled assembly could, in theory, be shared among all the application domains in the process. Runtime data such as the data structures the CLR uses to represent the assembly's classes, the code the CLR jit compiles while executing the assembly, and so on generally don't vary based on the application domain in which the assembly is loaded.

Domain-neutral code is a feature of the CLR that enables runtime data about an assembly to be shared among multiple application domains. The primary goal of domain-neutral code is to reduce the overall memory consumed by applications that use multiple application domains. This chapter describes how domain-neutral code affects extensible applications. I describe how domain-neutral code affects an application's architecture and how to enable domain-neutral code using the APIs available in the .NET Framework and the CLR hosting interfaces. As you'll see, however, you'll want to understand some consequences of domain-neutral code before enabling the feature.

Domain-Neutral Assembly Architecture

As stated, the goal of domain-neutral code is to reduce the overall working set used by a process. To get a general idea of how this goal is accomplished, consider the scenario discussed earlier in which an extensible application loads several of the same .NET Framework assemblies and its host runtime assembly into every application domain. In this situation, only the add-in assemblies are specific to a particular application domain, as shown in Figure 9-1.

Operating System Process

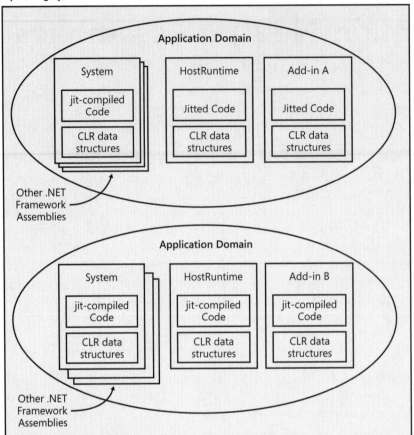

Figure 9-1   Extensible applications often load many of the same assemblies into each application domain.

As you can see, separate copies of all the "common" assemblies are loaded into every application domain. This approach results in significant duplication of the same runtime data. For example, each application domain has a copy of the native code that is compiled as the assembly is executed. Clearly, this could be optimized in scenarios in which this code is the same across all application domains. To reduce this duplication, the runtime data for an assembly is shared across all application domains if that assembly is loaded domain neutral. In Figure 9-2, you can see that only a single copy of the .NET Framework assemblies and the host runtime assembly are loaded into the process. The runtime data, including the jit-compiled native code and the CLR data structures used to represent the assembly in memory, is shared among all the application domains in the process.

In many ways, this sharing of runtime data is analogous to the way the operating system shares static code pages for DLLs that are loaded by multiple processes.

Operating System Process

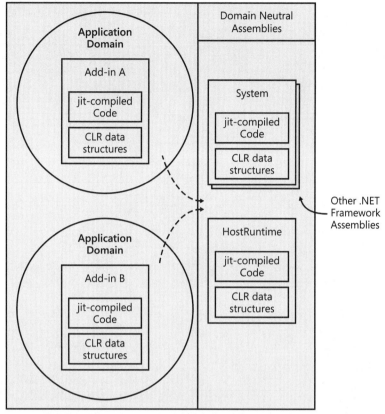

Figure 9-2   Domain-neutral assemblies are shared among all the application domains in a process.

It's important to remember that only the runtime data created by the CLR, such as the native code for the assembly, is shared between application domains, not the instances of the types created by the assembly itself. For example, say an assembly contains a method that creates a data structure that maintains a relationship between customer identifiers and instances of Customer objects. Clearly, sharing data such as this across multiple application domains would violate application domain isolation.

Implications of Using Domain-Neutral Code

At this point, domain-neutral code sounds like a panacea. After all, with all the working set savings, why aren't all assemblies loaded domain neutral? Not surprisingly, you should consider some implications of using domain-neutral code when deciding which (if any) assemblies to load domain neutral. These implications, which follow, are primarily related to performance, security, and flexibility:

■ Domain-neutral assemblies cannot be unloaded from a process.

■ Access to static member variables is slower.

- Initialization of types is slower in some scenarios.

- The set of security permissions granted to a domain-neutral assembly must be the same for every application domain.

- If an assembly is loaded domain neutral, all of its dependencies must be as well.

These points are described in more detail in the following sections.

Domain-Neutral Code Cannot Be Unloaded

Because the jit-compiled code and other CLR runtime data for a domain-neutral assembly is used by all application domains within a process, that assembly cannot be unloaded without shutting down the entire process. In most scenarios, the inability to unload a domain-neutral assembly is the biggest downside to using domain-neutral code. The fact that a domain-neutral assembly cannot be unloaded is the primary reason why the add-in assemblies in extensible applications aren't typically loaded domain neutral. Instead, most extensible applications load only the .NET Framework assemblies and the assembly containing the application domain manager as domain neutral. These assemblies are used in every application domain anyway, so the inability to unload them doesn't affect the overall design of the application.

Access to Static Member Variables Is Slower

To preserve the isolation properties of application domains, each domain must have a copy of the assembly's static member variables. Otherwise, a change made to a static variable in one application domain would be visible in all other application domains. Because each application domain has its own copy of static variables, the CLR must maintain a lookup table that maps the application domain in which the static variable is accessed to the correct copy of the variable. Calling through this level of indirection is clearly slower than accessing the variable directly.

Initialization of Types Can Be Slower

When an assembly is loaded domain neutral, any aspect of its execution that might produce different results in different application domains must be factored out and isolated per domain. Access to static variables is an excellent example of this, as described in the previous section. Type initializers (also known as class constructors or static constructors) are another example. The CLR runs a type's initializer in every application domain.

The CLR supports two different semantics for type initializers: *precise* and *relaxed*. The semantics for precise type initialization require that the initializer is run before the first access to any of the type's static or instance fields, methods, or properties. In contrast, types that use relaxed initialization are only guaranteed to be initialized before the first access to one of the type's static fields. Implementing precise initialization requires more runtime checks and more levels of indirection to maintain application domain isolation for domain-neutral assemblies, so the initialization of types requiring precise semantics will be slower if an assembly is loaded domain neutral. Even so, it's unlikely that this difference in performance will have a substantial impact on your application unless you rely on type initializers to do significant amounts of work.

> **Note** The choice of whether a type requires precise or relaxed initialization semantics is up to the language compiler you are using. In general, if a type initializer does nothing but initialize static variables, the compiler can emit a type initializer with relaxed semantics (*beforefieldinit* in MSIL). However, if a type initializer does more than just initialize static variables, precise semantics is required.

Security Policy Must Be Consistent Across All Application Domains

As I describe in Chapter 10, an application domain might define security policy that affects the set of security permissions granted to assemblies loaded in the domain. When an assembly is loaded domain neutral, the set of security permissions granted to the assembly must be the same for all application domains in the process. Ideally, the CLR would proactively check to make sure the grant set is consistent across application domains and fail to load the assembly if an inconsistency is found. Unfortunately, this is not the case. Instead, differences in the set of granted permissions show up as runtime errors, so it's best to design your security policy at the same time you're thinking about which assemblies to load domain neutral. In Chapter 10, I discuss the details of how to define security policy, including how to make sure your domain-neutral assemblies are granted the same set of permissions in all domains.

The Set of Domain-Neutral Assemblies Must Form a Closure

The set of assemblies loaded domain neutral must form a complete closure. That is, all assemblies referenced by a domain-neutral assembly must also be loaded domain neutral. In theory, the CLR could enforce this restriction when an assembly is loaded by proactively locating all of its dependencies and checking whether you've specified they should be loaded domain neutral as well. However, the performance impact of proactively checking an assembly's references in this fashion is prohibitive. Instead, the CLR enforces that the set of domain-neutral assemblies forms a closure at run time by checking each assembly as it is referenced. If a domain-neutral assembly makes a reference to an assembly that is not in the set of domain-neutral assemblies, the CLR throws a *FileLoadException*, so it's up to you to make sure that the assemblies you load domain neutral form a closed set. For this reason, it's generally best to use domain-neutral loading only on assemblies that you can statically analyze ahead of time—that is, the set of assemblies you know you'll load into your application versus the set of add-in assemblies that will be loaded into your application dynamically.

Domain-Neutral Code and Assembly Dependencies

The native code that the JIT compiler produces for an assembly can be shared across application domains only if that code is the same as the code that would be produced if the assembly were compiled in each application domain separately. An assembly's references influence the native code that is generated because the JIT compiler must emit code to call from one assembly to another. The native code for a given assembly can be shared across application domains only if that assembly has exactly the same set of assembly references in every application domain. An assembly's dependencies are statically recorded in metadata when the assembly is compiled. Those references will obviously be consistent in all application domains, but remember that an application domain might contain version policy that can cause a different version of a dependency to be loaded at run time, so any version policy that can affect the dependencies of a domain-neutral assembly must be the same in all application domains.

Each time an assembly you've specified as domain neutral is loaded into an application domain, the CLR checks to make sure that its set of dependencies is consistent with the other application domains already in the process. If an inconsistency is found, the native code for that assembly cannot be shared with the application domain in which the assembly is loaded. Instead, the CLR will generate a new copy of the native code specifically for that application domain. For example, consider a scenario in which you've specified that an assembly named *Statistics* should be loaded domain neutral. *Statistics* depends on an assembly called *Probability*. *Statistics* and version 5.0.0.0 of *Probability* have already been loaded by two application domains, as shown in Figure 9-3.

Operating System Process

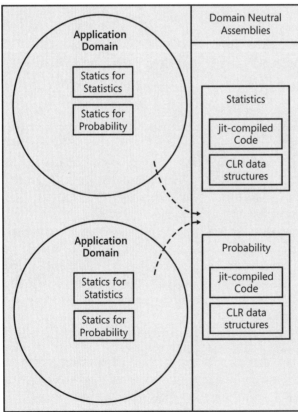

Figure 9-3   Native code can be shared only when an assembly's dependencies are consistent.

In this case, the native code for *Statistics* can be shared because *Statistics* references the same version of *Probability* in both application domains. (I'm assuming all of the other dependencies for *Statistics* are the same as well.) Now add another application domain to the scenario. This new application domain has version policy that redirects all references to *Probability* from version 5.0.0.0 to version 6.0.0.0. Because *Statistics* has a different set of dependencies in this new application domain, the native code that was previously generated in the process cannot be used. This situation is shown in Figure 9-4.

Operating System Process

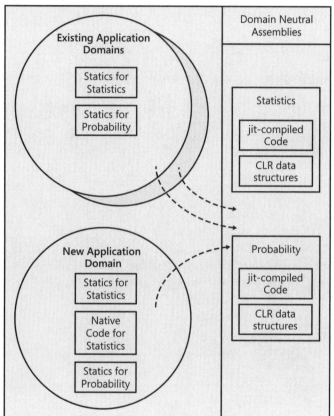

Figure 9-4   Native code cannot be shared if an assembly has a different set of dependencies.

In Figure 9-4, you can see that a separate copy of the native code for *Statistics* has been created for use by the new application domain. As a result, you've lost the working set savings associated with sharing native code across application domains. However, there's another downside to this situation as well. Because *Statistics* was specified to be domain neutral, it has all the properties of a domain-neutral assembly except the code sharing. That is, static variable access and type initialization will still be slower, security policy must be consistent with the other domains in the process, and so on. You can see in Figure 9-4 that even though the native code cannot be shared, a separate copy of the static variables of *Statistics* has been made in the new domain. In short, you've ended up with a worst-case scenario: not only have you lost the working set savings that you hoped to gain by loading *Statistics* domain neutral, but you are still left with the limitations associated with domain-neutral code.

Fortunately, you can avoid this situation by making sure that the version policy associated with the application domains in your process is consistent for those assemblies you wish to load domain neutral. The easiest way to ensure your version policy is consistent is to use an application domain manager to hook all calls to *AppDomain.CreateDomain*, as discussed in Chapter 6.

Specifying Which Assemblies Are Loaded Domain Neutral

You can use three sets of APIs to specify which assemblies you'd like to load domain neutral:

- *CorBindToRuntimeEx*
- The *LoaderOptimization* APIs
- The CLR hosting interfaces

CorBindToRuntimeEx and the *LoaderOptimization* APIs were introduced in .NET Framework 1.0, whereas the hosting interfaces for working with domain-neutral assemblies are new to .NET Framework 2.0.

CorBindToRuntimeEx

CorBindToRuntimeEx is the function used to initialize the CLR in a process. The *startupFlags* parameter to *CorBindToRuntimeEx* is used to configure various aspects of the CLR, including which assemblies should be loaded domain neutral. The valid domain-neutral settings are given by the *STARTUP_FLAGS* enumeration from mscoree.idl:

```
typedef enum {
  // Other flags omitted...
  STARTUP_LOADER_OPTIMIZATION_SINGLE_DOMAIN = 0x1<<1,
  STARTUP_LOADER_OPTIMIZATION_MULTI_DOMAIN = 0x2<<1,
  STARTUP_LOADER_OPTIMIZATION_MULTI_DOMAIN_HOST = 0x3<<1,

  // Other flags omitted...
} STARTUP_FLAGS;
```

These flags offer very coarse options for controlling domain-neutral loading. Each flag is tailored for a specific scenario, as described in the following list:

- **STARTUP_LOADER_OPTIMIZATION_SINGLE_DOMAIN** The *SINGLE_DOMAIN* setting specifies that no assemblies are loaded domain neutral. As its name implies, this setting is geared toward applications that have only one application domain.

- **STARTUP_LOADER_OPTIMIZATION_MULTI_DOMAIN** All assemblies are loaded domain neutral when you pass *STARTUP_LOADER_OPTIMIZATION_MULTI_DOMAIN* to *CorBindToRuntimeEx*. This setting is best for those applications that always load the same set of assemblies into all application domains.

■ **STARTUP_LOADER_OPTIMIZATION_MULTI_DOMAIN_HOST**   The *MULTI_DOMAIN_HOST* setting causes all assemblies with strong names to be loaded domain neutral. Assemblies with weak names are loaded into each application domain separately. This is the setting that .NET Framework 1.0 and .NET Framework 1.1 offer for extensible applications such as those I've been discussing throughout this book. This setting works great for extensible applications in which the host runtime has a strong name, but the add-in assemblies don't (the .NET Framework assemblies all have strong names). Of course, it's overly restrictive to assume that an add-in won't have a strong name. To solve this problem, the CLR added support for specifying an exact list of assemblies to load domain neutral using the hosting interfaces. I discuss that approach later in this section.

> **Note**   Saying that "no assemblies are loaded domain neutral" when you specify *STARTUP_LOADER_OPTIMIZATION_SINGLE_DOMAIN* isn't completely accurate. Regardless of the settings you specify, the CLR always loads mscorlib domain neutral. mscorlib is granted full trust by default security policy, and it doesn't reference any other assemblies so it's not subject to the security and version policy complications described here.

The following example uses *CorBindToRuntimeEx* to specify that all assemblies with strong names should be loaded domain neutral:

```
hr = CorBindToRuntimeEx(
  L"v2.0.41013",
  L"wks",
  STARTUP_LOADER_OPTIMIZATION_MULTI_DOMAIN_HOST,
  CLSID_CLRRuntimeHost,
  IID_ICLRRuntimeHost,
  (PVOID*) &pCLR);
```

One advantage of specifying domain-neutral settings using the values from *STARTUP_FLAGS* is that you don't have to worry about whether the set of assemblies you are supplying forms a full closure. Clearly, the set of no assemblies and the set of all assemblies form a closure. In addition, loading all assemblies with strong names domain neutral forms a closure, too, because an assembly with a strong name can only reference other assemblies with strong names—a reference from an assembly with a strong name to one with a weak name is not allowed.

The *STARTUP_LOADER_OPTIMIZATION* flags specify domain-neutral loading behavior for all application domains in the process. To specify different behavior per application domain, you must use the loader optimization API.

The Loader Optimization API

The loader optimization API is a managed API that enables you to set the same values for domain-neutral loading that *CorBindToRuntimeEx* does. The one difference is that the loader optimization API enables you to specify different values per application domain. The loader optimization API consists of the following components:

- The *System.LoaderOptimization* enumeration

- The *System.LoaderOptimizationAttribute* custom attribute

- The *LoaderOptimization* property on *System.AppDomainSetup*

The *LoaderOptimization* enumeration defines the same values for managed code that the *STARTUP_FLAGS* enumeration does for unmanaged code, with the addition of a new value, *NotSpecified*:

```
public enum LoaderOptimization
{
    NotSpecified            = 0,
    SingleDomain            = 1,
    MultiDomain             = 2,
    MultiDomainHost         = 3
}
```

NotSpecified works the same as if you didn't specify a value at all. Specifying *NotSpecified* at the process level defaults to *SingleDomain*. If specified at the application domain level, *NotSpecified* indicates that the process-wide settings should be used.

In terms of domain-neutral loading, the *LoaderOptimizationAttribute* is the managed equivalent to *CorBindToRuntimeEx* in that it enables you to specify the domain-neutral loading behavior for all application domains in the process. To specify the domain-neutral settings using the *LoaderOptimizationAttribute*, place the attribute on your application's *main* method and pass a value from the *LoaderOptimization* enumeration to its constructor as shown in the following example:

```
[LoaderOptimization(LoaderOptimization.MultiDomainHost)]
static void Main(string[] args)
{
}
```

If you specify the *LoaderOptimizationAttribute* on a method other than *main*, the CLR simply ignores it.

Domain-neutral settings can also be specified on a per–application domain basis using the *AppDomainSetup* object passed to *System.CreateDomain*. *AppDomainSetup* has a property called *LoaderOptimization* that accepts a value from the *System.LoaderOptimization* enumeration. Note that it is possible to specify domain-neutral settings both at the process level (using the *LoaderOptimizationAttribute* or *CorBindToRuntimeEx*) and at the application domain level (using the *LoaderOptimization* property of *AppDomainSetup*). When domain-neutral settings are specified in both places, the value that is specific to the application domain takes precedence (unless the per-domain setting is *NotSpecified*, as described earlier). In other words, the process-wide settings are used only in those application domains for which a specific setting wasn't provided.

Domain-Neutral Assemblies and the CLR Hosting Interfaces

In practice, the domain-neutral settings offered by *CorBindToRuntimeEx* and the loader optimization API were not granular enough for most extensible applications. In general, the most attractive option for extensible applications was to cause all assemblies with strong names to be loaded domain neutral. This worked great for the .NET Framework assembly and the application's host runtime, but was suboptimal if an add-in with a strong name was loaded into the process. Such an add-in would be loaded as domain neutral, and therefore couldn't be unloaded and was subject to the other restrictions described earlier in the chapter.

The CLR hosting interfaces in .NET Framework 2.0 solve this problem by letting CLR hosts supply an exact list of the assemblies to be loaded domain neutral. This list is supplied by implementing the *GetDomainNeutralAssemblies* method of *IHostControl*. *GetDomainNeutralAssemblies* returns the list of assemblies to load domain neutral in the form of a pointer to an *ICLRAssemblyReferenceList* interface, as shown in the following definition from mscoree.idl:

```
interface IHostControl : IUnknown
{
    // Other methods omitted…
    HRESULT GetDomainNeutralAssemblies(
        [out] ICLRAssemblyReferenceList **ppReferenceList);
}
```

Recall from Chapter 8 that *ICLRReferenceAssemblyList* pointers are obtained by passing an array of strings representing the assemblies in your list to the *GetCLRAssemblyReferenceList* method of *ICLRAssemblyIdentityManager*.

Although *GetDomainNeutralAssemblies* gives you the flexibility to load specific assemblies domain neutral, you must take on the burden of making sure the list you supply forms a complete closure. The only way to ensure you're supplying a closed set is to use ildasm.exe or another tool to analyze each assembly's dependencies statically. If the set of assemblies you supply doesn't form a closure, you'll see *FileLoadExceptions* at run time as discussed earlier.

The following sample provides an implementation of *GetDomainNeutralAssemblies* that returns a specific set of assemblies to load domain neutral. In this sample, I've taken the approach that most extensible applications use. Specifically, I've indicated that all of the .NET Framework assemblies and the assembly containing the host's application domain manager (*BoatRaceHostRuntime* in this case) should be loaded domain neutral. This achieves the goal of sharing the jit-compiled code and CLR runtime data structures for the assemblies I expect to load into every application domain, while still allowing me to load strong-named add-ins into the process and unload them later.

```
const wchar_t *wszDomainNeutralAssemblies[] = {
    L"BoatRaceHostRuntime, PublicKeyToken=38c3b24e4a6ee45e",
    L"mscorlib, PublicKeyToken=b77a5c561934e089",
    L"System, PublicKeyToken=b77a5c561934e089",
    L"System.Xml, PublicKeyToken=b77a5c561934e089",
    L"System.Data, PublicKeyToken=b77a5c561934e089",
    L"System.Data.OracleClient, PublicKeyToken=b77a5c561934e089",
```

```
        L"System.Runtime.Remoting, PublicKeyToken=b77a5c561934e089",
        L"System.Windows.Forms, PublicKeyToken=b77a5c561934e089",
        L"System.Web, PublicKeyToken=b03f5f7f11d50a3a",
        L"System.Drawing, PublicKeyToken=b03f5f7f11d50a3a",
        L"System.Design, PublicKeyToken=b03f5f7f11d50a3a",
        L"System.Runtime.Serialization.Formatters.Soap,
         PublicKeyToken=b03f5f7f11d50a3a",
        L"System.Drawing.Design, PublicKeyToken=b03f5f7f11d50a3a",
        L"System.EnterpriseServices, PublicKeyToken=b03f5f7f11d50a3a",
        L"System.DirectoryServices, PublicKeyToken=b03f5f7f11d50a3a",
        L"System.Management, PublicKeyToken=b03f5f7f11d50a3a",
        L"System.Messaging, PublicKeyToken=b03f5f7f11d50a3a",
        L"System.Security, PublicKeyToken=b03f5f7f11d50a3a",
        L"System.ServiceProcess, PublicKeyToken=b03f5f7f11d50a3a",
        L"System.Web.Mobile, PublicKeyToken=b03f5f7f11d50a3a",
        L"System.Web.RegularExpressions, PublicKeyToken=b03f5f7f11d50a3a",
        L"System.Web.Services, PublicKeyToken=b03f5f7f11d50a3a",
        L"System.Configuration.Install, PublicKeyToken=b03f5f7f11d50a3a",
        L"Accessibility, PublicKeyToken=b03f5f7f11d50a3a",
        L"CustomMarshalers, PublicKeyToken=b03f5f7f11d50a3a",
        L"cscompmgd, PublicKeyToken=b03f5f7f11d50a3a",
        L"IEExecRemote, PublicKeyToken=b03f5f7f11d50a3a",
        L"IEHost, PublicKeyToken=b03f5f7f11d50a3a",
        L"IIEHost, PublicKeyToken=b03f5f7f11d50a3a",
        L"ISymWrapper, PublicKeyToken=b03f5f7f11d50a3a",
        L"Microsoft.JScript, PublicKeyToken=b03f5f7f11d50a3a",
        L"Microsoft.VisualBasic, PublicKeyToken=b03f5f7f11d50a3a",
        L"Microsoft.VisualBasic.Vsa, PublicKeyToken=b03f5f7f11d50a3a",
        L"Microsoft.VisualC, PublicKeyToken=b03f5f7f11d50a3a",
        L"Microsoft.Vsa, PublicKeyToken=b03f5f7f11d50a3a",
        L"Microsoft.Vsa.Vb.CodeDOMProcessor, PublicKeyToken=b03f5f7f11d50a3a",
        L"Microsoft_VsaVb, PublicKeyToken=b03f5f7f11d50a3a",
        L"mscorcfg, PublicKeyToken=b03f5f7f11d50a3a",
        L"vjswfchtml, PublicKeyToken=b03f5f7f11d50a3a",
        L"vjswfccw, PublicKeyToken=b03f5f7f11d50a3a",
        L"VJSWfcBrowserStubLib, PublicKeyToken=b03f5f7f11d50a3a",
        L"vjswfc, PublicKeyToken=b03f5f7f11d50a3a",
        L"vjslibcw, PublicKeyToken=b03f5f7f11d50a3a",
        L"vjslib, PublicKeyToken=b03f5f7f11d50a3a",
        L"vjscor, PublicKeyToken=b03f5f7f11d50a3a",
        L"VJSharpCodeProvider, PublicKeyToken=b03f5f7f11d50a3a",
    };

    // ...


    HRESULT STDMETHODCALLTYPE CHostControl::GetDomainNeutralAssemblies(
                            ICLRAssemblyReferenceList **ppReferenceList)
    {
        // Get a pointer to an ICLRAssemblyIdentityManager using a helper class
        // called CLRIdentityManager. This class was defined in Chapter 8.
        CCLRIdentityManager *pIdentityClass = new CCLRIdentityManager();
        ICLRAssemblyIdentityManager *pIdentityInterface =
        pIdentityClass->GetCLRIdentityManager();

        DWORD dwCount = sizeof(wszDomainNeutralAssemblies)/
        sizeof(wszDomainNeutralAssemblies[0]);

        // Call GetCLRAssemblyReferenceList passing in the array of
        // strings identifying the assemblies you'd like to load domain neutral.
```

```
    HRESULT hr = pIdentityInterface->
        GetCLRAssemblyReferenceList(wszDomainNeutralAssemblies,
                                    dwCount,
                                    ppReferenceList);
    pIdentityInterface->Release();
    delete pIdentityClass;
    return S_OK;
}
```

The assembly names you supply to indicate which assemblies to load domain neutral can be partial. That is, the *PublicKeyToken*, *Version*, and *Culture* elements are all optional, just as they are when you use one of the assembly loading APIs to load an assembly given a partial name. (See Chapter 7 for details on how to use the loading APIs.) If you omit a value for one of the optional elements, the CLR treats that element as a wildcard when determining whether an assembly should be loaded domain neutral. For example, the preceding code provides a value for *PublicKeyToken* but not for *Version* or *Culture*. In this case, the CLR will load domain neutral all versions and all cultures of the assembly with the given name and *PublicKeyToken*.

Most CLR hosts that specify an exact list of assemblies using *GetDomainNeutralAssemblies* do not also supply domain-neutral settings using *CorBindToRuntimeEx* or the loader optimization APIs. It is possible to do so, however. If you do specify domain-neutral settings using more than one of the techniques I've described in this chapter, the results are combined. The following list describes which assemblies are loaded domain neutral when you specify both a specific list and one of the values for either *STARTUP_FLAGS* or the *LoaderOptimization* enumeration:

- If the host passes *STARTUP_LOADER_OPTIMIZATION_SINGLE_DOMAIN* (load no assemblies domain neutral), only the assemblies returned from *GetDomainNeutral-Assemblies* would be loaded domain neutral.

- If the host passes *STARTUP_LOADER_OPTIMIZATION_MULTI_DOMAIN* (load all assemblies domain neutral), all assemblies would be loaded domain neutral, regardless of what is returned from *GetDomainNeutralAssemblies*.

- If the host passes *STARTUP_LOADER_OPTIMIZATION_MULTI_DOMAIN_HOST* (load only strong-named assemblies domain neutral), all strong-named assemblies plus those returned from *GetDomainNeutralAssemblies* would be loaded domain neutral.

In this section, I've described both managed and unmanaged APIs for specifying which assemblies to load domain neutral. As discussed earlier, however, the features available to you through the various APIs are not the same. Specifically,

- The managed APIs enable you to specify domain-neutral settings per application domain, whereas the unmanaged APIs do not.

- The unmanaged APIs enable you to provide a specific list of assemblies to load domain neutral, whereas the managed APIs do not.

In practice, I think you'll find that returning a specific list of assemblies using *GetDomain-NeutralAssemblies* more closely matches most application requirements than the coarse settings offered by either *CorBindToRuntimeEx* or the loader optimization APIs. In particular,

GetDomainNeutralAssemblies enables you to implement the behavior most requested by extensible applications: the ability to load the .NET Framework assemblies and the host runtime assembly domain neutral while not loading any add-ins domain neutral regardless of whether they have a strong name.

Determining Whether an Assembly Has Been Loaded Domain Neutral

.NET Framework 2.0 introduces an API you can use to determine whether a given assembly was loaded domain neutral. The *AssemblyIsDomainNeutral* method on *System.Diagnostics.Loader* takes an assembly in the form of an instance of the *System.Reflection.Assembly* class and returns a *boolean* value indicating whether the assembly was loaded domain neutral, as shown in the following example:

```
using System;
using System.Text;
using System.Reflection;
using System.Diagnostics;

namespace DomainNeutralExample
{
    public class Program
    {
        [LoaderOptimization(LoaderOptimization.MultiDomainHost)]
        static void Main(string[] args)
        {
            Assembly a = Assembly.Load("Alinghi");

            Console.WriteLine(a.FullName +
                " is loaded domain neutral: " +
                Loader.AssemblyIsDomainNeutral(a).ToString());
        }
    }
}
```

Summary

Domain-neutral code is a feature of the CLR aimed at reducing the overall working set required by processes consisting of multiple application domains. The working set is reduced by sharing the jit-compiled code and other CLR runtime data structures for a given assembly across application domains. However, there are some restrictions placed on assemblies loaded domain neutral. For example, a domain-neutral assembly might only reference other domain-neutral assemblies. In addition, an assembly's dependencies must be exactly identical between application domains for the assembly's native code to be shared. The set of assemblies to load domain neutral is specified by a set of APIs provided by the .NET Framework and the CLR hosting interfaces. The most flexible, and therefore the most widely used, of these APIs is the *GetDomainNeutralAssemblies* method on the *IHostControl* interface. *GetDomainNeutralAssemblies* enables a host to specify the exact set of assemblies to be loaded domain neutral.

Chapter 10

Extending the CLR Security System to Protect Your Extensible Application

Microsoft .NET Framework applications run in a variety of different environments with a range of security considerations. For example, an environment in which code is dynamically downloaded to a machine and executed has different security considerations than a locked-down environment in which only code that has been explicitly approved and installed by an administrator is allowed to run. Because the CLR supports application models that allow code to be run in such varied environments, the CLR security system must be flexible enough to enable the providers of application models to enforce the security constraints they desire.

Throughout this book, I've talked about the techniques you can use to define new application models for managed code by writing CLR hosts and other extensible applications. Defining a new application model necessarily requires you to think about the security requirements for the environment in which your application will be running. A solid security design is critical for an extensible application primarily because much of the code that is loaded into an extensible application comes from unknown sources. The add-ins that will be loaded into your process will most likely be written by someone other than yourself. As a result, you don't know the origin of the code, which .NET Framework APIs it uses, whether it calls out into unmanaged code, and so on. As you'll see throughout this chapter, you can specify which operations can be performed by code running in the application domains you create. It's best to take a conservative approach to security when writing an extensible application that will execute assemblies from unknown sources. Securing your process from malicious access is important not only to protect your own data, but also to protect access to resources on the machine on which your application is running.

Fortunately, extensibility has been a key design goal of the CLR security system from the beginning. Nearly all of the system's core features can be extended and customized by individual applications. Throughout this chapter, I show you how to take advantage of these extensibility points to secure your extensible application. I begin by providing an overview of the CLR Code Access Security (CAS) system and the various ways it can be extended. Then I use these concepts to add security features to the cocoon deployment host I built in Chapter 8.

An Overview of Code Access Security

A thorough description of the CAS system is beyond the scope of this chapter. CAS is so broad and so detailed that entire books have been dedicated to the subject. In this section, I focus on the three main concepts in CAS (evidence, policy, and permissions) and describe them from the perspective of their use in extensible applications.

Perhaps the best way to begin describing CAS is by looking back at the original motivation behind the creation of the feature and the scenarios it is meant to enable. The primary goal of CAS is to enable what is referred to as *partially trusted code*. In the partial trust model, the range of operations that code can perform is related to how much it is trusted by the machine administrator and by the host that owns the process in which it is running. The level of trust, and therefore the operations the code can perform, can be very granular and ranges from no trust to fully trusted. Code with no trust is completely restricted—it can't even run. Code that is fully trusted is allowed to do anything it wants. Allowing levels of trust between full and none is where CAS provides its value. For example, a machine administrator might dictate that a given piece of code can access only a certain portion of the file system and display some user interface, but it can't do anything else, such as access the network, print documents, or store data in the registry.

Indeed, the motivation behind CAS and the partial trust model is to provide a more granular model than the "all or nothing" model used in many existing operating system security models. Consider the case of a control that is downloaded from an Internet site and executed on a local machine. In the purely native code security model, the administrator (and the user) have only two choices when determining how much to trust the control. They can decide either to trust it completely or not trust it at all. Trusting the control completely allows the control to have full access to the machine. Not trusting the control means it won't even be installed. The .NET Framework recognizes that there are many scenarios in which a more middle-of-the-road approach is desired. That is, code can be trusted to perform some operations but not others. These are the scenarios that CAS enables.

In addition to providing a more granular trust model, CAS differs from the existing Microsoft Windows operating system security model in another key way: security decisions in CAS are based on code identities, not user identities. That is, CAS grants code the permission to perform certain operations based on characteristics of the code itself, not based on the user who is logged on to the machine when the code is running. For example, an administrator or host can grant code the permission to access the file system based on whether the assembly has a strong name associated with a particular cryptographic key pair. In contrast, administrators of the Windows security system make decisions about which portions of the file system can be accessed based on the user who is running the code. The characteristics of the code that can be used to make security decisions in CAS are called *evidence*. Evidence is one of the primary concepts in CAS, as you'll see in the next section.

The Core Concepts: Evidence, Permissions, and Policy

The CAS system is built around the following three primary concepts: evidence, permissions, and policy.

- **Evidence** As described, security decisions in CAS are based on characteristics of the code called evidence. Evidence is associated with an assembly and comes from two main sources: the CLR and the extensible application that is loading the assembly.

■ **Permissions**   A *permission* represents the right to access a given resource in the system. For example, the .NET Framework includes a permission called *FileIOPermission* that defines which portion of the file system an assembly can access. Authors of extensible applications can also define their own permissions to protect access to application-specific resources.

■ **Policy**   Policy is the mapping between evidence and permissions. CAS policy is a collection of rules (expressed in what are called *code groups*) that describe which permissions are granted to the assembly based on the evidence associated with that assembly. For example, a policy statement can specify that "all code downloaded from *www.cohovineyard.com* can execute on my machine, but it cannot access any resources such as the file system or registry." Policy can be defined both by the administrator of the machine and the extensible application that hosts the assembly.

These concepts all work together to determine the set of operations an assembly can perform. Evidence is the input to policy, which specifies which permissions are granted as shown in Figure 10-1.

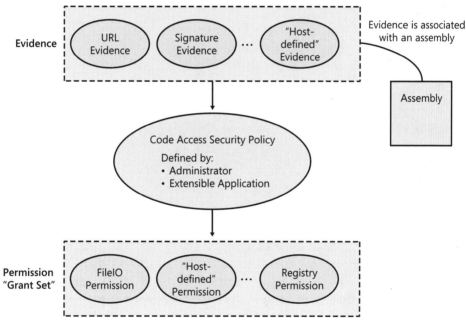

Figure 10-1   Code Access Security policy grants permissions to an assembly based on evidence.

As you've seen, all three of these primary concepts are extensible. In the next few sections, I describe these concepts in more detail and talk about when you might want to define custom evidence, write a custom permission, or author CAS policy statements for an extensible application.

Evidence

As discussed, the evidence describing an assembly comes from two main sources: the CLR and the extensible application that is hosting the assembly. The CLR assigns a fixed set of evidence to an assembly when it is loaded. This evidence can include the assembly's location on the file system or on the Internet, its strong-name signature, the identity of the assembly's publisher, and so on. Evidence assigned by the host can include these forms of evidence as well, but a host can also define application-specific evidence classes. For example, later in the chapter, I define application-specific evidence that identifies an assembly as contained in a cocoon file from the sample built in Chapter 8.

Evidence, like all of the core concepts in the CAS system, is implemented as managed objects. The evidence that is natively understood by the CLR is represented by managed classes, including the following from the *System.Security.Policy* namespace:

- *Application Directory*
- *Gac*
- *Hash*
- *PermissionRequestEvidence*
- *Publisher*
- *Site*
- *StrongName*
- *Url*
- *Zone*

> **Note**   An assembly can also provide evidence about itself. However, this evidence is weaker in the sense that any evidence provided by the CLR or the hosting application can always override it.

Let me make the concept of evidence more concrete by giving a specific example. The evidence for a given assembly can be discovered using the *Evidence* property on *System.Reflection.Assembly*. The *Evidence* property is an object of type *System.Security.Policy.Evidence* that contains a collection of all the evidence associated with an assembly. The program in Listing 10-1 loads an assembly and enumerates its evidence using the *Evidence* property from the *Assembly* class.

Listing 10-1   Evidencedisplay.cs

```
using System;
using System.Text;
using System.Reflection;
using System.Security.Policy;
using System.Collections;
```

```
namespace EvidenceDisplay
{
   class Program
   {
      static void Main(string[] args)
      {
         // Load an assembly.
         Assembly a = Assembly.Load("Utilities");

         // Get and display its evidence.
         Evidence ev = a.Evidence;
         IEnumerator e = ev.GetEnumerator();

         while (e.MoveNext())
         {
            Console.WriteLine(e.Current);
         }
      }
   }
}
```

The preceding program generates the following output:

```
<System.Security.Policy.Zone version="1">
<Zone>MyComputer</Zone>
</System.Security.Policy.Zone>

<System.Security.Policy.Url version="1">
<Url>file:///C:/temp/Evidence/Evidence/bin/Debug/Utilities.dll</Url>
</System.Security.Policy.Url>

<StrongName version="1"
Key="00240000048000009400000006020000002400005253413100040000010001005 71ED9EF397800C456148B4
CB3F5F1DC73223B883C62E1A7804E80CA2084FEE41D26B233AAF044BA8D6322D1BD78E448F07DFD4B06510A2C87D
1D7DC86F89EAE304A327737B290B9AC20BEB84F132C8B95A7868A8938562027803333381D8DD2A9E4D66A41E1A83
D01F7CE5C01DAC8A4CB9FBD02EEBEBEAB870D8EB291E4FCA6"
Name="Utilities"
Version="1.0.1613.31500"/>

<System.Security.Policy.Hash version="1">
<RawData>4D5.......0000000000000</RawData>
</System.Security.Policy.Hash>
```

As you can see, the CLR has assigned evidence to the *Utilities* assembly describing the zone and file location from which it originated, its strong-name signature, and a hash of the assembly's contents (I've abbreviated the output to display only a portion of the hash).

Evidence on its own merely describes an assembly. To make any use of evidence, policy must be defined that maps that evidence to a set of permissions. The next section describes CAS policy in more detail, including its role in extensible applications.

Policy

CAS policy is expressed as a collection of code groups that define the mapping between evidence and the set of permissions to grant the assembly. Each code group consists of a *membership condition* and a *policy statement*. A membership condition is a qualifier that defines the specific condition that an assembly's evidence must satisfy to be granted the specified set of permissions. The set of permissions to be granted, along with some attributes that describe how these permissions are merged with those from other code groups, is specified in the policy statement. Figure 10-2 shows a sample code group. This group grants all code downloaded from *www.cohowinery.com* the permission to execute and to read and write to the c:\temp directory in the file system.

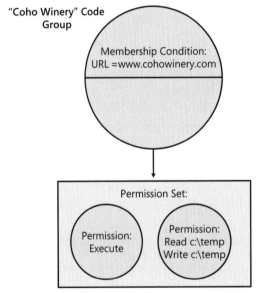

Figure 10-2   Code groups consist of a membership condition and a policy statement.

The code groups that constitute CAS policy are arranged in a hierarchy. That is, the code groups form a tree in which a code group can have other code groups as children. The code group at the top of a CAS policy tree always has a membership condition of *all code*, meaning that every assembly qualifies regardless of its evidence. The All Code code group then has children that define the mappings between specific pieces of evidence and a permission set to grant. An example of a policy tree is shown in Figure 10-3.

When evaluating policy for a given assembly, the CLR takes the assembly's evidence and compares it against the membership conditions for all code groups in the policy tree. The permission set specified by each code group for which the assembly's evidence qualifies is added to the overall set of permissions that will be granted to the assembly. For example, the policy tree in Figure 10-3 contains two code groups (other than the All Code group). One group (the Coho Winery code group) grants permissions based on the fact that an assembly originated from *www.cohowinery.com*. The second code group (the Coho Strong Name code group) grants permissions based on whether the given assembly was signed with a specific strong-name key (the Coho Winery key).

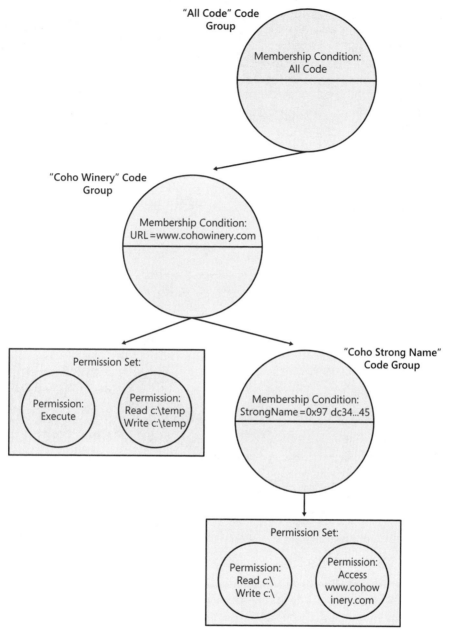

Figure 10-3   Code groups are arranged in a hierarchy.

To illustrate how the permission sets from multiple code groups are typically combined, assume the CLR is evaluating policy for an assembly from *www.cohowinery.com* that is signed with the Coho Winery key. The evaluation process begins at the top of the tree. After satisfying the membership condition for All Code, the CLR asks the Coho Winery code group whether the assembly's evidence passes the URL membership condition specified in that code group. Because the assembly originated from *www.cohowinery.com* (recall that the CLR automatically assigns this evidence), the permissions that grant the right to execute and to read and write from c:\temp are added to the assembly's grant set. Next, the CLR tests the membership condition for the Coho Strong Name code group. This membership condition passes as well because the assembly is signed with the proper key. As a result, the permission to read and write anywhere on c:\ and the permission to programmatically access the *www.cohowinery.com* site are granted to the assembly as well. The overall set of permissions granted to the assembly includes the following rights:

- Execute
- Read and Write to c:\ (this is a superset of the permission to read and write only from c:\temp)
- Access *www.cohowinery.com*

In this example, the permissions granted by each qualifying code group were combined (using the mathematical union operation) to form the final grant set. It's typically the case that permission sets are combined in this fashion, but other options are possible. The behavior for how different permission sets are combined is determined by the types of code groups in the policy tree and by the attributes on their policy statements. In our example, all code groups were *union code groups*. However, there are other types of code groups, including *first match* code groups, which define different rules for how permission sets are combined.

As with all of the core concepts in CAS, the code groups and membership conditions discussed here are represented as managed objects. The .NET Framework provides membership conditions that correspond to the types of evidence natively understood by the CLR. For example, the *ZoneMembershipCondition* class in *System.Security.Policy* corresponds to *Zone* evidence, the *StrongNameMembershipCondition* is used to test *StrongName* evidence, and so on. In addition, the CAS policy system is extensible and allows custom code groups and custom membership conditions to be defined. I take advantage of this capability later in the chapter when I define a custom membership condition to test whether evidence is present that identifies an assembly as coming from a cocoon file.

Policy Levels　The hierarchy of code groups just described constitutes a *policy level*. The CAS policy system has four such levels:

- **Enterprise**　Enterprise CAS policy is specified by a system administrator, typically using the .NET Framework Configuration tool, and deployed to the machines in an enterprise using any number of software distribution tools.
- **Machine**　Administrators can also define CAS policy that applies to all applications running on a given machine. Machine-level CAS policy is also typically specified using the .NET Configuration tool.
- **User**　CAS policy can also be specified for particular users on a machine. This level of policy enables an administrator to grant different sets of permissions to different types of users, for example.

- **Application domain**   CAS policy can be specified by the creator of each application domain. By default, each new domain has no such policy. The ability to provide custom policy per application domain is one of the primary techniques an extensible application can use to customize the CAS system. Later in the chapter, I define application domain CAS policy for the domains I create as part of the cocoon CLR host.

The CLR evaluates all four of these policy levels to determine the set of permissions that should be granted to an assembly. The four grant sets that result from evaluating the individual policy levels intersect to determine the assembly's final grant set as shown in Figure 10-4.

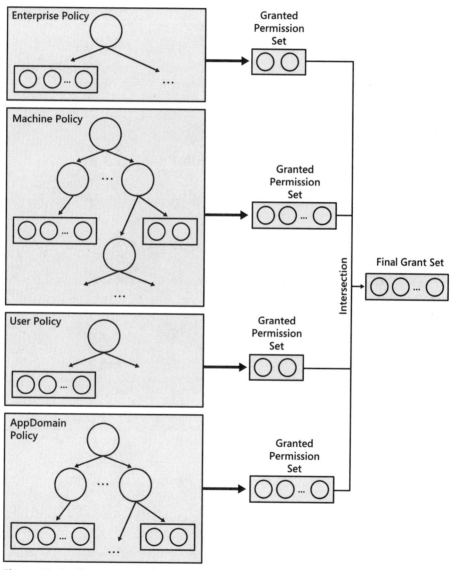

Figure 10-4   The grant sets from each policy level intersect to determine the set of permissions granted to the assembly.

The intersection of the grant sets from the individual policy levels results in a least-common-denominator approach to determining the final set of permissions granted to the assembly. As a result, no level can force a particular permission to be granted. A permission must be granted by all other levels for it to be part of the final grant set.

The caspol.exe tool that ships with the .NET Framework SDK contains some options you can use to evaluate the enterprise, machine, and user policy levels statically for a given assembly. These options are useful both to understand how the policy system works in general and to diagnose why the policy system isn't granting an assembly the set of permissions you expect. The -rsp (stands for "resolve permissions") flag to caspol.exe displays the results of evaluating policy for the assembly you provide. For example, the following output was generated by running *Caspol −rsputilities.dll* from a command prompt:

```
Microsoft (R) .NET Framework CasPol 2.0.40301.9
Copyright (C) Microsoft Corporation 1998-2004. All rights reserved.

Resolving permissions for level = Enterprise
Resolving permissions for level = Machine
Resolving permissions for level = User

Grant = <PermissionSet class="System.Security.PermissionSet"
    version="1">

<IPermission class="System.Security.Permissions.EnvironmentPermission,
    mscorlib, Version=2.0.3600.0, Culture=neutral,
    PublicKeyToken=b77a5c561934e089"
    version="1"
    Read="USERNAME"/>

<IPermission class="System.Security.Permissions.FileDialogPermission,
    mscorlib, Version=2.0.3600.0, Culture=neutral,
    PublicKeyToken=b77a5c561934e089"
    version="1"
    Unrestricted="true"/>

<IPermission class="System.Security.Permissions.SecurityPermission,
    mscorlib, Version=2.0.3600.0, Culture=neutral,
    PublicKeyToken=b77a5c561934e089"
    version="1"
    Flags="Assertion, Execution, BindingRedirects"/>

<IPermission class="System.Security.Permissions.UIPermission,
    mscorlib, Version=2.0.3600.0, Culture=neutral,
    PublicKeyToken=b77a5c561934e089"
    version="1"
    Unrestricted="true"/>

<IPermission class="System.Drawing.Printing.PrintingPermission,
    System.Drawing, Version=2.0.3600.0, Culture=neutral,
    PublicKeyToken=b03f5f7f11d50a3a"
    version="1"
    Level="DefaultPrinting"/>
```

```
<IPermission class="System.Diagnostics.EventLogPermission,
   System, Version=2.0.3600.0, Culture=neutral,
   PublicKeyToken=b77a5c561934e089"
   version="1">
   <Machine name="." access="Instrument"/>
</IPermission>

</PermissionSet>
```

As you can see from this output, the intersection of the enterprise, machine, and user policy levels grants the *Utilities* assembly the permission to read the USERNAME environment variable, display user interface, use the printer, write to the event log, and so on .

> **Note** As discussed, the core concepts of CAS are all represented as managed objects. So their on-disk representation is just the serialized form of the managed object. You can see this representation both in the preceding output from caspol.exe and in the output from the evidence display program listed earlier in the chapter. Running **caspol -rgs** determines the final grant set for the assembly and outputs it using .NET serialization. The policy trees that represent the enterprise, machine, and user policy are also serialized to disk in this way. For example, you can look at the serialized form of the machine policy tree by looking at the security.config file in the %windir%\microsoft.net\framework\v2.0.41013\config directory. The .NET Configuration tool simply edits the managed objects in memory and persists them to disk files using .NET Framework serialization.

Although caspol.exe can't be used to evaluate application domain CAS policy, it is useful to help debug extensible applications nonetheless. For example, you might expect that the code in your application domain should get a specific set of permissions as specified by your application domain CAS policy. However, if the enterprise, machine, or user level doesn't also grant the permission you do at the application domain level, the permission will not be included in the assembly's final grant set. Using caspol.exe to evaluate the grant set produced at the enterprise, machine, and user levels is a great way to diagnose these sorts of issues.

Default CAS Policy   The .NET Framework ships with default security policy for the enterprise, machine, and user levels. Generally speaking, default policy grants full trust to all code that is installed on the local machine and to all assemblies that ship as part of the .NET Framework. Code that is loaded from the Internet, an intranet, or file shares gets a reduced set of permissions. As demonstrated, it's useful to understand the contents of the enterprise, machine, and user levels of policy because policy does have an effect on the permission you'll grant as part of your extensible application. CAS policy, whether it's the default policy shipped with the .NET Framework or a set of policy explicitly provided by an administrator, is best viewed with the .NET Configuration tool. Figure 10-5 shows the code group hierarchy representing machine policy as displayed in the Configuration tool.

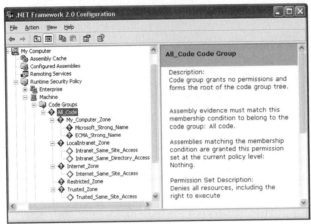

Figure 10-5   The .NET Configuration tool makes it easy to view security policy for the enterprise, machine, and user levels.

Permissions

As described, a permission represents the right to access a particular resource. Permissions are implemented as managed objects just as the other core concepts of the CAS system are. As demonstrated, permissions are granted to an assembly as a result of evaluating CAS policy based on the evidence associated with that assembly. In the next section, I discuss how the CLR enforces that the resources protected by a permission cannot be accessed by unauthorized code.

The .NET Framework includes several permissions that protect the resources on a typical computer. I gave some examples of these permissions earlier when I discussed the results of evaluating security policy for a particular assembly using caspol.exe. The list of permissions included with the .NET Framework includes the following:

- *FileIOPermission*
- *RegistryPermission*
- *EnvironmentPermission*
- *ReflectionPermission*
- *WebPermission*
- *SocketPermission*
- *UIPermission*
- *SecurityPermission*

As with most aspects of the CAS system, the set of permissions that can be granted to an assembly is completely extensible. If you have a resource to protect that isn't covered by one of the .NET Framework permissions, you simply write your own. The permissions you write can be granted by CAS policy and are enforced by the CLR just as the .NET Framework permissions are. I won't cover the details of how to write a custom permission in this book, but more information and examples can be found in the .NET Framework SDK and in any of a number of books dedicated to CAS.

Runtime Enforcement of Permissions: Permission Demands and the Stack Walk

At a high level, a security system performs the following three activities to ensure the protection of a particular resource:

1. Authentication

2. Authorization

3. Enforcement

Authentication, or the secure identification of the entity attempting to access a protected resource, is accomplished in CAS through the assignment of evidence to an assembly. The assignment of rights to the secure identity, or authorization, corresponds to the evaluation of CAS policy. In the last few sections, I discussed how evidence is used by the policy system to determine the set of permissions an assembly is granted. In this section, I show how the CLR enforces that a given assembly can access only the resources for which it has permission.

The enforcement of permissions by the CLR is done using three techniques: validation, verification, and stack walks. Validation and verification refer to the steps taken to ensure the correctness of an assembly. Validation ensures that the assembly's metadata and intermediate language (IL) stream are well formed. That is, the metadata doesn't include pointers to random memory locations in the file and that all IL instructions performed by the assembly are correctly formed. Verification ensures that the code in the assembly is type safe. In Chapter 5 I discuss the importance of type safety in ensuring that the isolation boundary provided by an application domain is sound. The final technique used to enforce the correctness of the CAS system is the stack walk. Simply put, a stack walk ensures that the assembly attempting to access a particular resource (and all of its descendents on the call stack) has been granted the permission required to access the resource.

The process of enforcing permissions through a stack walk begins with the *demand* of a permission by the class library that provides the managed API over the protected resource. This process works as follows. Resources protected by CAS permissions always have a managed API that is used to access them. For example, the .NET Framework includes a set of APIs to access the file system. These APIs, contained in the *System.IO* namespace, protect access to the file system using the *FileIOPermission*. Similarly, the .NET Framework APIs for accessing the registry protect the underlying resource using *RegistryPermission*. These class libraries protect resources by issuing a demand for the appropriate permission. For example, Figure 10-6 shows a class library containing a class called *File* that applications use to access the file system. The *Read* method on the *File* class issues a demand for *FileIOPermission* before reading the contents of the file.

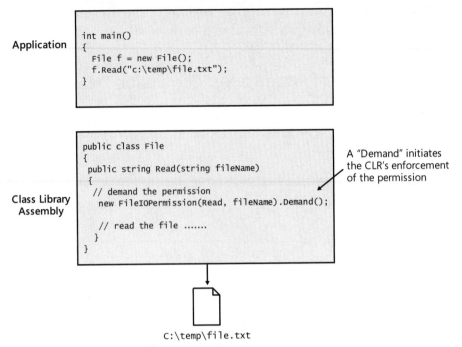

Figure 10-6   Class library authors demand permissions to protect resources.

A permission demand is an indication to the CLR that it should check to make sure that the caller attempting to access the resource has been granted the appropriate permission. In other words, the demand of a permission initiates a stack walk. When walking the stack, the CLR checks the assembly issuing the demand and all other assemblies in the call stack to make sure that they have been granted the appropriate permission, *FileIOPermission*, in this case. If all assemblies have the proper grant, the demand passes and execution proceeds. However, if any assembly in the call chain has not been granted the required permission, execution stops and an instance of *System.SecurityException* is thrown. The process of walking the stack in response to a demand for a permission is shown in Figure 10-7.

In the general case, a stack walk involves checking all callers on the stack as I've just described. However, CAS involves various concepts that can introduce variations on the basic stack walk. For example, demands such as *link demands* and *inheritance demands* check only an assembly's immediate caller instead of all callers on the stack. In addition, you can use various APIs to control how the stack walk is performed. Examples of these stack walk modifiers include the *assert*, the *deny*, and the *permit only*.

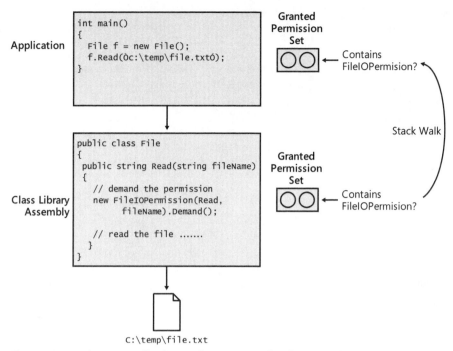

Figure 10-7   The CLR walks the stack to ensure all callers have been granted the demanded permission.

There is much more to the CAS system than what I have presented here. However, this introduction should provide enough background for you to be able to add the basic CAS concepts to an extensible application. Now that I've covered the basics, take a look at the specific APIs the .NET Framework provides for customizing evidence, permissions, and policy.

Customizing the Code Access Security System Using a *HostSecurityManager*

The *HostSecurityManager* class in the *System.Security* namespace provides the infrastructure through which an extensible application can customize the CAS system for individual application domains. By providing a class derived from *HostSecurityManager*, an extensible application can assign evidence to assemblies as they are loaded, supply a CAS policy tree for an application domain, and so on. Table 10-1 lists the members of *HostSecurityManager*.

Table 10-1   The Members of *HostSecurityManager*

Method	Description
DomainPolicy	A property through which an extensible application can supply an application domain CAS policy level.
ProvideAssemblyEvidence	A method used to supply evidence to assemblies as they are loaded. Extensible applications implement this method to supply host-specific evidence to augment the evidence provided by the CLR.

Table 10-1 The Members of *HostSecurityManager*

Method	Description
DetermineApplicationTrust	A method by which extensible applications can decide whether an application defined by a formal manifest is allowed to run. Note: I don't cover the topic of application manifests at all in this book. Refer to the .NET Framework SDK for more information on this property.
Flags	A set of flags of type *HostSecurityManagerFlags* through which the extensible application tells the CLR which CAS customizations it is interested in supplying. For example, the CLR won't consult your *HostSecurityManager* implementation for an application-domain-level policy tree unless this property includes the *HostSecurityManagerFlags.HostPolicyLevel* flag.

A *HostSecurityManager* is part of the application domain manager infrastructure that extensible applications use to customize new application domains. When initializing a new application domain, the CLR checks to see whether an implementation of *HostSecurityManager* has been provided for the new domain by accessing the *HostSecurityManager* property on the domain's application domain manager.

Now that I've covered the core concepts of the CAS system and have taken a first look at the *HostSecurityManager* class, I will go ahead and write an extensible application that extends CAS to enforce application-specific security requirements.

Code Access Security in the Cocoon Host

In Chapter 8, I wrote a CLR host called runcocoon.exe that enabled a new deployment model called a cocoon. Recall that the cocoon deployment model allowed you to package all the files in your application (minus the .NET Framework assemblies) into a single OLE-structured storage file. Runcocoon.exe customized how the CLR loads assemblies by providing an assembly loading manager using the CLR hosting interfaces to run the applications contained in cocoon files. In this section, I extend the host built in Chapter 8 to use the CAS system to restrict the set of operations that can be performed by applications contained in cocoons.

Before I get into the implementation details of how to customize CAS, allow me to establish some security requirements for runcocoon.exe. In particular, the enhancements I make in this chapter will enforce that code running as part of a cocoon application has the following characteristics:

■ It can reference only other assemblies contained in the cocoon and the .NET Framework assemblies. No other assemblies will be granted the permission to execute. A *SecurityException* will be raised if an attempt is made to load such an assembly.

■ It will have permission only to execute, display user interface, and read and write files to a temporary scratch space referred to as isolated storage. (I describe a bit more about isolated storage later in the chapter when I build the policy tree that grants the appropriate permission.)

I use the infrastructure provided by a *HostSecurityManager* to enforce these requirements. In particular, I supply an application domain CAS policy tree that grants the assemblies in the cocoon the permission only to execute, display user interface, and manipulate isolated storage. The assemblies in the cocoon will be identified to the CAS system using custom evidence and a custom membership condition. Modifying runcocoon.exe to incorporate CAS requires the following steps:

1. Create an initial implementation of a class derived from *HostSecurityManager*.

2. Create custom evidence used to authenticate the assemblies in the cocoon.

3. Create a membership condition that can recognize the custom evidence.

4. Create an application-domain-level CAS policy tree that grants the appropriate permissions.

5. Assign the custom evidence to the assemblies in the cocoon.

The following sections describe these steps in detail.

Step 1: Provide an Initial Implementation of *HostSecurityManager*

The customizations I'd like to achieve are centered around the implementation of a host security manager. Plugging the initial implementation of a host security manager into the CAS system requires three initial steps: (1) derive a class from the *HostSecurityManager* base class, (2) implement the *Flags* property to tell the CLR which customizations I am interested in participating in, and (3) return an instance of the host security manager from the application domain manager.

The host security manager will participate in two of the customizations offered by *HostSecurityManager*: it provides custom evidence for assemblies and an application-domain-level CAS policy tree. So I must return the *HostSecurityManagerFlags.HostAssemblyEvidence-* and *HostSecurityManagerFlags.HostPolicy*-level flags from the host security manager's implementation of the *Flags* property. The initial implementation looks like this:

```
public class CocoonSecurityManager : HostSecurityManager
{
    public override HostSecurityManagerFlags Flags
    {
        get
        {
            return (HostSecurityManagerFlags.HostAssemblyEvidence |
                HostSecurityManagerFlags.HostPolicyLevel);
        }
    }
}
```

Providing the CLR with an instance of the host security manager is just a matter of creating a new instance of *CocoonSecurityManager* and returning it from the *HostSecurityManager* property of the application domain manager. The following snippet shows the application domain manager class implemented in Chapter 8 with an implementation of the *HostSecurityManager* property added.

```
public class CocoonDomainManager : AppDomainManager, ICocoonDomainManager
{
    public override HostSecurityManager HostSecurityManager
    {
        get
        {
            // Return a new instance of the security manager.
            return new CocoonSecurityManager();
        }
    }
    // The rest of the class omitted…
}
```

Now that I've got the basic infrastructure in place, I will go ahead and fill in the details of the implementation.

Step 2: Create Custom Evidence

Recall that the CLR associates various types of evidence, including evidence describing the assembly's origin and any signatures it might have, with an assembly automatically as the assembly is loaded. However, none of the evidence the CLR assigns by default is sufficient to tell you that an assembly was loaded from a cocoon file, so I implement my own evidence for this purpose.

Implementing the custom evidence is very straightforward because any managed class can be used to represent evidence associated with an assembly. The custom evidence I implement in the runcocoon.exe host is a simple managed type called *EvCocoon*:

```
public class EvCocoon
{
};
```

The real work comes in implementing a membership condition to recognize this evidence and in constructing a code group that uses that membership condition to assign permissions, as you'll see in the next few sections.

Step 3: Create a Custom Membership Condition

Classes that represent custom evidence aren't generally useful without a corresponding membership condition that recognizes the evidence during policy evaluation. Earlier in the chapter, I discussed how the .NET Framework provides membership conditions that recognize the various types of evidence that the CLR natively understands, such as strong names, URLs, and so on. In this section, I do the same by providing a membership condition called *Cocoon-MembershipCondition* that recognizes the *EvCocoon* custom evidence object.

All membership conditions must implement the *IMembershipCondition* interface. *IMembership-Condition* derives from two other interfaces: *ISecurityEncodable* and *ISecurityPolicyEncodable*. The members on *IMembershipCondition* are shown in Table 10-2.

Table 10-2   The Methods on *IMembershipCondition*

Method	Description
Check	Given a collection of evidence, *Check* looks to see whether the collection contains the evidence the membership condition is looking for. In the sample implementation, *Check* will look for evidence of type *EvCocoon*.
Copy	Returns an exact copy of the instance of the membership condition on which it is called.
ToXml from *ISecurityEncodable*	Provides an XML representation of the membership condition.
FromXml from *ISecurityEncodable*	Creates the membership condition from the XML representation.
ToXml(policyLevel) from *ISecurityPolicy-Encodable*	Provides an XML representation of the membership condition specific to the requested policy level.
ToXml(policyLevel) from *ISecurityPolicy-Encodable*	Creates the membership condition from the XML representation for a specific policy level.

The *Check* method is the heart of a membership condition. The CLR calls *Check* during policy resolution to determine whether the set of evidence associated with an assembly satisfies the criteria required by the membership condition. If *Check* returns true, the CLR adds the permissions granted by the code group containing the membership condition. The implementation of *Check* in *CocoonMembershipCondition* enumerates the collection of evidence passed in looking for an instance of *EvCocoon*. The implementation of *CocoonMembershipCondition* is shown in the following listing:

```
public class CocoonMembershipCondition : IMembershipCondition
    {
        public bool Check(Evidence evidence)
        {
            if (evidence == null)
                return false;

            // Loop through the evidence looking for an instance of
            // EvCocoon.
            IEnumerator enumerator = evidence.GetHostEnumerator();
            while (enumerator.MoveNext())
            {
                Object obj = enumerator.Current;

                if (obj is EvCocoon)
                {
                    // We've found cocoon evidence!
```

```
                return true;
            }
        }
        return false;
    }

    public IMembershipCondition Copy()
    {
        return new CocoonMembershipCondition();
    }

    public override bool Equals(Object o)
    {
        CocoonMembershipCondition that = (o as CocoonMembershipCondition);

        if (that != null)
        {
            return true;
        }
        return false;
    }

    // The Cocoon membership condition cannot be specified in
    // security XML configuration files.
    public SecurityElement ToXml()
        { throw new NotSupportedException(); }
    public void FromXml(SecurityElement e)
        { throw new NotSupportedException(); }
    public SecurityElement ToXml(PolicyLevel level)
        { throw new NotSupportedException(); }
    public void FromXml(SecurityElement e, PolicyLevel level)
        { throw new NotSupportedException(); }
};
```

The *ToXml* and *FromXml* methods are called by the CLR during policy administration to translate the membership condition to and from an XML representation. You must implement these methods if you'd like your membership condition to be included in the enterprise, machine, and user policy levels because the definition of those policy levels is persisted to XML files stored on disk. In the sample case, however, the *CocoonMembershipCondition* will appear only in the custom application-domain-level policy tree. So I've chosen not to implement the methods required to translate a *CocoonMembershipCondition* to and from XML.

Step 4: Create an Application-Domain-Level Policy Tree

The custom evidence and custom membership condition I've built in the last few sections provide all the pieces I need to create a CAS policy tree that grants the appropriate permissions to assemblies loaded out of a cocoon.

A central element of the policy tree is a code group that grants the appropriate permissions to all assemblies that pass the membership condition implemented by *CocoonMembershipCondition*. Recall that I want assemblies in cocoon files to be able to execute, display user interface, and store files using isolated storage. These three permissions are represented, respectively, by the *SecurityPermission*, *UIPermission*, and *IsolatedStorageFilePermission* permissions from the *System.Security.Permissions* namespace. These permissions are grouped together into a *PermissionSet* object that is passed, along with an instance of the *CocoonMembershipCondition* class, to the constructor of the *System.Security.Policy.UnionCodeGroup* as shown in the following snippet:

```
// Create the permission set granted to assemblies that satisfy
// the custom membership condition. Grant the permission to execute,
// display UI, and access IsolatedStorage.
PermissionSet pSet = new PermissionSet(PermissionState.None);

// Add permission to execute.
pSet.AddPermission(new SecurityPermission(SecurityPermissionFlag.Execution));

// Add permission to display UI.
pSet.AddPermission(new UIPermission(PermissionState.Unrestricted));

// Add permission to store 10k of data in isolated storage.
IsolatedStorageFilePermission isoStorePermission = new
 IsolatedStorageFilePermission(PermissionState.None);
isoStorePermission.UsageAllowed =
 IsolatedStorageContainment.DomainIsolationByUser;
isoStorePermission.UserQuota = 10000;
pSet.AddPermission(isoStorePermission);

// Create a code group with the custom membership condition and grant set.
UnionCodeGroup cocoonCG =  new UnionCodeGroup(
    new CocoonMembershipCondition(), new PolicyStatement(pSet));
```

The policy tree needs more than just this one code group, however. Recall that the set of permissions granted to an assembly is the intersection of the permission grants from each of the four policy levels, so I must grant a set of permissions to all assemblies allowed to run in the application domain. Although the code group I've just built covers the assemblies in the cocoon, I must also add code groups that grant permissions to the .NET Framework assemblies. Without such a code group, the .NET Framework assemblies wouldn't be granted any permissions and, hence, wouldn't be allowed to run, even though the default security policy has granted them full trust! In addition, the host runtime assembly (*CocoonHostRuntime*) must also have permission to run in the application domain. Given the need to grant permissions to these other assemblies, the final policy will have several other code groups, as shown in Figure 10-8.

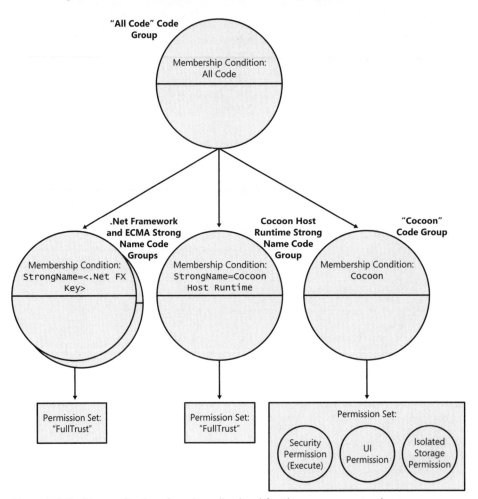

Figure 10-8   The application domain policy level for the runcocoon.exe host

As you can see in the figure, the policy tree contains code groups that grant full trust to the .NET Framework and *CocoonHostRuntime* assemblies based on the public key pair that was used to generate their strong names. This is accomplished in code using instances of *System.Security.Policy.StrongNameMembershipCondition*. Creating an instance of *StrongName-MembershipCondition* requires the public key used when the assembly was signed. The sn.exe utility from the .NET Framework SDK has options that enable you to extract the public key from a strong-named assembly and format that key in a way that makes it easy to paste into source code as an array of bytes. For example, to obtain the public key used for *CocoonHostRuntime*, I'd use the –e option:

```
C:\sn -e CocoonHostRuntime.dll CocoonPublicKey.snk
```

Now, given the key contained in cocoonpublickey.snk, I can use the –o option to translate that key into a form that's easy to use in source code:

```
C:\sn -o CocoonPublicKey.snk CocoonPublicKey.csv
```

Finally, I can define the public key in source code using the contents of cocoonpublickey.csv like this:

```
private static byte[] s_CocoonHostRuntimePublicKey =
{
      0,   36,    0,    0,    4, 128,    0,    0, 148,    0,    0,    0,
      6,    2,    0,    0,    0,   36,    0,    0,   82,   83,   65,   49,
      0,    4,    0,    0,    1,    0,    1,    0, 241, 255, 223,   68,
    103,   53,   57, 194,   68, 246,   41,   44, 219, 236, 159,   34,
    224, 176, 134, 172, 137,   77,   26, 145, 228, 143, 130,   16,
     75,   36, 135,   78, 188, 240,   60, 158, 191,   99, 180,   73,
    195, 154,   43,   24, 231, 230,   59,   49, 123, 233,   45, 148,
     56,    6, 192,   62, 100, 214,   15, 121,    2, 187, 167,   54,
    124,   15, 222,   25, 189, 129, 195,   28, 141, 227, 254, 209,
    189, 241,   48, 114, 192, 210, 132, 218,   80,   70, 248, 240,
    163,   79, 121, 196,   44,   83,   64, 217,   55,   19,   31, 204,
    104, 138,   91,   82, 208,   10,   72, 112, 214,   44, 127,   47,
    186,   72,   80, 101, 227, 240, 184,   27, 181,   50, 137, 147,
    173, 222, 101, 231
};
```

Given the definitions of the necessary public keys, all that's left is to construct the final policy tree and return it from the host security manager's implementation of *DomainPolicy* as shown in the following listing:

```
public class CocoonSecurityManager : HostSecurityManager
{
    private static byte[] s_msPublicKey =
    {
          0,   36,    0,    0,    4, 128,    0,    0, 148,    0,    0,    0,    6,    2,
          0,    0,    0,   36,    0,    0,   82,   83,   65,   49,    0,    4,    0,    0,
          1,    0,    1,    0,    7, 209, 250,   87, 196, 174, 217, 240, 163,   46,
        132, 170,   15, 174, 253,   13, 233, 232, 253, 106, 236, 143, 135,
        251,    3, 118, 108, 131,   76, 153, 146,   30, 178,   59, 231, 154,
        217, 213, 220, 193, 221, 154, 210,   54,   19,   33,    2, 144,   11,
        114,   60, 249, 128, 149, 127, 196, 225, 119,   16, 143, 198,    7,
        119,   79,   41, 232,   50,   14, 146, 234,    5, 236, 228, 232,   33,
        192, 165, 239, 232, 241, 100,   92,   76,   12, 147, 193, 171, 153,
         40,   93,   98,   44, 170, 101,   44,   29, 250, 214,   61, 116,   93,
        111,   45, 229, 241, 126,   94, 175,   15, 196, 150,   61,   38,   28,
        138,   18,   67, 101,   24,   32, 109, 192, 147,   52,   77,   90, 210,
        147
    };

    private static byte[] s_ecmaPublicKey =
    {
          0,    0,    0,    0,    0,    0,    0,    0,    4,    0,    0,    0,
          0,    0,    0,    0
    };
```

```csharp
private static byte[] s_CocoonHostRuntimePublicKey =
{
    0,  36,   0,   0,   4, 128,   0,   0, 148,   0,   0,   0,
    6,   2,   0,   0,   0,  36,   0,   0,  82,  83,  65,  49,
    0,   4,   0,   0,   1,   0,   1,   0, 241, 255, 223,  68,
  103,  53,  57, 194,  68, 246,  41,  44, 219, 236, 159,  34,
  224, 176, 134, 172, 137,  77,  26, 145, 228, 143, 130,  16,
   75,  36, 135,  78, 188, 240,  60, 158, 191,  99, 180,  73,
  195, 154,  43,  24, 231, 230,  59,  49, 123, 233,  45, 148,
   56,   6, 192,  62, 100, 214,  15, 121,   2, 187, 167,  54,
  124,  15, 222,  25, 189, 129, 195,  28, 141, 227, 254, 209,
  189, 241,  48, 114, 192, 210, 132, 218,  80,  70, 248, 240,
  163,  79, 121, 196,  44,  83,  64, 217,  55,  19,  31, 204,
  104, 138,  91,  82, 208,  10,  72, 112, 214,  44, 127,  47,
  186,  72,  80, 101, 227, 240, 184,  27, 181,  50, 137, 147,
  173, 222, 101, 231
};

public override PolicyLevel DomainPolicy
{
    get
    {
        PolicyLevel pol = PolicyLevel.CreateAppDomainLevel();

        pol.RootCodeGroup.PolicyStatement = new PolicyStatement(
            new PermissionSet(PermissionState.None));

        // Create membership condition for the MS platform key.
        UnionCodeGroup msKeyCG =
            new UnionCodeGroup(
                new StrongNameMembershipCondition(new
                    StrongNamePublicKeyBlob(s_msPublicKey),
                    null, null),
                    new PolicyStatement(
                        new PermissionSet(PermissionState.Unrestricted)));

        // Add this code group as a child of the root.
        pol.RootCodeGroup.AddChild(msKeyCG);

        // Create membership condition for the ECMA key.
        UnionCodeGroup ecmaKeyCG =
            new UnionCodeGroup(
                new StrongNameMembershipCondition(new
                    StrongNamePublicKeyBlob(s_ecmaPublicKey), null, null),
                    new PolicyStatement(
                        new PermissionSet(PermissionState.Unrestricted)));

        // Add this code group as a child of the root.
        pol.RootCodeGroup.AddChild(ecmaKeyCG);

        // Create membership condition for the key that
        // signed CocoonHostRuntime.
        UnionCodeGroup hostKeyCG =
            new UnionCodeGroup(
                new StrongNameMembershipCondition(
```

```
                    new StrongNamePublicKeyBlob(
                        s_CocoonHostRuntimePublicKey),
                        null, null),
                    new PolicyStatement(
                        new PermissionSet(PermissionState.Unrestricted)));

            // Add this code group as a child of the root.
            pol.RootCodeGroup.AddChild(hostKeyCG);

            // Create the permission set I'll grant to assemblies
            // that satisfy the custom membership condition. Grant the
            // permission to execute, display UI, and access
            // IsolatedStorage.
            PermissionSet pSet = new PermissionSet(PermissionState.None);

            // Add permission to execute.
            pSet.AddPermission(
                new SecurityPermission(SecurityPermissionFlag.Execution));

            // Add permission to display UI.
            pSet.AddPermission(
                new UIPermission(PermissionState.Unrestricted));

            // Add permission to store 10k of data in isolated storage.
            IsolatedStorageFilePermission isoStorePermission =
                new IsolatedStorageFilePermission(PermissionState.None);
                isoStorePermission.UsageAllowed =
                    IsolatedStorageContainment.DomainIsolationByUser;
                isoStorePermission.UserQuota = 10000;
                pSet.AddPermission(isoStorePermission);

            // Create a code group with the custom membership
            // condition and grant set.
            UnionCodeGroup cocoonCG =
                new UnionCodeGroup(new CocoonMembershipCondition(),
                new PolicyStatement(pSet));

            // Add this code group as a child of the root.
            pol.RootCodeGroup.AddChild(cocoonCG);

            return pol;
        }
    }
}
```

Now that I've built the policy tree, let's revisit the initial security requirements to see how they are satisfied. There were two requirements. The assemblies in a cocoon file (1) can reference only other assemblies contained in the cocoon and the .NET Framework assemblies, and (2) will have the permission only to execute, display user interface, and store files in isolated storage. The first requirement is satisfied because the policy tree does not have a code group that grants any permissions to assemblies other than the assemblies in the cocoon, the .NET Framework assemblies, and the *CocoonHostRuntime*. If an attempt is made to load any other assembly into the application domain, the policy tree will grant it no permissions. Because the final grant set for an assembly is determined by intersecting the permission grants from each of the four policy levels, the fact that I've granted no permissions will cause the assembly's final grant set to be empty. Without at least the permission to execute, the assembly won't run in the application domain. The second requirement is satisfied by the code group that I specifically built to grant permissions to assemblies in cocoons. That code group grants only the permissions I want. Again, because the overall grant set is determined by intersection, I am guaranteed that no other policy level can grant more permissions than I'd like.

> **Note**   *System.AppDomain* has a method called *SetAppDomainPolicy* that can also be used to associate a CAS policy tree with an application domain. *SetAppDomainPolicy* is now deprecated in favor of using the *PolicyLevel* property introduced in .NET Framework 2.0. However, if your extensible application must run on versions of the .NET Framework earlier than .NET Framework 2.0, you'll need to use *SetAppDomainPolicy* instead.

Step 5: Assign Custom Evidence to Assemblies in the Cocoon

The final step in adding CAS support to runcocoon.exe is to associate the custom evidence type (*EvCocoon*) with all assemblies that are loaded out of cocoon files. I do this using the *ProvideAssemblyEvidence* method on the host security manager. Because I returned the value *HostSecurityManagerFlags.HostAssemblyEvidence* from the *Flags* property of *CocoonHostSecurity-Manager*, the CLR will call *ProvideAssemblyEvidence* each time an assembly is about to be loaded into an application domain. *ProvideAssemblyEvidence* takes as input an instance of *System.Reflection.Assembly* identifying the assembly about to be loaded and an instance of *System.Security.Policy.Evidence* representing the collection of evidence that has been assigned to the assembly so far. That is, the set of evidence that the CLR has automatically assigned as part of loading the assembly. The implementation of *ProvideAssemblyEvidence* is free to modify this evidence in any way. The modified evidence is then returned from the method. The definition of *ProvideAssemblyEvidence* is as follows:

```
public class HostSecurityManager
{
    // The rest of the class definition omitted...

    public override Evidence ProvideAssemblyEvidence(
        Assembly loadedAssembly,
        Evidence evidence);
}
```

Evidence has several methods that enable you to manipulate the contents of an evidence collection. One of these methods, called *AddHost*, is specifically designed to allow extensible applications to add evidence to an existing evidence collection. I use *AddHost* to add an instance of *EvCocoon* to the collection of evidence passed to *ProvideAssemblyEvidence*. I then return the modified collection.

Before I can finish the implementation of *ProvideAssemblyEvidence*, however, I must consider one more important design point. The implementation of *ProvideAssemblyEvidence* must add an instance of the *EvCocoon* evidence only to those assemblies that are loaded from the cocoon. However, given that *ProvideAssemblyEvidence* will be called for every assembly that is loaded into the application domain, how can I determine which calls to *ProvideAssemblyEvidence* are for assemblies contained in cocoons? The only thing I have to work with is the instance of the *Assembly* class passed to *ProvideAssemblyEvidence*. Given that, I must be able to determine whether an assembly comes from a cocoon through some property or method on *Assembly*.

The best way to solve this problem requires revisiting how assemblies are loaded by run-cocoon.exe. Recall from Chapter 8 that runcocoon.exe uses the CLR hosting interfaces to implement an assembly loading manager whose sole purpose is to load assemblies from the cocoon. It is the assembly loading manager, specifically the implementation of *IHost-AssemblyStore::ProvideAssembly*, that knows when an assembly is being loaded from a cocoon. What I need is some mechanism for *ProvideAssembly* (in the unmanaged portion of the host) to communicate the fact that an assembly was loaded from a cocoon to the implementation of *ProvideAssemblyEvidence* (in the managed portion of the host). This mechanism exists in the form of the *pContext* parameter to *ProvideAssembly* and the *HostContext* property on *Assembly*. Here's the definition of *ProvideAssembly* from mscoree.idl:

```
interface IHostAssemblyStore: IUnknown
{
    HRESULT ProvideAssembly
            (
            [in] AssemblyBindInfo *pBindInfo,
            [out] UINT64          *pAssemblyId,
            [out] UINT64          *pContext,
            [out] IStream         **ppStmAssemblyImage,
            [out] IStream         **ppStmPDB);
    // Rest of the interface definition omitted...
}
```

To pass context information to managed code, the implementation of *ProvideAssembly* will set a specific value into **pContext* each time an assembly is loaded from a cocoon. This value can then be retrieved in *ProvideAssemblyEvidence* using the *HostContext* property on *Assembly*. Here are the relevant parts of the implementation of *ProvideAssembly* from Chapter 8:

```
static const int CocoonAssemblyHostContext = 5;

HRESULT STDMETHODCALLTYPE CCocoonAssemblyStore::ProvideAssembly(
                    AssemblyBindInfo *pBindInfo,
                    UINT64           *pAssemblyId,
                    UINT64           *pContext,
                    IStream          **ppStmAssemblyImage,
                    IStream          **ppStmPDB)
{

    // Portions of the implementation omitted…
```

```
    *pContext = 0;

    // Try to load the assembly from the cocoon. If the assembly is
    // contained in the cocoon, S_OK will be returned.
    HRESULT hr = m_pStreamIndex->GetStreamForBindingIdentity(
        pBindInfo->lpPostPolicyIdentity,
        pAssemblyId,
        ppStmAssemblyImage);

    if (SUCCEEDED(hr))
    {
        // Set the host context to indicate this assembly was loaded
        // from a cocoon. This data will be used in the host security manager's
        // implementation of ProvideAssemblyEvidence to associate the custom
        // evidence with the assembly.
        *pContext     = CocoonAssemblyHostContext;
    }


    return hr;
}
```

Now that I can easily determine which assemblies came from cocoons, the implementation of *ProvideAssemblyEvidence* is straightforward:

```
public class CocoonSecurityManager : HostSecurityManager
{
    // Portions of the class implementation omitted…
    static int CocoonAssemblyHostContext = 5;

    public override Evidence ProvideAssemblyEvidence(Assembly loadedAssembly,
    Evidence evidence)
    {
        if (loadedAssembly.HostContext == CocoonAssemblyHostContext)
        {
            // Add an instance of the cocoon evidence class to the list of host
            // evidence. This evidence will cause the check in
            // CocoonMembershipCondition to pass during policy evaluation,
            // thereby granting the permissions specified in the app-domain-
            // level policy.
            evidence.AddHost(new EvCocoon());

            // Add evidence that identifies this assembly as coming from
            // the MyComputer zone. Without this evidence, the assembly would
            // get no permissions at the machine level, so the grant based on
            // cocoon evidence would get canceled out. In essence, providing
            // this evidence causes the assembly to get "FullTrust" (through
            // default policy), which I then lock back down through Cocoon
            // evidence.
            evidence.AddHost(new Zone(SecurityZone.MyComputer));
        }

        return evidence;
    }
}
```

There is one subtlety in the preceding code that I haven't explained. Notice that in addition to associating *EvCocoon* evidence with assemblies that come from cocoons, I also associate evidence representing the *MyComputer* zone. The reason I must do this is as follows. Assemblies loaded from an assembly loading manager (*IStream**), such as those contained in cocoons, don't get much of the default evidence that the CLR typically associates with assemblies as they are loaded. Because the CLR doesn't know where the contents of an assembly represented by an *IStream** originated, it cannot assign evidence describing the URL, zone, and so on, so these assemblies have no evidence that would cause the enterprise, machine, and user policy levels to grant them any permissions whatsoever (through default policy). Given this, the permissions I grant through the application-domain-level CAS policy don't appear in the final grant set; they are intersected out of the final result because the other policy levels have granted nothing.

I can solve this in a few ways. First, I could modify enterprise, machine, or user policy to grant permissions to assemblies based on *EvCocoon* evidence. Although this approach would work, it's cumbersome because it requires the default CAS policy files to be edited on every machine on which I want to run an application contained in a cocoon. The other approach is to assign additional evidence to cocoon assemblies that will cause them to be granted permissions by the enterprise, machine, or user level. That is the approach I've taken in the preceding code. By granting evidence representing the *MyComputer* zone, I cause the assemblies in the cocoon to be granted full trust by the default CAS policy at the machine level. Then, when full trust is intersected with the grants I supply at the application domain policy level, the grants form the final set of permissions granted to the assembly.

At first glance it might seem dangerous to associate evidence that will cause a cocoon assembly to be granted full trust at the machine level. However, because the assembly's final grant set is determined through an intersection of the grant sets from each level, you can effectively narrow down the grant set from full trust to only those permissions specified at the application domain level.

Assigning Evidence Using the Assembly Loading APIs

Assigning evidence using *ProvideAssemblyEvidence* is convenient because it enables you to assign evidence to all assemblies from a single location. In this way, you can be sure that no assemblies will be loaded into the domain without you having a chance to customize their evidence. However, you can also assign evidence to an assembly at the time you load it using one of the assembly loading APIs. Recall from Chapter 7 that the assembly loading APIs, such as *Assembly.Load* and *AppDomain.Load*, all have a parameter that enables you to specify evidence to associate with the assembly. It's generally more convenient to assign evidence using a host security manager as described. However, if you have a simple scenario in which you don't need a host security manager (or application domain manager) for any other reason, or if you have context at the point the assembly is loaded that is required to generate the proper evidence, supplying evidence using one of the assembly loading APIs is a perfectly viable solution.

As you'd expect, the parameter that enables you to supply evidence using one of the assembly loading APIs is of type *System.Security.Policy.Evidence* as shown in the following definition of *Assembly.Load*:

```
static public Assembly Load(AssemblyName assemblyRef,
                           Evidence assemblySecurity)
```

Listing 10-2 creates a new evidence collection, adds an instance of *EvCocoon* to the collection, and passes it to *Assembly.Load*.

Listing 10-2   Evidenceload.cs

```
using System;
using System.Reflection;
using System.Security;
using System.Security.Policy;
using System.Collections;

namespace EvidenceDisplay
{
    [Serializable]
    class EvCocoon
    {
    }

    class Program
    {
        static void Main(string[] args)
        {
            Evidence cocoonEvidence = new Evidence();
            cocoonEvidence.AddHost(new EvCocoon());
            cocoonEvidence.AddHost(new Zone(SecurityZone.Intranet));

            // Load an assembly.
            Assembly a = Assembly.Load("Utilities",cocoonEvidence);

            // Assembly a is now loaded and ready to use...
        }
    }
}
```

The evidence you pass to the assembly loading APIs is merged with the evidence supplied by the CLR in the following ways:

- All types of evidence you pass that are not also supplied by the CLR are simply added to the evidence collection. Thus, the final collection contains both the evidence you supplied along with that provided by the CLR.

- If you supply a type of evidence that is also supplied by the CLR, your evidence will supersede the evidence already in the collection. For example, when you load an assembly from the local machine, the CLR will assign it evidence of type *System.Security.Policy.Zone* representing the *MyComputer* zone. If you supply zone evidence in your call to the assembly loading APIs, representing *Intranet*, for example, the final collection of evidence associated with the assembly will have *Zone* evidence representing *Intranet*.

Remember, too, that if you are using an assembly loading API that loads an assembly into an application domain other than the one in which you're currently running, the CLR must be able to serialize your custom evidence type across the application domain boundary. This is why the *EvCocoon* type in Listing 10-2 is marked with the *[Serializable]* custom attribute.

Putting It All Together

Now that I've implemented all the pieces required to incorporate CAS into the runcocoon.exe host, let's take a step back and see how all these pieces fit together. Figure 10-9 shows the sequence of steps that occur at run time to grant a set of permissions to the assemblies in a cocoon application.

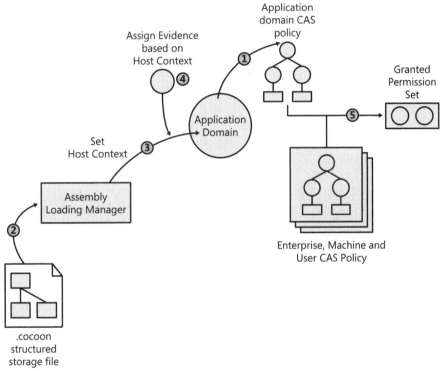

Figure 10-9   Code Access Security in the runcocoon.exe host

The following points explain these steps in greater detail:

1. An application domain is created in which to run the application contained in the cocoon. When the application domain is created, the CLR accesses the *DomainPolicy* property on the host security manager (implemented by *CocoonHostSecurityManager*) to access the CAS policy tree associated with the new domain.

2. As the application is running, the assembly loading manager gets called to load assemblies from the cocoon.

3. The implementation of *IHostAssemblyStore::ProvideAssembly* sets a special value into the host context parameter (**pContext*) to indicate that a particular assembly was loaded from the cocoon.

4. The implementation of *ProvideAssemblyEvidence* in *CocoonHostSecurityManager* accesses the *HostContext* property on the instance of *Assembly* it is passed to determine whether a given assembly is being loaded from a cocoon. I add an instance of *EvCocoon* to the evidence collection for all assemblies coming from cocoon files.

5. As the assembly is loaded, the CLR evaluates CAS policy with that assembly's evidence at the enterprise, machine, user, and application domain levels. The grant sets from each level are intersected to determine the final set of permissions granted to the assembly.

Associating Evidence with an Application Domain

So far, I've described evidence as being associated solely with assemblies. Although this is clearly the most common scenario, it's also possible to associate evidence with an application domain. Application domain evidence is evaluated by CAS policy and a permission set is granted, just as it is done for assembly evidence. The CLR considers the permission set associated with the application domain while walking the stack to ensure that a particular permission demand is enforced. In essence, the application domain becomes another caller when viewed from the perspective of the CLR's stack walk. Figure 10-10 shows how the stack walk is affected by application domain evidence. In the figure, the assembly that issues the permission demand and all its descendents on the call stack are checked for the required permission. In addition, the permission set associated with the application domain is checked as well.

Application domain evidence can be used to grant a permission set that will restrict the operations that code running in the domain can perform. To see where this is useful, consider the case of an extensible application that is hosting code downloaded from a particular Web site. Let's say that such an application has a requirement that no code downloaded from the site will be granted more permissions than would be associated with the site's URL itself. This requirement can be enforced by associating evidence with the application domain that represents the site from which the code running in the domain came. Even if the downloaded code were granted more permission, because of a particular signature perhaps, the evidence and resulting permission set on the application domain will limit what that code can do.

Application domain evidence typically isn't used if you've already defined a CAS policy tree for your domain. The same restrictions you are enforcing through application domain evidence can also be specified using a policy tree. Application domain evidence is useful in scenarios such as the one described previously when your security requirements are straightforward enough to be expressed with application domain evidence without having to construct an entire policy tree.

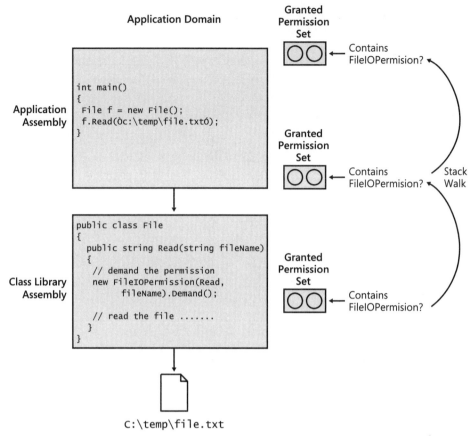

Figure 10-10 Associating evidence with an application domain creates an additional permission set that is evaluated as part of the CAS stack walk.

Evidence is associated with an application domain using the *securityInfo* parameter either to *AppDomain.CreateDomain* or the implementation of *CreateDomain* provided by your application domain manager. (See Chapter 5 for more information about the role of an application domain manager in extensible applications.) For reference, here's the definition of *CreateDomain* from *System.AppDomainManager*:

```
public class AppDomainManager : MarshalByRefObject
{
        public virtual AppDomain CreateDomain (string friendlyName,
                                               Evidence securityInfo,
                                               AppDomainSetup appDomainInfo)
        {
        }
}
```

Listing 10-3 shows how to use application domain evidence. This example creates a type called *TextWriter* in a new application domain. *TextWriter* has a *Write* method that writes a text string to the specified file. *Write* accesses the file using the types from the *System.IO* namespace, which demand *FileIOPermission* to protect the file system properly. The application domain in which *TextWriter* is loaded is created with evidence representing the *Internet* zone. Permission to access the file system (*FileIOPermission*) is not granted to the *Internet* zone through default policy, so this application will fail with a security exception, even if the application is run from the local machine.

Listing 10-3   Appdomainevidence.cs

```
using System;
using System.Security;
using System.Security.Policy;
using Utilities;

namespace AppDomainEvidence
{

    class Program
    {
        static void Main(string[] args)
        {
            // Create evidence representing the Internet zone.
            Evidence internetEvidence = new Evidence();
            internetEvidence.AddHost(new Zone(SecurityZone.Internet));

            // Create a new domain with the "Internet" evidence.
            AppDomain ad = AppDomain.CreateDomain("Custom Evidence Domain",
                internetEvidence);

            // Create an instance of the TextWriter class in the new
            // application domain.
            TextWriter w = (TextWriter) ad.CreateInstanceAndUnwrap(
                "Utilities","Utilities.TextWriter");

            // Call a method on TextWriter that writes text to a file.
            // This method demands FileIOPermission. This operation
            // will fail with a security exception because callers in
            // the Internet zone are not granted FileIOPermission through
            // default CAS policy.
            w.Write("file.txt", "Hello World!");

        }
    }
}
```

The *AllowPartiallyTrustedCallers* Attribute

As described, one of the primary goals of CAS is to enable scenarios in which code can be partially trusted. Even so, by default, a given assembly must be fully trusted to call a method in another assembly. Although this might seem counter to the spirit of CAS, the goal of this default is to force the author of an assembly to think explicitly about what is required to expose APIs to partially trusted callers. Specifically, an assembly author should perform a full security audit, including an analysis to determine that permission demands are used appropriately, before exposing APIs to callers with partial trust. In other words, the full trust default requires the author of a class library to take explicit action to enable partially trusted callers. The explicit action that is required is the annotation of the assembly with the *System.Security.AllowPartiallyTrustedCallersAttribute* custom attribute.

It's useful for you to have an understanding of the *AllowPartiallyTrustedCallers* attribute for extensible applications that grant partial trust to the code they host. For example, the assemblies I load out of the cocoon files are partially trusted because I grant only *SecurityPermission* (to execute), *UIPermission*, and *IsolatedStorageFilePermission* so assemblies in cocoon files can call only methods in other assemblies that are annotated with *AllowPartiallyTrustedCallers*. Any attempt to call a method in an assembly without this attribute results in a *Security-Exception* with the following text:

```
System.Security.SecurityException: That assembly does not allow partially
trusted callers.
```

Many of the .NET Framework class libraries are accessible by add-ins with partial trust because they are already annotated with *AllowPartiallyTrustedCallers*. In addition, you might need to use the *AllowPartiallyTrustedCallers* attribute yourself if, as part of your extensible application, you provide class libraries that are meant to be used by the add-ins you host. Be sure you consider the security ramifications of exposing your assembly to partially trusted callers before annotating your assembly with *AllowPartiallyTrustedCallers*. The best place to find up-to-date information about the prerequisites for using *AllowPartiallyTrustedCallers* can be found on the Microsoft Developer Network Web site (*http://www.msdn.microsoft.com*).

Summary

The CAS system has several extensibility points that enable it to be customized to meet the security requirements of a range of different environments. Authors of extensible applications can control the set of permissions granted to the assemblies running in their application domains by providing a CAS policy tree that maps an assembly's evidence to a set of granted permissions. The permissions granted by the extensible application are intersected with those granted at the enterprise, machine, and user policy levels to determine the final set of permissions that control which resources the assembly can access.

The *HostSecurityManager* class in the *System.Security* namespace provides the infrastructure needed for extensible applications to customize CAS. By providing a class that derives from *HostSecurityManager*, authors of extensible applications can supply evidence for assemblies loaded into their application domains and supply application domain CAS policy.

Chapter 11

Writing Highly Available Microsoft .NET Framework Applications

Throughout this book, I've discussed a number of techniques you can use to customize the CLR for use in a variety of application scenarios. In this chapter, I cover the support the CLR provides for application scenarios that require a high degree of availability—that is, scenarios in which the process must live for a very long time. These scenarios include servers such as database or e-mail servers and operating system processes.

As the CLR continues to be used in more environments with requirements for long process lifetimes, it must provide a set of features that a host can use to ensure that the process stays alive in the face of exceptional conditions such as out of memory or stack overflow errors. As I demonstrate, the CLR leverages the concept of application domain isolation and ensures that a domain can always be unloaded without leaking resources, even in conditions of resource failure. By ensuring that domains can always be safely unloaded, the CLR provides a construct that hosts can use to remove code from the process that has encountered an error that prevents it from continuing to run normally. In this way, the host can isolate faulty code without affecting the integrity of the process itself.

The ability to guarantee that an application domain can be unloaded without leaking resources requires the CLR to expose some new infrastructure to the authors of class libraries. This new infrastructure includes concepts such as *safe handles*, *critical finalizers*, and *constrained execution regions*. As the author of an extensible application, you can choose to use these new concepts to make your host runtime code more reliable in the face of resource exhaustion and other exceptional conditions. In addition, an understanding of these new concepts can help you decide how to deal with add-ins that might not have been explicitly written with this new infrastructure in mind.

In addition to the infrastructure required to unload an application domain cleanly, the CLR provides the ability for a CLR host to customize how various exceptional conditions affect the process. For example, by default, a failure to allocate memory will cause the CLR to throw a *System.OutOfMemoryException*. If this exception occurs while executing an add-in, the host might not be confident that the add-in was written to handle the exception correctly. As a result, the host can choose to *escalate* this exception and cause the entire thread on which the exception occurred to be aborted instead. Furthermore, if the exception occurs while the add-in is known to be editing state that is shared across multiple threads, it's likely that the integrity of that state cannot be guaranteed. So a host might decide it's safer to unload the entire application domain to guarantee the integrity of the process. The act of dictating how exceptions are handled in this way is referred to as customizing *escalation policy*.

This chapter covers all of the concepts the CLR introduces in Microsoft .NET Framework 2.0 aimed at enabling you to incorporate the CLR safely into application models with high availability requirements. I start by describing in more detail the motivation behind a reliability model based on unloading application domains. Next, I describe the CLR hosting interfaces you can use to customize escalation policy. Finally, I look at a variety of topics you can use in your own code to ensure that your application runs properly in the face of exceptional conditions such as resource failures.

Application Domain Isolation and Process Lifetimes

At first glance, it might seem unnecessary to build a complex infrastructure just to make sure that a process doesn't crash in the face of exceptional conditions. After all, it would seem easier to simply write your managed code such that it handled all exceptions properly. In fact, this is the path the CLR team started down when it first began the work to make sure that managed code could work well in environments requiring long process lifetimes. However, it was quickly determined that writing large bodies of code to be reliable in the face of all exceptions is impractical. As it turns out, the CLR's model for executing managed code could, in theory, cause exceptions to be thrown on virtually any line of code that is executed. This situation is primarily caused by the fact that memory can be allocated, and other runtime operations can occur, in places where you wouldn't expect. For example, memory must be allocated any time *Microsoft intermediate language* (MSIL) code needs to be jit-compiled or a value type needs to be boxed. The following code snippet simply inserts an integer into a hash table:

```
hashtable.Add("Entry1", 5);
```

However, because the signature of *HashTable.Add* specifies that the second parameter is of type *Object*, the CLR must create a reference type by boxing the value "5" before adding it to the hash table. The act of creating a new reference type requires memory to be allocated from the garbage collector's heap. If memory is not available, the addition of the value 5 into the hash table would throw an *OutOfMemoryException*. Also, consider the following example that saves the value of an operating system handle after using PInvoke to call Win32's *CreateSemaphore* API:

```
IntPtr semHandle = CreateSemaphore(...);
```

In this case, if the call to *CreateSemaphore* were to succeed but an exception were to be thrown before the value of the handle could be stored in the local variable, that handle would be leaked. Resource leaks such as these can add up over time to undermine the stability of the process. Furthermore, conditions such as low memory can prevent the CLR from being able to run all cleanup code that you might have defined in *finally* blocks, finalizers, and so on. The failure to run such code can also result in resource leaks over time.

It's also worth noting that even if it were practical for all of the Microsoft .NET Framework assemblies and the assemblies you write as part of your extensible application to handle all exceptional conditions, you'd never be able to guarantee that the add-ins you host are written with these conditions in mind. So the need for a mechanism by which the host can protect the process from corruption is required.

The first two releases of the CLR (in .NET Framework 1.0 and .NET Framework 1.1) didn't have the explicit requirement to provide a platform on which you could guarantee long process lifetimes mainly because there weren't any CLR hosts at the time that needed this form of reliability model. The primary CLR host at the time was Microsoft ASP.NET. High availability is definitely a requirement in Web server environments, but the means to achieve that reliability have been quite different. Historically, at least on the Microsoft platform, Web servers have used multiple processes to load balance large numbers of incoming requests. If the demand were high, more processes would be created to service the requests. In times of low demand, some processes either sat idle or were explicitly killed. This method of achieving scalability works well with Web applications because each request, or connection, is stateless; that is, has no affinity to a particular process. So subsequent requests in the same user session can be safely redirected to a different process. Furthermore, if a given process were to hang or fail because of some exceptional condition, the process could be safely killed without corrupting application state. To the end user, a failure of this sort generally shows up as a "try again later" error message. Upon seeing an error like this, a user typically refreshes the browser, in which case the request gets sent to a different process and succeeds.

Although achieving scalability and reliability through process recycling works well in Web server scenarios, it doesn't work in some scenarios, such as those involving database servers where there is a large amount of per-process state that makes the cost of starting a new process each time a failure occurs prohibitive. Just as the ASP.NET host drove the process recycling model used in the first two releases of the CLR, Microsoft SQL Server 2005 has driven the .NET Framework 2.0 design in which long-lived processes are a requirement.

As described, the CLR's strategy for protecting the integrity of a process is to always contain failures to an application domain and to allow that domain to be unloaded from the process without leaking resources. Let's get into more detail now by looking at the specific techniques the CLR uses to make sure that failures can always be isolated to an application domain.

Failure Escalation

Given that failures caused by resource exhaustion or other exceptional conditions can occur at virtually any time, hosts requiring long process lifetimes must have a strategy for dealing with such failures in such a way as to protect the integrity of the process. In general, it's best to assume that the add-ins running in your host haven't been written to handle all exceptions properly. A conservative approach to dealing with failures is more likely to result in a stable process over time. The host expresses its approach to handling failures through the escalation policy I described in the chapter introduction. In this section, I describe escalation policy as it fits into the CLR's overall reliability model. Later in the chapter, I discuss the specific CLR hosting interfaces used to express your escalation policy.

In .NET Framework 2.0, all unhandled exceptions are allowed to "bubble up" all the way to the surface, thereby affecting the entire process. Specifically, an exception that goes unhandled will terminate the process. Clearly, this end result isn't acceptable when process recycling is too expensive.

> **Note**   Allowing all unhandled exceptions to affect the process in this way is new to .NET Framework 2.0. In the first two versions of the CLR, various unhandled exceptions were "swallowed" by the CLR. These exceptions didn't necessarily bring down the process, but rather often resulted in silent failures or corruption of the process. In .NET Framework version 2.0, the CLR team decided it would be much better to allow these exceptions to surface, thereby making the failures more apparent and easier to debug.

CLR hosts can use escalation policy to specify how these types of failures should be handled and what action the CLR should take when certain operations take longer to terminate than desired. For example, a thread might not ever abort if the finalizer for an object running on that thread enters an infinite loop, thereby causing the thread to hang. The specific failures that can be customized through escalation policy are as follows:

- **Failure to allocate a resource**   A resource, in this case, typically refers to memory or some other resource managed by the operating system, but stack overflows or other exceptional conditions are also considered resource failures.

- **Failure to allocate a resource in a critical region of code**   A critical region is defined as any block of code that might be dependent on state shared between multiple threads. The reason that a failure to allocate a resource while in a critical region is called out explicitly is as follows. Code that relies on state from another thread cannot be safely cleaned up by terminating only the specific thread on which it is running. In other words, if only one of the threads that is cooperating to edit shared state is terminated, the integrity of that state cannot be guaranteed. Later I show that a host can elect to take more conservative steps to guarantee the integrity of the process when shared state is being edited. For example, the SQL Server host uses escalation policy to abort the thread on which a failure to allocate a resource occurs. However, if that thread is in a critical region when the failure occurs, SQL Server decides that it is safer to abort the entire application domain just in case any cross-thread state has become corrupted. It's also worth noting that the CLR hosting interfaces provide a mechanism by which the add-ins running in a process are prevented from sharing state across threads altogether. This mechanism, known as *host protection*, is the subject of Chapter 12. One important question regarding shared state remains: how does the CLR determine whether code is in a critical region? That is, how does the CLR know that a given piece of code is relying on state from another thread? The answer lies in the CLR's ability to detect that code it is executing is waiting on a synchronization primitive such as a mutex, event, semaphore, or any other type of lock. If code that encounters a resource failure is in a region of code that depends on a synchronization primitive, the CLR assumes that the code depends on synchronized access to shared state.

> **Note**   The CLR's ability to detect when code is waiting on a synchronization primitive requires some additional help from the host. The *System.Threading* namespace in the .NET Framework includes several classes for creating primitives such as mutexes and events. The CLR can keep track of these locks because they are created directly in managed code. However, add-ins that have been granted full trust in the Code Access Security (CAS) system (or more specifically, those that have been granted the ability to call native code) can use PInvoke to create synchronization primitives by calling Win32 APIs. Locks acquired in this way are outside the realm of managed code and are therefore unknown to the CLR. As a result, any code waiting on such a lock won't be reported as belonging to a critical region of code should a resource failure occur. So, to make sure the CLR can identify all locks held by managed code, don't grant add-ins the ability to access native code. More details on how to use the CAS system to prevent access to native code can be found in Chapter 10.

- **Fatal runtime error**   Despite all the infrastructure aimed at increasing the reliability of the process, it's still conceivable that the CLR can enter a state in which it encounters a fatal internal error that prevents it from continuing to run managed code. Were this to happen, the host could use escalation policy to determine which actions to take. For example, the host might decide to exit the process at this point, or it might determine that sufficient work can be done that doesn't require managed code. In this case, the host can choose to tell the CLR to disable itself. I describe more about how to disable the CLR later in the chapter when I discuss the specific escalation policy interfaces.

- **Orphaned lock**   I've described how a failure to allocate a resource in code that is waiting on a synchronization primitive is likely to leave the application domain in an inconsistent state. Another scenario in which this can occur is when a synchronization primitive is created but never freed because the code that initially created the lock is terminated. For example, consider the case in which a synchronization primitive such as a *Mutex* or a *Monitor* is created on a thread that is aborted before the lock is freed. The lock is considered *orphaned* and can never be freed. Too many orphaned locks can eventually result in resource exhaustion. So the CLR considers an abandoned lock a failure and allows the host to specify the action to take as a result.

Given these failures, a host can choose to take any of a number of actions. The specific actions that can be taken are the following:

- **Throw an exception**   Throwing an exception is the default action the CLR takes when a resource failure occurs. For example, a stack overflow causes a *StackOverflowException* to be thrown, failure to allocate memory causes an *OutOfMemoryException* to be thrown, and so on.

- **Gracefully abort the thread on which the failure occurred**   The CLR provides two flavors of thread aborts: a *graceful* abort and a *rude* abort. The CLR initiates a graceful abort by throwing a *ThreadAbortException* on the thread it is terminating. When aborting a thread gracefully, the CLR gives the add-in a chance to free all resources by running all code contained in *finally* blocks.

- **Rudely abort the thread on which the failure occurred**   In contrast to graceful aborts, the CLR makes no guarantees about which, if any, of an add-in's cleanup code it will run. It's best to assume that no code in *finally* blocks will be run during a rude abort. Rude thread aborts are typically used to remove threads from the process that haven't gracefully aborted in a host-specified amount of time.

- **Gracefully unload the application domain in which the failure occurred**   There are graceful and rude techniques used to unload an application domain just as there are to abort a thread. A graceful application domain unload involves gracefully aborting all threads in the domain, then freeing the CLR data structures associated with the domain itself. In addition, when gracefully unloading an application domain, the CLR will run all finalizers for objects that lived in the domain. Chapter 5 provides more details on the specific steps taken by the CLR to gracefully unload an application domain.

- **Rudely unload the application domain in which the failure occurred**   A rude application domain unload involves rudely aborting all threads in the domain before freeing the data structures associated with the application domain. Just as rude thread aborts are often used to terminate threads that take too long to gracefully abort, rude application domain unloads are typically used to forcefully remove an application domain from a process that has timed out during the course of a normal shutdown. When rudely unloading an application domain, the CLR does not guarantee that any object finalizers will be run (with the exception of critical finalizers that I discuss later in the chapter).

- **Gracefully exit the process**   In extreme circumstances, such as when a critical failure occurs internal to the CLR, the host might choose to exit the process entirely. Through escalation policy, the host can choose to exit the process either gracefully or rudely. When exiting the process gracefully, the CLR attempts to gracefully unload all application domains. That is, an attempt is made to run all code in *finally*s and finalizers to give the host and the add-ins a chance to finish any processing necessary for a clean process shutdown, such as flushing any buffers, properly closing files, and so on.

- **Rudely exit the process**   A rude process exit makes no attempt at an orderly shutdown—all application domains are rudely unloaded and the process terminates. In a way, a rude process exit is the equivalent of calling the *TerminateProcess* API in Win32.

- **Disable the CLR**   Instead of exiting the process entirely, a host can choose to disable the CLR. Disabling the CLR prevents it from running any more managed code, but it does keep the process alive, thereby enabling the host to continue doing any work that doesn't require managed code. For example, if a critical error were to occur in the CLR while running in the SQL Server process, the SQL host could choose to disable the CLR, but continue running all stored procedures, user-defined types, and so on that were written in T-SQL (native code), which doesn't require any of the facilities of the CLR to run properly.

In addition to specifying which actions to take in the face of certain failures, escalation policy also enables a host to specify timeouts for certain operations and to indicate which actions should occur when those timeouts are reached. This capability is especially useful to terminate code that appears to be hung, such as code in an infinite loop or code waiting on a sychronization primitive that has been abandoned. A host can use escalation policy to specify a timeout for thread abort (including an abort in a critical region of code), application domain unload, process exit, and the amount of time that finalizers are allowed to run.

Finally, escalation policy can be used to force any of the operations for which timeouts can be specified to take a certain action unconditionally. For example, a host can specify that a thread abort in a critical region of code should always be escalated to an application domain unload.

Now that I've covered the basic concepts involved in escalation policy, let's look at a specific example to see how a host might use those concepts to specify a policy aimed at keeping the process alive in the face of resource failures or other exceptional conditions. Figure 11-1 is a graphical representation of an escalation policy similar to the one used in the SQL Server 2005 host.

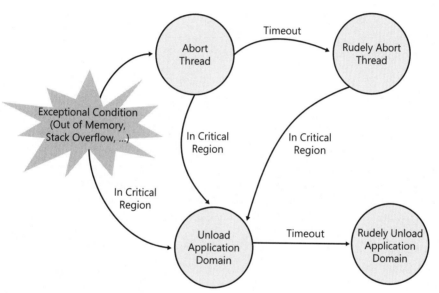

Figure 11-1   Escalation policy is the host's expression of how failures in a process should be handled.

The key aspects of this policy are as follows:

1. All exceptional conditions are automatically escalated to thread aborts, unless the failure occurs in a critical region of code, in which case the failure is escalated to an application domain unload.

2. If a thread doesn't gracefully abort in a specified amount of time, the thread is rudely aborted. Also, if a thread abort is initiated in a critical region of code, the thread abort is escalated to an application domain unload.

3. If an application domain doesn't gracefully unload in a specified amount of time, the application domain is rudely unloaded.

Critical Finalization, *SafeHandles*, and Constrained Execution Regions

One of the key pieces of infrastructure needed to ensure that application domains can be unloaded without leaking resources is the capability to guarantee that any native handles held by managed code will be closed properly. Several classes in the .NET Framework (not to mention those written by third parties, including those you might have written yourself) logically act as a wrapper around a native resource. For example, the file-related classes in the *System.IO* namespace hold native file handles, and the classes in *System.Net* maintain native handles that represent open network sockets. Traditionally, these native handles have been closed using a combination of the Dispose design pattern and object finalizers. However, as I've described, the CLR does not guarantee that finalizers will be run when rudely unloading an application domain. If a class that holds a native resource requires a finalizer to run to free the handle, that handle will be leaked when an application domain is rudely unloaded. For this reason, the CLR has introduced some new infrastructure in .NET Framework 2.0 that can be used to guarantee that native handles such as these will always be released, regardless of how the application domain is terminated.

The concepts of critical finalization, safe handles, and constrained execution regions work together to ensure that native handles can always be released. Simply put, a critical finalizer is a finalizer that the CLR will always run. Furthermore, a critical finalizer is always guaranteed to complete. Any type that derives from *System.Runtime.ConstrainedExecution.CriticalFinalizerObject* receives the benefits of critical finalization. One such type is *System.Runtime.InteropServices.SafeHandle* (and its derivatives). A *SafeHandle* is a wrapper around a native handle that relies on critical finalization to ensure that the native handle will always be freed. All of the classes in the .NET Framework that hold native handles have been rewritten in version 2.0 to use *SafeHandles* to wrap those handles. The handles held by those classes will always be freed.

What is it about a critical finalizer that enables the CLR to make the guarantee that it will always be run and that it will always complete? The answer lies in the concept known as a *constrained execution region (CER)*. A CER is a block of code in which the CLR guarantees that exceptions such as *OutOfMemoryException* or *StackOverflowException* are never thrown because of a lack of resources. Given this guarantee, you can be sure that the code in the CER will always complete (assuming it handles normal application exceptions, that is).

To guarantee that resource failures will never occur in a CER, the CLR must do two things:

1. Prepare the CER.
2. Restrict which operations can be performed inside a CER.

When preparing a CER, the CLR moves the allocation of all resources, such as memory, to a point just before the type containing the CER is created. For example, all code in a CER is jit-compiled before the CER is entered, thereby ensuring that enough memory exists to create the native code needed to execute the methods in the CER. If the creation of a type in a CER succeeds, you can guarantee it will run without failing because of a lack of resources. Note that preparing a type isn't just a matter of looking at the resource needs of the type; it also requires preparing all types referenced in the CER (recursively) as well. Also, preparing a CER ensures it will run only if the code in the CER doesn't allocate additional memory by creating new reference types, boxing value types, and so on. So code in a CER is restricted from performing any operations that can allocate memory. In .NET Framework 2.0, there is no mechanism in the CLR to enforce that code in a CER follows these restrictions. However, there likely will be in future releases. For now, the primary way to make sure that code in a CER doesn't allocate additional resources is by code review.

Given this understanding of CERs, step back and see how this all relates to safe handles. Safe handles guarantee the release of the native handles they wrap because all code in an instance of *SafeHandle* runs in a CER. If there are enough resources available to create an instance of *SafeHandle*, there will be enough resources available to run it. In short, the CLR moves the allocation of all resources required for a critical finalizer up to the point where the object containing the finalizer is created, rather than waiting to allocate the resources at the point the finalizer must run.

Given that critical finalizers are guaranteed always to run, why not just make all finalizers critical? Or even better, why invent a new separate notion of a "critical" finalizer at all, and simply guarantee that all finalizers will complete successfully? Although this might seem tempting on the surface, there are two primary reasons why this wouldn't be practical. The first is performance: preparing a type (and its dependencies) takes time. Furthermore, the CLR might jit-compile code that is never even executed. The second reason that critical finalization can't become the default behavior is because of the restrictions placed on code running in a CER. The inability to cause memory to be allocated dramatically limits what can be done in a CER. Imagine writing a program that never used *new*, for example.

One final aspect of critical finalization worth noting is that critical finalizers are always run after normal finalizers. To understand the motivation for this ordering, consider the scenario of the *FileStream* class in *System.IO*. Before .NET Framework 2.0, *FileStream*'s finalizer had two key tasks: it flushed an internal buffer containing data destined for the file and closed the file handle. In .NET Framework 2.0, *FileStream* encapsulates the file handle using a *SafeHandle*, thus uses critical finalization to ensure the handle is always closed. In addition, *FileStream* maintains its existing finalizer that flushes the internal buffer. For *FileStream* to finalize properly, the CLR must run the normal finalizer first to flush the buffer before running the critical finalizer, which closes the file handle. The ordering of finalizers in this way is done specifically for this purpose.

Specifying Escalation Policy Using the CLR Hosting Interfaces

CLR hosts specify an escalation policy using the failure policy manager from the CLR hosting interfaces. The failure policy manager has two interfaces: *ICLRPolicyManager* and *IHostPolicyManager*. As their names imply, *ICLRPolicyManager* is implemented by the CLR and *IHostPolicyManager* is implemented by the host.

Hosts obtain a pointer of type *ICLRPolicyManager* by calling the *GetCLRManager* method on *ICLRControl*. The pointer to an *ICLRPolicyManager* can then be used to call methods that specify timeouts for various operations, the actions to take when failures occur, and so on. The *IHostPolicyManager* interface is used by the CLR to notify the host of actions taken as a result of escalation policy. The CLR obtains a pointer to the host's implementation of *IHostPolicyManager* using *IHostControl::GetHostManager*. The actions taken on failures are then reported to the host by calling methods on *IHostPolicyManager*.

The next few sections describe how to specify escalation policy using *ICLRPolicyManager* and how to receive notifications by providing an implementation of *IHostPolicyManager*.

Setting Policy Using *ICLRPolicyManager*

Escalation policy consists of three primary concepts: failures, actions, and operations. These concepts were described in general terms earlier in the chapter when I described how escalation policy fits into the CLR's overall infrastructure to support hosts with requirements for long process lifetimes. *Failures* refer to exceptional conditions such as the failure to allocate a resource. *Actions* describe the behavior that the CLR should take when a failure occurs. For example, a host can specify an action of thread abort given a failure to allocate a resource. *Operations* serve two purposes in the failure policy manager. First, they specify the operations for which timeouts can be specified, such as thread aborts, application domain unloads, and process exit. Second, a host can use operations to escalate the actions taken on failures. For example, a host can specify that a failure to allocate a resource in a critical region of code should always be escalated to an application domain unload.

In terms of the hosting interfaces, these concepts are represented by three enumerations: *EClrFailure*, *EPolicyAction*, and *EClrOperation*. Values from these enumerations are passed to the methods of *ICLRPolicyManager* to define escalation policy. The methods on *ICLRPolicyManager* are described in Table 11-1.

Table 11-1 The Methods on *ICLRPolicyManager*

Method	Description
SetActionOnFailure	Enables a host to specify the action to take for a given failure.
SetTimeout	Enables a host to specify a timeout value (in milliseconds) for given operations such as a thread abort or application domain unload.
SetActionOnTimeout	Enables a host to specify which action should be taken when a timeout for a particular operation occurs.
SetTimeoutAndAction	Enables a host to specify both a timeout value and a subsequent action in a single method call. *SetTimeoutAndAction* is a convenience method that combines the capabilities of *SetTimeout* and *SetActionOnTimeout*.
SetDefaultAction	Enables a host to specify the default action to take for a particular operation. *SetDefaultAction* is primarily used to override the CLR default behavior for a given action.
SetUnhandledExceptionPolicy	As described, the behavior of unhandled exceptions is different in .NET Framework 2.0 than it is in .NET Framework 1.0 and .NET Framework 1.1. In particular, unhandled exceptions in .NET Framework 2.0 result in process termination. This behavior isn't desirable for hosts with requirements for long process lifetimes, so *SetUnhandledExceptionPolicy* enables a host to turn off this behavior so that unhandled exceptions do not cause the process to exit.

CLR hosts typically use the following steps to specify escalation policy using *ICLRPolicyManager*:

1. Obtain an *ICLRPolicyManager* interface pointer.

2. Set the actions to take when failures occur.

3. Set timeout values and the actions to take when a timeout occurs.

4. Set any default actions.

5. Specify unhandled exception behavior.

Step 1: Obtain a *ICLRPolicyManager* Interface Pointer

As described in Chapter 2, CLR hosts obtain interface pointers to the CLR-implemented managers using the *ICLRControl* interface. The *ICLRControl* interface is obtained by calling the *Get-CLRControl* method on the *ICLRRuntimeHost* pointer obtained from the call to *CorBindToRuntimeEx*. Given a pointer of type *ICLRControl*, simply call its *GetCLRManager* method passing the IID corresponding to *ICLRPolicyManager*(*IID_ ICLRPolicyManager*) as shown in the following code sample:

```
// Initialize the CLR and get a pointer of
// type ICLRRuntimeHost.
ICLRRuntimeHost *pCLR = NULL;
HRESULT hr = CorBindToRuntimeEx(
```

```
      L"v2.0.41013",
      L"wks",
      STARTUP_CONCURRENT_GC,
      CLSID_CLRRuntimeHost,
      IID_ICLRRuntimeHost,
      (PVOID*) &pCLR);

// Use ICLRRuntimeHost to get the CLR control interface.
ICLRControl *pCLRControl = NULL;
pCLR->GetCLRControl(&pCLRControl);

// Use ICLRControl to get a pointer to the failure policy
// manager.
ICLRPolicyManager* pCLRPolicyManager = NULL;
hr = pCLRControl->GetCLRManager(IID_ICLRPolicyManager,
                              (PVOID*)&pCLRPolicyManager);
```

Step 2: Set Actions to Take on Failures

Given an interface pointer of type *ICLRPolicyManager*, a host can now specify which actions the CLR should take given specific failures by calling *SetActionOnFailure*. As can be seen from the following method signature, *SetActionOnFailure* takes two parameters. The first parameter is a value from the *EClrFailure* enumeration describing the failure for which an action is specified. The second parameter is a value from the *EPolicyAction* enumeration describing the action itself.

```
interface ICLRPolicyManager: IUnknown
{
    HRESULT SetActionOnFailure(
        [in] EClrFailure failure,
        [in] EPolicyAction action);

    // Other methods omitted…
}
```

The values for *EClrFailure* correspond directly to the failures described earlier in the overview of escalation policy. Specifically, the failures for which an action can be specified are the failure to allocate a resource, the failure to allocate a resource in a critical region of code, a fatal error internal to the CLR, and an abandoned synchronization primitive. Here's the definition of *EClrFailure* from mscoree.idl:

```
typedef enum
{
    FAIL_NonCriticalResource,
    FAIL_CriticalResource,
    FAIL_FatalRuntime,
    FAIL_OrphanedLock,
    MaxClrFailure
} EClrFailure;
```

The meaning of many of the values from *EPolicyAction* should also be clear from the overview of escalation policy presented earlier in the chapter. Here's the definition of *EPolicyAction* from mscoree.idl:

```
typedef enum
{
    eNoAction,
    eThrowException,
    eAbortThread,
    eRudeAbortThread,
    eUnloadAppDomain,
    eRudeUnloadAppDomain,
    eExitProcess,
    eFastExitProcess,
    eRudeExitProcess,
    eDisableRuntime,
    MaxPolicyAction
} EPolicyAction;
```

Values from *EPolicyAction* that likely require additional explanation are these:

- **eNoAction and eThrowException**   These values are the defaults for various operations that can be customized through escalation policy. For example, *eThrowException* is the default action for all resource failures. Because these values are defaults, they are primarily used to reestablish default behavior if you had changed it earlier.

- **eFastExitProcess**   In addition to the graceful and rude methods for terminating a process, escalation policy enables a host to specify a third alternative called a *fast process exit*. The CLR does not run any object finalizers during a fast exit, but it does run other cleanup code such as that in *finally* blocks. A fast exit is a compromise between a graceful exit and a rude exit both in terms of how quickly the process terminates and in the amount of add-in cleanup code the CLR attempts to run.

With the exception of *eClrFailure.FAIL_FatalRuntime*, all of the values in *EPolicyAction* are valid actions for any of the failures indicated by *EClrFailure*. *FAIL_FatalRuntime* is a special case in that when a fatal error occurs, the only actions that can be taken are to exit the process or disable the CLR. Specifically, the following values from *EPolicyAction* are valid when calling *SetActionOnFailure* for a fatal runtime failure:

- *eExitProcess*

- *eFastExitProcess*

- *eRudeExitProcess*

- *eDisableRuntime*

Now that you understand the parameters to *SetActionOnFailure*, let's look at some example calls to see how particular actions can be specified for given failures. The following series of calls to *SetActionOnFailure* specifies a portion (minus the timeout aspects) of the escalation policy shown in Figure 11-1.

```
hr = pCLRPolicyManager->SetActionOnFailure(FAIL_NonCriticalResource,
                                           eAbortThread);

hr = pCLRPolicyManager->SetActionOnFailure(FAIL_CriticalResource,
                                           eUnloadAppDomain);

hr = pCLRPolicyManager->SetActionOnFailure(FAIL_OrphanedLock,
                                           eUnloadAppDomain);

hr = pCLRPolicyManager->SetActionOnFailure(FAIL_FatalRuntime,
                                           eDisableRuntime);
```

In particular, these lines of code specify the following actions:

1. All failures to allocate a resource cause the thread on which the failure occurred to be aborted.

2. If the failure to allocate a resource occurs in a critical region of code, the failure is escalated to an application domain unload. Recall that a resource failure in a critical region has the potential to leave the application domain in an inconsistent state. Hence, a conservative approach is to unload the entire application domain.

3. The detection of an abandoned lock also causes the application domain to be unloaded. As with a resource failure in a critical region, an orphaned lock is a pretty good indication that application domain state probably isn't consistent.

4. Instead of exiting the process if a fatal internal CLR error is detected, the CLR is disabled, thereby enabling the host to continue any processing unrelated to managed code.

Step 3: Set Timeouts and the Actions to Take for Various Operations

The ability to specify timeout values for operations such as thread aborts and application domain unloads is a key element in the host's ability to describe an escalation policy that will keep a process responsive over time. As shown in Table 11-1, *ICLRPolicyManager* has three methods that hosts can use to set timeouts: *SetTimeout*, *SetActionOnTimeout*, and *SetTimeoutAndAction*. Each of these methods enables a host to specify a timeout value in milliseconds for an operation described by the *EClrOperation* enumeration. The definition of *EClrOperation* is as follows:

```
typedef enum
{
    OPR_ThreadAbort,
    OPR_ThreadRudeAbortInNonCriticalRegion,
    OPR_ThreadRudeAbortInCriticalRegion,
    OPR_AppDomainUnload,
```

```
    OPR_AppDomainRudeUnload,
    OPR_ProcessExit,
    OPR_FinalizerRun,
    MaxClrOperation
} EClrOperation;
```

Timeouts can be specified only for a subset of the values in *EClrOperation*. For example, it wouldn't make sense to specify a timeout for any of the operations that represent rude thread aborts or application domain unloads because those operations occur immediately. The values from *EClrOperation* for which a timeout can be specified are as follows:

- *OPR_ThreadAbort*

- *OPR_AppDomainUnload*

- *OPR_ProcessExit*

- *OPR_FinalizerRun*

In general, hosts that require a process to live for a long time are likely to want to specify timeout values for at least *OPR_ThreadAbort*, *OPR_AppDomainUnload*, and *OPR_FinalizerRun* because there are no default timeout values for these operations. That is, unless a host specifies a timeout, attempts to abort a thread or unload an application domain could take an infinite amount of time. The CLR does have a default timeout for *OPR_ProcessExit*, however. If a process doesn't gracefully exit in approximately 40 seconds, the process is forcefully terminated.

The following series of calls to *SetTimeoutAndAction* specifies timeout values and the actions to take for the operations indicated by the escalation policy specified in Figure 11-1.

```
    hr = pCLRPolicyManager->SetTimeoutAndAction (OPR_ThreadAbort, 10*1000,
                                                 eRudeAbortThread);
    hr = pCLRPolicyManager->SetTimeoutAndAction (OPR_AppDomainUnload,  20*1000,
                                                 eRudeUnloadAppDomain);
```

In particular, these statements specify the following:

1. If an attempt to abort a thread doesn't complete in 10 seconds, the thread abort is escalated to a rude thread abort.

2. If an attempt to unload an application domain doesn't complete in 20 seconds, the unload is escalated to a rude application domain unload.

Step 4: Set Any Default Actions

The *SetDefaultAction* method of *ICLRPolicyManager* can be used to specify a default action to take in response to a particular operation. In general, this method is used less than the other methods on *ICLRPolicyManager* because the CLR's default actions are sufficient and because escalation is usually specified in terms of either particular failures or timeouts. However, if you'd like to change the defaults, you can do so by calling *SetDefaultAction* with a value for *EPolicyAction* describing the action to take in response to an operation defined by a value from

EClrOperation. For example, the following call to *SetDefaultAction* specifies that the entire application domain should always be unloaded whenever a rude thread abort occurs in a critical region of code:

```
hr = pCLRPolicyManager->SetDefaultAction (OPR_ThreadRudeAbortInCriticalRegion,
                                           eUnloadAppDomain);
```

SetDefaultAction can be used only to escalate failure behavior; it cannot be used to downgrade the action to take for a given operation. For example, it's not valid to use *SetDefaultAction* to request an action of *EAbortThread* for an operation of *OPR_AppDomainUnload*. Table 11-2 describes which values from *EPolicyAction* represent valid actions for each operation from *EClrOperation*.

Table 11-2   Valid Combinations of Actions and Operations for *SetDefaultAction*

Value of *eClrOperations*	Valid Values from *EPolicyAction*
OPR_ThreadAbort	*eAbortThread*
	eRudeAbortThread
	eUnloadAppDomain
	eRudeUnloadAppDomain
	eExitProcess
	eFastExitProcess
	eRudeExitProcess
	eDisableRuntime
OPR_ThreadRudeAbortInNonCriticalRegion	*eRudeAbortThread*
OPR_ThreadRudeAbortInCriticalRegion	*eUnloadAppDomain*
	eRudeUnloadAppDomain
	eExitProcess
	eFastExitProcess
	eRudeExitProcess
	eDisableRuntime
OPR_AppDomainUnload	*eUnloadAppDomain*
	eRudeUnloadAppDomain
	eExitProcess
	eFastExitProcess
	eRudeExitProcess
	eDisableRuntime
OPR_AppDomainRudeUnload	*eRudeUnloadAppDomain*
	eExitProcess
	eFastExitProcess
	eRudeExitProcess
	eDisableRuntime

Table 11-2   Valid Combinations of Actions and Operations for *SetDefaultAction*

Value of *eClrOperations*	Valid Values from *EPolicyAction*
OPR_ProcessExit	eExitProcess
	eFastExitProcess
	eRudeExitProcess
	eDisableRuntime
OPR_FinalizerRun	eNoAction
	eAbortThread
	eRudeAbortThread
	eUnloadAppDomain
	eRudeUnloadAppDomain
	eExitProcess
	eFastExitProcess
	eRudeExitProcess
	eDisableRuntime

Step 5: Specify Unhandled Exceptions Behavior

The change in the way unhandled exceptions are treated in .NET Framework 2.0 was implemented to make application exceptions more obvious and easier to debug. Previously, the CLR caught, and thereby hid, unhandled exceptions; often this completely masked the problem such that the end user or developer wasn't even aware the error occurred. Enabling unhandled exceptions always to be visible makes it possible for these errors to be discovered and fixed. Although this is a positive step in general, hosts that require the process to live for a long time would rather have unhandled exceptions masked in these cases rather than having the process terminated. As I've shown, escalation policy provides the host with the means to unload any code that might be in a questionable state because of an unhandled exception. The *SetUnhandledExceptionPolicy* method on *ICLRPolicyManager* enables the host to revert to the behavior for treating unhandled exceptions that was implemented in versions of the .NET Framework earlier than version 2.0. The definition of *SetUnhandledExceptionPolicy* is shown here:

```
interface ICLRPolicyManager: IUnknown
{
    HRESULT SetUnhandledExceptionPolicy(
        [in] EClrUnhandledException policy);

    // Other methods omitted…
}
```

As you can see, hosts specify their desired behavior with respect to unhandled exceptions by passing a value from the *EClrUnhandledException* enumeration to *SetUnhandledExceptionPolicy*. *EClrUnhandledException* has two values as shown in the following definition from mscoree.idl:

```
typedef enum
{
    eRuntimeDeterminedPolicy,
    eHostDeterminedPolicy,
} EClrUnhandledException;
```

The *eRuntimeDeterminedPolicy* value specifies the .NET Framework 2.0 behavior, whereas the *eHostDeterminedPolicy* value specifies that unhandled exceptions should not be allowed to proceed to the point where the process will be terminated.

The following call to *SetUnhandledExceptionPolicy* demonstrates how a host would use the API to specify that unhandled exceptions should not result in process termination:

```
pCLRPolicyManager->SetUnhandledExceptionPolicy(eHostDeterminedPolicy);
```

Receiving Notifications Through *IHostPolicyManager*

Hosts that specify an escalation policy using *ICLRPolicyManager* can receive notifications whenever an action was taken as a result of that policy. These notifications are sent to the host through the *IHostPolicyManager* interface. Table 11-3 describes the methods the CLR calls to notify the host of actions taken as a result of escalation policy.

Table 11-3   **The Methods on *IHostPolicyManager***

Method	Description
OnDefaultAction	Notifies the host that an action was taken in response to a particular operation. The action taken and the operation to which it applied are passed as parameters.
OnTimeout	Notifies the host that a timeout has occurred. The operation that timed out and the action taken as a result are passed as parameters.
OnFailure	Notifies the host that a failure has occurred. The particular failure that occurred and the action taken as a result are passed as parameters.

To receive these notifications, a host must complete the following two steps:

1. Provide an implementation of *IHostPolicyManager*.

2. Register that implementation with the CLR.

These steps are described in more detail in the next two sections.

Step 1: Provide an Implementation of *IHostPolicyManager*

To provide an implementation of *IHostPolicyManager*, simply write a class that derives from the interface and implement the *OnDefaultAction*, *OnTimeout*, and *OnFailure* methods. As described earlier, the CLR calls these methods for informational purposes only. Although no direct action can be taken in the implementation of the methods, it is useful to see when your escalation policy is being used by the CLR. This information can be helpful in tuning your policy over time. The following code snippet provides a sample definition for a class that implements *IHostPolicyManager*:

```
class CHostPolicyManager : public IHostPolicyManager
{
public:
    // IHostPolicyManager
    HRESULT STDMETHODCALLTYPE OnDefaultAction(EClrOperation operation,
                                              EPolicyAction action);
    HRESULT STDMETHODCALLTYPE OnTimeout(EClrOperation operation,
                                        EPolicyAction action);
    HRESULT STDMETHODCALLTYPE OnFailure(EClrFailure failure,
                                        EPolicyAction action);

    // IUnknown
    virtual HRESULT STDMETHODCALLTYPE QueryInterface(const IID &iid,
                                                     void **ppv);
    virtual ULONG STDMETHODCALLTYPE AddRef();
    virtual ULONG STDMETHODCALLTYPE Release();
};
```

Step 2: Notify the CLR of Your Implementation Using *IHostControl*

After you've written a class that implements *IHostPolicyManager*, you must notify the CLR of your intent to receive notifications related to escalation policy. As with all host-implemented interfaces, the host returns its implementation when the CLR calls the *GetHostManager* method on *IHostControl* (refer to Chapter 2 for a refresher on how the CLR discovers which managers a host implements). The following partial implementation of *IHostControl::GetHostManager* creates an instance of the class defined earlier when asked for an implementation of *IHostManager*:

```
HRESULT STDMETHODCALLTYPE CHostControl::GetHostManager(REFIID riid,void **ppv)
{
    if (riid == IID_IHostPolicyManager)
    {
      // Create a new instance of the class that implements
      // IHostPolicyManager.
      CHostPolicyManager *pHostPolicyManager = new CHostPolicyManager();
      *ppv = (IHostPolicyManager *) pHostPolicyManager;
      return S_OK;
    }

    // Checks for other interfaces omitted…

    return E_NOINTERFACE;
}
```

Now that I've notified the CLR of the implementation of *IHostPolicyManager*, it will call the implementation each time an action is taken in response to the escalation policy defined using *ICLRPolicyManager*.

Guidelines for Writing Highly Available Managed Code

In many cases, the capability to specify an escalation policy is required primarily to protect against add-ins that weren't written explicitly with high availability in mind. For example, I've discussed how a host can cause a resource failure to be escalated to a request to unload an entire application domain if the code in question happens to be updating shared state when the resource failure occurs. Ideally, these situations would never occur in the first place, and hence, the escalation policy wouldn't be needed. After all, terminating an application domain likely results in some operations failing and having to be retried from the user's perspective. Although you generally can't guarantee that all the add-ins you load into your host will be written with high availability in mind, you can follow some guidelines when writing your own managed code to ensure that the situations causing an application domain to be unloaded are kept to a minimum and that no resources you allocate are leaked if an application domain unload does occur.

In particular, the following guidelines can help you write code to function best in environments requiring long process lifetimes:

- Use *SafeHandle*s to encapsulate handles to native resources.
- Use the synchronization primitives provided by the .NET Framework.
- Ensure that all calls you make to unmanaged code return to the CLR.
- Annotate your libraries with the *HostProtectionAttribute*.

Use *SafeHandle*s to Encapsulate All Native Handles

As described earlier in the chapter, *SafeHandle*s leverage the concepts of critical finalization and constrained execution regions to ensure that native handles are properly released when an application domain is unloaded. In general, you probably won't have to make explicit use of *SafeHandle*s because the classes provided by the .NET Framework that wrap native resources all use *SafeHandle*s on your behalf. For example, the classes in *Microsoft.Win32* that provide registry access wrap registry handles in a *SafeHandle*, and the file-related classes in *System.IO* use *SafeHandle*s to encapsulate native file handles. However, if you are accessing a native handle in your managed code without using an existing .NET Framework class, you have two options for wrapping your native handle in a *SafeHandle*. First, the .NET Framework provides a few classes derived from *System.Runtime.InteropServices* for wrapping specific types of handles. For example, the *SafeFileHandle* class in *Microsoft.Win32.SafeHandles* encapsulates a native file handle. There are also classes that wrap Open Database Connectivity (ODBC) connection handles, COM interface pointers, and so on. However, if one of the existing *SafeHandle*-derived classes doesn't meet your needs, writing your own is relatively straightforward.

Writing a class that leverages *SafeHandle* to encapsulate a new native handle type requires the following four steps:

1. Create a class derived from *System.Runtime.InteropServices.SafeHandle*.

2. Provide a constructor that enables callers to associate a native handle (typically represented by an IntPtr) with your *SafeHandle*.

3. Provide an implementation of the *ReleaseHandle* method.

4. Provide an implementation of the *IsInvalid* property.

IsInvalid and *ReleaseHandle* are abstract members that all classes derived from *SafeHandle* must implement. *IsInvalid* is a *boolean* property the CLR accesses to determine whether the underlying native handle is valid and therefore needs to be freed. The *ReleaseHandle* method is called by the CLR during critical finalization to free the native handle. Your implementation of *ReleaseHandle* will vary depending on which Win32 API is required to free the underlying handle. For example, if your *SafeHandle*-derived class encapsulates registry handles, your implementation of *ReleaseHandle* will likely call *RegCloseKey*. If your class wraps handles to device contexts used for printing, your implementation of *ReleaseHandle* would call Win32's *DeleteDC* method, and so on.

Both *IsInvalid* and *ReleaseHandle* are executed within a constrained execution region, so make sure that your implementations do not allocate memory. In most cases, *IsInvalid* should require just a simple check of the value of the handle, and *ReleaseHandle* should require only a PInvoke call to the Win32 API required to free the handle you've wrapped.

The following class is an example of a *SafeHandle* that can be used to encapsulate many types of Win32 handles. In particular, this class works with any handle that is freed using Win32's *CloseHandle* API. Examples of handles that can be used with this class include events, processes, files, and mutexes. My *SafeHandle*-derived class, along with a portion of the definition of *SafeHandle* itself, is shown here:

```
[SecurityPermission(SecurityAction.InheritanceDemand, UnmanagedCode=true)]
[SecurityPermission(SecurityAction.LinkDemand, UnmanagedCode=true)]
public abstract class SafeHandle : CriticalFinalizerObject, IDisposable
{
    public abstract bool IsInvalid { get; }
    protected abstract bool ReleaseHandle();

    // Other methods on SafeHandle omitted…
}

public class SafeOSHandle : SafeHandle
{
        public SafeOSHandle(IntPtr existingHandle, bool ownsHandle)
                : base(IntPtr.Zero, ownsHandle)
        {
            SetHandle(existingHandle);
        }
```

```
    // Handle values of 0 and -1 are invalid.
    public override bool IsInvalid
    {
        get { return handle == IntPtr.Zero || handle == new IntPtr(-1); }
    }

    [DllImport("kernel32.dll"), SuppressUnmanagedCodeSecurity]
    private static extern bool CloseHandle(IntPtr handle);

    // The implementation of ReleaseHandle simply calls Win32's
    // CloseHandle.
    override protected bool ReleaseHandle()
    {
        return CloseHandle(handle);
    }
}
```

Several aspects of *SafeOSHandle* are worth noting:

- **SafeHandle is derived from CriticalFinalizerObject.**   By deriving from *CriticalFinalizer-Object*, the finalizers for all *SafeHandle* classes are guaranteed to be run, even when a thread or application domain is rudely aborted.

- **All classes derived from *SafeHandle* require the permission to call unmanaged code.**   *SafeHandle* is annotated with both an *InheritanceDemand* and a *LinkDemand* that require the ability to call unmanaged code. In practice, partially trusted callers likely wouldn't be able to derive from *SafeHandle* anyway because the implementation of *ReleaseHandle* often involves calling a Win32 API through PInvoke, which requires the ability to access unmanaged code.

- **The constructor has an *ownsHandle* parameter.**   The *ownsHandle* parameter is set to false in scenarios where you are using an instance of *SafeHandle* to wrap a handle you didn't explicitly create yourself. When *ownsHandle* is false, the CLR will not free the handle during critical finalization.

- **The call to CloseHandle is annotated with SuppressUnmanagedCodeSecurityAttribute.**   Generally, calls through PInvoke to unmanaged APIs cause the CLR to perform a full stack walk to determine whether all callers on the stack have permission to call unmanaged code. However, the dynamic nature of the stack walk can cause additional resources to be required, which should be avoided while running in a CER. The *SuppressUnmanagedCodeSecurityAttribute* has the effect of moving the security check from the time at which the method is called to the time at which it is jit-compiled. This happens because *SuppressUnmanagedCodeSecurityAttribute* causes a link demand to occur instead of a full stack walk. So the security check happens when the method is prepared for execution in a CER instead of while running in the CER, thereby avoiding potential failures when the method is executed.

Use Only the Synchronization Primitives Provided by the .NET Framework

I've shown how hosts can use the escalation policy interfaces to treat resource failures differently if they occur in a critical region of code. Recall that a critical region of code is defined as any code that the CLR determines to be manipulating state that is shared across multiple threads. The heuristic the CLR uses to determine whether code is editing shared state is based on synchronization primitives. Specifically, if a resource failure occurs on a thread in which code is waiting on a synchronization primitive, the CLR assumes the code is using the primitive to synchronize access to shared state. However, this heuristic is useful only if the CLR can always detect when code is waiting on a synchronization primitive. So it's important always to use the synchronization primitives provided by the .NET Framework instead of inventing your own. In particular, the *System.Threading* namespace provides the following set of primitives you can use for synchronization:

- *Monitor*
- *Mutex*
- *ReaderWriterLock*

If you synchronize access to shared state using a mechanism of your own, the CLR won't be able to detect that you are editing shared state should a resource failure occur. So the escalation policy defined by the host for resource failures in critical regions of code will not be used, thereby potentially leaving an application domain in an inconsistent state.

Ensure That Calls to Unmanaged Code Return to the CLR

Throughout this chapter, I've discussed how the CLR relies on the ability to abort threads and unload application domains to guarantee process integrity. However, in some cases a thread can enter a state that prevents the CLR from being able to abort it. In particular, if you use PInvoke to call an unmanaged API that waits infinitely on a synchronization primitive or performs any other type of blocking operation, the CLR won't be able to abort the thread. Once a thread leaves the CLR through a PInvoke call, the CLR is no longer able to control all aspects of that thread's execution. In particular, all synchronization primitives created out in unmanaged code will be unknown to the CLR. So the CLR cannot unblock the thread to abort it. You can avoid this situation primarily by specifying reasonable timeout values whenever you wait on a blocking operation in unmanaged code. Most of the Win32 APIs that allow you to wait for a particular resource enable you to specify timeout values. For example, consider the case in which you use PInvoke to call an unmanaged function that creates a mutex and uses the Win32 API *WaitForSingleObject* to wait until the mutex is signaled. To ensure that your call won't wait indefinitely, your call to *WaitForSingleObject* should specify a finite timeout value. In this way, you'll be able to regain control after a specified interval and avoid all situations that would prevent the CLR from being able to abort your thread.

Annotate Your Libraries with the *HostProtectionAttribute*

In Chapter 12, I discuss how hosts can use a feature called *host protection* to prevent APIs that violate various aspects of their programming model. For example, hosts can use the host protection feature to prevent an add-in from using any API that allows it to share state across threads. If an add-in is not allowed to share state in the first place, the host portion of escalation policy dealing with critical regions of code will never be required, thus resulting in fewer application domain unloads (or whatever other action the host specified).

For host protection to be effective, all APIs that provide capabilities identified by a set of host protection categories must be annotated with a custom attribute called the *HostProtectionAttribute*. Refer to Chapter 12 for more a complete description of the host protection categories and how to use *HostProtectionAttribute* to annotate your managed code libraries properly.

Summary

.NET Framework 2.0 is the first version in which the CLR needs to provide a solution for hosts whose reliability model requires long process lifetimes. These requirements were primarily driven by the integration of the CLR into SQL Server 2005 and the anticipation of other hosts with similar requirements in the future. Before .NET Framework 2.0, CLR hosts that required high availability used a model based on process recycling. This model worked great for hosts such as ASP.NET in which virtually no per-process state was kept, so it really didn't matter which process was used to process a particular incoming request.

To support hosts for which a process recycling model is inadequate, the .NET Framework 2.0 version of the CLR introduces a reliability model based on application domain recycling. In this model, the CLR guarantees that an application domain can be unloaded from a process without leaking any resources. If the integrity of an application domain becomes questionable because of an exceptional condition such as the failure to allocate a resource, the application domain can simply be removed from the process without affecting the integrity of the process. One of the technical challenges of the application domain recycling model is to provide the guarantee that handles to native resources, such as files and kernel objects held by managed code, can always be freed when an application domain is unloaded. Providing this guarantee requires the introduction of new infrastructure in the form of critical finalization, *SafeHandles*, and constrained execution regions. These three new concepts work together to guarantee that the code required to free a handle to a native resource will always be run, regardless of how quickly an application domain must be unloaded.

Another critical piece of the CLR's design to support long process lifetimes is the notion of escalation policy. CLR hosts use the hosting interfaces to specify a set of rules known as escalation policy that dictate the actions taken by the CLR in the face of various exceptional conditions. Hosts can tailor these actions to their specific requirements to guarantee process integrity.

As you'll see in the next chapter, hosts can use another new .NET Framework 2.0 feature called host protection to restrict the set of APIs an add-in can use, thereby reducing the possibility of having to unload an application domain to maintain process integrity at all.

Chapter 12

Enforcing Application-Specific Programming Model Constraints

As the managed code programming model becomes more widely adopted both within Microsoft and in the community in general, the range of capabilities available through managed class libraries will continue to grow. This trend will become even more apparent in future versions of the Microsoft Windows operating system when more and more of the existing Microsoft Win32 API is superseded with managed class libraries. However, not all of the capabilities available to add-ins through managed class libraries are appropriate in all hosting scenarios. For example, the ability to display a user interface doesn't fit at all in server scenarios, and the ability to call a managed API that will cause the process to exit isn't appropriate in hosting scenarios that require long process lifetimes.

What's required is a mechanism for an extensible application to block certain categories of functionality that don't fit with its overall programming model. The CLR hosting interfaces offer a feature called *host protection* that is designed specifically for this purpose. Because host protection is exposed through the CLR hosting interfaces, your application must be a full CLR host to use the feature.

The host protection feature identifies categories of functionality that are deemed of interest in various hosting scenarios. Hosts can then indicate that certain categories of functionality are not allowed within the host's process. Examples of host protection categories in Microsoft .NET Framework 2.0 include the ability to share state or perform synchronization across threads, the ability to affect the host's process or any of its threads, the ability to display user interface, and so on.

Given the identification of the host protection categories, two steps are necessary to enable a host to prevent categories of functionality from being used in their process. First, the .NET Framework class libraries must be annotated with a custom attribute called the *HostProtection-Attribute* that identifies which APIs belong to which categories. For example, the *System.Threading.Thread* class has several methods that would allow an add-in to affect how threads are created and used within a process. These members have all been marked with the *Host-ProtectionAttribute*, indicating that they belong to the threading category. *HostProtectionAttribute* is typically applied to types and members, but can also be applied to entire assemblies, value types, and delegates as well. Also, members of interfaces can also be annotated. In this case, all implementations of those methods in derived classes are automatically considered annotated as well. The annotation of the .NET Framework class libraries has been done as part of the version

2.0 release. The host must then enable host protection by indicating which categories of functionality should be blocked. This is done using the host protection manager in the CLR hosting interfaces. Specifically, the host asks the CLR for an interface of type *ICLRHostProtectionManager* through which it tells the CLR which categories should be blocked.

The host protection feature in its current form has been designed specifically with the requirements of the Microsoft SQL Server 2005 host in mind. This design is apparent in two ways. First, the host protection categories that have been defined in .NET Framework 2.0 are designed specifically to meet the needs of the SQL programming model. Second, not all of the .NET Framework class libraries have been annotated with the *HostProtectionAttribute*. Only those assemblies that SQL Server 2005 allows in its process have been annotated. (SQL Server uses an assembly loading manager to restrict which .NET Framework assemblies can be loaded, as described in Chapter 8.) The methods and types in an assembly that has not been annotated cannot be blocked using host protection. As time goes on, I expect both that the number of host protection categories will be expanded to meet the needs of other hosts and that the number of managed code libraries that are annotated with *HostProtectionAttribute* will increase. Nevertheless, if your hosting requirements are similar to those of SQL Server, you might find the current host protection categories adequate.

The goals of host protection are often confused with the goals of Code Access Security (CAS) for obvious reasons—both are techniques used to prevent a particular class or method from being used in a process. However, the motivation behind these two features is quite different. CAS is about protecting your process and the machine on which it is running from malicious access to protected resources, whereas host protection is merely about enforcing specific characteristics of a given host's programming model. The difference between CAS and host protection can best be seen by looking at the consequences that could occur were each feature to be compromised. A vulnerability in CAS (or its use) results in unauthorized access to a protected resource, or a *security vulnerability*. In contrast, compromising host protection results only in a violation of the programming model. Such a violation can cause the host to perform poorly or even to crash, but it does not allow unauthorized access to a protected resource. There is one case in which CAS and host protection are directly related, however. When a host specifies that certain categories of functionality should be blocked, those categories are blocked only for partially trusted assemblies. Assemblies granted full trust are exempt from host protection—they can use any API they want.

This chapter describes how to use host protection to limit the functionality available to the add-ins you load into your extensible application. I start by describing the host protection categories. The description of each category includes a list of the types, methods, and properties that are currently identified as belonging to that category using the *HostProtectionAttribute*. After the categories are described, I show you how to use *ICLRHostProtectionManager* to tell the CLR which categories should be blocked.

The Host Protection Categories

The host protection categories are defined by the *HostProtectionResource* enumeration from the *System.Security.Permissions* namespace:

```
[Flags, Serializable]
    public enum HostProtectionResource
    {
        None                        = 0x0,
        Synchronization             = 0x1,
        SharedState                 = 0x2,
        ExternalProcessMgmt         = 0x4,
        SelfAffectingProcessMgmt    = 0x8,
        ExternalThreading           = 0x10,
        SelfAffectingThreading      = 0x20,
        SecurityInfrastructure      = 0x40,
        UI                          = 0x80,
        MayLeakOnAbort              = 0x100,
        All                         = 0x1ff,
    }
```

Given that host protection has initially been designed with SQL Server 2005 in mind, the best way to understand the motivation behind the host protection categories is to think of them in the context of the SQL Server programming model. Two aspects of the SQL Server programming model drove the definition of these categories: reliability and scalability. Recall from Chapter 11 that the basis of the CLR's reliability design in .NET Framework 2.0 is the ability to shut down an application domain without leaking any resources, so one of the host protection categories (*MayLeakOnAbort*) is used to annotate code that cannot be guaranteed to free all resources when an application domain is unloaded. In addition, many of the host protection categories are aimed at preventing an add-in from inadvertently limiting the scalability of the host process. The SQL Server scheduler is highly tuned toward providing the highest degree of scalability possible. Any attempts by an add-in to block synchronizing access to shared state, or to affect how threads behave in the process, can limit the ability of SQL Server to scale. SQL Server add-ins such as user-defined types and stored procedures that are written in native code (using the T-SQL programming language) don't have the ability to perform operations that limit scalability in this way. Many of the host protection categories are designed to ensure that SQL Server add-ins written in managed code don't have those capabilities either.

The next several sections describe the individual host protection categories in detail. For each category, I describe the motivation for the category and the characteristics of the .NET Framework APIs that belong to that category. Each section also includes a full list of the .NET Framework APIs that belong to the particular category.

Synchronization

The synchronization host protection category includes APIs that allow an add-in to synchronize access to a particular resource explicitly across multiple threads. For example, many of the collection classes in the *System.Collections* namespace have a method called *Synchronized* that returns an instance of the collection to which only one thread can have access at a time. In addition, the *System.Threading* namespace includes several types that can be used to create and hold various types of operating system locks such as mutexes and semaphores. Synchronizing access to a resource means that at least one thread must wait if multiple threads are trying to access the resource simultaneously. Waiting on a resource limits scalability and should be avoided when possible in scenarios requiring high throughput. Hosts can block access to the APIs in the synchronization category to prevent an add-in from limiting scalability by waiting for access to a resource. In addition, synchronization can also hurt both scalability and reliability by causing the host to terminate an entire application domain instead of just an individual thread. Chapter 11 discusses how a host can specify policy that will cause the CLR to unload an entire application domain when a thread that is holding a lock receives a *ThreadAbortException*, for example.

The set of .NET Framework APIs that belongs to the synchronization host protection category is listed in Table 12-1.

Table 12-1   Properties and Methods with the Synchronization *HostProtectionAttribute*

Type	Property or Method
System.Collections.ArrayList	*Synchronized*
System.Collections.Generic.SortedDictionary<K, V>	*SyncRoot { get }*
System.Collections.Generic.Stack<T>	*SyncRoot { get }*
System.Collections.Hashtable	*Synchronized*
System.Collections.Queue	*Synchronized*
System.Collections.SortedList	*Synchronized*
System.Collections.Stack	*Synchronized*
System.IO.TextReader	*Synchronized*
System.IO.TextWriter	*Synchronized*
System.Threading.AutoResetEvent	All methods and properties
System.Threading.EventWaitHandle	All methods and properties
System.Threading.Interlocked	All methods and properties
System.Threading.ManualResetEvent	All methods and properties
System.Threading.Monitor	All methods and properties
System.Threading.Mutex	All methods and properties
System.Threading.ReaderWriterLock	All methods and properties
System.Threading.Semaphore	All methods and properties

Table 12-1   Properties and Methods with the Synchronization *HostProtectionAttribute*

Type	Property or Method
System.Threading.Thread	*Start*
	Join
	SpinWait
	ApartmentState { set }
	TrySetApartmentState { set }
	SetApartmentState
	BeginCriticalRegion
	EndCriticalRegion
System.Threading.ThreadPool	All methods and properties
System.Threading.Timer	All methods and properties
System.ComponentModel.AttributeCollection	All methods and properties
System.ComponentModel.ComponentCollection	All methods and properties
System.ComponentModel.EventDescriptorCollection	All methods and properties
System.ComponentModel.ISynchronizeInvoke	*BeginInvoke*
System.ComponentModel.PropertyDescriptorCollection	All methods and properties
System.Diagnostics.TraceListener	All properties and methods
System.Data.TypedDataSetGenerator	All properties and methods
System.Xml.XmlDataDocument	All properties and methods
System.Diagnostics.Process	All properties and methods
System.Text.RegularExpressions.Group	*Synchronized*
System.Text.RegularExpressions.Match	*Synchronized*
System.Diagnostics.EventLog	*SynchronizingObject*
System.Diagnostics.PerformanceCounter	All properties and methods
System.Diagnostics.PerformanceCounterCategory	All properties and methods
System.Timers.Timer	All properties and methods

Shared State

The sharing of state between threads is related to synchronization in that access to the shared state must be synchronized for that state to remain consistent, so the shared state host protection category exists for many of the same reasons that the synchronization category does. The most obvious example of an API that allows you to share state between threads is the *Alloc-DataSlot* (and related) APIs on *System.Threading.Thread*. These APIs essentially provide a managed-code view of the thread local store feature of Win32.

The complete set of APIs in the shared state category is listed in Table 12-2.

Table 12-2   Properties and Methods with the *SharedState HostProtectionAttribute*

Type	Property or Method
System.Threading.Thread	*AllocateDataSlot*
	AllocateNamedDataSlot
	FreeNamedDataSlot
	GetData
	SetData
System.Diagnostics.Debug	*Listeners { get }*
System.Diagnostics.Trace	*Listeners { get }*
System.Data.TypedDataSetGenerator	All properties and methods
System.Diagnostics.Process	All properties and methods
System.Diagnostics.ProcessStartInfo	All properties and methods
System.Diagnostics.PerformanceCounter	All properties and methods
System.Diagnostics.PerformanceCounterCategory	All properties and methods

External Process Management

The external process management category contains APIs that add-ins can use to manipulate processes other than the host process itself. The APIs in this category can't affect the integrity or the reliability of the host process specifically, but they can have an indirect effect through the ability to create and manipulate other processes on the system. For example, SQL Server runs best when it is one of just a few processes on a system and it can therefore take advantage of the majority of the system's resources, including memory. The presence of many other processes competing for the same resources can adversely affect SQL Server performance. The *Process* class in the *System.Diagnostics* namespace is a great example of a class that can be used to affect other processes. *Process* has methods that allow an add-in to create and kill processes, interact with processes through the standard input and output streams, and so on.

Table 12-3 lists the types in the external process management category.

Table 12-3   Properties and Methods with the *ExternalProcessMgmt HostProtectionAttribute*

Type	Property or Method
System.ComponentModel.LicenseManager	All properties and methods
System.Diagnostics.Process	All properties and methods

Self-Affecting Process Management

Whereas the APIs in the external process management category cannot affect the host's process directly, the APIs in the self-affecting process management category can, so the APIs in this category can directly affect the stability of the host.

The APIs in the self-affecting process management category are all in the *System.Diagnostics* namespace and are all either on the *Process* class or its relatives. The self-affecting process APIs allow an add-in to affect characteristics of the host process, including its priority and the processor affinity of threads running in the process. The full list of self-affecting process APIs is given in Table 12-4.

Table 12-4 Properties and Methods with the *SelfAffectingProcessMgmt* HostProtectionAttribute

Type	Property or Method
System.Diagnostics.Process	All properties and methods
System.Diagnostics.ProcessStartInfo	All properties and methods
System.Diagnostics.ProcessThread	All properties and methods

Self-Affecting Threading

Whereas the APIs in the self-affecting process management category can directly affect various aspects of the host's process, the APIs in the self-affecting threading category can affect specific threads running within the host process. Examples of APIs in this category are those on *System.Threading.Thread* that allow a thread's priority to be altered, its COM apartment state to be set, and so on.

As I mentioned in the beginning of this chapter, the line between which APIs are blocked using CAS and which are blocked using host protection can often be blurry. For example, the *System.Threading.Thread.Abort* method can clearly be used to affect the threads in a process, so you'd expect *Abort* to be annotated with *HostProtectionAttribute*, identifying it as belonging to the self-affecting threading category. It is not, however. Instead, to be called, *Abort* demands a CAS permission (*SecurityPermission.ControlThread*). In this particular case, *Abort* was not annotated with *HostProtectionAttribute* because it already has a CAS demand. There are many cases in which a method or type that was protected using CAS wasn't annotated with *HostProtectionAttribute* even though it logically belonged to one of the host protection categories, so a host must use a combination of CAS, as described in Chapter 10, and host protection to ensure that no inappropriate APIs can be used in the process.

The list of APIs in the self-affecting threading category is given in Table 12-5.

Table 12-5 Properties and Methods with the *SelfAffectingThreading* HostProtectionAttribute

Type	Property or Method
System.Security.Principal.WindowsImpersonationContext	All properties and methods
System.Threading.Thread	*Priority { set }*
	IsBackground { set }
	ApartmentState { set }
	TrySetApartmentState { set }
	SetApartmentState

External Threading

The external threading category contains those APIs that can affect threads in the host process but cannot directly impact the host's stability. In most cases, the external threading APIs are those that allow an add-in to start an asynchronous operation such as reading from a network socket or a file.

Many of the types in the *System.Threading* namespace are also included in the external threading category, as shown in Table 12-6.

Table 12-6   Properties and Methods with the *ExternalThreading* *HostProtectionAttribute*

Type	Property or Method
System.ICancelableAsyncResult	*Cancel*
System.IO.FileStream	*BeginRead*
	BeginWrite
System.IO.Stream	*BeginRead*
	BeginWrite
System.Threading.AutoResetEvent	All methods and properties
System.Threading.CancellationRegion	*SetNonCancelable*
	SetCancelable
System.Threading.CancellationSignal	*CancelSynchronousIO*
System.Threading.EventWaitHandle	All methods and properties
System.Threading.Interlocked	All methods and properties
System.Threading.ManualResetEvent	All methods and properties
System.Threading.Monitor	All methods and properties
System.Threading.Mutex	All methods and properties
System.Threading.ReaderWriterLock	All methods and properties
System.Threading.Semaphore	All methods and properties
System.Threading.Thread	*Start*
	Join
	SpinWait
	AllocateDataSlot
	AllocateNamedDataSlot
	FreeNamedDataSlot
	GetData
	SetData
	CurrentUICulture { set }
	Name { set }
	BeginCriticalRegion
	EndCriticalRegion

Table 12-6   Properties and Methods with the *ExternalThreading* *HostProtectionAttribute*

Type	Property or Method
System.Threading.ThreadPool	All methods and properties
System.Threading.Timer	All methods and properties
System.ComponentModel.ISynchronizeInvoke	*BeginInvoke*
System.Data.ProviderBase.DbConnectionInternal	*BeginOpen*
System.Data.SqlClient.SqlCommand	*BeginExecuteNonQuery*
	BeginExecuteXmlReader
	BeginExecuteReader
System.Data.SqlClient.SqlConnection	*BeginOpen*
System.Data.SqlClient.SqlDependency	All constructors
System.Net.Authenticator	*BeginAuthenticate*
	BeginAcceptAuthRequest
System.Net.Dns	*BeginGetHostByName*
	BeginResolveToAddresses
	BeginResolve
System.Net.FileWebRequest	*BeginGetRequestStream*
	BeginGetResponse
System.Net.FtpWebRequest	*BeginGetRequestStream*
	BeginGetResponse
System.Net.HttpListener	*BeginGetContext*
System.Net.HttpWebRequest	*BeginGetRequestStream*
	BeginGetResponse
System.Net.IPAddress	*BeginResolveToAddresses*
System.Net.Mail.SmtpClient	*SendAsync*
System.Net.NetworkInformation.Ping	*SendAsync*
System.Net.Security.NegotiateStream	*BeginClientAuthenticate*
	BeginServerAuthenticate
	BeginRead
	BeginWrite
System.Net.Security.SslStream	*BeginClientAuthenticate*
	BeginServerAuthenticate
	BeginRead
	BeginWrite
System.Net.Sockets.NetworkStream	*BeginRead*
	BeginWrite

Table 12-6 Properties and Methods with the *ExternalThreading HostProtectionAttribute*

Type	Property or Method
System.Net.Sockets.Socket	BeginSendFile
	BeginConnect
	BeginDisconnect
	BeginSend
	BeginSendTo
	BeginReceive
	BeginReceiveFrom
	BeginAccept
System.Net.Sockets.TcpClient	BeginConnect
System.Net.Sockets.TcpListener	BeginAcceptSocket
	BeginAcceptTcpClient
System.Net.Sockets.UdpClient	BeginSend
	BeginReceive
System.Net.WebClient	OpenReadAsync
	OpenWriteAsync
	DownloadStringAsync
	DownloadDataAsync
	DownloadFileAsync
	UploadStringAsync
	UploadDataAsync
	UploadFileAsync
	UploadValuesAsync
System.Net.WebRequest	BeginGetResponse
	BeginGetRequestStream

Security Infrastructure

There are only two types in the security infrastructure host protection category, as shown in Table 12-7. These types allow an add-in to manipulate different aspects of the underlying Windows security system, including how impersonation is done and how security principals are managed.

Table 12-7 Properties and Methods with the *SecurityInfrastructure HostProtectionAttribute*

Type	Property or Method
System.Security.Principal.WindowsImpersonationContext	All properties and methods
System.Security.Principal.WindowsPrincipal	All properties and methods

User Interface

The number of types and methods in the user interface category is surprisingly small given the breadth of UI-related class libraries in the .NET Framework. There are two reasons for this. First, many of the types that allow the display of user interface are already protected by CAS permissions. In many cases, those types have not been annotated with *HostProtection-Attribute* as well. Also, recall that only the .NET Framework assemblies that SQL Server 2005 allows in its process have been annotated with the *HostProtectionAttribute*. This automatically eliminates *System.Windows.Forms*, one of the primary class libraries for building applications with user interfaces. As it stands in .NET Framework 2.0, only the user interface–related classes in the *System.Console* class are included in the user interface host protection category, as shown in Table 12-8.

Table 12-8   Properties and Methods with the UI *HostProtectionAttribute*

Type	Property or Method
System.Console	*Error { get }*
	In { get }
	Out { get }
	Beep
	ReadKey
	KeyAvailable { get }
	OpenStandardError
	OpenStandardInput
	OpenStandardOutput
	SetIn
	SetOut
	SetError
	Read
	ReadLine
	WriteLine
	Write

"May Leak on Abort"

As discussed in Chapter 11, the ability to unload an application domain without leaking any resources is a core concept in the CLR's design to provide a system that can execute predictably in scenarios requiring high availability. The "may leak on abort" host protection category is used to identify those types and methods that are not guaranteed to be leakproof when an application domain is unloaded. A type or method can leak resources if it doesn't adhere to the guidelines for writing reliable managed code that were outlined in Chapter 11. For example, if a type maintains a handle to an operating system resource without wrapping it using the *SafeHandle* class, the CLR cannot guarantee that the handle will not be leaked in all abort and shutdown scenarios. Hosts should be aware that they must block the "may leak on abort" host protection category if they require a highly available system.

The list of methods and types that can leak resources on abort or shutdown is given in Table 12-9.

Table 12-9   Properties and Methods with the *MayLeakOnAbort HostProtectionAttribute*

Type	Property or Method
System.Reflection.Assembly	Load(byte[] rawAssembly,...)
	LoadFile
	LoadModule
System.Reflection.Emit.AssemblyBuilder	All properties and methods
System.Reflection.Emit.ConstructorBuilder	All properties and methods
System.Reflection.Emit.CustomAttributeBuilder	All properties and methods
System.Reflection.Emit.EnumBuilder	All properties and methods
System.Reflection.Emit.EventBuilder	All properties and methods
System.Reflection.Emit.FieldBuilder	All properties and methods
System.Reflection.Emit.MethodBuilder	All properties and methods
System.Reflection.Emit.MethodRental	All properties and methods
System.Reflection.Emit.ModuleBuilder	All properties and methods
System.Reflection.Emit.PropertyBuilder	All properties and methods
System.Reflection.Emit.TypeBuilder	All properties and methods
System.Reflection.Emit.UnmanagedMarshal	All properties and methods

Using the Host Protection Manager

CLR hosts specify which host protection categories they'd like to block using the host protection manager from the CLR hosting interfaces. The host protection manager has just one interface, *ICLRHostProtectionManager*. As its name indicates (following the naming convention used throughout the hosting interfaces), *ICLRHostProtectionManager* is implemented by the CLR, not by the host. A host obtains an *ICLRHostProtectionManager* interface pointer from the CLR through the standard CLR control object described in Chapter 2. Given this pointer, a host then calls its *SetProtectedCategories* method to specify which host protection categories to block. Here's the definition of *ICLRHostProtectionManager* from mscoree.idl:

```
interface ICLRHostProtectionManager : IUnknown
{
    HRESULT SetProtectedCategories([in] EApiCategories categories);
};
```

The host specifies which categories to block by performing an OR operation on values from the *EApiCategories* enumeration. *EApiCategories* is the unmanaged equivalent of the

System.Security.Permissions.HostProtectionResource enumerations used to specify the host protection categories in managed code:

```
typedef enum
{
    eNoChecks                   = 0,
    eSynchronization            = 0x1,
    eSharedState                = 0x2,
    eExternalProcessMgmt        = 0x4,
    eSelfAffectingProcessMgmt   = 0x8,
    eExternalThreading          = 0x10,
    eSelfAffectingThreading     = 0x20,
    eSecurityInfrastructure     = 0x40,
    eUI                         = 0x80,
    eMayLeakOnAbort             = 0x100,
    eAll                        = 0x1ff
} EApiCategories;
```

As you can see, enabling host protection is relatively straightforward. The real challenge with this feature is not in writing the code required to enable it, but rather in the analysis to determine which host protection categories should be blocked in your particular scenario.

Now that I've covered the details of the host protection features, let's enable it in one of our existing example hosts.

Host Protection in the Cocoon Deployment Model

In Chapter 8, I wrote a CLR host called runcocoon.exe that executes applications contained in OLE-structured storage files called cocoons. In this section, I extend runcocoon.exe to use host protection to prevent the assemblies contained in cocoon files from using any of the .NET Framework APIs that are annotated with *HostProtectionAttribute*. Remember that only partially trusted assemblies are prevented from accessing members blocked by host protection, so the extensions I made to runcocoon.exe in Chapter 10 apply here as well. In that chapter, I used an application domain CAS policy tree to assign a partial level of trust to all assemblies loaded from a cocoon. Because those assemblies are only partially trusted, they're subject to the host protection settings I'll add to runcocoon.exe in this section. I won't list the entire source for the runcocoon.exe host again here. Instead, I'll just provide those portions of the implementation that are specific to host protection. A complete source code listing can be found on this book's companion Web site.

Enabling host protection in runcocoon.exe requires two steps:

1.   Obtaining the *ICLRHostProtectionManager* interface from the CLR

2.   Using *SetProtectedCategories* to specify which categories to block

These two steps are described in more detail in the next sections.

Step 1: Obtaining the *ICLRHostProtectionManager* Interface Pointer

As described in Chapter 2, all of the primary hosting interfaces implemented by the CLR are obtained using the *GetCLRManager* method on *ICLRControl*. The following code snippet initializes the CLR with *CorBindToRuntimeEx*, and then uses *ICLRControl::GetCLRManager* to get the CLR's implementation of *ICLRHostProtectionManager*:

```
int wmain(int argc, wchar_t* argv[])
{
   HRESULT hr = S_OK;

// Start the .NET Framework 2.0 version of the CLR.
   ICLRRuntimeHost *pCLR = NULL;
   hr = CorBindToRuntimeEx(
      L"v2.0.41013",
      L"wks",
      STARTUP_CONCURRENT_GC,
      CLSID_CLRRuntimeHost,
      IID_ICLRRuntimeHost,
      (PVOID*) &pCLR);
   assert(SUCCEEDED(hr));

   // Get the CLRControl object.
   ICLRControl *pCLRControl = NULL;
   hr = pCLR->GetCLRControl(&pCLRControl);
   assert(SUCCEEDED(hr));

   // Ask the CLR for its implementation of ICLRHostProtectionManager.
   ICLRHostProtectionManager *pCLRHostProtectionManager = NULL;
   hr = pCLRControl->GetCLRManager(IID_ICLRHostProtectionManager,
(void **)&pCLRHostProtectionManager);
   assert(SUCCEEDED(hr));

   // Rest of the host's code omitted... }
```

Step 2: Specifying Which Host Protection Categories to Block

Now that I have a pointer of type *ICLRHostProtectionManager*, I simply need to call its *SetProtectedCategories* method to specify which categories I'd like to block. The following call to *SetProtectedCategories* blocks the full set of host protection categories:

```
// Block all host protection categories.
hr = pCLRHostProtectionManager->SetProtectedCategories (
         (EApiCategories)(
            eSelfAffectingProcessMgmt |
            eSelfAffectingThreading |
            eSynchronization |
            eSharedState |
            eExternalProcessMgmt |
            eExternalThreading |
            eSelfAffectingProcessMgmt |
            eSelfAffectingThreading |
```

```
            eSecurityInfrastructure |
            eMayLeakOnAbort |
            eUI));
    assert(SUCCEEDED(hr));
```

Now that I've enabled host protection, all attempts by cocoon assemblies to access protected APIs will result in an exception of type *System.Security.HostProtectionException*. The *HostProtectionException* has fields that describe which categories the host has blocked and which category contains the method that caused the exception to be thrown. For example, the following exception text resulted from a cocoon assembly attempting to call *Console.WriteLine*, which belongs to the UI host protection category:

```
System.Security.HostProtectionException: Attempted to perform an operation that was
    forbidden by the CLR host.
The protected resources (only available with full trust) were:
All
The demanded resources were: UI
```

> **Note**   Just as host protection and CAS appear similar on the surface, their implementations are very similar as well. The fact that *HostProtectionAttribute* is in the *System.Security.Permissions* namespace and that *HostProtectionException* is in *System.Security* gives a clear hint that their underlying implementations are very similar to CAS. In fact, both host protection and demands for CAS permissions are implemented using the same infrastructure within the CLR. When a host enables host protection using *ICLRHostProtectionManager*, the CLR introduces a link demand for a permission of type *System.Security.Permissions.HostProtectionPermission* into the code that is jit-compiled for each protected method. The failure of this link demand is what causes the *Host-ProtectionException* to be thrown.

Summary

Host protection enables a host to prevent partially trusted add-ins from using APIs that don't fit well with the host's programming model. Although on the surface the goals of host protection seem very much like those of CAS, the two features have different motivations. CAS is a mechanism used to protect a resource from unauthorized access, whereas host protection is aimed at constraining an add-in to adhere to a host's programming model.

Host protection consists of a set of categories that define capabilities deemed of interest to hosts, a custom attribute for grouping APIs into those categories, and a hosting interface that hosts use to specify which categories of functionality don't fit their programming model. The .NET Framework class libraries have been annotated with the custom attribute (the *HostProtectionAttribute*) to indicate which types and methods belong to which host protection categories. After determining which categories apply to its scenario, a host uses the *ICLRHostProtectionManager* interface to prevent the APIs belonging to those categories from being used in the process.

Chapter 13

Managing How the CLR Uses Memory

The hosting of the CLR within Microsoft SQL Server 2005 has required the CLR to take a new approach to obtaining the resources it historically has obtained directly from the operating system. Specifically, a new level of abstraction has been added to the Microsoft .NET Framework 2.0 CLR that enables a host to supply the CLR with resources such as memory, threads, and synchronization primitives. This abstraction layer is made available to hosts in the form of new managers in the CLR hosting API. If the CLR is hosted and the host has indicated the desire to supply the CLR with a specific type of resource by implementing the appropriate manager, the CLR will call the host to obtain the resource instead of getting it directly from the operating system.

The CLR hosting API includes managers that enable the host to supply the CLR with the basic primitives it needs to allocate and free memory, create and destroy executable tasks, queue work items to a thread pool, create synchronization primitives, and so on. The CLR's new approach to obtaining the basic resources it needs to run programs is very powerful because it enables the CLR to be integrated into environments with very specific requirements for resource management. In this chapter, I discuss the APIs a host can use to supply the CLR with the primitive functions it needs to manage memory. In Chapter 14, I discuss how a host can use the CLR hosting API to integrate the CLR into environments with specific threading and concurrency requirements.

To gain a better understanding of the scenarios in which a host might want to provide the hosting managers that enable it to replace the basic primitives the CLR uses to create and manage resources, consider SQL Server requirements. In many ways, SQL Server behaves like an operating system on machines on which it runs. For example, SQL Server closely manages all the memory it uses, it can be run in a mode in which it manually schedules executable tasks on fibers instead of leaving all scheduling up to the operating system, and so on. These custom subsystems are highly tuned to provide the highest overall throughput and performance in the most critical SQL Server scenarios. The primary challenge in integrating the CLR into SQL Server 2005 was getting two systems that were designed independently to cooperate on issues related to resource management in such a way that the overall solution doesn't adversely affect SQL Server scalability and performance requirements.

Memory management provides a good example illustrating the changes required by the CLR to ensure a seamless integration with SQL Server 2005. SQL Server operates within a configurable amount of memory. In many cases, SQL Server is the only application running on a given server and is therefore configured to use most all of the machine's physical memory. A key design goal of SQL Server is never to allocate more memory than it is configured to use.

Although it is certainly possible, given the operating system's virtual memory system, allocating more memory than is physically available causes memory pages to be swapped out to disk only to be reloaded later when they are needed. Paging in the virtual memory system introduces a performance cost that is unacceptable in many SQL Server scenarios. In other words, if the request to execute a particular query would cause the operating system to page, SQL Server is designed to fail the request rather than incur the performance cost associated with demand paging. SQL Server tracks all memory allocations made in the process to ensure it never exceeds the amount of memory it is configured to use. If a request to allocate memory would cause SQL to exceed its configured limit, that request is denied. This approach works great as long as SQL Server is the only entity in the process that is allocating memory.

However, the introduction of the CLR into the process means that there is an additional entity making requests for memory. Clearly, for SQL Server to be able to track all memory allocated in the process accurately, all of the CLR's requests for memory must go through SQL Server instead of directly to the operating system. This is where the CLR hosting APIs come into play. By implementing a memory manager using the CLR hosting API, SQL Server can intercept all memory requests and handle them as it sees fit. In this way, SQL Server is able to track all memory requests in the process accurately regardless of whether they are initiated by SQL Server or by the CLR. In addition, if a memory request initiated by the CLR would cause SQL Server to exceed its configured limit, SQL Server can return a failure to the CLR indicating that no more memory is available. In this way, SQL Server can regulate the amount of memory the CLR can use. The redirection of the CLR's memory requests through the hosting API and into SQL Server is shown in Figure 13-1.

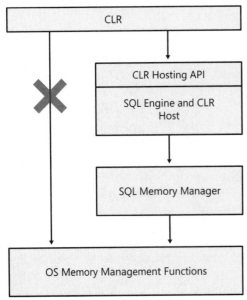

Figure 13-1   The CLR redirects all requests for memory through the hosting API while running inside SQL Server.

The CLR hosting API exposes two managers that hosts can use to configure how the CLR uses memory in the process. The first of these managers enables a host to supply the CLR with basic memory allocation primitives, whereas the second hosting manager provides functions a host can use to configure the CLR's garbage collection. I cover both of these managers in detail throughout the chapter.

Integrating the CLR with Custom Memory Managers

If you need to constrain or otherwise customize how the CLR uses memory, use the CLR hosting API to implement a memory manager. Implementing a memory manager enables you to customize the following aspects of how memory is managed in your process:

- Virtual memory management
- Heap management
- File mapping functions
- Reporting the current memory load to the CLR

These capabilities are provided by the three interfaces that make up a memory manager: *IHostMemoryManager*, *IHostMalloc*, and *ICLRMemoryNotificationCallback*. As the primary interface in the hosting manager, *IHostMemoryManager* is the interface the CLR asks the host for during initialization. The CLR determines whether a host implements the memory manager by passing the IID for *IHostMemoryManager* to the *GetHostManager* method of the host's implementation of *IHostControl*. (Refer to Chapter 2 for a complete description of how the CLR determines which managers a particular host implements.)

In the next several sections, I provide the details on how to use the capabilities offered by the three interfaces that comprise the memory manager.

Virtual Memory Management

The CLR relies on the features provided by Microsoft Win32 virtual memory management functions to allocate the memory it needs for its garbage collection heaps and to store other internal CLR data structures. If you implement a memory manager in your host, you must provide the CLR with a set of virtual memory management functions that map to those provided by Win32. As you can see in Table 13-1, *IHostMemoryManager* has a set of methods whose names match those of the Win32 virtual memory functions. When you implement a memory manager, the CLR will use the virtual memory methods provided by your implementation of *IHostMemoryManager* instead of calling those provided by Win32.

Table 13-1   The Methods on the *IHostMemoryManager* Interface

Method	Description
VirtualAlloc	Equivalent to the *VirtualAlloc* API in Win32.
VirtualFree	Equivalent to the *VirtualFree* API in Win32.
VirtualQuery	Equivalent to the *VirtualQuery* API in Win32.
VirtualProtect	Equivalent to the *VirtualProtect* API in Win32.
CreateMalloc	Returns an interface of type *IHostMalloc* that the CLR will use to access methods needed to manage memory in heaps. I describe this method in more detail in the "Heap Management" section later in this chapter.
GetMemoryLoad	The CLR calls this method to get an indication of the current memory load on the system. I describe this method in more detail later in this chapter in the section called "Reporting Memory Status to the CLR."
RegisterMemoryNotificationCallback	The CLR calls this method to register a callback you can use to notify the CLR of the current memory load on the system. I describe this method in more detail later in this chapter in the section called "Reporting Memory Status to the CLR."
NeedsVirtualAddressSpace	The CLR calls *NeedsVirtualAddressSpace* to determine whether space is available to map a file on disk into memory. I describe this later in the "File Mapping" section of this chapter.
AcquiredVirtualAddressSpace	The CLR reports the memory it has allocated to map disk files into memory by calling *AcquiredVirtualAddressSpace*. I describe this later in the "File Mapping" section of this chapter.
ReleasedVirtualAddressSpace	After the CLR has freed the memory it needed to map files into memory, it notifies the host by calling *ReleasedVirtualAddressSpace*.

Most of the parameters to the *VirtualAlloc*, *VirtualFree*, *VirtualQuery*, and *VirtualProtect* methods on *IHostMemoryManager* map directly to those provided by the Win32 APIs of the same name. The one notable exception is the *eCriticalLevel* parameter to *IHostMemoryManager::VirtualAlloc*, which is unique to the virtual memory management functions provided by the CLR hosting API. Here's the definition of the *VirtualAlloc* method on *IHostMemoryManager* from mscoree.idl:

```
interface IHostMemoryManager : IUnknown
{
    // Other methods omitted...

    HRESULT VirtualAlloc([in] void*      pAddress,
                         [in] SIZE_T     dwSize,
                         [in] DWORD      flAllocationType,
                         [in] DWORD      flProtect,
                         [in] EMemoryCriticalLevel eCriticalLevel,
                         [out] void**    ppMem);
}
```

Hosts are free to deny the CLR's request for more memory by returning the *E_OUTOFMEMORY* HRESULT from their implementation of *VirtualAlloc*. However, depending on how critical the CLR's need for more memory is when it calls *VirtualAlloc*, it might not be able to complete certain operations if the request for more memory is denied. The consequences of denying a request for more memory are communicated to the host using *eCriticalLevel*. Typically, the failure to allocate memory causes the CLR to abort the specific task[1] it is executing at the time. In more extreme cases, the failure to obtain more memory can cause the CLR to unload the current application domain or even terminate the entire process. Each time the CLR calls *VirtualAlloc*, it passes in a value from the *EMemoryCriticalLevel* indicating whether a failure to obtain the requested memory will cause the task, application domain, or process to be terminated. Here's the definition of *EMemoryCriticalLevel* from mscoree.idl:

```
typedef enum
{
    eTaskCritical = 0,
    eAppDomainCritical = 1,
    eProcessCritical = 2
} EMemoryCriticalLevel;
```

Given that a host can use a memory manager to supply the CLR with implementations of *VirtualAlloc* and *VirtualFree*, it's relatively easy to see how SQL Server uses the CLR hosting API to make sure that it never exceeds the amount of memory it is configured to use. SQL Server implementation of *IHostMemoryManager* records both the sizes of all memory allocations that are made through *VirtualAlloc* and the amount of memory freed by each call to *VirtualFree*. The difference between the two values is the amount of virtual memory the CLR is using at any one time. This total, combined with the virtual memory allocated by SQL Server, is always kept under the amount that SQL Server is configured to use.

Throughout this section, I haven't said anything about how a host's implementation of the virtual memory management methods on *IHostMemoryManager* should behave, other than to allocate (or deny) and free the memory that is requested by the CLR. With the exception of these basic requirements, the host is free to implement these methods any way it sees fit. This freedom is a very powerful aspect of the abstraction provided by the CLR hosting API. In some cases, a host might choose simply to delegate the calls to the virtual memory methods on *IHostMemoryManager* to their Win32 equivalents after doing any bookkeeping that is necessary. A host's implementation of these methods need not do that, however. If a host has specific requirements around the timing of memory allocations, the locations from which the memory comes, and so on, it can use the abstraction provided by the hosting APIs to hide these details from the CLR.

---

1. In this context, the term *task* refers to either an operating system thread or a host-provided fiber as described in Chapter 14.

The management of virtual memory is only one part of the overall picture, however. In the next section, you'll see how a host can use a memory manager to supply the CLR with the primitives it uses to manage memory allocated in heaps.

Heap Management

In addition to the virtual-memory APIs described in the previous section, the CLR also relies on a set of functions that enable it to manage memory in heaps. A host provides the CLR with these functions through the *IHostMalloc* interface. As you can see from Table 13-2, *IHostMalloc* contains methods that correspond to heap management APIs provided by Win32.

Table 13-2   The Methods on the *IHostMalloc* Interface

Method	Description
Alloc	Allocates memory from the heap
DebugAlloc	The debug version of *Alloc*
Free	Releases memory previously allocated with *Alloc* or *DebugAlloc*

The CLR obtains the *IHostMalloc* interface from the host by calling the *CreateMalloc* method on *IHostMemoryManager*. *CreateMalloc* takes a set of flags that identify the characteristics needed in the heap that is returned as shown in the following definition from mscoree.idl:

```
interface IHostMemoryManager : IUnknown
{
    HRESULT CreateMalloc([in] DWORD dwMallocType,
                         [out] IHostMalloc **ppMalloc);

    // Other methods omitted...
}
```

The valid flags to *CreateMalloc* are represented by the *MALLOC_TYPE* enumeration:

```
typedef enum
{
    MALLOC_THREADSAFE = 0x1,
    MALLOC_EXECUTABLE = 0x2,
} MALLOC_TYPE;
```

The *MALLOC_THREADSAFE* flag indicates that the CLR must be able to safely allocate and free data in the heap from multiple threads simultaneously. The current version of the CLR always sets this value. The CLR sets the *MALLOC_EXECUTABLE* flag when it intends to store executable code in the heap. It sets this, for example, when it dynamically creates and stores the code it uses as part of the COM Interoperability layer. The *MALLOC_EXECUTABLE* flag exists so the host and the CLR can properly use the No Execute (NX) feature available on some processors today. Essentially, NX enables memory pages to be marked with a bit that prevents executable code from being stored and run from the page. By marking pages in this way, the potential for security vulnerabilities is reduced when a page is not explicitly intended to contain executable code. Specifically, NX helps mitigate the vulnerability whereby a malicious party writes code into random locations in memory and causes it to be executed.

In the same way that all requests for virtual memory come through *IHostMemoryManager*, all requests to allocate memory from a heap come through *IHostMalloc*. If you are implementing a memory manager for the purposes of restricting the amount of memory the CLR can use, remember to account for the memory allocated through *IHostMalloc* when determining how much memory the CLR has requested.

File Mapping

The CLR uses the Win32 memory-mapped file APIs when loading and executing assemblies. Because the process of mapping a file requires address space, the CLR must keep the host informed of all memory allocated while mapping files. The methods used to communicate information about file mappings to the host are the *NeedsVirtualAddressSpace*, *AcquiredVirtualAddressSpace*, and *ReleasedVirtualAddressSpace* methods on *IHostMemoryManager*. Here are the definitions of those methods from mscoree.idl:

```
interface IHostMemoryManager : IUnknown
{
    HRESULT NeedsVirtualAddressSpace(
        [in] LPVOID startAddress,
        [in] SIZE_T size
        );

    HRESULT AcquiredVirtualAddressSpace(
        [in] LPVOID startAddress,
        [in] SIZE_T size
        );

    HRESULT ReleasedVirtualAddressSpace(
        [in] LPVOID startAddress
        );
}
```

The CLR maps files into memory using the Win32 *MapViewOfFile* API. All address space acquired by calling *MapViewOfFile* is reported to the host by calling *AcquiredVirtualAddressSpace*. If the host is using a memory manager to keep track of the amount of address space used by the CLR, it must include the address space reported through *AcquiredVirtualAddressSpace* in its totals. If the CLR's call to *MapViewOfFile* fails because of low address space conditions, the CLR tells the host that it needs additional address space by calling *NeedsVirtualAddressSpace* and passing in the start address and size of the address space it needs. If the host is able to make the address space available, it returns the *S_OK HRESULT* from *NeedsVirtualAddressSpace*. The CLR will then try to call *MapViewOfFile* again, assuming that the required address space is now available. After the CLR unmaps a file using the Win32 *UnmapViewOfFile* API, it notifies the host that the virtual address space used by the file mapping is now free by calling *ReleasedVirtualAddressSpace*.

Reporting Memory Status to the CLR

One of the heuristics the CLR uses to determine when to perform a garbage collection is the amount of memory pressure currently on the system. If memory pressure is high (signifying that very little memory is available), the CLR will do a garbage collection and return all the memory it can to the system. The CLR uses two Win32 APIs to determine the current memory load: *GlobalMemoryStatus* and the memory resource notification created with *CreateMemory-ResourceNotification*. Hosts that implement a memory manager can provide replacements for these APIs so that a host's own impression of the current memory load can be used to influence when garbage collections occur.

The *GetMemoryLoad* Method

The equivalent of the Win32 *GlobalMemoryStatus* API is the *GetMemoryLoad* method on *IHostMemoryManager*. The CLR will call *GetMemoryLoad* periodically to determine the memory load on the system from the host's perspective. The host returns two values from *GetMemory-Load*, as shown in the following definition from mscoree.idl:

```
interface IHostMemoryManager : IUnknown
{
    // Other methods omitted...
    HRESULT GetMemoryLoad([out] DWORD* pMemoryLoad,
                          [out] SIZE_T *pAvailableBytes);
}
```

The first parameter, *pMemoryLoad*, is the percentage of physical memory that is currently in use. This parameter is equivalent to the *dwMemoryLoad* field of the *MEMORYSTATUS* structure returned from *GlobalMemoryStatus*. The *pAvailableBytes* parameter is the number of bytes that are currently available for the CLR to use.

The exact behavior of the CLR in response to the values returned from *GetMemoryLoad* isn't defined and is likely to change between releases. That is, returning specific values doesn't guarantee that a specific amount of memory will be freed or even that a garbage collection will be done immediately. All that is guaranteed is that the CLR considers the values returned from *GetMemoryLoad* when determining the timing of the next garbage collection.

The *ICLRMemoryNotificationCallback* Interface

The CLR calls the *GetMemoryLoad* method on *IHostMemoryManager* when it wants to determine the current memory load on the system. As a host, you have no control over when *Get-MemoryLoad* is called. However, you can be more proactive about notifiying the CLR of the current memory status by calling the methods on an interface provided by the CLR called *ICLRMemoryNotificationCallback*.

The process of reporting memory status through this callback is as follows. After the CLR obtains your memory manager by calling *IHostControl::GetHostManager*, it calls the *RegisterMemoryNotificationCallback* method on *IHostMemoryManager*, passing in an interface pointer of type *ICLRMemoryNotificationCallback*. The definition of *RegisterMemoryNotificationCallback* is shown here:

```
interface IHostMemoryManager : IUnknown
{
    // Other methods omitted...
        HRESULT RegisterMemoryNotificationCallback(
            [in] ICLRMemoryNotificationCallback * pCallback);
}
```

A host's implementation of *RegisterMemoryNotificationCallback* should save a copy of the *ICLRMemoryNotificationCallback* interface pointer it is given by the CLR. At any time, the host can call back through *ICLRMemoryNotificationCallback* to report memory status to the CLR. *ICLRMemoryNotificationCallback* has a single method called *OnMemoryNotification* as shown in the following definition from mscoree.idl:

```
interface ICLRMemoryNotificationCallback : IUnknown
{
    HRESULT OnMemoryNotification([in] EMemoryAvailable eMemoryAvailable);
}
```

Memory status is reported to the CLR by passing a value from the *EMemoryAvailable* enumeration:

```
typedef enum
{
    eMemoryAvailableLow = 1,
    eMemoryAvailableNeutral = 2,
    eMemoryAvailableHigh = 3
} EMemoryAvailable;
```

The most useful value from *EMemoryAvailable* is the *eMemoryAvailableLow*. When this value is passed, the CLR will perform a garbage collection in an attempt to make more storage available to the system. The current version of the CLR doesn't take any action at all when it receives either *eMemoryAvailableNeutral* or *eMemoryAvailableHigh* from the host.

Configuring the CLR Garbage Collector

The CLR hosting APIs offer two more interfaces that hosts can use to monitor and configure how the CLR uses memory. These two interfaces, *ICLRGCManager* and *IHostGCManager*, comprise the hosting interface's garbage collection manager. The *ICLRGCManager* interface enables a host to initiate garbage collections, gather various statistics related to collections, and partition the garbage collector's heap for optimal performance. Hosts can receive notifications about the timing of garbage collections by providing the CLR with an interface of type *IHostGCManager*. I discuss the role of *IHostGCManager* in more detail later in the chapter in the section entitled "Receiving Notifications Through the *IHostGCManager* Interface."

CLR hosts obtain an interface pointer of type *ICLRGCManager* through the standard mechanism used to obtain hosting interfaces from the CLR—that is, by calling the *GetCLRManager* method on the CLR's implementation of *ICLRControl*, as shown in the following sample main program. (Refer to Chapter 2 for a detailed discussion of how both the host and the CLR exchange pointers to the various interfaces in the hosting API.)

```
int wmain(int argc, wchar_t* argv[])
{
   HRESULT hr = S_OK;

   // Start .NET Framework version 2.0 of the CLR.
   ICLRRuntimeHost *pCLR = NULL;
   hr = CorBindToRuntimeEx(
      L"v2.0.41013",
      L"wks",
      STARTUP_CONCURRENT_GC,
      CLSID_CLRRuntimeHost,
      IID_ICLRRuntimeHost,
      (PVOID*) &pCLR);

   assert(SUCCEEDED(hr));

   // Get the CLRControl object. Use this to get the pointer of
   // type ICLRGCManager.
   ICLRControl *pCLRControl = NULL;
   hr = pCLR->GetCLRControl(&pCLRControl);
   assert(SUCCEEDED(hr));

   // Get a pointer to an ICLRGCManager.
   ICLRGCManager *pCLRGCManager = NULL;
   hr = pCLRControl->GetCLRManager(IID_ICLRGCManager,
                                   (void **)&pCLRGCManager);
   assert(SUCCEEDED(hr));

   // The ICLRGCManager pointer is now ready to use...

   // Remember to release it.
   pCLRGCManager->Release();

   // The rest of the host's code is omitted...
}
```

Once the host has a pointer of type *ICLRGCManager*, it can use the methods on that interface to customize various aspects of how the garbage collector works. Table 13-3 provides an overview of the methods on *ICLRGCManager*.

Table 13-3   The Methods on the *ICLRGCManager* Interface

Method	Description
Collect	Enables a host to initiate a garbage collection
GetStats	Returns various statistics about the garbage collections that have occurred so far in the process
SetGCStartupLimits	Enables a host to partition the garbage collection heap to optimize overall performance for its specific scenario

The next several sections describe how to use the methods in Table 13-3.

Partitioning the Garbage Collector's Heap

The CLR garbage collector uses the notion of generations to optimize the collector based on the expected lifetime of managed objects in the heap. A complete description of how the garbage collector uses generations is described in many other texts, so I won't repeat it here. If you're looking for a great reference on the CLR's garbage collector, refer to Chapter 19 in *Applied Microsoft .NET Framework Programming* by Jeffery Richter (Microsoft Press, 2002).

The *SetGCStartupLimits* on *ICLRGCManager* can be used to specify how much of the garbage collection heap is to be used for generations 0 and 1. The garbage collection heap is divided into segments. The managed objects in generations 0 and 1 are stored in the same segment. The objects in generation 2 are sometimes stored in the same segment as generations 0 and 1, but not always. The decision about where the objects in generation 2 and the objects in the large object heap live is a CLR implementation detail that can change over time. The relationship between segments and generations is shown in Figure 13-2.

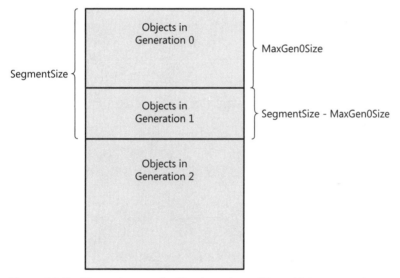

Figure 13-2   The garbage collection heap is partitioned into segments.

SetGCStartupLimits enables you to supply two values that control how the garbage collection heap is partitioned, as shown in the following definition from mscoree.idl:

```
interface ICLRGCManager : IUnknown
{
    // Other methods omitted...
    HRESULT SetGCStartupLimits([in] DWORD SegmentSize,
                               [in] DWORD MaxGen0Size);
}
```

The *SegmentSize* parameter to *SetGCStartupLimits* controls the size of the segments in the garbage collection heap. The value you supply to this method must be a multiple of 1 MB and at least 4 MB. The *MaxGen0Size* specifies the size of the space used to store objects in generation 0.

MaxGen0Size must be at least 64 KB. Both *SegmentSize* and *MaxGen0Size* are specified in bytes. Given values for *SegmentSize* and *MaxGen0Size*, the CLR computes the amount of space to use for generation 1 as shown in Figure 13-2. Both values you supplied through *SetGCStartupLimits* can be set only once—subsequent calls are ignored. The following sample call to *SetGCStartup-Limits* sets the segment size to 8 MB and the maximum size of generation 0 to 128 KB:

```
hr = pCLRGCManager->SetGCStartupLimits(8*1024*1024,128*1024);
```

Now that you know how to partition the garbage collection heap using *SetGCStartupLimits*, take a look at how you might use the statistics returned from *ICLRGCManager::GetStats* to determine which values for *SegmentSize* and *MaxGen0Size* might work best for your application.

Gathering Garbage Collection Statistics

The ability to partition the garbage collection heap isn't of much use if you don't know which values for *SegmentSize* and *MaxGen0Size* make sense in your application. Settling on the right values will likely take several iterations, but the *GetStats* method on *ICLRGCManager* can help you get started. *GetStats* returns a structure that contains various statistics about how the garbage collector is performing in your process. By looking at the values returned from *GetStats*, you can start to establish patterns that can help you optimize the performance of the garbage collector by adjusting how the heap is partitioned using *SetGCStartupLimits*.

GetStats returns a structure of type *COR_GC_STATS* as shown in the following definition from mscoree.idl:

```
interface ICLRGCManager : IUnknown
{
    HRESULT GetStats([in][out] COR_GC_STATS *pStats);
}
```

The *COR_GC_STATS* structure contains fields that report both the number of collections that have occurred and the current status of the memory used by the garbage collector. *COR_GC_STATS* is defined in gchost.idl in the .NET Framework SDK:

```
typedef struct _COR_GC_STATS
{
    ULONG       Flags;

    SIZE_T      ExplicitGCCount;
    SIZE_T      GenCollectionsTaken[3];

    SIZE_T      CommittedKBytes;
    SIZE_T      ReservedKBytes;
    SIZE_T      Gen0HeapSizeKBytes;
    SIZE_T      Gen1HeapSizeKBytes;
    SIZE_T      Gen2HeapSizeKBytes;
    SIZE_T      LargeObjectHeapSizeKBytes;
    SIZE_T      KBytesPromotedFromGen0;
    SIZE_T      KBytesPromotedFromGen1;
} COR_GC_STATS;
```

Notice from the definition of *GetStats* that the *pStats* parameter is marked as both an in and an out parameter. When calling *GetStats*, you must first populate the *Flags* fields of *COR_GC_STATS* to indicate which of the statistics you'd like populated. Based on the flags you set, the CLR fills in the appropriate fields of the structure that you passed in. The valid values for the *Flags* field are given by the *COR_GC_STAT_TYPES* enumeration from gchost.idl:

```
typedef enum
{
    COR_GC_COUNTS      = 0x00000001,
    COR_GC_MEMORYUSAGE = 0x00000002,
} COR_GC_STAT_TYPES;
```

If *COR_GC_COUNTS* is added to the *Flags* field of *COR_GC_STATS*, the CLR populates the fields of *COR_GC_STATS* that describe the number of collections that have occurred so far in the process. These fields are *ExplicitGCCount* and *GenCollectionsTaken*. *ExplicitGCCount* indicates the number of times that a garbage collection has been explicitly initiated either through a call to *ICLRGCManager::Collect* or through the *Collect* method on the *System.GC* class in the .NET Framework class libraries. The *GenCollectionsTaken* array describes the number of collections that have occurred per generation. Element 0 of *GenCollectionsTaken* contains the number of collections done in generation 0, element 1 contains the number of collections done in generation 1, and so on.

Setting *COR_GC_MEMORYUSAGE* in the *Flags* field of *COR_GC_STATS* causes the CLR to return the values that provide insight into how the garbage collector is using memory in the process. The fields returned when *COR_GC_MEMORYUSAGE* is set are as follows:

- *CommittedKBytes*

- *ReservedKBytes*

- *Gen0HeapSizeKBytes*

- *Gen1HeapSizeKBytes*

- *Gen2HeapSizeKBytes*

- *LargeObjectHeapSizeKBytes*

- *KBytesPromotedFromGen0*

- *KBytesPromotedFromGen1*

These fields describe the total amount of memory that has been committed and reserved by the garbage collector, the number of bytes currently used to store the objects in each generation, and the number of bytes promoted from generation 0 to generation 1 and from generation 1 to generation 2.

The following sample call sets both *COR_GC_COUNTS* and *COR_GC_MEMORYUSAGE* to return all of the statistics available from *GetStats*:

```
COR_GC_STATS stats;
stats.Flags = COR_GC_COUNTS | COR_GC_MEMORYUSAGE;

hr = pCLRGCManager->GetStats(&stats);
// The stats structure now contains values for the full set
// of garbage collection statistics.
```

Using the statistics returned from *GetStats* to tune the CLR garbage collector requires several iterations and an extensive amount of testing. It's very easy to hurt performance instead of help it if you're not careful. If you see that an excessive number of generation 0 collections are happening in your particular scenario, you might try adjusting the amount of space the CLR is using to store generation 0 objects. However, be sure you follow up with enough benchmarking to ensure you aren't inadvertently making matters worse.

Initiating Garbage Collections

The CLR uses several heuristics to determine when to initiate a garbage collection. For example, a collection is done when generation 0 is full. These heuristics work great for the vast majority of application scenarios, and the general guidance is to leave it up to the CLR to determine the optimal time to do a collection. That said, available APIs enable you to force a garbage collection to happen. The CLR hosting API offers the ability to initiate a garbage collection by calling the *Collect* method on *ICLRGCManager*. *Collect* takes a single parameter that identifies the generation you'd like collected, as shown in the following definition from mscoree.idl:

```
interface ICLRGCManager : IUnknown
{
    HRESULT Collect([in] LONG Generation);
    // Other methods omitted...
}
```

To force a collection for a particular generation, simply pass the number of that generation (0, 1, or 2) as the *Generation* parameter. You can force all generations to be collected by passing –1.

As with all techniques available to configure the CLR garbage collector, use the ability to initiate collections programmatically with care. Just the act of preparing for a garbage collection can be an expensive operation. To prepare, the CLR must bring all threads to a known safe state and ensure that several internal data structures cannot be modified while the collection is performed. Calling *Collect* too often can easily degrade performance by causing the CLR unnecessarily to bring itself to a state in which it's safe to perform a collection. Again, be sure to test thoroughly to make sure you're not hurting performance when you intend to make it better.

> **Note**   The CLR hosting APIs from .NET Framework 1.0 and .NET Framework 1.1 include an interface in gchost.idl called *IGCHost*. This interface has many of the same capabilities that *ICLRGCManager* now has. *IGCHost* is now deprecated and should not be used going forward. Always use *ICLRGCManager* instead.

Receiving Notifications Through the *IHostGCManager* Interface

In Chapter 14, you'll see that the CLR hosting APIs provide a set of interfaces that enable a host to integrate the CLR with custom task-scheduling schemes. To schedule tasks most efficiently, a host must know when the CLR suspends a thread either to do a garbage collection or for other activities. A host can use the knowledge of when a thread is about to be suspended to avoid scheduling any tasks on that thread until the CLR is ready to let the thread run again.

The CLR notifies the host when a thread is about to be suspended (and when it resumes) by calling methods on the host's implementation of *IHostGCManager*. The methods on *IHostGC-Manager* are shown in Table 13-4.

Table 13-4   The Methods on the *IHostGCManager* Interface

Method	Description
ThreadIsBlockingForSuspension	Notifies the host that the thread making this call is about to block for a garbage collection or other activity. At this point, the host should not schedule any managed code to run on the thread.
SuspensionStarting	Notifies the host that a thread suspension is beginning.
SuspensionEnding	Notifies the host that a thread suspension is ending. *SuspensionEnding* includes a parameter that indicates for which generation garbage was collected while the thread was suspended.

Hosts provide the CLR with an implementation of *IHostGCManager* using the standard technique employed for all of the hosting interfaces implemented by the host. Specifically, a host must do the following:

1. Define a class that derives from *IHostGCManager*.

2. Return an instance of that class when the CLR calls the host's implementation of *IHost-Control::GetHostManager*, passing in the interface identifier for *IHostGCManager* (*IID_IHostGCManager*).

I provide many more details on how to integrate the CLR with a custom scheduler in Chapter 14.

Summary

The interfaces that make up the memory manager enable a host to control closely how the CLR uses memory in a process. These interfaces effectively form an abstraction layer between the CLR and the operating system by enabling the host to provide the basic memory management primitives for which the CLR typically relies on the operating system. By implementing a memory manager, a host can control basic functions such as the use of virtual memory and the management of heaps. SQL Server 2005 uses a memory manager to ensure that memory allocated by the CLR doesn't cause SQL Server to exceed the amount of memory it is configured to use.

Hosts can also affect the CLR's use of memory using the interfaces that constitute the garbage collection manager. The *ICLRGCManager* interface enables the host to optimize how the garbage collector functions by partitioning the garbage collection heap in ways that best fit the memory usage patterns of the host. Configuring the garbage collector requires extensive iteration and testing. It's surprisingly easy to hinder performance inadvertently if you haven't done sufficient benchmarking.

Chapter 14

Integrating the CLR with Custom Schedulers and Thread Pools

In Chapter 13, I describe how hosting the CLR within Microsoft SQL Server 2005 requires the CLR hosting API to act as an abstraction layer through which the CLR directs all requests to allocate and free memory. In this chapter, I show how the same approach has been taken to enable SQL Server 2005 to supply the basic primitives needed by the CLR to create and manage tasks, manipulate synchronization primitives, and queue work items to a thread pool. The managers that implement these abstractions are the task, synchronization, and thread pool managers.

Integrating how the CLR works with tasks, synchronization primitives, and the thread pool is required to meet the performance and scalability requirements of SQL Server 2005. One scenario of particular interest is a mode of execution termed fiber mode. In fiber mode, SQL Server uses cooperatively scheduled fibers to achieve high throughput on multiprocessor machines. These fibers are managed by the SQL Server custom scheduler and can be moved freely between threads to get the maximum amount of work done given the number of currently available threads. The ability to run in an environment where tasks are scheduled cooperatively is completely new to the CLR. In both Microsoft .NET Framework version 1.0 and .NET Framework version 1.1, the CLR assumed it was running in an environment in which code was preemptively scheduled directly by the operating system. As you'll see, one of the primary capabilities of the task manager is to enable the host to insulate the CLR from the knowledge of whether the underlying scheduling mechanism is preemptive or cooperative.

Without a doubt, the interaction between the host and the CLR through the task and synchronization managers is much more complex than with any other hosting interfaces I've described in this book. In effect, the use of these two managers enables you to control, at a very basic level, how managed code is executed in your process. Several intricacies involved are hard to get right, especially in a way that maintains acceptable performance. In this chapter, I provide an overview of the capabilities that are available by introducing the basic concepts and the interfaces involved. If you choose to take advantage of some of these capabilities in your application, you'll likely find the CoopFiber sample in the .NET Framework version 2.0 SDK very helpful. CoopFiber is a CLR host that uses the task and synchronization managers to implement a managed-code fiber library. Even if you don't need to make use of the hosting managers described in this chapter, understanding their capabilities provides great insight into how the CLR is implemented internally.

The Task Abstraction

As described, the task manager enables a host to insulate the CLR from both the basic unit of execution and the approach with which that unit of execution is scheduled. To achieve this abstraction, the CLR hosting API introduces the notion of a *task*. All communication between the CLR and host is done in terms of tasks. The host's implementation of the task manager maps the notion of a task to an underlying unit of execution such as a thread or a fiber. The task abstraction is shown conceptually in Figure 14-1.

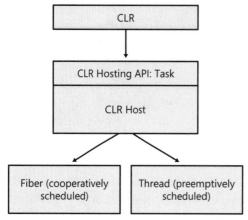

Figure 14-1   CLR hosts map the notion of a task to an underlying scheduling primitive such as a thread or a fiber.

The task abstraction is leveraged to the full extent in SQL Server 2005 in that a task needn't be mapped to the same underlying construct every time SQL Server runs. Specifically, SQL Server 2005 maps tasks either to threads or fibers based on whether SQL Server 2005 is configured to run in fiber mode.

Controlling the Execution of Tasks

The primary purpose of the task manager is to enable the host to provide the CLR with the basic primitives it needs to create, execute, abort, and otherwise manage tasks in the process. In scenarios in which a host does not provide an implementation of the task manager, the CLR calls the Microsoft Win32 API *CreateThread* each time it needs to create a thread, it calls the Win32 *SetPriority* API to adjust a thread's priority, and so on. However, when a host provides the CLR with a task manager, all such calls are sent to the host instead of directly to the operating system. In this way, the host can deeply integrate the CLR's management of tasks with its own.

The following four interfaces comprise the task manager:

- *IHostTaskManager*

- *ICLRTaskManager*

- *IHostTask*

- *ICLRTask*

IHostTaskManager is the primary interface in the task manager. That is, it is the interface the CLR will ask the host for during startup by passing the IID for *IHostTaskManager* to the *GetHostManager* method on the host's implementation of *IHostControl*. Hosts express their desire to provide an implementation of the task manager by returning a valid interface of type *IHostTaskManager* when asked. Generally speaking, *IHostTaskManager* provides the CLR with a set of methods it can use to create individual tasks and to notify the host of special situations, including periods of time when the CLR cannot tolerate a thread abort or when calls transition into and out of the CLR when an add-in uses PInvoke or COM interoperability. Table 14-1 describes the methods on *IHostTaskManager*.

Table 14-1   The Methods on *IHostTaskManager*

Method	Description
GetCurrentTask	Returns the task that is currently running on the thread from which *GetCurrentTask* is called.
CreateTask	Enables the CLR to create a new task.
Sleep	Causes the current task to sleep for a given number of milliseconds. The CLR calls this method when an add-in calls *System.Threading.Thread.Sleep*, for example.
SwitchToTask	Notifies the host that it should switch out the currently running task. In SQL Server fiber mode, calls to *SwitchToTask* cause the fiber representing the current task to be unscheduled or taken off the thread on which it is currently running.
SetLocale	Notifies the host that the culture has been changed. The CLR calls *SetLocale* when an add-in sets the *System.Threading.Thread.CurrentCulture* property, for example. By notifying the host of changes made to the culture, the CLR gives the host a chance to adjust any culture-related state it maintains internally. For example, SQL Server 2005 has its own notion of culture that is used for sorting database tables and so on. Calls to *SetLocale* enable SQL Server to stay in sync with changes to culture made by the add-ins it is hosting.
SetUILocale	Notifies the host that the UI culture has been changed. The CLR calls *SetUILocale* when an add-in sets the *System.Threading.Thread.CurrentUICulture* property. By notifying the host of changes made to the UI culture, the CLR gives the host a chance to adjust any culture-related state it maintains internally.

Table 14-1   The Methods on *IHostTaskManager*

Method	Description
LeaveRuntime	In the section "Hooking Calls That Enter and Leave the CLR" later in this chapter, I describe how the CLR calls methods on *IHostTask-Manager* to enable the host to hook calls that transition between managed and unmanaged code. Calls to *LeaveRuntime* notify the host that a transition from managed to unmanaged code is about to occur. A transition from managed to unmanaged code would occur if an add-in were to use PInvoke to call a method in a Win32 DLL, for example.
EnterRuntime	*EnterRuntime* is called to notify the host that a previous transition from managed to unmanaged code (as indicated by a previous call to *LeaveRuntime*) is now returning. See "Hooking Calls That Enter and Leave the CLR" later in this chapter for more details on how the calls to *LeaveRuntime* and *EnterRuntime* are related.
ReverseEnterRuntime	Transitions between managed and unmanaged code can be nested. *ReverseEnterRuntime* notifies the host that a previously identified transition from managed to unmanaged code has initiated a call back into managed code. See "Hooking Calls That Enter and Leave the CLR" later in this chapter for more details about how such transitions can be nested.
ReverseLeaveRuntime	Notifies the host that a nested transition is going back out to unmanaged code from managed code. See "Hooking Calls That Enter and Leave the CLR" for more details.
BeginThreadAffinity	At times, the CLR requires the current task not be moved to a different physical thread. If SQL Server 2005 is running in fiber mode, this affinity requirement specifically means that the current fiber should not be rescheduled on a different thread. The CLR calls *BeginThreadAffinity* to notify the host that a period of time in which thread affinity is required is beginning. There are various points during the initialization of the CLR when thread affinity is required.
EndThreadAffinity	Calls to *EndThreadAffinity* notify the host that a period requiring thread affinity is ending. The host is now free to reschedule the current task on a different physical thread if desired.
BeginDelayAbort	As you saw in Chapter 11, the ability to abort a thread or unload an application domain is key to the CLR's ability to support hosts that require long process lifetimes. There are periods of time, however, when the CLR cannot tolerate a thread abort. The CLR calls *BeginDelayAbort* to notify the host when such a period of time begins.
EndDelayAbort	Calls to *EndDelayAbort* notify the host that the CLR is now able to tolerate thread aborts again. Each call to *BeginDelayAbort* has a corresponding call to *EndThreadAbort*.
SetCLRTaskManager	Provides the host with a pointer to the CLR's implementation of *ICLRTaskManager*.

After the CLR obtains a pointer to the host's implementation of *IHostTaskManager* by calling *IHostControl::GetHostManager*, it gives the host a pointer to its implementation of *ICLRTask-Manager* by calling the *SetCLRTaskManager* method on *IHostTaskManager*. *ICLRTaskManager* is the mirror image of *IHostTaskManager* in that it provides the host with a set of methods for controlling the CLR's basic task-related functions. The methods on *ICLRTaskManager* are shown in Table 14-2.

Table 14-2   The Methods on *ICLRTaskManager*

Method	Description
CreateTask	Enables the host to create a new task. As you'll see later in the section entitled "The Life Cycle of a Task," either the CLR or the host can initiate the creation of a new task.
GetCurrentTask	Returns the CLR's notion of the task running on the calling thread.
SetUILocale	Notifies the CLR that the UI culture has been changed by the host. In most cases, a host will call this if the UI culture has been changed by some unmanaged code (either by the host or by an unmanaged add-in) running in the host's process. *ICLRTaskManager::SetUILocale* is the mirror image of *IHostTaskManager::SetUILocale*.
SetLocale	Notifies the CLR that the culture has been changed. *ICLRTaskManager::SetLocale* is the mirror image of *IHostTaskManager::SetLocale*.
GetCurrentTaskType	The CLR creates a few threads itself regardless of whether the host has provided an implementation of the task manager. Examples of these threads include those used for garbage collection and those used to control debugging. Hosts can use *GetCurrentTaskType* to determine whether the current task is one of the special tasks that the CLR creates directly. See the sidebar "CLR Threads Created Independently of the Hosting API" for more details on the threads the CLR creates itself.

The other two interfaces in the task manager, *IHostTask* and *ICLRTask*, represent individual tasks that have been created in the process. As shown in Figure 14-2, each process contains one instance each of *IHostTaskManager* and *ICLRTaskManager* and many instances of *IHost-Task* and *ICLRTask*. Each task created in the process is represented by a matched pair of *IHost-Task* and *ICLRTask* implementations. As their names suggest, *IHostTask* is the view of the task as implemented by the host and *ICLRTask* is implemented by the CLR.

Process

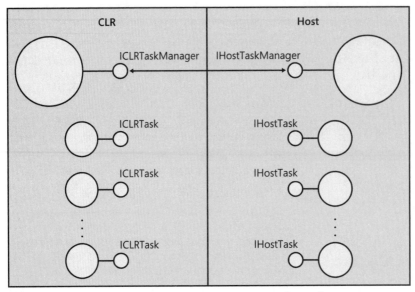

Figure 14-2 A matched pair of *IHostTask* and *ICLRTask* interfaces represents each task in the process.

IHostTask and *ICLRTask* provide operations that the CLR and the host, respectively, can use to manipulate a specific task. Tables 14-3 and 14-4 describe the methods on these two interfaces.

Table 14-3 The Methods on *IHostTask*

Method	Description
Start	Instructs the host to begin execution of the task.
Alert	Wakes a task up so it can be aborted. The CLR will call *Alert* when aborting a thread or unloading an application domain.
Join	Blocks the current task either until the task on which *Join* is called terminates or a specified interval of time passes.
SetPriority	Sets the task's priority. One scenario in which the CLR calls *SetPriority* is when an add-in adjusts a task's priority using the *Priority* property on *System.Threading.Thread*.
GetPriority	Gets the task's priority.
SetCLRTask	When called by the CLR, associates an implementation of *ICLRTask* with this instance of *IHostTask*.

Table 14-4   The Methods on *ICLRTask*

Method	Description
SwitchIn	Notifies the CLR that the host is scheduling this task to run. In fiber mode, calls to *SwitchIn* indicate that the fiber representing this task is about to begin executing on a physical thread.
SwitchOut	Notifies the CLR that this task is being unscheduled. In fiber mode, calls to *SwitchOut* indicate that the fiber representing this task is being removed from running on a physical thread.
GetMemStats	Returns a structure of type *COR_GC_THREAD_STATS* that contains statistics about the amount of memory allocated by this task.
Reset	Clears all internal state related to a task that is to be reused. The CLR allows its representation of a task to be reused to prevent the host from paying the cost of re-creating large numbers of tasks. A host calls *Reset* in preparation for task reuse. One example of state that is cleared is all data stored on the task when an add-in calls *System.Threading.Thread.Alloc(Named)DataSlot*.
ExitTask	Notifies the CLR that the task is exiting normally.
Abort	Notifies the CLR that the task is being aborted.
RudeAbort	Notifies the CLR that the task is being rudely aborted. Refer to Chapter 11 for details on the differences between an abort and a rude abort.
NeedsPriorityScheduling	Notifies the host that the task must be rescheduled. One of the challenges in integrating the CLR into SQL Server 2005 is to ensure that the SQL Server scheduler doesn't schedule tasks in such a way as to interfere with the CLR's garbage collector. Specifically, if the CLR is attempting to get all tasks to a state in which it is safe to perform a garbage collection, but a given task isn't being scheduled frequently enough to make progress toward a safe state, the garbage collector can end up waiting for an unacceptable amount of time before it can proceed with a collection. The return value from *NeedsPriorityRescheduling* indicates to the host that the task should be rescheduled as soon as possible. A host can use this information to place the task near the beginning of the scheduling queue instead of at the end, for example.
YieldTask	Causes the CLR to attempt to bring the task to a state in which it will yield. This method is used in an attempt to get long-running code to give up the CPU in scenarios in which the host uses co-operative task scheduling.
LocksHeld	Returns the number of locks (synchronization primitives) currently held by the task.
SetTaskIdentifier	Associates a host-defined identifier with the task. This identifier is used primarily to group related tasks together in debugger output. The CLR simply passes this identifier on to the debugger. The identifier isn't used internally at all.

Now that I've described the basic capabilities offered by the task manager, take a look at how the specific interfaces are used during the typical life cycle of a task.

The Life Cycle of a Task

In general, the life cycle of a task consists of three primary phases:

1. The task is created.

2. Tasks are repeatedly switched in and out as they execute.

3. The task terminates.

Figure 14-3 shows the relationship between these phases over time for a host that is running the CLR on cooperatively scheduled fibers.

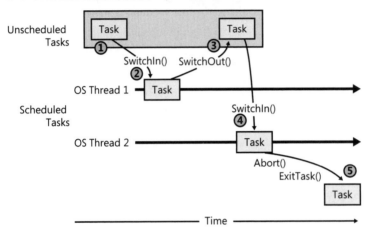

Figure 14-3   The typical life cycle of a task

The numbered steps in Figure 14-3 are described in the following points:

1. Tasks are in the unscheduled, or "not-running," state when they are first created. The creation of a new task is typically initiated by the CLR, but a host can create a new task as well. The CLR creates a new task by calling the *CreateTask* method on *IHostTask-Manager*. Next, the CLR creates an instance of *ICLRTask* to associate with the new task the host has just created. The link between the CLR's representation of the task and the host's representation is established when the CLR passes its instance of *ICLRTask* to the *SetCLRTask* method of the *IHostTask* that represents the new task. When all the interfaces are in place, the CLR calls the *Start* method on *IHostTask* to move the task to a state in which it can be scheduled.

2. At some point, the host will schedule the task for execution. The host calls the *SwitchIn* method on *ICLRTask* to notify the CLR that the task is about to be scheduled.

3. Later, the host might decide to switch the task out or remove it from the thread and place it back in a nonrunning state. A host might choose to do this if the running task blocks on a synchronization primitive, is waiting for I/O to complete, and so on. A host notifies the CLR that a task is being switched out by calling *ICLRTask::SwitchOut*.

4.   The next time the task is scheduled, it's quite possible it can be scheduled to run on a different physical thread than it ran on previously. This is shown in Figure 14-3 when the task that first ran on OS Thread 1 is placed on OS Thread 2 when rescheduled.

However, in some scenarios the CLR requires thread affinity for a given task. Periods of thread affinity are defined when the CLR calls *IHostTaskManager::BeginThreadAffinity* and *IHostTaskManager::EndThreadAffinity*. In this particular diagram, when the time comes to reschedule it, the host must schedule the task back on OS Thread 1 if the task requires thread affinity.

5.   Eventually, a CLR task ends permanently. This generally happens when the code running on the task reaches its natural end. In this scenario, the host calls *ICLRTask::ExitTask* to notify the CLR that the task is ending and that the implementation of *ICLRTask* can be destroyed. Tasks can also end in aborts or rude aborts as indicated, respectively, by calls to the *Abort* or *RudeAbort* methods of *ICLRTask*. It is also possible to reuse an implementation of *ICLRTask* instead of destroying it when the task it currently represents terminates. To reuse a task, a host calls *ICLRTask::Reset* to reset the CLR's representation of the task to a clean state. The instance of *ICLRTask* can then be reused in the future to represent a new task.

CLR Threads Created Independently of the Hosting API

When an add-in or other managed code running in a process requests that a new task be created (by using *System.Threading.Thread*, for example), that request is mapped by the CLR to the host through the task manager as discussed. However, not all threads the CLR creates in a process are redirected through the host in this way. Regardless of whether it is hosted or not, the CLR always creates a few threads for its internal implementation using the Win32 API. These threads include the following:

- The threads for performing garbage collections
- A thread for interacting with debuggers
- A thread that gates access to the thread pool
- An internal timer thread

The threads the CLR creates without the aid of the host are represented by the values from the *ETaskType* enumeration (minus the *TT_USER* value). Here's its definition from mscoree.idl:

```
typedef enum ETaskType
{
    TT_DEBUGGERHELPER = 0x1,
    TT_GC = 0x2,
    TT_FINALIZER = 0x4,
    TT_THREADPOOL_TIMER = 0x8,
    TT_THREADPOOL_GATE = 0x10,
```

```
    TT_THREADPOOL_WORKER = 0x20,
    TT_THREADPOOL_IOCOMPLETION = 0x40,
    TT_ADUNLOAD = 0x80,
    TT_USER = 0x100,
    TT_THREADPOOL_WAIT = 0x200,

    TT_UNKNOWN = 0x80000000,
} ETaskType;
```

Hooking Calls That Enter and Leave the CLR

In addition to the ability to provide an abstraction over the basic unit of execution and the method of scheduling, the task manager also enables a host to intercept all calls that transition between managed and unmanaged code. Transitions out of managed code occur when an add-in (or your host runtime assembly) accesses a Win32 DLL through either PInvoke or COM interoperability. Transitions into managed code occur when code in a Win32 DLL calls into managed code either through reverse PInvoke[1] or COM interoperability.

The ability to hook these transitions is important to hosts that employ cooperative scheduling because once a call leaves the CLR for unmanaged code, the thread on which that call is made is no longer under the CLR's (or the host's) control. As a result, the host can no longer schedule cooperative tasks to run on that thread. Instead, the host must allow the thread to be scheduled preemptively by the operating system until it returns to managed code, at which point the thread can be used again by the host's cooperative scheduler.

The CLR notifies the host of transitions into and out of managed code through a series of calls to the following methods on *IHostTaskManager*:

- *LeaveRuntime*
- *EnterRuntime*
- *ReverseEnterRuntime*
- *ReverseLeaveRuntime*

You can easily guess how *LeaveRuntime* and *EnterRuntime* are used: the CLR calls *LeaveRuntime* each time a call transitions out of managed code and *EnterRuntime* when that call returns. The use of *ReverseEnterRuntime* and *ReverseLeaveRuntime* isn't quite so obvious, however. These calls exist to support the nested transitions between managed and unmanaged code.

Here is an example to give you an idea of how these methods are used when transitions into and out of the CLR are nested. Figure 14-4 shows the sequence of calls that occur when three transitions are nested.

---

1. By *reverse PInvoke*, I'm referring to the scenario in which a Win32 DLL calls into managed code through a delegate that had been previously marshaled out to native code as a function pointer.

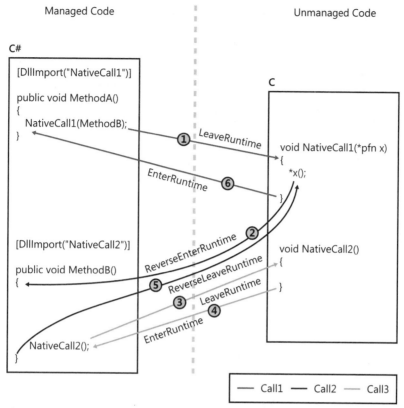

Figure 14-4   Nested calls between managed and unmanaged code

The sequence of calls the CLR makes to the methods on *IHostTaskManager* to notify the host of the transitions shown in Figure 14-4 is as follows:

1. The PInvoke call from *MethodA* to *NativeCall1* initiates the sequence of transitions. The CLR calls *LeaveRuntime* to notify the host that control is transferring from managed code to unmanaged code. Notice that *NativeCall1* takes a parameter that is a function pointer. *MethodA* passes an instance of *MethodB* as this parameter.

2. The implementation of *NativeCall1* calls the function identified by the function pointer it is passed. In this case, the function pointer is to a managed method (*MethodB*), so calling through the function pointer causes a call from unmanaged code to managed code. This transition is nested because the call the CLR previously identified through a call to *LeaveRuntime* (the call from *MethodA* to *NativeCall1*) has not completed. The CLR calls *ReverseEnterRuntime* to notify the host of this nested transition back into managed code.

3. *MethodB* uses PInvoke to transition back out to unmanaged code using a call to *NativeCall2*. Because the call to *NativeCall2* initiates a new series of transitions from managed to unmanaged code, the CLR notifies the host of this transition by calling *LeaveRuntime*.

4. *NativeCall2* returns to the CLR with no further nesting. *EnterRuntime* is called to indicate that the previous call to *LeaveRuntime* is now returning.

5. The executing of *MethodB* is now complete. Upon return from *MethodB*, control will transfer back out to unmanaged code. Because the call to *MethodB* occurred within a nested transition, its transition from managed code to unmanaged code is communicated by a call to *ReverseLeaveRuntime*. The call to *ReverseLeaveRuntime* completes the transition that started in step 2 with a call to *ReverseEnterRuntime*.

6. The call from managed code to unmanaged code that initiated this whole sequence is now complete. The CLR notifies the host of the return from *NativeCall1* back into managed code by calling *EnterRuntime*.

As you can see, nested transitions such as the sequence shown in Figure 14-4 can result in multiple interleaved calls to *LeaveRuntime*, *EnterRuntime*, *ReverseLeaveRuntime*, and *Reverse-EnterRuntime*. Figure 14-5 shows how the sequence of calls used to notify the host of the transitions that occur in Figure 14-4 would be represented on the call stack. Notice that calls to *LeaveRuntime* and *EnterRuntime* are always paired, as are calls to *ReverseEnterRuntime* and *ReverseLeaveRuntime*.

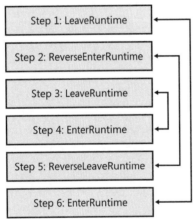

Figure 14-5 A stack representing nested transitions between managed and unmanaged code

The Synchronization Manager

In the last few sections, I've shown how SQL Server 2005 implements a task manager to integrate the execution of managed code with SQL Server's custom scheduler. Although the capabilities offered by the task manager provide many of the basic features that are needed, the task manager alone doesn't provide all that's required to achieve a high-performance integration between the two products. Specifically, the use of synchronization primitives, either by the CLR or by the managed add-ins it executes, has a direct impact on scalability.

For example, say the CLR needs to synchronize access to a resource from multiple threads. The traditional way to accomplish such synchronization is to use a Win32 API, such as

CreateEvent, to obtain an object that can be used for synchronization. However, if such a lock were taken on a thread without informing SQL Server, the thread that is currently waiting on the synchronization primitive would be blocked, and therefore would be unavailable for SQL Server to schedule. As a result, the overall efficiency of the system is reduced.

What's needed instead is a way for the host to supply the CLR with the synchronization primitives it typically gets from the operating system. In this way, if the CLR were to block waiting for a synchronization primitive to be signaled, SQL Server could unschedule that blocked task, thereby making the thread available for other tasks to run. At some later point in time, SQL Server would reschedule the blocked task to give it a chance to obtain the lock and become unblocked. The ability to supply the CLR with synchronization primitives in this way is exactly the role of the synchronization manager in the CLR hosting API. By providing the CLR with the basic primitives it needs to synchronize access to resources, the host is not only able to detect cases of contention, but also to consider the locks taken by managed code when determining how to resolve a deadlock. The synchronization manager enables the CLR to create the following types of synchronization primitives through the host:

- Critical sections

- Semaphores

- Monitors

- Reader/writer locks

- Auto-reset events

- Manual-reset events

Support for these primitives is provided by the six interfaces that comprise the synchronization manager. In addition to interfaces that represent specific types of synchronization primitives, the synchronization manager also includes two interfaces that enable the creation and exchange of ownership data for individual primitives. The following points provide an overview of the interfaces that make up the synchronization manager.

- **IHostSyncManager**   As the primary interface in the synchronization manager, *IHostSyncManager* is the interface the CLR asks the host for at startup through a call to *IHostControl::GetHostManager*. In addition to its role as the primary interface, *IHostSyncManager* contains the methods the CLR uses to create individual synchronization primitives. These methods include *CreateSemaphore*, *CreateMonitorEvent*, *CreateAutoEvent*, and so on.

- **ICLRSyncManager**   After the CLR obtains a pointer of type *IHostSyncManager* from the host, it provides the host with an implementation of *ICLRSyncManager* by calling *IHostSyncManager::SetCLRSyncManager*. Hosts use *ICLRSyncManager* to determine which task owns a particular synchronization primitive.

- **IHostSemaphore**   Semaphores are represented in the CLR hosting API by the *IHostSemaphore* interface. The CLR uses methods on *IHostSemaphore* to wait for a particular semaphore to become available and to release the semaphore when it is no longer needed.

- **IHostManualEvent** Manual reset events are represented by the *IHostManualEvent* interface. In addition to providing the CLR with manual reset events, *IHostManualEvent* is also used in the implementation of reader/writer locks. *IHostManualEvent* has methods corresponding to the operations that are typically performed on events created using the Win32 API. For example, *IHostManualEvent* enables the CLR to wait on the event and to set or reset the event.

- **IHostAutoEvent** Auto reset events are represented by the *IHostAutoEvent* interface. As with *IHostManualEvent*, *IHostAutoEvent* contains methods for waiting on the event and for setting the event. In addition to their use as stand-alone synchronization primitives, auto-reset events are also used in the implementation of monitors and reader/writer locks.

- **IHostCrst** The CLR manages critical sections created by the host using the *IHostCrst* interface. *IHostCrst* has methods that enable the CLR to enter and leave the critical section. In addition, *IHostCrst* also contains a spincount used to implement lightweight locks when the critical section isn't contested.

Replacing the CLR's Thread Pool

The final threading-related hosting manager to cover is the thread pool manager. As discussed in Chapter 5, and as you are probably aware from your own experience with .NET Framework programming, the CLR provides a process-wide thread pool that makes it easier to write scalable multithreaded applications. By providing an implementation of the thread pool manager, you are able to replace the CLR's thread pool with your own implementation.

The requirement to be able to supply a custom thread pool comes from the integration of the CLR into SQL Server 2005, as many of the other threading-related requirements have. As you've seen throughout this chapter, SQL Server closely manages how threads are used in its process, including the number of threads that are created. If the CLR would continue to implement its own pool of threads while running in SQL Server, several threads wouldn't be under the control of SQL Server. Given requirements for scalability in SQL Server, any threads running in the process that are not integrated with the custom scheduling mechanism of SQL Server can throw off the internal optimizations of SQL Server, and performance can be hampered.

The thread pool manager consists of a single interface called *IHostThreadpoolManager*. The CLR asks the host if it wants to provide a custom thread pool implementation by calling the host's implementation of *IHostControl::GetHostManager*, passing the IID for *IHostThreadpool-Manager*. If an implementation of *IHostThreadpoolManager* is provided, the CLR directs all requests to queue items to a thread pool to the host. In addition to the method used to queue work items to the host's thread pool, *IHostThreadpoolManager* also contains methods that enable the CLR to set and query various values related to the size of the thread pool, as shown in Table 14-5.

Table 14-5   The Methods On *IHostThreadpoolManager*

Method	Description
QueueUserWorkItem	Queues a work item to the thread pool. *QueueUserWorkItem* has the same signature as the Win32 API with the same name.
SetMaxThreads	Sets the maximum number of threads that can be created in the thread pool. Hosts are not required to honor the CLR's request to set the size of the thread pool. If a host wishes to keep the size of the thread pool under its own control, it should return the *E_NOTIMPL HRESULT* from *SetMaxThreads*.
GetMaxThreads	Returns the maximum number of threads that will be created in the thread pool.
GetAvailableThreads	Returns the number of threads that are currently available to service requests.
SetMinThreads	Sets the minimum number of threads that will be created in the thread pool. As with *SetMaxThreads*, hosts are not required to honor the CLR's request to alter any aspect of the thread pool's size.
GetMinThreads	Returns the minimum number of threads that will be created in the thread pool.

Summary

SQL Server 2005 can run in a mode in which it leverages the notion of fibers to improve scalability when running on machines with multiple processors. When running in fiber mode, SQL Server implements a custom scheduler that assigns fibers to physical threads using an algorithm designed to utilize each thread fully to achieve maximum overall throughput. The integration with SQL Server 2005 marks the first time the CLR is required to run in an environment in which tasks are cooperatively scheduled. Until this time, the CLR has been used only in environments in which threads were preemptively scheduled directly by the operating system.

To integrate the CLR with SQL Server 2005 so that scalability isn't hindered, all scheduling-related activities must be managed directly by SQL Server. The CLR hosting API provides an abstraction called the task manager that hosts can use to supply the CLR with the basic primitives it needs to create and manage how tasks behave in the process. By using the primitives supplied by the host instead of going directly to the operating system, the CLR makes the host (SQL Server 2005, in this case) aware of all threading-related activities that occur in the process such that the execution of managed tasks can be integrated with the host's custom scheduler.

In addition to the primitives needed to control the execution of managed code, the CLR hosting API offers two more abstractions that are needed to integrate the CLR seamlessly with custom schedulers. The first of these abstractions is the synchronization manager. SQL Server 2005 uses a synchronization manager to supply the CLR with synchronization primitives such as events, monitors, and semaphores. Redirecting the requests for such primitives through the host is required for the host to optimize its custom scheduler based on whether a given task is blocked waiting for a synchronization primitive to become available. The final threading-related manager provided by the CLR hosting API is the thread pool manager. Hosts can use the thread pool manager to replace the CLR's custom implementation of the thread pool. The need to cause the CLR to use the host's thread pool also comes from the fact that SQL Server 2005 must be aware of all threads that are currently executing in the process.

The threading, synchronization, and thread pool managers consist of several interfaces with numerous complex methods. Making use of these managers in your own application requires extensive design and testing. This chapter provides an introduction to what is possible. If your scenario requires you to integrate the CLR with a custom scheduler or thread pool, you'll likely find the CoopFiber sample in the .NET Framework SDK an invaluable resource.

Index

A

About the Author

Steven Pratschner is a Program Manager on the .NET Compact Framework team at Microsoft. Before joining the .NET Compact Framework team, Steven worked on the CLR for the full .NET Framework for several years. During that time, Steven worked on various features of the CLR, including the versioning system, hosting, and security. Steven has written articles and presented at numerous conferences on a variety of topics related to .NET Framework programming.

Before coming to Microsoft, Steven worked as a software developer for a number of small software companies. He started writing software for the Microsoft platform back when OS/2 and Windows 3.0 were becoming popular. Steven has computer science degrees from North Dakota State University and Santa Clara University.

Steven has twin 10-year-old daughters with whom he loves to spend time whenever he can. He also recently married his high school sweetheart on a beach in Hawaii. Steven's hobbies include sailing his boat on Puget Sound and reading books about U.S. history.

What do you think of this book?
We want to hear from you!

Do you have a few minutes to participate in a brief online survey? Microsoft is interested in hearing your feedback about this publication so that we can continually improve our books and learning resources for you.

To participate in our survey, please visit:

www.microsoft.com/learning/booksurvey

And enter this book's ISBN, 0-7356-1988-3. As a thank-you to survey participants in the United States and Canada, each month we'll randomly select five respondents to win one of five $100 gift certificates from a leading online merchant.* At the conclusion of the survey, you can enter the drawing by providing your e-mail address, which will be used for prize notification *only*.

Thanks in advance for your input. Your opinion counts!

Sincerely,

Microsoft Learning

Learn More. Go Further.

To see special offers on Microsoft Learning products for developers, IT professionals, and home and office users, visit: *www.microsoft.com/learning/booksurvey*